Heal Yourself with Gemstones

Gemstones have been used throughout history to actualize hidden potential and aid in the healing process. They make excellent healing tools because they carry, concentrate, and amplify vibrational energy.

Now, *Gems of the Seven Color Rays* shows you how to use the vibrational power of gemstones to work with color-ray energy. Our auras are composed of color-ray energy, a part of the spectrum of life energy. Learn to use gemstones to strengthen your aura and bring your body back into a healthy balance.

For example, blue-ray energy helps you use your mind more effectively. Wear a blue sapphire necklace to eliminate old, dysfunctional habit patterns. Clearing away this mental clutter with blue sapphire will open your mind to communication with spirit.

Bring yourself into alignment with the positive forces in the universe by identifying and altering your energy patterns. This book shows you how to use the power of gemstones to create lasting, positive life changes!

D1473266

About the Author

William Stuber (Sequim, Washington) is a writer with an uncanny ability to read peoples' energy, thoughts, and motivations. He has initiated research into the effects of gemstones and developed new color-ray energy healing techniques. As a result, he has mastered the use of gemstones to clear weaknesses.

Stuber has spent the last twenty-six years developing his spiritual abilities, giving him an innovative view of life. He works easily with people interested in the occult, mind development, healing arts, and spirituality.

Audiences have enjoyed his weekend healing retreats and gemstone workshops. He has also written and performed for numerous poetry readings, plays, shows, ads, and seminars.

Stuber was part of a team of specialists that combined the use of gemstones with Reiki, acupuncture, and sound and light therapy. He teaches classes on gem healing and performs diamond and gemstone therapy on local health professionals seeking to achieve breakthroughs. Stuber travels extensively to present his work.

To Write to the Author

If you wish to contact the author or would like more information about this book, please write to the author in care of Llewellyn Worldwide and we will forward your request. Both the author and publisher appreciate hearing from you and learning of your enjoyment of this book and how it has helped you. Llewellyn Worldwide cannot guarantee that every letter written to the author can be answered, but all will be forwarded. Please write to:

William C. Stuber
℅ Llewellyn Worldwide
P.O. Box 64383, Dept. 1-56718-685-8
St. Paul, MN 55164-0383, U.S.A.

Please enclose a self-addressed stamped envelope for reply,
or $1.00 to cover costs. If outside U.S.A., enclose
international postal reply coupon.

Many of Llewellyn's authors have websites with additional information and resources. For more information, please visit our website at:
http://www.llewellyn.com

William C. Stuber

GEMS OF THE
7 *Color Rays*

A Comprehensive Guide to Healing with Gems

2001
Llewellyn Publications
St. Paul, Minnesota 55164-0383, U.S.A.

FIRST EDITION
First Printing, 2001

Book design and editing by Astrid Sandell
Cover design by Anne Marie Garrison
Color insert design by Anne Marie Garrison
Photography by William C. Stuber

Library of Congress Cataloging-in-Publication Data
Stuber, William C.
    Gems of the seven color rays : a comprehensive guide to healing with gems /
William C. Stuber. — 1st ed.
       p. cm.
    Includes bibliographical references and index.
    ISBN 1-56718-685-8
       1. Precious stones—Psychic aspects. 2. Precious stones—Therapeutic use.
3. Gems—Psychic aspects. 4. Gems—Therapeutic use. I. Title.

BF1442.P74 S78 2000
133'.25538—dc21
                                                      99-057920

Llewellyn Publications
A Division of Llewellyn Worldwide, Ltd.
P.O. Box 64383, Dept. 1-56718-685-8
St. Paul, MN 55164-0383, U.S.A.
www.llewellyn.com

 Printed in the United States of America on recycled paper

Dedicated to Herold and Joan Klemp,
whose example gave me the faith to complete this work.

Contents

Part III: Supporting Therapies

Acknowledgments

I want to thank Michael Katz for his inspiration and for his pioneering work in *Gemisphere Luminary* (Gemisphere Publishing, 1997). I extend my special thanks to him for his work in the field of gem healing. I very much appreciate Gemisphere for the publications they released—especially on the therapeutic use of gemstones—as these have inspired me and furthered my research into the application of gems.

Special thanks to Charlotte Sykes for her proofing and attention to detail in the initial edit. Thanks to Douglas Stuber for his read and his notes. Thanks also to Irene Stuber, who helped get this book finished. I would like to acknowledge Janene Jurgenson, Fran Hamilton, Nisa Flemming, Maureen Thompson, Richard Folker, and Al Harris, all of whom gave me their support during the research and development process.

Part I

Understanding the
Color Ray Model

W e are about to embark on a journey into a vast interior world, a personal world made of cerebral energy. We shall use our ability to imagine and together explore this world. As we travel to different levels of the mind, you will learn something about how these areas operate and the laws by which they are governed. Like a vast internal sea, your world offers many experiences that await an adventurous soul. Together, we will explore the possibilities of how this world can become a larger universe in which consciousness expands to meet the coming of ever more exciting possibilities.

Consciousness is like a ship destined to discover as many amazing sights and sounds as recorded by any explorer who has pioneered a new world. New things are being created as we speak, and the manifestations that occur within this everchanging realm are purely for your benefit. If our mission is successful, we shall discover a clear sense of the positive potential of love in action, the vision to see a better future than we thought achievable, and the motivation and ability to use the energy centers of this universe for the greater good.

As we explore, we will find that we can learn to change our state of being, our concepts, and our thoughts in order to allow ourselves to realize a more vital experience of the world within. In fact, all of us live in our own

1
Color Me Gemstone

subjective world. Our attitudes affect the way we are. Whereas one person may move to a new town and find nothing there to enjoy, another more adaptable person may move to the same town and find a wide variety of interesting things to admire. The decisions we make, from the earliest age on, completely govern the way we experience this world. If we are to experience joy in our lives, we must first find it within.

Our state of being, our ship, is fully integrated. The emotions and thoughts that follow from our pattern of action create our circumstances. If we learn to master the forces at work in our lives, we can enjoy the benefits of a new freedom, we can live more thoroughly. Our reactions control our ship's course until we become free of reaction and begin to master the winds and currents.

Circumstances, whether good or bad, are the result of our state of being. On one hand, we could learn how to enjoy profound inner freedom from someone who spent years as a prisoner of war in a concentration camp in Nazi Germany during World War II. On the other hand, we could learn what life is like in the narrow confines of a world no bigger than a packing crate from a person who has all the advantages of material wealth. Life is not what you have or even who you know—life is what you make of it. The circumstances do not make the person; rather, the state of being you generate within produces your subjective experience. It is entirely possible for a person to feel young after a ninety-year journey; just as likely, a person can experience symptoms of old age after only thirty or forty years.

Our reaction to each experience we encounter is within our control if we can learn to direct it. We, as soul, can captain our ship and the many crew teams (mind, body, and emotions) on board. The crew can take care of the necessary tasks required to pilot the vessel and we can enjoy the trip, if we can maintain a vision without interfering with their jobs. A few may require retraining, but most have the ability to do their jobs efficiently. In order to get the various members in harmony and heading in an agreeable direction under the guidance of soul (our individual spiritual being), we must learn to trust our crew and remain clear-headed enough to stay in command of the bridge. For this purpose, we have tools available to us in many forms, and gemstones are among the most powerful and effective when used with clear intention and knowledge as to their application.

To learn to maximize our enjoyment of life and create a state of being in which we master the inner seas of life, we must learn to live life fully and overcome fear. Fear blocks the experience of love. As we learn to move forward without succumbing to fear, our experience is more positive. Our crew is depending on us to remove blocks and self-imposed limits. Gemstones can help you gain control over inner reactions and can teach you to become flexible so that you can instantly redirect energy as needed to safely pass through troubled waters.

Through continued interaction with gemstones, you can learn to direct light and sound energy and to become resilient, expressive, and loving in whatever you do. Together, we shall explore the nature of color-ray energy. Anyone who continues this journey beyond the farthest edges of their known universe will directly contact the source of color-ray energy. This energy will stretch you and recreate your agenda to include further exploration of unknown areas of the mind. Gemstones, when used intentionally with love, will cause you to accept a level of abundance not previously attainable. Awareness of the power of light and the workings of your ambition that runs on color-ray energy will double and redouble in the presence of this energy. You may realize a life mission and actualize your dreams. By mastering color-ray energy, you will no longer be tied to old patterns of behavior that limit your potential.

Gemstones are powerful, compact carriers of vibrational energy. Gemstones are used as healing tools because they carry, concentrate, and amplify vibrational energy. The energies within have vibration, and if you change an energy's vibration, you change its effect. You can learn to manipulate energies on your own, without the aid of tools, but you can more rapidly learn how to identify and alter energy patterns by practicing gemstone healing. Use gemstones to learn the art of directing internal energy in a similar, yet more powerful way than you could use light, sound, and other forms of external energy to clear blocks that interrupt the flow of energy within your body and cause physical energy depletion.

Understand that all internal processes and functions are initiated, motivated, directed, and controlled by vibrational energy, energy that emanates in a particular wavelike pattern. Just as a tuning fork will act to cause a sympathetic resonance in the string of a guitar, inducing a hum of the same pitch, a gemstone will cause the human form to resonate in sympathetic harmony with the gemstone's vibrations.

Intention is the key to using gemstones to make desired changes. Decide exactly what changes you wish to make and hold on to your intention to make those changes. Find which gemstone will help you, and you will find this an easy process.

Using Spherical Gemstones

This book refers primarily to the use of the spherical form of gemstones to bring much larger amounts of color-ray energy into your life to create major life changes that remove fear and doubt leaving inner harmony and balance, and to bring you into alignment with positive forces in the universe. Pointed crystal formations can also be used to create changes in your aura or physical body, but these changes may force you out of balance. Spheres, on the other hand, will interact with a person in such a way that at no time will you be thrown out of balance from the gemstone's influence. Your body will let you know when you have had enough color energy, and the gentle yet persistent influence can be removed until the energy has been assimilated. Thus, you will not be moved into changes that would not be supported by your inner makeup. Spheres are safer and easier to use than terminated crystals, and allow experimentation without disruption.

Spheres can be used in necklaces or alone. Worn as necklaces, they will affect the whole person. When placed on the body or held in the aura, single spheres will focus their effects on a small local area. Gemstone spheres will saturate the aura with beneficial color-ray energy and will never deplete the aura of beneficial energies. In the natural crystal shape, gemstones are capable of draining all or part of the auric energy from an individual.

Angular gemstones will focus the energies that pass through them in one direction. This effect is not desirable when working with most gemstones. Directed energies will rapidly fill or deplete the aura. This rapid alteration of the aura can send a person into severe reactions. Each of us has become accustomed to our own vibrations and our auras as they are. If changed too suddenly, our vibrations will be highly unstable and our sense of who we are can be deeply shaken. One learns best in gradual changes.

Gemstone necklaces are also made from chips that are not spherical or pointed. Certain stones like citrine, tourmaline, and aquamarine can be worn effectively in necklaces made of chips because of their high vibrational makeup. Chip necklaces, especially those of therapeutic quality, are highly charged and should be monitored in order to control their effects. Once you are aware of what it feels like to be fully charged by a gemstone, you will always be able to tell when you have had enough. Once experience teaches us to be aware of the presence of too much gemstone influence, we can monitor ourselves quite effectively.

Gemstones are surprisingly powerful. Many wearers report dramatic changes after only one application. Some of the effects are subtle and may not be obvious to the wearer, but even the subtle effects are quite powerful and wearing gemstones is an invitation for change. It is best to make comprehensive change in a safe environment with the support of those who have some experience in this.

All gemstones are carriers of color energy, and each has its own distinct vibration. For each color of the spectrum, one specific gemstone is the primary carrier of that color ray. The primary color-ray–bearing gemstones provide the benefit of being able to infuse the body with that color ray to a higher concentration than is possible with other gemstones.

Everyone responds to one color ray that most supports their well-being. The color ray that best builds their strengths is their "strength ray," and it is preferable to begin your introduction to gemstone healing by working with this ray. Most people will be instantly drawn to the stone carrying the color that is their strength ray as soon as they touch or visualize that stone. They will see its color as the most beautiful of colors. The primary color-ray–bearing stone of that color will stand out as the one stone that feels best to them. If you are not sure which is your strength color ray, contact a gemstone therapist in your area for assistance, or consider the characteristics listed here and decide which are most like you. The gemstones will guide you.

Why Gemstone Healing Works

As recent advances in scientific methods and technology have enabled us to look ever more closely at the fundamental physical laws that govern our makeup, we have begun to realize that matter is not actually solid. In fact, matter and energy are different forms of the same "thing." Furthermore, matter is energy stored. The "particles" that make up matter are as much like energy waves as they are solid particles. In other words, we are made up of energy. We have also come to find out that we do not think the same. Advanced studies in psychology have shown that we are all different. Each of us is made from the same energy, yet we are all different, and we all react differently to similar circumstances. As we employ a new set of tools —ones more powerful and more able to interact with the fundamental energy of our bodies—such as gemstones, we learn to understand how we can live and thrive according to our personal blueprints.

Personal blueprints are records within soul of our potential to use energy to a far greater capacity than commonly known, and we can use this signature vibrational blueprint to redesign our bodies to perform excellently with greater ease. Adjusting the vibrations of the many parts of us both large and small to be harmonious with our blueprints will result in a total feeling of strength, well-being, and harmony. We accomplish this by adjusting our balance of color to match blueprints.

Gemstones are the most powerful transmitters of vibrational energy known to man. They have been effectively used throughout history by those trained in their application in order to actualize hidden potentials and heal wounds. They have been used to heal emotional sicknesses. Mental prowess can be developed through the informed use of these tools. For those interested in going further with the process, gemstones can be used to explore our basic beliefs about ourselves. We can learn to change beliefs that limit us, and we can learn to develop new beliefs that set us free. Ultimately, we can learn to demonstrate the power of love, which is the greatest power for life.

You may ask how gemstones accomplish this. How can we come to understand our fundamental nature? How can we begin to remove blockages in our ability to become all that we can be? How can we limit our susceptibility to disease and degeneration? How can we learn to understand and direct the energy that makes up our being? Simply put, how can we become true to soul, and congruent with the love within our true selves?

While there are certainly no simple answers to these questions, those who are willing to explore the many uses of these transmitters of vibrational energy will find that working with gemstones will lead to answers. Of one thing we can be sure, however: gemstones are being used ever more widely to delve into the workings of the human energy mystery. As to the relative safety of the spherical gemstones, be confident that as powerful as these tools may be, we will not be able to effect any changes that we are not already capable of effecting without these tools. Gemstones simply focus our abilities the same way they focus light to create laser beams. They can be used to store and interact with our patterns the same way they are used to store and interact with information in the form of computer data. They can provide the stimulus to create new experiences.

For too long we have lived as victims of the belief that we are too ignorant to understand ourselves and develop and heal ourselves. It is time to heal. It is time to move on and take responsibility for our own personal world.

About the Author

I have been working with gemstones as part of a research group of specialists with diverse backgrounds in the fields of counseling, social work, gemology, acupuncture, Chinese medicine, cranial sacral treatment, Reiki, Bach Flower Remedies, neurolinguistic programming (NLP), naturopathic medicine, music therapy, healing with light, anthropology, psychology, sound health engineering, regression therapy, dream work, past-life analysis, and others. Together, we have built a set of premises for understanding and applying vibrational healing. At times, the gemstones themselves have shown us how to proceed.

We have come to learn that the more we understand and use these tools, the more we are able to take advantage of their benefits to us. I make no guarantee that you, the reader, will be able to achieve any of the changes described in this book. I present this material only to document the incredible results my colleagues and I have enjoyed. Color-ray therapy works. Perhaps it is the use of our own energy, and focused clear intention combined with the unshakable belief we hold that absolutely nothing is impossible, which have facilitated the changes we have made in ourselves and others as described in this book. In no way would this fact change my belief that anyone who sets out on the path of self-discovery with an open heart and a true love for life can achieve phenomenal results with the aid of gemstones.

I shall endeavor to describe our primary model, which is based on the premise that all matter is made up of energy, and as such can be transformed. This energy is the basic building block of the physical universe and can be differentiated according to its vibration. It can be seen by some as colors in an aura around the body and can be photographed by Kirlian photography, while others can hear this energy or feel it. Our physical, emotional, causal, and mental bodies can be equated to sheaths worn by soul so that it might have protection from the coarse energies of this multidimensional world. These sheaths are not us, but protect us and are the mechanisms by which we come to know and experience our world. We are, in fact, soul. As soul, we can perceive, learn, and know. We can gain experience in this world through the use of our bodies and the various tools life has provided for us.

All energy can be divided into spectrums. Some are visible, some are audible, others are tangible, and yet others are known to us only through their effects or through instruments that document their effects. In other words, we know these different spectrums by direct experience, using the senses and capabilities of the physical and other bodies.

The energies we are primarily concerned with here are in the visible and audible spectrums. All light energy can be divided into one

2 *Energy Has a Hue*

of the eight color rays. These can be seen as the seven rainbow colors, or as white if comprised of all seven colors equally. The rate of vibration of any energy determines which color ray it is identified with (i.e., blue, red, or green) on the physical plane. Likewise, color-ray energy exists on other levels as well. Each spectrum of visible energy on each level can be divided into these color rays. Thus, the blue color ray is manifest in physical matter, physical light, astral matter, astral light, causal matter, causal light, and so forth.

Matter, whether visible or invisible, is made up of energy. This energy is stored in the form of atoms and molecules. All atoms and molecules are made of energies, which can be described as combinations of the different vibrational energies that can be affected by color-ray energy. Matter is formed in our bodies according to the blueprints we hold in our cells, organs, bones, and other body systems. All our physical abilities, including the ability to assimilate nutrients, discharge waste, grow, develop, and do all the other functions we perform as physical beings, are the result of the application of these energies. How well we perform these tasks is determined by our blueprints.

As emotional beings we have a sheath made of emotional energies. This sheath is carried around with us and occupies the same space as our physical sheath. This emotional sheath is made from astral blueprints and has a form different from the physical in some respects. Emotional blueprints determine how we react emotionally to stimuli of all kinds—physical, mental, and causal. Further, our minds are also present in the form of a sheath. While it is true that we have a brain that receives our sensory data, the actual mental processes take place within our mental sheaths.

They are the result of the movement and storage of color-ray energies on the mental level, just as the causes for the patterns of behavior we employ are stored in our causal sheath and when employed, are made up of causal level color-ray energies.

In other words, we are actually living in several sheaths. Each of these performs a different set of functions—functions that we are quite familiar with. We just aren't aware of how it all works. Once we use gemstones as described in this book to experience how this works, we will be able to create new abilities and generate all kinds of new results in our lives. Though at this time you may find it hard to believe, you can become so capable that you are limited only by your imagination.

At first this information may be difficult to visualize on the physical level and may be almost impossible to understand on the causal or mental levels. Understanding the functions of different sheaths is not critical to the use of gemstones. You need understand the differences between levels only gradually as you begin to be introduced to the different stones and how they work. Through the use of the stones you will become familiar with blueprints and their constituent color rays. Also, you will come to understand the sheaths and be able to identify them separately with the continued use of vibrational tools such as gemstones.

You already do understand something about energy. After all, every time you listen to music you hear energy. Every time you see a painting you experience color rays. Every time you use your sense of touch you feel vibrations. You need to understand how to more accurately identify what is happening and put this understanding into your own language. This new language will allow you to begin to identify the actual process that goes on within you to create thoughts, behaviors, emotions, and physical action. You can learn to understand how these processes work and to alter them for your benefit. Be reassured: this learning is safe, fun, and exciting. It may be spiritual. It is in alignment with the instruction in the Bible "Know thyself, that ye may someday know Me."

I will not instruct you to use these tools for any purpose other than to know yourself, so that you may purify yourself. After all, the body you inhabit is like a temple if you make it so.

You can learn to understand feelings. When you experience an emotion, you react not to what is happening outside, but to the energy that is present in the emotional sheath as it filters through this sheath in the form of energy vibrations. Your very thoughts are packets of energy stored in the mind. So, do not let this new language fool you. You are being asked only to divide the activities going on in these different sheaths into their constituent parts so that we can distinguish the steps in the process. You can become conscious of these distinctions by using gemstones.

The reason to develop the understanding of blueprints and the way they govern our use of energy is to gain control of this mechanism. Imagine if you can that you are a person who gets a headache every time you see your mother-in-law and spend more than five minutes with her. Now imagine that there is a specific mental process going on within your mental sheath in reaction to this stimulus. Each time you see this person, you initiate this process. The result is a headache. Suppose you could actually visualize this process. See exactly how it happens. Suppose you could modify the process so that every time you spent time with your mother-in-law you felt truly inspired and energized. Gemstones can teach you how to do this.

This is not magic—it is the act of gaining control over the processes already constantly going on inside you. Gemstones will help highlight these processes and even slow them down so that you can actually begin to understand what is happening, step by step. That's right—you can learn why life seems to repeat itself. You can gain control of the dials and valves that direct your life. It is your ship, learn the ways of the ocean and the stars, and you will never be lost or without hope.

Introduction to our Primary Colors

Characteristics of the different color-ray personalities may vary. Few people will have all or most of the following characteristics as listed under their color ray. This is primarily due to the fact that few individuals are in touch with their true natures. Once a person works with the gemstones and focuses on removing inner blockages to clear energy flow, they will discover their fundamental nature and begin to recognize the qualities of color-ray energy in themselves and other people such that they will become able to identify another's primary color ray as well as their own. With this in mind, read these descriptions and see if you can read the primary color ray of your friends. Let your decision as to your primary color ray wait until you have tried the exercises in this book.

Red-ray individuals are persuasive and self-assured. They can be the life of the party and often are quite content to challenge the group. They make great leaders and lovers. Inner strength can give red-ray people the edge where courage is required. They may be relied on to carry the day when they believe in their work. They enjoy being noticed but are also quite content to be on their own. They make good athletes and coaches. They can inspire others with their strong beliefs. They usually have strong opinions and can have trouble seeing others' points of view. Anger could be a problem as they try to connect with others, but have difficulty understanding another's process. Red-ray people who have learned patience can be very strong and grace all with their heartfelt beliefs. It is heart that will bring a red-ray person from persuasion to true inner strength. Where compassion enters the heart, simple passion turns into devotion. Disappointment with others will turn to acceptance.

Orange-ray people are spontaneous and lively. They are often the first in a group to decide their course in any given circumstance, and can influence others with their enthusiasm. They like to meet challenges and make good salespeople or travel agents. They are often outgoing, but may enjoy their own world of joyful fantasy when not encouraged by life or family. Their ability to step off into the unknown may make them popular in some circles, however risk-taking may not always be their best solution. Orange-ray people can be very genuine and can also be willful or self-absorbed if they do not learn how to relate to others. Those who can practice discrimination and go with the flow will be natural seers or mystics. Unlike the indigo person, their idea of mysticism is more a form of direct knowing. Orange-ray people can be quite amazing in their candor particularly when explaining their purposes. To excel, they must learn the difference between their latest idea and a well-founded decision based on the commitment that comes from the ability to see the big picture in the light of love.

Yellow-ray people are always busy. They like to be involved with setting goals and making plans. They are good at seeing the potential of situations and make good consultants. They can be trusted and will lend credibility to whomever they befriend. Seeing the future, they make good explorers, though they will often choose roles that call more on their ability to communicate as an equal. They like to get to completion with projects and are unhappy in circumstances or relationships that stagnate. If yellow-ray people can avoid the pitfalls of pride or alienation and learn to use their creativity with gratitude and focus they may become the most inspiring poets or artists. Much of what the finest artists do involves paring down the elements of their art until they have an expression that is so simple, so elegant, so fine that the world recognizes itself in the art. Yellow-ray people must learn the art of eliminating the unnecessary to reveal the essential. To overcome the apparent wall of meaninglessness, the yellow-ray person must cut to the essential. Sometimes silent, these outgoing people love excitement.

Green-ray people are comfortable with themselves. When well grounded and harmonious, their environment will become an extension of their character. They make excellent healers and are often able to see the cause for other peoples' physical conditions. Unlike most artists, they relate to others through their connection with the whole. They can often help others to find the most satisfying activities or careers. They make good counselors because they can understand and relate to introverts as well as extroverts. If a green-ray person can learn to overcome the natural drive to control life and learn generosity, they can achieve a deep serenity and emulate inner peace. Service is the key. Self-indulgence is their undoing. If a green-ray person finds their mission in life, they can inspire even the most reserved opponents with their commitment.

Blue-ray people can be very intelligent. They usually relate to others by sharing their concepts. They are good at understanding patterns and are usually well organized. They make good engineers and designers. They are usually precise and can see distinctions between similar ideas easily. They are always interested in cataloging their experiences and are mentally well structured. Often dispassionate or aloof, they can still make great teachers if they can overcome vanity and learn humility and receptivity. A self-realized blue-ray person is truly a blessing, for they are capable of true charity and compassion when devoted to a larger cause than their own. Truth and wisdom are their beacons and should never be compromised. When they can be true to themselves, no obstacle will be too great for the blue-ray person to move beyond. They see their course but must not forget to look up.

Indigo-ray people are intuitive. They can figure out what is missing or give clues to help resolve unsolvable problems. Look to the indigo person to have thought out all the angles from which to approach a problem in a simple, elegant way. They manipulate energy well. They speak in terms of correlation and metaphor when relating to others. They would do well as scientists or writers and are often found in contemplation and like to develop an overview from a private perspective. They may protect their fears as they have some difficulty trusting others or believing others can understand them. Their thoughts can run deep, though they may talk about superficial things to avoid conflict. An indigo-ray person must avoid their fears. It may not be easy for an indigo-ray person to know that fear is at work when they insulate themselves using rationalization. Simplifying their truth will set them free. If they can learn to motivate themselves, the future may hold great promise for their inventions and they can excel in structural engineering with surprising insight and creativity. They can make things work like no one has before.

Violet-ray people who have found their own values are wise. They take their time, get to know people gradually, and are often loyal. They like to work with symbols and make good psychologists or mathematicians. They also tend to stay in positions for the long haul and become managers or owners of real estate or other stable businesses. They will always choose their circumstances carefully and are tolerant and patient when life is well stabilized. When they find their center, violet-ray people can be charming, even charismatic. When they have found an inner sense of joy, they can weather any storm. If they can learn detachment from their own strong symbols and ideals, a deep joy and freedom can be developed. Only through detachment will violet-ray people find a wholeness or a feeling of being at home within themselves. They must learn balance and develop integrity before they can allow anyone else what is necessary for growth, otherwise they may continually fight or rebel, cutting all ties or trying to win with control rather than love.

The most rare, white-ray people are integrated and self-assured. They mix well with all people. They are usually comfortable working with many different kinds of people. They make good diplomats, chairmen, or judges as they can usually see everyone's point of view in any discussion. As observers, they are often capable of objective detachment. They may find it difficult to be like others. Yet, they may, in rare instances, be able to develop the qualities of all the other color rays and integrate them into their way of relating to life. If they are able to take this process to its natural conclusion, they will be truly great architects and capable of taking large and unique projects to a manifest conclusion. Foundation is important to white-ray persons. If you are white ray by nature, then do not be in a hurry, for you must learn many skills before you can bring to fruition something that would challenge you. Be persistent, overcome the tendency toward a judgmental attitude, and be open to all possibilities, and you will find your inner strength.

When you have finished reading the chapters that follow, come back to this chapter and see if you can better identify you primary color ray. This is your strength ray. It will help you develop your most important traits as well as helping you master your most challenging life obstacles. For some people, their primary ray is not the first color ray they identify as their strength ray. Go ahead and work with the one that seems best suited to you and you will soon discover if it is your primary ray. It may take months of working with the ray that first reveals itself as the strength ray before you can realize your true nature. The first ray you recognize is your strength ray. Read the chapter for this ray often and follow the leads you get from working with the gemstones as described in that chapter, and you will be able to develop a great ability to work with your color ray.

If you have no guess as to your strength ray, work with the orange ray first. Orange gemstones will help you to find balance and discover your primary ray. Its presence will begin processes within you that balance any major imbalances in your system that might be making it impossible to immediately recognize either your strength or primary color ray. Give it time. Major changes are best done gradually. Persist, and all you wish for will be yours.

Aspects of Our Color-Ray Path

Each of the various color rays provides a different spiritual path for those who were created with that particular dominant ray. Find your color ray and look for indications of improvement. Also see where the inner strength of your particular color ray lies. On the next pages, some symbols for meditation and the corresponding power animals are given, along with musical notes, body organs, planets, and zodiac signs for each ray. Do not assume that the zodiac sign of your birth will relate to the color ray under which you originated. Our sun signs and the relative positions of the planets at our birth do not correspond to the prime color rays but do correlate to our individual mission in this life. Look instead for the deeper significance of the color-ray symbols as they relate to your inner struggles.

Imagine, if you will, that all souls were created and when they enter into the lower universes for the first time to take on a physical body, they enter through one of eight portals. Each of these portals is like a gate. It has a primary color and vibration. Our color is that color ray for the duration of our time in the lower worlds. This vibration holds keys to our spiritual renaissance, the freedom we seek. Throughout our existence, we search for the keys and abilities that will allow us to return to this gate and be given access to the heavenly worlds beyond. Cultivate your strength ray and you will begin to see your way home.

Red

Path to Self-Realization: grace
Primary Spiritual Goal: purification, immortality
Positive Mental Attributes: tolerance, patience, focus
Positive Emotional Attributes: acceptance, passion
Negative Mental Attributes: guilt, blame, disappointment
Negative Emotional Attributes: passivity/anger, rebellion/wrath
Symbols: cross
Power Animal: lion
Musical Note: do
Body Organs: kidneys
Planet: Mars
Zodiac Sign: Taurus
Material: fire
Numbers: 6, 13, 20

Orange

Path to Self-Realization: surrender
Primary Spiritual Goal: spiritual presence, valor, soul perception
Positive Mental Attributes: discrimination, initiative, spontaneity
Positive Emotional Attributes: happiness, joy, enthusiasm
Negative Mental Attributes: confusion, disillusionment
Negative Emotional Attributes: lust, withholding/victim
Symbols: five-pointed star

Power Animal: butterfly
Musical Note: re
Body Organs: lungs
Planet: Sun
Zodiac Sign: Aries
Material: sulfur, wood
Numbers: 5, 12, 19

Yellow

Path to Self-Realization: gratitude
Primary Spiritual Goal: creativity, individuation
Positive Mental Attributes: focus, inspiration, inventiveness
Positive Emotional Attributes: strength, courage, individuality
Negative Mental Attributes: pride/rebellion, alienation
Negative Emotional Attributes: shame/humiliation,
     disregard/meaninglessness
Symbols: eight-petal lotus
Power Animal: eagle
Musical Note: me
Body Organs: heart
Planet: Mercury
Zodiac Sign: Leo
Material: mercury, gold
Numbers: 1, 8, 15

Green

Path to Self-Realization: contentment
Primary Spiritual Goal: harmony, serenity, peace
Positive Mental Attributes: temperance, balance, equilibrium
Positive Emotional Attributes: generosity, willingness, empathy
Negative Mental Attributes: greed, control, austerity
Negative Emotional Attributes: indolence, gluttony, cowardice
Symbols: fulcrum, cube
Power Animal: fish
Musical Note: fa
Body Organs: intestines, spleen
Planet: Venus
Zodiac Signs: Libra, Pisces
Material: water
Numbers: 4, 11, 18

Blue

Path to Self-Realization: charity
Primary Spiritual Goal: devotion, compassion
Positive Mental Attributes: reciprocity, intelligence, acuity
Positive Emotional Attributes: humility, heart wisdom, purity
Negative Mental Attributes: vanity, arrogance, false modesty
Negative Emotional Attributes: envy/indulgence, aloofness/disdain
Symbols: caduceus, lovers
Power Animal: wolf
Musical Note: so
Body Organs: sense organs, sensory part of brain
Planet: Moon
Zodiac Signs: Capricorn, Virgo
Material: earth
Numbers: 2, 9, 16

Indigo

Path to Self-Realization: mercy, forgiveness
Primary Spiritual Goal: integration, wisdom, justice
Positive Mental Attributes: intuition, synthesis, structure
Positive Emotional Attributes: caring, perseverance
Negative Mental Attributes: perfectionism, prejudice, judgment
Negative Emotional Attributes: disdain/hate and bitterness
Symbols: egg
Power Animal: frog
Musical Note: la
Body Organs: liver, skeletal
Planet: Saturn
Zodiac Signs: Cancer, Sagittarius
Material: silica, calcium
Numbers: 7, 14, 21

Violet

Path to Self-Realization: joy
Primary Spiritual Goal: freedom, abundance
Positive Mental Attributes: detachment, centeredness, fairness
Positive Emotional Attributes: responsive, fortunate, inclusive
Negative Mental Attributes: attachment, worry, projection
Negative Emotional Attributes: fear and despondence, defeatism
Symbols: iris, angel
Power Animal: bear
Musical Note: ti
Body Organs: adrenal glands (endocrine)
Planet: Jupiter
Zodiac Sign: Aquarius
Material: clay
Numbers: 3, 10, 17

White

Path to Self-Realization: integration (wholeness)

Primary Spiritual Goal: initiation and foundation

Positive Mental Attributes: spontaneity, cycles of fertility, potential

Positive Emotional Attributes: clarity, receptivity, directness

Negative Mental Attributes: oppression of self, idle curiosity

Negative Emotional Attributes: coldness, emptiness, bankruptcy

Symbols: snowflakes

Power Animal: man

Musical Note: all notes

Body Organs: skin

Planet: Uranus

Zodiac Sign: Gemini

Material: air

Numbers: 0, 22

Welcome Companions on Our Road

The next section of chapters in this book are designated by color and describes many commonly used therapeutic gemstones of the respective color. As energetic beings, we require a balance of all the color rays. Gemstones are powerful amplifiers and focusers of the color-ray energy. These tools will help individuals learn how to regulate and distribute the flow of color-ray energies within the physical and subtle bodies. Once this energy is fully understood, any person can begin to work with these energies without the aid of these tools.

Therapeutic gemstones are of incalculable help in the process of safely breaking down personal energy blocks and tuning the physical and subtle bodies to optimal performance of the many physical, supraphysical, emotional, causal, mental, subconscious, and spiritual operations without losing oneself in the influences of energies. A few remarkable individuals tap a modest portion of the energy available to them, but most of us make use of only a tiny fraction of what is possible. Gemstones teach us, and as we learn we can become masters of the use of energy.

Read this book through once, and then simply take the time to practice the exercises in these chapters one segment at a time. Add your own exercises as you conceive of them, and the peace and harmony that comes with the practice of grace and love will fill your life. All spiritual unfoldment occurs as a person is ready. Gemstones cannot direct the spiritual forces of love, but they can teach us to be ready. This journey takes time, but gemstones may be welcome companions when the road becomes rocky.

Part II

The Color-Ray Carriers

Let us journey first into the heart of the red ray. As we enter the red portal from which all souls who are of the red ray enter the worlds of materiality, we are struck with the profound importance of the spiritual lessons of this ray—survival, strength, courage, and passion. In this purely red vibration area we find the elemental aspects of personality that reflect the divine qualities of red. We begin to recognize that red is this planet's most-absorbed color. As we realize that red light is absorbed by things, we are shown how the other colors within light, like green and blue, are reflected from the surfaces of the objects of our world.

Our eyes have receptors that receive the impression of either red, green, or blue. All other colors are seen as combinations of these three, just as the three colors of video tubes in a video projector project thousands of colors produced from only red, green, and blue. Thereby, we learn that the red ray is one of the three prime color rays for this planet. It is most important for our survival. For example, our eyes can differentiate well over four-hundred shades of red. By comparison, we are capable of differentiating only some forty shades of blue. In our discussion of insights into the characteristics of this ray, we shall be concerned with primary red, though many other shades have characteristics in common.

3 Red Ray Stones

Red is the ray of strength. It provides wearers the key to greater courage when the vibration of red flows freely within. Courage comes from the strength of knowing who we are. To learn who we are, we must abandon all limitations and preconceived notions of who we think we are. One who lacks courage would not consider taking such a bold and adventurous path through unknown territory to recreate their mind and body. Red ray energy encourages it.

You do not need to recreate your life to find love. You need only learn compassion, and your life will never be the same. The red ray can bring more compassion into your life. We can learn much about the value of compassion, which opens the heart to make love strong. Love is a weak force when compassion is not demonstrated. An open heart is the first prerequisite to true love. True love is a most powerful force.

Passion is the territory of the red ray. Look for passion, and the red ray will be the guide. It supports all who desire a deep passion for everything that life has to offer. Passion here refers not simply to the desire for sex, but to a deeply felt desire for life and the fullness it offers.

Use the red ray to clear away feelings of inadequacy. Learn how to stand tall. Learn to make decisions. Learn to know what is good for you and those you love. The red opens the door to inner confidence. It builds the physical strength as it improves mental stamina and resolve.

If red is your primary color ray, you will want to work with each and every one of the red and pink gemstones. They will help you develop composure and the serenity that comes from being at home wherever you are. For those who need the experience of strength, ruby will teach the inner process of becoming a spiritual warrior, one who is courageous enough to live in accord with their spiritual purpose.

Your strength may be used for the good of all—not to create a perfect world, but to maintain an inner focus on the positive as it manifests in the world. Red supports a belief in this positive force. Tremendous strength is required to hold fast to a belief in the absolute, the omnipresent, and the omnipotent qualities of spirit. Most people would like to believe, but they feel a strain when challenged with the idea of acting on that belief at all times. Most people prefer to complain about situations in life, asking "Where is the fairness in life?" Blaming people and circumstances in life for their own inner weakness is a common trait of those who prefer to exhibit their weakness rather than change it. Nearly all of us blame sometimes. The challenge of the red ray is to give with passion.

To have compassion for the struggles of people caught in the web of life, you must have great inner strength. Allow the red ray stones to teach inner strength. Allow them to work with your feelings of fear and weakness. Commit to giving up all limitations and avoidance of personal responsibility for your subjective world. Do this, and inner strength will be yours. Passion will be yours. When you find inner strength, you can walk among the crises that are all around and feel compassion, never being drawn into negative thinking. Imagine not having a thought of scarcity. Imagine not feeling oppressed or overwrought. Imagine being in a world where life is a spiritual experience, and where understanding and compassion follow your every perception. Imagine these things are possible, and the red ray will open your heart to their reality.

Ruby

Imagine a great giant whose heart is overflowing with love. This being is called to your side by ruby. As it comes into your aura, you become aware that it will teach you to love. As you learn of human love, you will begin to understand selfless love as well. Perfect love may be yours as you follow this gentle but powerful guidance.

Ruby is the primary carrier of the red ray. Do not underestimate its strength. It is intense and will act on your deepest parts with a kind of love that you may not be familiar with. Choose ruby carefully, and use the most translucent variety you can afford. A single high-quality stone of deep red color will do more good than a whole necklace of the lesser-quality ruby. Ruby has the power of a freight train. As long as it is on the pure red-ray track, its vibrations will carry you a long way.

The red ray will most support those whose main color ray is red. For these people, strength is derived largely from their feelings, and ruby will help them sustain a higher level of and a more fulfilling type of feelings without becoming out of balance.

Ruby teaches detached love and moves us to accept divine will. This force drives us to experience a greater abundance of love through giving. Whatever love we are able to give out, it will amplify. It generates desire, as well, and desire tempered by love is indeed a transformational force. Even when we find ourselves overwhelmed by forces that seek to harm us or disrupt our lives, we still can come from a place of love. In this way, we will not be scorched by the fire when we walk through the red-hot coals of life's tests. We may cross the rough waters in a storm and though we may get wet, we will not be filled with fear.

We may even learn to give up fear. After all, we experience pain only to the degree to which we resist the reality of what is there. We resist reality to the degree to which we are afraid of what will happen to us if we go with it. To be free of suffering, we need only give up fear. Once we give up all fear, we need never give up another thing.

As we learn to trust ruby's strength it will show us how illusion captures the imagination. A free imagination is a great power. If we listen and are willing to learn, we will start to understand that nothing "bad" ever really happens to us. Granted, we do not always expect what happens. We don't always like what happens. We simply learn that all experiences have a gift for us. Ruby supports this attitude. It demands that we adopt a positive attitude, realizing our potential in love. Negative attitudes slowly burn in the presence of ruby. With a positive attitude, we can indeed walk the coals that appear able to destroy.

Nothing happens to us that we have not attracted by having strong feelings about it. Ruby will intensify strong feelings. You will not be able to mistake them. If you experience strong negative feelings, ruby will intensify them until you begin to understand that the attitudes you hold on to that cause those feelings can be subtly changed until they generate more positive feelings. By having strong, positive feelings, you will attract the experiences of life that bring joy and the intense pleasure of a love without expectation of what you must have in return.

Approach decisions to change attitudes that generate strong feelings carefully. First, place a ruby in the center of the chest just below the protrusion of bone at the sternum and determine whether a feeling is negative by reviewing how that feeling motivates you. Sometimes even anger can be positive if it motivates one to growth. Second, trace negative, destructive feelings to the attitude that engendered them. Third, carefully write down exactly what you believe and your attitude toward life. Fourth, place a single ruby on the brow, between the eyes, just above the eyebrows, and a third ruby one inch below the navel. After you have allowed this placement to begin working for a few minutes, look again at what you have written. Try to determine how you could change your attitude slightly to allow more positive, growth-enhancing feelings to attach themselves to this attitude.

For facilitating change, this stone is unparalleled. It will go to work immediately on the emotional hotbeds of self-hatred and guilt. Disruption of these negative areas may lead us to a kind of love we are not used to experiencing. If we are not willing to let these go, we will find ourselves burning our feet as we cross the hot coals of passion. We will find the storms of life ripping our sails.

At first you may wish to work with single rondels—flattened spheres— a common shape for ruby beads. You can tape one on any point that you intuitively feel needs the red ray drawn into it. I suggest you not try chakras or other points located along your body's center line until you have experimented with points located on extremities or along the left or right side of the body. Changes that result from center line placements are usually deeper and more global within the context of one's life than those resulting from placements on other points. Note that for most wearers, left-side placements will affect issues related to the feminine side and right-side placements usually bring up issues affecting masculine energies.

For physical regeneration, there will likely be several points on the abdomen that can use the red ray. These will be points of reflexive connectedness to certain organs or body systems. Between one and sixteen rubies can work on a single organ area at one time.

Locate the troubled organ. Then choose a single ruby and hold the ruby between the thumb and first finger. Ask your body if it would like a ruby. Notice if your body resists or accepts the ruby as you move it toward the abdomen. If it accepts the ruby, apply it where it seems to want to go (use tape if necessary). Do not be concerned about precision. Your intuition will be correct ninety-five percent of the time. An incorrect placement will not cause harm. It will still add to the treatment, though it will be less effective than those placed directly over a target point. When you have placed as many stones as you feel your body wants, allow these stones to remain for a few minutes while paying attention to physical sensations and breathing.

Ruby is very effective for treating weakened muscle groups. Especially affected are muscles associated with weightlifting and other forms of strenuous physical exercise. Most of these muscle groups are the same on both the right and left sides of the body, and the function of the mirror group on the opposite side of the body is identical. For treating muscle points located on the arms or legs, it usually is best to use a ruby on both arms or both legs at the same point and at the same time.

Muscle groups along the spine, or chest-muscle groups, are best treated by also treating the opposing muscles, so that a balance is maintained. Place a single ruby on each group and allow it to remain for two to six hours. Muscles can take a sustained gradual infusion of the ruby-directed red ray.

Single rubies are very effective when used on the life-path points. These points, located where the Achilles tendon meets the calf muscle on the back of the lower leg, are central to the flow of energies that you can direct to create a new life path or to more fully realize the path you are on. This point is about five to eight inches up the back of the leg from the floor, when standing. On an average male of five feet, ten inches in height, this point would be approximately six and three-quarters inches up from the floor. Wear a ruby on both legs for three hours or less and expect to realize a change in your relationship with the future.

Wear rubies only until they begin to "itch" or feel uncomfortable. You may notice yourself getting very irritable or having a hard time with your emotions. Whatever your symptoms are, you will notice an unusual urge to tear the rubies off. Go ahead. You may wish to wear them for only a few minutes to an hour at first.

Once we have used ruby to point out and help us deal with issues, we are ready to build our physical stamina to allow us to sustain a greater output of energy. We all are capable of using red energy to build our inner storehouse as sound as a fortress. Ruby will provide a large amount of red energy. This energy builds life force, *chi* as it's known in China. Life force will seek to express itself. It cannot easily be blocked. It freely builds the strength of the inner fortress made of chi as long as we do not insist on leaving breaches in the wall. Fortress walls are of red-ray building blocks in combination with other color rays. Each building block is supported by others and is formed and held together by a self-directed attitude. For example, when you have allowed some thoughts of unworthiness to enter your mind as the fortress is being rebuilt, the wall will be built mislaying some of the red-ray building blocks leaving a breach. See the information on red coral in chapter 13 ("Treasures of the Deep") for more information on building an inner fortress of positive color-ray energy.

We may be blocking our life force in ways we were taught in the early months of life. At that age, we gave all we had, whether it was in the form of crying or laughter. When we expressed our needs simply, our "gods"— our parents and other guardians at the time—may have told us "shhhhh" or "stop it." Perhaps we cried out for love and got set down and left alone. Our parents probably were doing the best they could, but we were aware of feeling small and rejected. We may have learned that giving all does not result in joy or acceptance.

Now, when things don't go well, we may find ourselves quitting. We may be afraid of rejection or abandonment. We may even despise our needs. We may come to despise ourselves if our needs seem to bring us only bad responses.

Ruby will encourage us to rethink the decisions we made as toddlers. A youth often makes important life decisions at too young an age. An adult can learn that there is more than one way to look at things.

The life force as directed by ruby will drive us to trust and be vulnerable. Trust is essential to getting needs met. We may be pushed to expand our world by this force. It may cause us to change everything. Better that we change than become increasingly bitter and resentful.

As ruby works with us, we will become more capable of expressing ourselves. Our emotional storms will slowly settle into passions for good, life-supporting purposes. We may become better able to protect ourselves from disruptive or harmful influences. For those who have trouble maintaining their psychic space, boundaries will become clearer. One will have greater tolerance for someone else's boundaries while holding strong their right to their own space.

When ruby is worn with frosted quartz, the almost overpowering effects of ruby will be moderated. You can stay better balanced and begin to see the causes for your tendency toward imbalance. With the assistance of quartz, balance will be easier to maintain.

When worn with rose quartz, ruby will open us up like a wind blowing open our closed inner doors. Our inner world can be likened to a mansion. Many of the hundreds of rooms have not been opened for years, if ever. Within each room is another world. As we reenter a room we discover the original purposes that set in motion a particular goal in our life.

We will uncover secrets about ourselves that we have kept well hidden. We will develop a greater capacity to love ourselves and to reject self-effacing behaviors.

For those who wear ruby with Biwa pearls and rhodocrosite spheres, a whole new way of relating to the emotional self will open up. You will be shown how to rebuild your every goal according to mature emotions. This process may take months, and it will not be easy. Patterns we have held onto tightly will be removed link by link and eventually replaced by new, self-affirming behaviors.

When you wear a full strand of high-quality rubies, the effects will be considerable. Even for those who are not open to changes in their emotional makeup, this strand will ignite a fire of desire and intensify their every emotion. Wear the strand with caution and be aware of the actions you take. You will not do things the same way you have in the past, and the difference will bring powerful insights. If you can relate differences to life decisions and discover the basis for those decisions, you can modify those decisions to allow more freedom.

For those whose main strength color is not red, wear more than a few rubies only when awake and for durations of perhaps twenty minutes or less, interspersing this with treatments of your main strength ray.

Ruby is highly effective, even in tiny amounts. For most, this powerful carrier of red ray energy is best used singly or in combination necklaces with white coral, Biwa pearl, or other red stones. A single three- or four-millimeter rondel or sphere of ruby, when placed on the body, will carry the red ray deep within. Place it on the sternum, or anywhere within three inches of the navel that "calls" for it, or on acupuncture point CV 21, which is located about six inches below either underarm on an average adult male. A single ruby will infuse the entire region within twenty to thirty minutes.

Using ruby as the first opening to an issue will prove the most direct movement into that issue. Ruby steals into an issue like a thief entering a jewelry store. It adores each aspect of an issue. Even as it is entering a special case to reveal a prize that is usually hidden from casual eyes, it gently opens the case and reverently appreciates its beauty. Such is the love within the red ray as it challenges our limitations.

The red ray is the key to courage, strength, and compassion, and ruby is the prime carrier of the red ray. Use it with clear intention. Do not wear this stone without either knowing what you want or being willing to receive and act on a new perspective. Think before choosing ruby. When you have a clear inner direction and have confronted inner obstacles, you can use ruby to give life to your dreams. Dreams can become reality, but you must be clear on how you wish to achieve them. Dreams must feel good when picturing them. Loving, warm feelings can then drive us to actualizing our greatest visions.

Positive feelings that are infused with red-ray energy are like tugboats. They can move even the largest ships. Goals are like large ships, beautiful and inviting. They cannot, however, go anywhere until a tugboat gets them safely out of the harbor. Once on the open seas and properly navigated, even the largest ships can cross the ocean. In fact, sometimes the largest ships provide the smoothest rides over rough seas. Dreams are like a harbor. If you wish to get out of the harbor of dreams, you must employ strong feelings, whereby even the largest goals can be put into service.

Let ruby develop your courage, stamina, strength, and desire, and you will be able to move large ships to far destinations.

Red Garnet (Rhodolite)

Rhodolite is the name given the reddish variety of garnet. It is mostly red, but carries the blue ray as well. High-quality rhodolite is readily available, so do not settle for inferior grades. You should endeavor to find stones that are perfectly spherical rather than poorly rounded. For garnet to have therapeutic effect, it must have clarity and deep color. Choose stones that sparkle with energy.

Garnet is very helpful for those who think they are not worth much to anyone. For those with a weak ego and little ability to take care of themselves, garnet will support maturation of the ego. As time passes, those who wear a necklace of garnet will find it increasingly easy to stand up for themselves. Their sense of who they are will become stronger as they take action to protect themselves and stand aside when harm seeks them out.

Those who suffer from a vague feeling of insufficiency also will be aided. Garnet will gradually highlight areas of the emotional body that carry bad feelings. These areas invariably are linked to areas in the mental body that conceal thoughts of self-derision. Others in our lives may have once—even repeatedly—said we were bad people. Only we can internalize these thoughts. Are we really so bad? Have we done our best and learned from our mistakes? Garnet will insist we reevaluate the verdicts of others. It will show us how to argue with diminutive thoughts. Each thought requires an exactly opposite thought to cancel it. Garnet energizes thoughts of positive self-image, and this allows cancellation of self-destructive thoughts. For each negative self-projection on the inner screen, garnet creates a positive character that stands up to it.

We may have been mean at one time. We may have done things about which we feel remorse. These facts do not prove a case against us and we can make amends for our wrongdoings. We are not our behaviors. Behaviors are changeable. What we were yesterday, we are no longer today. Garnet teaches us to stop generalizing and oversimplifying. It shows us when we are thinking that we should somehow be omnipotent. It teaches us to expect mistakes with positive assurance that mistakes are the stepping stones to success. Those who make the most mistakes test the most new decisions and become good decision makers who resolve even the most enervating, depressing, overwhelming circumstances and rise above like the phoenix to become something greater. That is who we are.

No tool will do your work for you, and this tool is no exception. You must take action and stand up for yourself. This effort may not require you to take dangerous risks, but it will certainly require you to set limits and speak up for your needs.

For those who are a little headstrong or who have a tendency to judge others, garnet would not be a useful tool. It is much more appropriate for those who do not know what their opinions are.

Garnet may help you improve your shield of protection. It can act like the magical shield of Greek mythology. It reflects trouble back to the sender.

We are not required to participate in all of life's many situations. We often are faced with situations that do not involve us and in which we do not have to take any part. Initially, new boundaries we set up with the help of garnet will be fairly rigid. These boundaries often will not work above the supraphysical level. Do not rely on them for protection against the caustic or deranged thoughts of those who may wish to harm you. Boundaries are only a start. Learning to back up your position may be a bit more difficult, but at least you will learn you have the right to stand up for yourself. Knowing when a boundary is crossed is the first step in self-protection.

Garnet in combination with ruby provides limited insight into the nature of heart conditions. Wearers may become aware of constrictions in the heart chakra before they manifest into physical conditions. Placing a strand of garnet over the heart may help improve certain conditions of poor blood circulation. Improved circulation, in combination with regular exercise and a good diet, can improve physical strength.

Garnet carries a very hard energy and is perfect for those who lack drive. A dense form of vibration, garnet is patterned in a way that supports predictability. This form may help those who easily lose sight of all sense of the familiar. Without a sense of the familiar, confusion repeatedly develops. Garnet will work on the fear that nothing remains the same and help to provide a sense of continuity. Garnet will show the wearer that within the fabric of impermanence is the eternal. It will describe a way for us to include self-directed change in our routine. We can set up healthy routines that include moderate change. This notion is paradoxical, for once a habit becomes a rut, it will no longer serve us, but without habits we have great difficulty connecting to the permanent, eternal, unchanging part of us within. Garnet shows us the key to the paradox of how to train the mind to a disciplined routine and include the discriminate use of change as intuition suggests it.

A life with no habit is a life with no self-discipline. Self-discipline is a prerequisite to healthy living. On the other hand it can also be our downfall to continue with habits that no longer serve us. Because of this, our habits must be carefully monitored, balancing change with disciplined routine. You must learn when discipline is helpful and when it no longer aids growth but instead cuts you off from the flow of life. Garnet teaches appropriate use of discipline and the benefits of a flexible discipline.

For those with a wistful nature who cannot get their feet on the ground or remain with a decision long enough to see it through, red garnet is a good influence. It allows you to stay with a resolution until you reach the point where you can bring about results. Holding a resolution until you can manifest new circumstances in your life could take years. Patience is improved when you do not question the process of manifestation as it is working. Wearers of garnet learn to question at the beginning of the process but hold back from further questioning and self-doubt once the process has moved to later stages.

Garnet can be worn all the time. The wearer can let it fill the aura and keep it filled. Even the four-millimeter size will be sufficient to maintain enough of the garnet vibration to maintain a solid sense of your own energy. You can keep its influence in the aura, even when not wearing the necklace, by putting your attention on the stone and its color. By allowing the constant presence of garnet, you will be rewarded with a new sense of purpose and clarity. Each of us has our own purpose and if we can be who we are, we can find our way, but it does not work in reverse. We cannot find our way in order to be who we are. Allow garnet to take you into who you are. As a guide it can especially help those who give away their being to avoid the challenge of facing who they are.

You can look to garnet as a mentor interface. A mentor is any life form that can teach how life works. All life forms can teach how their way of life works as they live it. Garnet connects us to those that can help us as mentors and to those who we can help. It creates a chain that is similar to an electronic interface. Garnet could be viewed as a great network of interlinking connections. Every end of this interlink is connected to a consciousness. Myriad ends are each connected to some living thing that could teach us something about how to make our life work. If we can send out clear messages over this network about what we want or need, the knowledge of how to get it will be provided by a mentor.

Garnet works directly with the interlink. The mind and body work like a computer, accessing the interlink to get whatever one wants. It has a central processor and several input devices, which include the senses. Then there is the higher self, which works like the programmer and user of the computer. The higher self can design and control the use of all programs to get incredible results in any area of life. It has full knowledge of the parameters of the program and can find others who are motivated to accomplish things. The computer, when not run by the programmer, can operate on automatic pilot. We all do some of this, at times operating the computer, other times allowing it to run itself. The question is why the higher self stays out of the process when it can do such a good job at taking charge. The answer has to do with hidden agendas, guilt, and honesty. The higher self cannot operate programs containing hidden agendas. The mind, on the other hand, loves to keep on going on its own, operating with or without these agendas.

Here is the cycle: when you run programs with hidden agendas, you get skewed results. Skewed results create guilt. Guilt is such a powerful negative force that it generates bad feelings. Bad feelings produce self-negation. Self-negation on a regular basis requires dishonesty. Dishonesty forces denial of the higher self. Denial forces the higher self to abandon the role of programmer (it cannot participate in destructive cycles.) Once the higher self is out of the role of programmer, the mind will continue to run programs with hidden agendas. It will tell itself that the results it is getting are good, but that the problems encountered are to be blamed on others. The mind will send out messages on the interlink that it needs others to blame for its incompetence. Others who are in guilt binds and are in deep denial that has created self-dishonesty will answer the call. The cycle renews. Each time it renews, it gets deeper.

Do you find yourself getting results you cannot feel entirely good about? Do you notice that your behavior seems to create feelings of inadequacy? Do you find yourself blaming others? Do you accuse others of having hidden agendas? Do you feel guilt when things go any other way than the way you planned?

If you answered yes to any of these, you are not alone. Millions of people feel their lives slipping away and their positive goals drifting off. This is one reason why cults and drugs and alcohol are in constant demand. The cycle is painful. Drugs and other distractions forestall the pain, only to defer it until later. Coming off drugs is difficult partially because one must go through this deferred pain.

Garnet is an ally. It can be your friend. It can teach you to desire self-esteem. It can begin a new cycle in your life, if you want it enough. This cycle leads to the higher self taking charge and becoming stronger rather than weaker in its programming skills.

Here is the new cycle: the higher self designs a program for your improvement. The mind has no hidden agendas. All your agendas, wants, needs, and expected outcomes are stated clearly. The message is sent out over the interlink. Other healthy life forms gladly reply. They participate in the mentor program with you. No guilt is generated because you and every one of these life forms is clear on the complete program. Results may be as one predicted or not. Either way the results are good because all are learning, no denial is necessary, and guilt is not present, so everyone feels good about the effort. Another program is designed for a new cycle.

This one is a better program and is based on the learning from the last. The call goes out and the cycle is renewed.

Garnet builds the self-esteem you need to start a program of regular growth, keeping all your agendas out in the open. Garnet builds an interlink with those who would participate in guilt-free, honest programs of growth. In this way, garnet is an excellent ally when you commit to positive change. It helps you to experience being positive.

Often, those who suffer low self-esteem feel ashamed when a friend or someone in their family is ashamed. Garnet helps you build a safe barrier to someone else's shame until you can develop an awareness of how to keep from taking on another's emotions. Without unnecessary shame, or other's shame, your self-image improves.

Garnet increases the desire for positive results. Garnet increases the awareness of self-defeating behaviors. In short, rhodolite garnet is the best supporting vibrational energy tool to shift one into a cycle of growth and away from any cycle of destructive self-negation.

Rhodonite

The specific color of rhodonite used for someone's therapy must be chosen with an eye to match it with the needs of the individual. This is simple to do; place the rhodonite against the person's chest and look at it. Try the different varieties, ranging from light pink to dark rose. If one variety of rhodonite appears more colorful, more vibrant, more beautiful against the person's chest than it did sitting on the table, then it is the correct variety. The person will usually be drawn to rhodonite if it can help them. It is immediately soothing to those who can use the emotional support.

Perhaps the person for whom the stone is intended should choose the most beneficial variety by its appeal to them. This choice can be a highly personal matter. Assume that the variety that looks and feels most pleasing to you is the correct variety for you to use.

Rhodonite has its greatest effect on the emotional body. It sends out lines of force in an elliptical orbit around the body. These lines of force are particularly helpful to those who have a hard time remaining in their physical bodies because of fear or trauma. It will relieve that disconcerting feeling of being out of touch or of not being quite "there." These lines of force connect areas of strength in the emotional sheath. Those who suffer from panic, emotional overload, or are frequently overwhelmed by fear and depression have significant areas of weakness in their astral body aura. As points of greater strength are interconnected, a feeling of well-being will develop.

Reintegration is a key part of the mission of rhodonite. It makes the reintegration of your suppressed parts easier. Wearers are gently served with soothing, emotional support. Total integration can be achieved in small, easily assimilated steps. The process could take months or years as an appropriately easy pace is accepted by the individual. Those whose identity has been shattered and display multiple personalities will require psychiatric help, but can find some comfort when wearing rhodonite.

For those who have taken psychoactive drugs, this realignment and reintegration of the emotional (astral) body would be quite helpful, though it may not represent a cure. Sometimes the astral body can become misshapen or contorted, and this condition can manifest as bone alignment problems. The action of rhodonite can be very helpful for this condition if worn all the time for several weeks or more. In these cases, until realignment can be effected, certain organs will remain weak or begin to degenerate as long as this distortion causes astral energies to be misdirected.

A variety of emotional problems can be traced to misalignment of the astral and other subtle sheaths. Chronic conditions of anger, hysteria, panic, depression, anxiety, insomnia, fatigue, or other more normal emotions that persist, but have no immediate cause, are always accompanied by misalignment. Long-term care, including continuous use of rhodonite, can help bring the bodies into harmony and will ultimately ease distortions and misalignments.

For cases where aberrations are severe, use rhodonite that is filled with black specks. The light-pink variety may appeal more to those who have need of emotional nurturing. Medium-pink varieties will assist in collapsed emotional boundary issues. Rose varieties will help the wearer to recapture lost feelings of abundance and freedom. Darker rose rhodonite helps one face deeper fears and panic. A more pure red variety will be preferred by those interested in protection from potentially damaging rays or psychic forces that may be at work on the astral body. Each color nourishes a different aspect of the emotional sheath.

In cases where greater emotional security is needed, you may wish to wear rhodonite with ruby to help create a firmer foundation. Any move toward greater security will occur gently and as you are able to assimilate the changes. For those who require a major restructuring in some area of their emotional lives, a strand of rhodonite worn with rose quartz, ruby, and other red ray stones will do the job over a period of perhaps a few months. The rhodonite will help the wearer maintain greater balance during the restructuring process. Restructuring takes place naturally as feelings of stress, anxiety, and fear are reduced in the presence of rhodonite.

Rhodonite eases the trace anxieties hidden in the fabric of their emotional sheath that resulted from emotional stress. It may help the wearer improve his sense of self-worth because it helps him deal more effectively and appropriately with his emotions. The wearer can learn to deal with strong emotions that otherwise would completely overwhelm any ability to reason and thereby shut down all contact with intuition. Maintaining balance is a key to self-control, therefore, clear quartz is a good supporting stone to use with rhodonite to ease anxiety.

The ability to control or at least modify and moderate emotions is part of the inner strength required to maintain healthy self-esteem. Rhodonite doesn't directly build self-esteem but it does teach you how to moderate or subdue excessive emotions by highlighting them and the consequences that follow from such excess.

Self-esteem comes to those who trust their inner strength. This trust develops over time. First, you must be able to choose your responses to life's situations. Look to ruby and rhodocrosite for help with this. Then you must be able to act with greater self-control. Rhodonite helps with emotional control by lowering inner pressure. Certain blue stones like lapis lazuli and sapphire help with mental control.

For those who have difficulty taking care of themselves, rhodonite is an ideal influence. Its subtle vibrations will support self-nurturing and emotional individuation. Like a layer of new skin, supple and firm, rhodonite will give the wearer a new look. The inner feeling of youth, an idealistic impervious self-assurance will precede you into a room.

The grounding effect of rhodonite is very helpful for those who are disoriented and prone to emotional highs and lows. Grounding will help those who feel out of control emotionally. At worst, someone who suffers from this condition is constantly disoriented. At best, a sufferer is unable to focus emotions, sustain them, or allow them to manifest his or her goals into physical results. Rhodonite will act to ground emotions so the individual can learn to safely, privately expose negative emotions and allow them to flow into the earth without harming anyone's emotional body. See the section on black onyx for more help with this.

As you wear rhodonite, you are able to reframe your experiences from the past that were of a destructive nature. You will learn to understand destructive behavior for what it is: defensive. You can learn to ease self-judgment and perhaps reach forgiveness. With persistence and the support of rhodonite, you can eradicate self-destructive patterns that stem from unbalanced defensive reactions that disturbed you or dominated past events.

A gentle process of changing the way you think of your situation and experiences from the past will begin and continue as long as the strand is kept on. Rhodonite eases harsh memories. Memories themselves are not directly affected, but the emotions attached to memories of traumatic events and past circumstances will change.

For memories that provoke anger, you may wish to include a black onyx sphere as every fifth bead on your necklace. Onyx furthers the ability of rhodonite to foster control of harmful anger or rage or any type of hysteria. This strand will help tremendously with managing anger problems as crises occur. Often, anger is part of a syndrome in which the person cannot distinguish their own world from that of others. This strand will aid the wearer in "owning" his own emotions and distinguishing them from those of others. Consider joining an anger management group as well as for greater support and longer lasting result, if anger has disrupted your life and the lives of those who are close to you.

Use only necklaces of one single variety of rhodonite when help with emotional control of the above symptoms or others like uncertainty, confusion, depression, or remorse is needed. Multiple varieties within one strand may be employed where the user has built an affinity with this stone and wishes to delve into more complex emotional reactions. Employ varieties which range from light pink through dark rose.

If clinical or manic depression is the diagnosis, include regular psychiatric consultations in your treatment plan. You should use rhodonite to support changes as they are carefully planned out in light of such counsel.

In cases where the emotions are not out of control, but the person is rarely feeling well emotionally, build a custom necklace from several rhodonite varieties. A rhodonite mixture will help the wearer work through unhappiness and discomfort when issues relate to many different current life conditions.

It may be best to rebuild all aspects of emotional strength where a person's emotions are simply depleted, missing, or unavailable. One must have long-term support for this condition. Test to be certain that emotional depletion is not a result of chronic physical pain or other more severe disorders. Include a physical checkup to test for physical causes in all cases of chronic emotional depletion or loss.

Rhodonite necklaces work like music therapy, gently reminding you of a better song. You may even discover a song in your heart after a time with this necklace. Singing can speed healing with rhodonite. Sing a song that speaks of the current trouble bothering your heart. Notice as rhodonite reveals the troubles of the past to the heart. As an old trouble arises, sing away the feelings. Make up your own lyrics to a popular melody, or just sing or hum a song that expresses the feelings in your heart.

Paintings and photographs are not as effective as songs. They are helpful, though, especially if the pictures are spoken of in a song or are relevant to one. Songs that paint accurate pictures of your feelings may be the best ones to sing. If your voice is not pleasing or sounds rough, you can use this singing technique when you are alone, however being in tune is not important to the results. Sing in the shower or by the nearest waterfall or highway, if the noise helps to make you less self-conscious. Wear headphones as you sing to music, and you will not hear your own voice as easily as you sing loudly. It is the act of putting the emotion into the words that releases the blockages. Sing as far off-key as you want if singing improves the emotional release. Although the car may be a good place to sing where others cannot hear, it is not safe to close the eyes or get into gestures that raise powerful emotions in a moving car. Emotional releases that follow singing may make driving unsafe.

The results from this exercise can be so remarkable that it can be worth making special preparations to achieve free and unhampered emotion while singing. Rhodonite makes great promises, but only by taking action do we teach the unconscious safe methods of clearing emotions. Listen to the promises of the stone. They are possible realities. Make the effort to prove to yourself that the safe and complete release of emotions will totally invigorate the emotional sheath. If you find yourself saying that this all sounds silly, then I guarantee that this exercise will bring results for you. Exercising the emotions will bring emotional strength and stamina. Workouts on a regular basis will guarantee greater joy.

Rhodonite helps wearers who believe they are well adjusted to free up emotions that are not easily expressed. I do not suggest that you should learn to emote more dramatically, rather I suggest that you learn to express feelings appropriately, and when possible with candor, in a balanced and harmonious way. Rhodonite will teach you to discern when to speak up and when to express emotions. Total expression is not always healing or sagacious.

Most of all, wearers will learn to feel their feelings within the heart center. They will learn to have greater control over their expression, how they appear, or react. A person may feel things more deeply when in control over their display of emotion. Like a great actor, we can learn to underplay our emotion and become all the more convincing for it.

Rhodocrosite

Quality is a most important consideration when working with rhodocrosite. Most rhodocrosite has a light pink color and a lot of white bands or areas of brown and white. Only the rare AAA-quality stones are translucent and have a deeper red-orange color. The very best stones have no white material, and all light directed at their surface flows easily through the deep red-orange material. These stones are a deep, dark color with no inclusions and total translucence. A stunning vibration is revealed to those who are ready for this mighty stone.

Stones containing large amounts of white material or other inclusions will be more harsh and will not be as effective in helping the wearer reach the higher planes of awareness. If possible, work with the finest-quality stones. Even small four- to six- millimeter rhodocrosite spheres will have a substantial effect if the quality is high. Wearers may also want to use ruby, rhodonite, Biwa pearl, or coral strands to help assimilate and process the changes that are expedited by rhodocrosite.

Rhodocrosite is a forceful gemstone indeed. Do not wear it unless you are asking for change or are "stuck." It acts primarily to bring an often deep and sometimes sudden change in your emotional makeup. Whenever it is worn, it acts like a tornado on any emotions that are not appropriate to or relevant to events in the present. It stirs up and intensifies any such emotion and incites you to review the original event that gave rise to that emotion and the associated feelings that accompanied it. This gemstone will keep energizing this set of feelings until you are able to detach from identification with the emotion and change your viewpoint, and thereby change your current emotion when reminded of past events. Ultimately, rhodocrosite will act on every emotion related to past events that remains upsetting within the subconscious mind.

Rhodocrosite is not recommended for the weak at heart. The powerful changes that begin the instant it is put on are for those who can handle deep and lasting change. If you can stay focused and direct the changes, you will be able to work through all sorts of issues, especially those giving rise to highly charged emotion.

Because of its effects on the emotions, rhodocrosite is well suited to those who have a strong connection to their intuitive natures. These individuals will be able to work through past events of extreme pain or trauma. For these individuals, changes that might have taken years often can be resolved within months. If your grasp of intuition is weak or shaky, try using indigo to assist in developing an active intuition and in strengthening the ability to direct it.

Rhodocrosite will penetrate those thoughts that were built on illusions related to past events. It works on the most deeply held issues, so wearers must be prepared to deal with these issues. You may be well advised to form a support team. Find one or more friends who will give accurate feedback. As you go through a process of significant change as initiated by rhodocrosite, share insights with these trusted persons. Sharing will help you to become detached and let go of harmful reactions.

One of the uses of rhodocrosite is to develop connections of truth. The wearer supports this mission to the degree she can honestly share her truth with confidants. The mission develops as pockets of truth seekers share their truth in groups that spring up across the planet. Larger political and social groups may become involved with this mission of change only when individuals and small groups take on the challenge first. Do not mistake this sharing for a superficial recounting of your long-standing views on the behavior of others. On the contrary, connections of truth require completely honest accounts of your current motivations, feelings, habits, negative thoughts, hidden agendas, stories about reality, and generally everything another person would need to know to see clearly why you act the way you do. This work cannot be done in a few sittings. It takes time and commitment.

Rhodocrosite goes to work first on behaviors that are based on a chain reaction like a thought-emotion-physical reaction-emotion-thought pattern. It singles out a destructive pattern and begins to unravel it by making you aware of the pattern and forcing you to look at how decisions made in the past no longer serve you. You will be challenged to make new decisions as reactions that have been normal in the past do not work. The longer the chain and the stronger the emotions within it, the greater the effects of this chain on our lives. Such chains may rule our decisions and actions. Over time, even deeply imbedded negative patterns will be completely disintegrated, one link at a time. Patterns with many negative feelings attached to them are very potent and disruptive. By making the effort to recognize and eradicate destructive patterns, you can avoid making the same decisions in the future and keep from recreating these patterns.

You will be forced to look at what you are doing before you will be able to repeat the pattern. You may repeat the pattern, but rhodocrosite will make the addition of a chink in one of the reactions. The next time this pattern is activated, you will have to notice the chink. Each time a negative pattern is repeated in the presence of rhodocrosite, a new chink will be placed. Each chink is like another reason to quit the pattern. Each chink reminds you of the observable costs of the pattern. Every negative pattern costs the person who engages in its repetition something precious, primarily the opportunity for freedom of choice. A long-standing negative pattern has cost plenty. Is it time to stop these patterns? If so, look to rhodocrosite for help.

Work with a high-quality strand of rhodocrosite for an extended time and expect to master your reactions. You can eliminate reactions that engage you without thinking in repetitive patterns. Learn to think before you react. Learn to decide how to act in each new situation, rather than repeating a habit without thought.

Rhodocrosite does much of its work on nonverbal levels. Time is needed to assimilate this work. Often, dream time is the only time you can allow for subconscious assimilation of such influences. While working with rhodocrosite, the wearer would be well advised to write down all dreams immediately upon awakening. Use a dream journal and review it each week to discover what dreams are telling you. These dreams will be invaluable in understanding the nature of your patterns and the exact way in which they were formed. Pay particular attention to symbols that represent events of the past. Often, these symbols will date the events in the dream and help the dreamer make correlations.

Putting down on paper the different correlations you discover will cement them in your consciousness. Writing them down will improve your symbol vocabulary. You can also make up symbols. Simply think of an answer you want, like "yes." Now give "yes" a symbol—perhaps an easy one like a hawk or a more unusual one like a paddle boat. Make sure the symbol gives you the feeling of the answer. Does the paddleboat make you feel the way the word "yes" does? Then simply expect life to provide such a paddleboat symbol when you should consider "yes."

For greatest results, you must expect to put out some effort. Take the time to explore the events of a dream. Was the house in which the dream took place familiar? Could it have been the house you lived in between ages four and ten? What time of year was it? Could this time in the year correlate with a certain time in the development of a pattern? Make the assumption that this dream is telling you something that will benefit you.

Even a bad dream could tell you something you could use to advantage. Besides, bad dreams can be an easy way of working out tough problems. It is better to learn from bad dreams than to learn from tough experiences in the awakened state.

Before bed, make the following declaration: "I will have a dream just before waking in the morning that will reveal the cause of a habit I want to change. As I awake, I will remember my dream and understand its significance." That's all you need say and then let it go. You can add something like, "I will remember any dream that will tell me something about a pattern." Then don't give it another thought.

Don't forget to write down every dream, even if you don't understand what it is telling you right away. Later, you will gain insights and clues that will bring the message clearer.

The following exercise may help you work with rhodocrosite to break up destructive patterns.

Imagine you are entering a wild, pink tornado with lightning flashing and thunder cracking. You are sure it will remove bad habits. You are sure it won't hurt you. With this image strongly on your inner screen, focus on the thoughts that are bothering you, and see the emotions and associated thoughts being sucked up by the powerful wind. You may hear laughing in the background as the clearing process begins. Let the wind carry the pictures of whatever problems you have. Look as hundreds, perhaps thousands, of pictures are drawn up by the mighty currents. As you watch the pictures rise up, let the certainty come over you that these pictures contain symbols and images of all your associations with a particularly destructive pattern. They are pictures of every way this pattern could, does, or has manifested in your life. Let them all go.

Denial has no place in this process. Rhodocrosite is too forceful to allow denial. If you deny that your behavior is inconsistent, if you refuse to admit that other's reactions are troublesome, and if you do not attempt to find out why this is or to make changes for the better, rhodocrosite will not be a good tool to begin using to initiate the process of change. Instead, begin the process of healing with a stone that can help you overcome denial and achieve balance. For a more gentle approach you can look to sodalite, rose quartz, citrine, or your primary color ray necklace. If you are unsure where to start, then begin with carnelian.

Denial serves an important purpose of self-protection. Do not remove denial unless you are firmly rooted in survival. If survival is in question, avoid rhodocrosite.

Changes in your emotional makeup will be thorough. You may even find that your physical appearance will change. Others may not relate to you in the same way. Your relationship to life will be different. You may find an increase in vitality as your emotional energy is released from its bondage to these patterns. You will no longer have to use your energy to keep these emotions contained. You will be amazed how much energy is held in a negative pattern. Holding onto patterns takes a lot of energy.

Anyone who displays few emotions, procrastinates all the time, hides their emotions, or cannot get up the desire to do very much is probably carrying more than one negative pattern. Most patterns contain some negative energy. This energy hangs within the mental sheath and causes subtle disruptions and it functions to attract other negative energies. If allowed to remain unchecked, these energies will attract people who also hold negative energies in their mental bodies. Detrimental experiences result when two or more people meet who harbor these energies. Releasing a pattern releases the held negative energy that can now no longer draw negative experiences into your life.

As with any of the gemstones, the wearer must do the work. It may not be easy to learn the art of the sculptor who cuts away all that is not the perfected or permanent to reveal the sculpture within the stone. Most of us are not master sculptors and may need assistance in determining what is the true way when given two apparently similar choices. Get help when the going gets tough. The challenge of rhodocrosite is to learn discrimination, to be in the moment. As the past is our friend, so may it become our master if we rely too heavily on it to make our decisions for us. This stone reminds us to awaken again to the childlike spirit of readiness and choose freshly and simply in the present. Spontaneity is the result of long association with rhodocrosite.

For those with a strong connection with spirit, the process will be filled with excitement. A successful conclusion to this process may take as long as six to ten months or more, during which time you must wear rhodocrosite for at least eight hours a day. You may be well advised to take some photos and keep notes, for you will need them to be able to recognize how you have changed after a year.

Rose Quartz

It is important to find rose quartz that has not been treated, dyed, or otherwise unnaturally altered. Rose quartz is fairly common, but stones with a strong, pure, natural color and clarity may be expensive and rare. Lower grades are often treated and dyed to look like better-quality stones. Therapeutic-quality stones are best, as the effects will be many times more nourishing and balancing to the astral body. Cloudy stones with inclusions and a dark or gray tint can be subtly harmful. Those with a slightly brownish quality to the pink are usable for easing the emotions but not for opening the heart. The best variety is completely translucent, comes in a slightly purple shade of pink, and is radiant. The color should be consistent though it need not be very dark.

Rose quartz is one of the most powerful tools available for working with the emotional (astral) self and is known for gently helping the wearer open the heart center. In this world of fear and superstition, an open heart can get a person hurt. Rose quartz helps the wearer to learn self-protection techniques to allow on to open the heart without fear. Hearts that are open and hold fear attract conflict. Eliminate fear, and love fills an open heart. In this way, rose quartz shows the path to spiritual development. It is a stone you can work with regularly for spiritual unfoldment.

Spiritual development is supported by taking care of oneself in every way. When we begin to express gratitude for the precious gift of life, then we can also help others. We can have a life to be grateful for only when we have taken responsibility for our feelings and have begun to create a life that nourishes us and all who draw near. It is up to us to create that life. Rose quartz can help us create the foundation for such a life. Its vibrations will show us the way to open the heart. It will teach us how to safely nourish the subtle sheaths.

Serving others may be the way to spiritual enlightenment and joy, yet if we do not appreciate the spiritual gifts hidden in life's challenges, we will have little to offer. Those we care for are best served when the heart is not burdened by fear of your own life challenges. Fear exists where love has retreated.

Rose quartz can help the wearer see the hand of divine love in every difficult situation. To learn to give uncompromising love, you must believe it is available and forthcoming at all times in all circumstances. After all, that which we do not value and nurture in ourselves can do little for others. Talk of love helps a little. Actual love helps all who suffer.

After we begin to see all that rose quartz can do for us, it will begin to powerfully affect our lives; however, we must make the changes. Rose quartz can only facilitate our own ability to expect things to be different and to act accordingly. Our own actions have brought us to where we are now, and until we take responsibility for our circumstances, nothing will change substantially for us. We must act like we believe in love for love to honor us with its presence. We must become trustworthy before loving people will trust us. We must become strong so we will not pour out our love until exhaustion sets in.

Learning to love yourself is one of the most important lessons you can learn. You must first love yourself before you can love others in a way that is beneficial to them. Rose quartz will produce supporting vibrations that fill our hearts to the degree of the intention we have to love ourselves.

If we truly desire the ascendant motion of spirit to fill us and raise us up out of our mire, we must become masters of the astral energies—not in order to force our will on others, but to champion the forces of good. Wearing a strand of rose quartz can help. Do not underestimate the strength of the astral forces, however, know that you can work with them as easily as you do the forces of gravity. First, you must see how astral forces work as they follow emotional tides. Notice how these forces follow your feelings. Then you can learn to create more of the emotions that will carry you to the higher worlds. Feelings of joy, love, and gratitude are the emotions that raise our vibrations. Once we are full of these, then they can spill over by contact to our loved ones.

Spiritual energy flows everywhere. It has been recognized throughout history. It has been given names like universal life energy, prana, etheric energy, manna, orgone energy, perpetual energy, the light, the word, aura, kirlean energy, the Holy Spirit, and many others. Feelings of love, joy and gratitude open the heart to this spiritual energy. This energy is responsible for sustaining life. We create our own blocks to this flow of energy.

Single pink quartz spheres can be used as placements over areas that hold emotional blockages. Blockages are areas where energy is kept from flowing freely. The physical body often will develop chronic pain, arthritis, "slipped" disks, hardness, tumors, stones, plaque, abnormal growths, weakness, or other signs of dis-ease in these areas. Rose quartz will not necessarily bring immediate relief or sudden healing. Over time, however, it will help the individual release physical energy blockages, liberating blocked emotions. As energy enters a physical area, the mind interprets the experience as acceptable or not acceptable. The mind stops energy from flowing through some areas. Rose quartz helps the wearer learn to deal with energy flowing into all areas of the physical body. Color-ray energy is good and brings life when allowed to flow freely. This stone checks the stopping action of the mind. Soon the emotions free as well. It helps you accept your emotions. It will also help you safely dissolve the astral aberrations that accompany denied or unexpressed emotions.

Pink-ray energy is an easy form of red-ray energy to absorb for those who are not easily able to embody the principals of the spiritual warrior. Warrior here refers to the ability to stand strong for what is right and guard the heart without having to resort to anger, violence, or destruction. Spheres of twenty- to two-hundred-millimeter high-grade rose quartz are excellent for increasing the amount of pink ray we can absorb. The following exercise can help with this process.

Sit calmly and comfortably with the sphere about two to three feet directly in front of you and about two inches above your line of sight. Practice singing different vowels; hold each one for as long as you can. Experiment with different tones until you find a pitch that deeply resonates the vibrations of the quartz, allowing them to move deep into areas of blockage. As you allow yourself complete freedom to move to different pitches and vowels, you will find one vowel that deeply enhances the feeling of closeness and presence to the quartz, and one pitch that resonates the vibrations allowing them to go deeper.

Sing this sound for several minutes as you visualize your body. Notice any areas that are tight or uncomfortable. Let go of the tension in these areas. Some areas may not want to relax at first. Some areas may not seem tense to you, though they are tight as a clenched fist. You may not be familiar with the feeling of looseness. Nevertheless, everyone will find some area that is uncomfortable. Allow the pink vibrations from the stone to fill this area, and know that within the next few hours, you will begin to release the emotions you have pent up in or around this area.

As the next few hours pass, notice if you have any emotions. Are any of them out of proportion? Ask others to give you feedback describing your emotional state and comparing it to your usual state. Soon you will become aware of the specific stuck emotion if you pay close attention. Write yourself a note or make an entry in your journal regarding the area of discomfort and the stuck emotion associated with it.

During the next few weeks, place your attention on the sphere and see yourself as someone who has complete freedom of movement, particularly in the stuck area, without pain or discomfort. Each time you become aware of some area of pain, write it down. Try to write down what was happening when you noticed the tightness. This may give you a clue as to the nature of the stuck emotions associated with that area. Come back to this exercise and repeat it for each new location in your body. This process may take some time, but you will find a great amount of stress can be released by using it.

These pent-up emotions result when we use our astral energies to do the work of our will. Right use of will at all times, without imposing on others' space, keeps the emotions free. Once we begin to repress our will or use it to control others, it is difficult to stop from repressing it all the time. All ability to act appropriately and effectively is lost when grief, resentment, or other powerful feelings are held in. Expressing these pent-up emotions in the liberating presence of the pink ray will allow their safe resolve. Rose quartz keeps others from being harmed by the release, and thus our will can be freed.

By wearing a strand of rose quartz spheres at night, one can continue this process in the dream state. Dreams can be an excellent place to resolve physical and emotional blockage. You may experience awful, or even violent, dreams at first. Do not be dismayed. Nightmares are an excellent way to learn to love the overly emotional parts of yourself—parts that have been neglected for so long that they become violent. We can release them to express themselves in dreams, rather than force them to hide and develop into depression or chronic illness. Repression creates illness, freedom allows abundant health. We all wish to be free, this type of quartz teaches us to handle the responsibility without encroaching on others or repressing ourselves.

Learning to achieve self-love is like attending a fitness class. You must work through the first few weeks of apparent torture to enjoy the years of good health that can result. Rose quartz is a great coach. Let it set the pace and choose the regime. Follow its lead. It will build an astral sheath that has fortitude.

You will find, after only a short time, that you are more spontaneously free of moods that seemed to move in and hang over you like thunderstorms for days. Your moods will leave as soon as you have resolved the associated emotions. Often, this can be as quick as the time it takes to stand up and stretch. You must exercise the emotional sheath before you can gain insight into its great potential. This sheath can change more rapidly than the physical body. Exercise regimes are taught by rose quartz. Listen carefully to dream symbology to get clues as to how to exercise and visualize the astral body becoming strong and full of love. When the astral body becomes healthy, the physical body will be easily able to accept and work through the release of energy blockages over time.

The wearer may find it helpful to wear this quartz with lapis lazuli to improve mental understanding of emotional freedom. The wearer may wish to wear a strand of four-millimeter indigo spheres to help them intuitively know what to do with unwanted emotions.

The force of love is greater than that of power. Only the force of love can overcome apparent obstacles and opposition resulting from power struggles. Strengthen your emotional sheath, and you will learn to express beauty and kindness in a way befitting someone whose grace can then shine like the sun.

For those who suffer from loneliness or lack of affection, rose quartz can be a true friend. It will always be there in times of trouble as well as during times of great joy. Its friendship strengthens the emotional sheath gradually, making it invincible to many forms of attack. It teaches you to let go of power struggles and look to love.

A deeper appreciation for the creative arts may result from regularly using rose quartz. Those who find painting, sculpture, music, or poetry a complete mystery may find their attitude changing. Once emotions open up and begin to flow freely, the heart center can better experience the world. You may find emotional perceptions are deeper, clearer, and more exhilarating than you thought possible. We think of our minds as the primary seat of perception and look to reason as the seat of decision-making power to logically remove unwanted feelings. Actually, our hearts make distinctions that our minds could not fathom and decisions made by soul, not the mind, using input from the heart are most likely to be in alignment with the path of love. The path of love is to freedom. Freedom provides us with the ability to choose our emotions. Power is the path followed by a mind confused by its own overinflated sense of importance, and this path leads to repression of oneself and oppression of others.

Devoted wearers of rose quartz learn compassion for the plight of others. Unless we have experienced this feeling, we may judge it to be a form of weakness. Yet, only the strongest of hearts can withstand seeing the passions and hopes of the less fortunate dashed, again and again. It is not easy to look at, and even more difficult to feel, the fears and desperation of the downtrodden. A heart filled with true compassion can help the weary find freedom. Helping another to find freedom is the fastest, surest way to find freedom yourself.

Those who have the fortitude to get down on their hands and knees and help those who are the lowest of the low to rise up will be able to understand the purpose of suffering. Jesus said the lowest shall be made to rise up and become the most high. We may not wish to follow the path of Jesus, but we can certainly learn something about the value of compassion from him. Children seem to know compassion, they will often be seen reaching out to those in need. A child could easily invite a homeless waif in for a meal. Children do it out of response to a perceived need. As adults we must learn compassionate love before we will reach out to those less fortunate.

Rose quartz teaches us to let love into our hearts and open our hearts to others. It teaches us to let go of the struggle for control and to ease out of the grip of fear. Work with it for a time. Devote yourself to the study of the heart. Take the time to find out what your heart is telling you and you will understand the reason it is the key to love.

Rubellite (Pink Tourmaline)

Samples of the clear, wine-pink tourmaline containing no other color like green, brown-red, blue, or black-green in them are fairly rare. This material is called rubellite and is available in chips and beads. Undrilled spheres are quite rare and expensive. Strands of like-colored pink tourmaline, spherical beads are nearly unaffordable. However, those who are drawn to rubellite can work very successfully with small chips worn in necklaces. You may wish to use a more balanced necklace, which could be made with approximately fifty-percent of its length composed of two- to four-inch sections of Biwa pearl or four-millimeter beads of mother-of-pearl with chips of rubellite in between.

The stone of the woman warrior, rubellite will help women develop their strength. Women must draw on a different source than men for their feminine energy to become powerful. The female power is magnetic, as opposed to the male power, which is electric. These two powers affect each other profoundly, though they are quite different. Although women can learn to use the electric male energy, their greatest accomplishments will result from the use of the magnetic female power.

There are twelve major energy centers in the human energy system called chakras. Each of these centers accepts and transmits energy. Much of this power is generated from the second and third chakras, located in the lower and central abdominal regions where preservation and sexual energy is concentrated. If you are able to move this power up into the heart center and out, and direct it in ways helpful to others, it will produce great results. If you become rooted in desire for power over others or sexual prowess, these two lower chakras will become focused on creating these instead, and you will soon become out of balance. Harmony will be lost. You will become like the lion without a lair. You will constantly have to win everything and will always need more. Power over others implies that the locus of attention is outside yourself. Magnetic power that is given from the heart, whenever given, multiplies in the giver as it draws the giver to those to whom one gives.

The female body is more equipped to channel this magnetic energy. Whether it is used for love or dominance/servitude is up to the wearer. If dominance is chosen, it may work well for a while, but the magnetic energy will create a strong negative pole, and the user eventually will come to a point where they are out of control. If subservience is chosen, a very weak pole will be created. If love is chosen, the positive pole will gradually be increased, and the result will be shared love that will be for the greater good of the whole as well as for the individual. Do not be deceived into thinking that love is going to cause subservience or dominance—although many say they love and cause these, it is not really love but power they use. Power creates lust, love creates peace and harmony.

What is truly good for the individual is good for the whole of humanity. Whatever you, as a woman, give out will be amplified by the rubellite in your aura. Be wary, for that which you give out will also be powerfully attracted to you. Like iron filings to a strong magnet, these results will be hard to separate from you once you have attracted them. Give love and love will find you. A magnet for love radiates beauty.

A woman must learn from rubellite to become like a tree. A woman who goes out chasing the world will tire. A tree allows the world to come to it. It does not use its energy to try to change the world. A healthy tree stands tall and beautifully, and simply finds many places in the soil to draw its nourishment from. It dominates the landscape by the economy of its effort. Wherever it sends out a root that easily grows, it multiplies that root. A tree draws all it needs like a magnet into the highest part of itself.

Men who wear rubellite may find peace and mutuality with their feminine side. They may begin to appreciate the feminine aspect. The magnetic energy will teach men to become more flexible. A man whose strength comes only from his ability to resist the forces of nature or who must constantly adjust the direction of the forces in his life is not really strong. He may find that he will become weak over time like a rock that splits a river. Though a rock is tough and will divide a river for many years, eventually it will be worn thin. Finally, it will fall and be digested by the river, never to divide it again. By contrast, the fish never seeks to divide the river. Though it is soft and easily crushed, the fish conquers the river by yielding to it, understanding it, and working with it to create a home for itself and its descendants.

Men must learn to yield to forces greater than themselves, in order to become coworkers with these forces and to help these intelligent forces bring positive energy into their life and into all beings.

Peace is found only through integration of both the masculine electricity (taught by the green tourmaline) and the feminine magnetism. Learn first the power that is like your gender. Then learn to master the force of the opposite gender. Magnetism protects as it repels all that is not in harmony with the positive force of its pole. Electricity propels as it creates a positive motion that can take us to the farthest reaches of the universe and beyond.

Rubellite will help protect you from forces that you are not attracting—forces that you have no use for and had previously let go. Just as magnetism repels other magnets that are influencing it by turning a like energy toward them, so one learns to repel nonharmonious energies.

Only when you have lost interest in the disharmony you attract or let in can you protect yourself from disharmony. You must learn to fully polarize the heart to attract only what is positive. First, learn to put your attention on your heart and there find the source of the power of love. Then, give up control of your heart to this power of love. Only when you no longer seek to control everything external to yourself can you stop paying attention to this disharmony and stop attracting it into your life. Only then can you use the feminine energy for self-protection.

The feminine form of protection is more like aikido than karate. In aikido, you use the force of the attacker to defeat the attacker. Go with this force and let the force itself defeat the attacker. Whatever force is used by the attacker, the defense is always to let the attacker defeat themselves. In karate, you defend with your own force. You rely on your ability to strike swiftly and with precision. In aikido, you use much less energy than in karate, and you primarily use whatever force is generated by the attacker himself. The magnetic force of the feminine pulls the attacker's energy slightly from the direction it was applied and suddenly the balance of the attacker is lost. Rubellite teaches the art of emotional and mental aikido. Once you become grounded in its use, you will never fear an onslaught of anger or persecution again.

A balance of the masculine and feminine aspects within the heart will be easier to achieve in the presence of rubellite, for this stone has the effect of creating a strong, positive resonance at that balance point. This balance point is where you have just the right amount of masculine and feminine energies. For one person, this percentage may be 60/40; for another, it may be 52/48. Each must find their own balance point. If you are searching for balance, rubellite will mark the balance point so it will be unmistakable.

Women have a difficult time believing that they can accomplish more with less effort than men normally do. They can. The key is to find the balance point. At times, women find the balance point without thinking about it. When they get control of the ability to stay in balance during challenges where they would habitually lose their balance, they will accomplish all that they set out to do. Women must be careful to choose their goals and set their sights on these goals only when in balance, otherwise they will find themselves pursuing goals that do not really afford them the opportunity to grow. Rubellite will highlight growth opportunities that truly support the individual. Women need simply wear a strand to bed at night and go to sleep with the intention of recalling the desire to grow in capability without having to lose balance in a dream. Upon rising, take time to analyze the dream remembered. Take the strand of rubellite off and set it in front of the paper on which you have written your dream. Ask the rubellite to show you a hint of the dream's meaning that day. Replace the strand around your neck. Later that day, some clue will come to you as to the meaning of your dream.

This technique can actually work with a blank page if you don't remember your dream on first awakening and, therefore, have nothing to write. Proceed as if the dream were written on the page and look for clues. Often this technique will help the wearer recall a clip from the dream after, or when, finding a clue that day. If the technique fails the first day, it is only because the answer is too simple. Try again the next night. This time add the suggestion that you will need some very obvious symbol to jar your memory and allow your subconscious to reveal the hidden meaning. Continue this technique and learn the feminine way of goal setting as opposed to the masculine.

Men should consider this stone a source of wisdom and balance only when worn with a concentrated internal focus. Be open to what is being taught. Listen, first of all. You may be led to things that initially make no sense to you. Take note, pay attention, and keep listening. Wear rubellite with purpose, and return to your internal center by wearing your favorite necklace after a short experiment with rubellite. Each use should be for a determined time and not an indefinite duration.

For instance, you may wish to be more effective during business consultations. You may put on your strand of rubellite and focus on this issue. Do a short, silent contemplation. Ask rubellite to show you a sign or symbol to guide you in this issue. Suppose that during your contemplation, you see the snake, silent and still in his dealings with his prey and with his brethren. Ask yourself what this symbol means in terms of the issue.

What does this have to do with being in charge of and directing negotiations at your next meeting, you may ask? You could dismiss the input of a snake as so unlikely that it does not warrant further consideration. You may, on the other hand, try being silent about your position while at the meeting, ready for a sudden strike during the upcoming negotiations. This tactic may bring you the results you wanted. You may find yourself congratulating the other side for being so insightful as to offer you such good terms. Silently, you will know they offered all you had wanted and more to get you to "settle" for their terms.

Silence often is seen as a weak approach, yet it may be the perfect technique for your situation. Through a willingness to understand the messages you receive from rubellite, you may increase your repertoire of moves to include some of the feminine approaches. Magnetic energy acts differently and gets results differently. Use it to resolve conflict. In business as in other areas, the more ways you can learn to resolve an apparent conflict, the more you will succeed.

Both men and women can learn much from rubellite. It is a subtle teacher, but a powerful ally. It will react faithfully to all attempts to go out of your habitual patterns. Each attempt to try something new will bring greater results. You may soon find you are looking at life in a completely different way. Using rubellite in focused sessions of short duration will allow you to assimilate the shift in consciousness that occurs the moment you place a strand of rubellite chips around your neck. You may miss the subtle shift if you do not take the opportunity to take the strand off and notice the change and then put it on again a bit later and remember the feeling and notice the influence.

Be open. Think of what you would like to have more of in your life when you wear rubellite. Wear it only when you are looking for specific input. It will bring results if you do not dismiss its influence. In fact, you may achieve more with less work. That is the feminine way.

Rubellite is a doorway. It will open into subtle areas of consciousness where you store untapped capabilities you have not previously utilized. An individual may ask "How will I recognize these capabilities if I have no knowledge of them?" The answer is going to sound too simple, but let it in. You need only believe you have discovered some mysterious capability while wearing rubellite, and that this new capability will be apparent when the need for its use arises.

Wear your strand for a few minutes each morning. If you have a trusted guide, ask for their help in making a leap of faith. Take off the strand and go about your business during the day and look for an opportunity to practice some new ability that will come to you as needed. Life will comply by offering new situations and new challenges. Now, as the opportunity arises, just watch yourself, notice the application of a new way of thinking.

Welcome each new challenge as a chance to discover some hidden capacity and soon you will be riding the wave of abundance that is the vibration of rubellite throughout your life even if you only wear the strand for a few minutes each morning.

Welcome to the blue-ray path, which leads through the maze of the mind. Prepare for a journey guided by the pure blue ray into the worlds of mental function. We must be careful to understand new distinctions unless we wish to remain forever in the confusion generated by our minds when we do not understand life because we are basing our lives on habit rather than on a higher knowledge. The blue ray will lead us directly into the maze, but if we hold off confusion and persist, we will begin to unravel the patterns of truth within the patterns of life.

Blue stones are the carriers of the blue ray, which regulates and circulates impulses—the vibrational equivalents of sensory data. Forming at the senses, impulses are transmitted to the brain where they are processed and categorized, and then either filed or acted upon.

Perceptions are the resultant knowledge derived from thoughts or ideas that form in the mind as it receives impulses. A perception is a bit of knowledge gleaned from observing what we think about a certain impulse or set of impulses. Our perceptions are possible primarily through the unconscious mind as it "observes" blue-ray energies flowing from sensory receptors to the mental function.

Left unattended, the mind will create habits. Habits are reactions that normally follow a pattern of thought that no longer leads

4
Blue
Ray
Stones

to new knowledge and is not directed by soul. The mind will choose what to do in response to such thoughts largely based on habit. Perceptions can, however, free the individual from habits. This process of learning to act on the basis of perceptions rather than on the habits that follow, not from knowledge but from thought patterns (often random and not directed or purposeful) that are generated by the undisciplined mind, allows for speedier reactions that produce mastery over the forces that direct manifestation. Simply, we can create what we want if we learn to base our actions on knowledge of truth rather than on fantasy or habit.

The process of receiving impulses, transmitting them to the brain, forming thoughts, choosing a response from the usual habit list, and reacting, can all happen without conscious thought and without producing new knowledge. Blue-ray energy expands the process to include conscious discipline of thought that results in greater knowledge through perception rather than thought that results in repeating a habit.

By opening to a greater flow of blue-ray energies, truth can be known. The ability to differentiate between illusion and truth is fundamental to an understanding of the spiritual reasons for life and the existence of soul. For those who are surprised by life and find the nature of things disturbing, confusing, mystifying, or upsetting, the free flow of blue-ray energies is undoubtedly constricted or blocked. Just as the blue ray helps the blood to flow through our veins, the essential flow of thoughts and impressions is built on blue-ray energy. Blue-ray energy opens the mind to new, more productive habits.

Blue sapphire, as carrier of the blue ray, is the most potent of the blue stones. Its crystal matrix, when shaped into rondel or spherical form, is unsurpassed in bringing the undifferentiated pure blue-ray energy into the bodies. Once you have brought in sufficient blue-ray energy, you can use the blue-ray energy to uplift thought, that is, to raise thought from the level of habit to that of an art form. Each gemstone described in the blue stones chapter helps us with a different aspect of refining and practicing a greater flow of blue-ray energy within our being.

The signature that a blue-ray energy stone carries is composed of energy from more than the one visible octave. Color-ray energy is primarily a vibration that is within the visible band of the spectrum, but it also exists on higher and lower harmonic wavelengths that are not visible. Aquamarine, for example, brings in blue-ray energy from several higher vibrational octaves. This particular vibration allows us to see the spiritual reason for perception and the other various bodily functions related to the processing of thought information and sensory data. The blue-ray energy from any one gemstone will be a combination of wavelengths of blue energy from the different octaves with small amounts of other colors within those octaves. The primary vibration within the visible spectrum is the most powerful of the bands, but the others have subtle transformative effects. Aquamarine will introduce us to this understanding in a way that words cannot.

Color-ray energy should be experienced for its properties to be appreciated. Experiment for yourself. The gift that comes from the natural use of blue-ray energy must be experienced to be useful. As you learn to use each color ray individually as amplified by a gemstone, you will learn how these color-ray energies function together. The use of the spherical form of a gemstone that carries the energy of a prime color ray affords a way to gradually and easily discover your own given ability to experience truth, always pristine and renewed. Follow the hints and exercises given here to begin your experience. Develop your own techniques as the blue-ray energy brings you closer to the source of its flow.

Blue Sapphire

The primary bearer of the blue ray, blue sapphire helps you make a connection between spirit and the higher mental functions. You may experience a deepening sense of your spiritual path and a certainty of the reality of the workings of spirit in your life when working with sapphire.

The workings of the mind will be apparent both in the higher mental development of "right" thinking and in the management of lower mental functions, which serve to manifest either constructive or destructive thought. Removing thought patterns and forms that do not serve you may be as easy as exposing them to the blue light.

Taking the lead, sapphire will give you the grand tour of your thought constructs, patterns, and choices. You can learn to map the mental body, giving rise to a deeper understanding of your life.

Try this exercise: place your attention on the inner screen, which is located between the eyebrows over the bridge of the nose. Fill the screen with a strong, pure blue light. Now step into this light. Instantly it saturates the body. Observe the cells of the head as they absorb the blue light. Watch as the blue light streams in through the throat and out through the forehead. It carries with it the bluest form of love.

This love is so powerful and profound that you could decide to give up all your negative thoughts to it. See the stream of negative thoughts being replaced by the blue love as the negative thoughts are carried on the out-stream into the deep blue ocean where they will no longer produce negative experiences for you. Realize that these negative thoughts were the best way you had of expressing your needs and your love of others. Also know that you are now capable of using a higher form of communication. You are capable of expressing your deepest needs directly to those who can help you meet those needs. You are being given a new power of discrimination. With it you will automatically begin to weed out those who cannot hear your honesty. You will begin to move toward people or animals you will be able to trust with all your sensitive thoughts and feelings about your life. You will be able to express the dreams you have shared with no one until now.

Sapphire is capable of piercing areas of mental dysfunction and denial. It is not a gentle tool when used to cut away unnecessary mental constructs. Like a precision knife used by a master surgeon, it will cut away only those portions of these constructs that no longer serve the individual. Sometimes called frozen fire, sapphire can feel like blue icicles as it stimulates and awakens parts of the mental body that may be suppressed. For some, this process may be uncomfortable and should be taken slowly. Wear sapphire for short periods at first. You may have no striking physical sensations; however, sapphire will not be dormant. It works from the deepest levels out. Awakening parts of the mind that are not used, it will greatly improve your ability to stay with self-discipline. Once the need for greater self-discipline has been digested and assimilated, it will work with mental structure. Sapphire will support the creation of new structures. These structures will be a firm mental foundation on which to base all positive mental activity.

Individuation is the process of becoming yourself, free from the mental suggestions of society to choose your own best path. Only when you become familiar and comfortable with using the parts of the mind that have not previously been available to them will you truly be able to understand your purpose in life. It is much easier to discipline yourself after you become clear about personal goals and direction. Developing goals and direction will be of great value for those who are disorganized, scattered, or in the extreme case, schizophrenic. It can also help those who are rigid or stuck in goals that do not work, especially those who do not allow themselves to try new things or activities that may require making mistakes.

Sapphire helps you reach out. Wearing a necklace of sapphire may help you to see others for what they are and appreciate their gifts. People who seemed to us to be one-dimensional or stereotypical now will appear as they truly are—multifaceted individuals with many good points. Thus, sapphire is a tool that helps in relationships. It teaches us how to be supportive of those we love. We will learn to show more compassion for others while at the same time remaining detached enough to follow our own path.

Sapphire helps you to see. It has a soothing effect on the eyes. It may help you see into situations and find the truth about their causes. After all, "what you see is what you get." Taking personal responsibility for your life is very powerful. The attitude that, "I create my world and can make it better," is the basis for positive change. Personal freedom comes from personal responsibility. Wearers may find their words will affect life more profoundly as they take more responsibility for the consequences their words create.

In ancient times, blue sapphire was worn when consulting the oracle or to open the third eye. This form of developing intuition and contact with the unseen inner forces is stimulated and enriched by sapphire. The darker blue varieties of sapphire are excellent for leading us into worlds beyond the physical and protecting us as it shows us the way. These other worlds are simply dimensions that intersperse our own. As mathematicians and scientists have theorized, we live in a multidimensional realm, just as atoms of blue ink float in water. We do not see the water, but we know it is there.

Similarly, our inner universe is multidimensional. You may begin to learn to cut away unnecessary patterns of behavior that arise from old thought progressions. This is a first step in freeing the mind to apprehend a greater truth. Blue sapphire will act as your torch, burning away the unwanted debris. Use it to light the way into areas of the mind that have remained dark. There is much to explore.

Recognition of your higher self may be more comfortable as you are eased into a state of quiet and at-one-ment. Like the mountains, sapphire will inspire a reverence that comes from the quiet splendor of majesty. Inspiration will be available to all who follow blue sapphire.

Most of us have the mistaken impression that moving into the higher-self consciousness should be easy. It should be like settling into a soft couch to watch your favorite TV program. Instead, it is more like stepping ever deeper into an abysmal dark cave with unknown, frightening animals inside. The mind instinctively knows its habits will be stripped away by these animals. It is afraid. Blue sapphire acts to reassure the mind. It works to uncover all the hidden agendas. It works to assure you that your whole person is served by your choice of actions. This means being illogical at times. It means not following the reaction patterns of old habits. Old habits will die, but the mind will not die. It will live on to create a whole new identity. It will survive the death of the old habits. The fear will be eased by forming better habits in the presence of the blue ray.

Once you become accustomed to the companionship of the blue ray, you will be shown the way into the vast areas of the unexplored mind. You will find it easier to gauge what would be an appropriate reaction to difficult situations instead of relying on habit. You will learn to regulate your response to difficult encounters.

All aspects of the mental function will be strengthened by a strand of rondels worn around the neck. This stone is especially useful for those who have difficulty concentrating, focusing, or organizing thoughts. Mental aberrations will begin to dissipate in the presence of the blue ray.

The mind will begin to more easily recognize the directions given by spirit. Those who choose to follow the direction will become aware of the origins of their thought patterns and mental aberrations. Soon they will no longer find themselves repeating old habit patterns that no longer serve them. They will better be able to control their destiny as they become aware of the origin and causes of their outmoded mental patterns.

The mind regulates the functions of the entire body. These functions are controlled by "valves" in the brain. The valves can be checked by the mind as it unconsciously observes their respective "gauges." These gauges allow us to know on a deeper level what is going on throughout the body and thus to control all body processes. The flow of energies that control these processes of mind and body are controlled by valves. Sapphire will show the nonconscious, instinctual mind how to regulate these valves and stay in touch with the gauges of the mind that indicate flow. One by one the gauges are highlighted and adjusted. As you become better able to control bodily functions, you will experience physical harmony during the life changes you go through. You will have effectively "tightened down the screws" that keep the settings on your valves from wandering. You will feel more in touch with your body as you begin to perceive subtle distinctions in physical performance hitherto unnoticed.

Thoughts exist in "rooms" in mental space that are compartmentalized to deal with the different thoughts. Imagine your mental body comprising a network of thoughts placed in rooms made up of spectrums of light. See these as small spheres of bright light connected to each other by tubes of rainbow light. As you look more closely, you see that areas of thought are regulated by large dials, which allow the seven colors to enter these areas in exact proportions.

As you begin to inspect these dials, you realize they are not set for optimum results. In fact, some gauges indicate certain valves are not open at all, and others are fully open when they should be restricting the flow. Colors may need adjustment. Picture a worker who wears a suit of powerful deep blue light. Watch him as he floats effortlessly to the various dials and turns the dials to settings appropriate to optimize mental functioning.

Notice that the pineal gland and the thyroid and other glands that regulate the body functions are eased into proper functioning as a result of these adjustments. See the worker continue to adjust dials throughout your mental body. He may have to tighten screws and cut or lengthen some of the tubes.

As he works, you will become aware of areas of the mind becoming filled with a bright light made of many colors. Each of these lights is individually balanced to a precise measure of the seven colors, each according to the blueprint given at birth.

The physical body will begin to become more aware of the original blueprint for the correct functioning of its various systems. It will begin to adjust itself to be in alignment with this new information. Soon a deep feeling of well-being will replace the feeling of unhappiness that accompanied the body when it was ruled by a mind filled with confusion and doubt.

Body fluids will begin to flow more easily. Oxygen will be brought to all areas of the body in greater abundance and will bring strength and energy to every cell.

You can learn to keep silent about changes until you have assimilated them thoroughly and to release ties that are not promoting health. You may find yourself easing into a state of quiet recognition. You may even begin to recall lessons learned in other lifetimes. These lessons will be applicable to all sorts of situations in your present life.

Remember—life is a gift you enjoy only if you open it.

Sapphire will open you up to gratitude for all the people and situations that have been provided for you. Every experience in your daily life is a lesson for your growth and benefit when you expect it to be. As you see how each situation in your life has added to your understanding of the way life works, you will grow. Life is change, and sapphire will help you anticipate change.

Resentments and anger will slip away as you learn how to differ with others in a healthy way. Once sapphire has helped you learn how to say everything you need to say when conflicts occur, you will no longer need to stew about conflict. When the conflict is over, you will be complete with everyone and have no need to harbor anger and resentments.

Simply put, sapphire will show you how to use your mind more effectively. You will become a better communicator after working with this stone. It will encourage broader use of mental capability rather than an out-of-balance reliance on just a few mental functions.

Sapphire works well with lavender, frosted quartz, and white coral. These stones will support the changes initiated by sapphire and allow the wearer to remain in balance while the mind is opened to greater awareness.

Effecting deeper changes in the mental body should not be expected without effort and direction on the part of the wearer. Try to use your imagination creatively. Visualize the blue ray entering your body on waves of sapphire vibration, which circulate throughout your entire body. You must direct the sapphire energy to obtain the deeper effects and broader results.

Go as far as you wish into the mental realm. Use stones like amethyst, citrine, and indigo to connect the mind with your higher spiritual nature. Soul must learn to work in the physical world, and mind must learn to cooperate with soul. Wearing these three stones with blue sapphire will bridge the gap between the mind and soul.

The ascetic Eastern religions teach you to ignore and finally to stop the mind. In the West, we have learned the many benefits of a healthy mind. Few of us have minds clear of unproductive thoughts, as diligent we may be. The art of quieting the mind is quite useful. When the mind is quiet, you can properly focus the attention. A quiet mind can be influenced by truth as it wells up inside.

Whatever you desire is available if you can concentrate and bring to bear all levels of the mind. This concentration is useless and can even be destructive without the direction of soul. Learn to focus the mind in cooperation with soul and you will have mastered the mind. This great tool we have been given is for a high spiritual purpose when used by an individual who is trained by blue sapphire, indigo, amethyst, and citrine.

Aquamarine

For those drawn to aquamarine it will be calming and soothing. It may ease pain and grief for those stricken with an unrelenting feeling of loss. Anger and frustration may be easier to handle as the wearer becomes accustomed to the vibrations of aquamarine. You may find a brighter outlook on life, and the effects of emotional trauma on the brain tissues will be gradually reversed. These benefits can be directly attributed to the higher-octave blue-ray energies as amplified by aquamarine.

This stone can be worn in chip or spherical form. The greater the mass of stones, the greater the effects. The darker the color of the aquamarine, the faster it will saturate the aura and its effectiveness will be deeper. It is advisable to avoid using stones that have been irradiated or dyed or both—common practices with gemstones, especially aquamarine. Its therapeutic effects, especially on the subtle mind and emotional sheaths, are distorted by such alteration of the surface or crystalline matrix.

Aquamarine is a powerful gem. Work with it gradually. If it raises the vibrations of the mental sheath too quickly, you could become unbalanced. If your body becomes uncomfortable when wearing this stone, it is advisable to put it aside for a time. Then use it for short durations and wait until smaller vibrational changes have been assimilated.

Although most stones can be cleansed of disharmonies by placing them in the sun for a few hours, aquamarine will fade if it is left in the sun for any time. It is advisable to cleanse this stone by placing it alternately in hot, then cold, then hot, then cold water. Cleanse the stones every few weeks if rarely used, daily if used for significant change, or more often if used in repeated therapeutic treatments. Salt water clears disharmony well.

Aquamarine will help clear and replace the negative energies that may accumulate in your aura. These may come from your own thoughts and emotions or the thoughts and emotions of others. The head, neck, and chest are filled with soothing blue light when a necklace of chips is worn for a few hours.

Understanding the blue ray and the benefits it brings to the mental aspect of your being will come to those who work with aquamarine. You will intuitively begin to practice forms of contemplation that gradually bring this understanding.

Imagine aquamarine as a gentle guide of immense power who takes you to a string of pools of crystal clear, light blue water. The pools flow from higher to lower levels of wisdom. Picture this series of pools with beautiful water flowing from pool to pool from the high spiritual planes down into the lower worlds. When you enter one of these pools in your imagination, the effects will be on the most subtle of levels. These pools are filled with the liquid vibrations of aquamarine. See yourself becoming purified; all disharmony not directly related to your spiritual path washes away. See yourself as whole and radiant as you step from the first pool and walk toward the second pool. Each successive pool washes you of the disharmony on that level. Harmony is yours as you proceed.

The energies of aquamarine will work with the brain tissues and allow them to sustain greater mental activity. Tension may be eased if you allow it to be released. The neck and shoulders will receive the blue ray in proportion to the amount they can accept and the amount of the aqua vibration you can direct to these areas. These areas often are holding large amounts of stress surrounding encapsulations of some of the deepest issues we face, especially areas where the neck joins to the shoulders and upper back.

Aquamarine works to open the higher chakras. After age five, your crown chakra and brow chakra are usually beginning to close. As you work with the energy of the stone, you should notice an easing of tightness in these areas. Once the chakras open, greater flow of higher-octave color-ray energies will change destructive thoughts patterns and encourage the use of the mental faculties for more spiritual contemplation.

You may find that you will seek the darker-colored aquamarine as you become accustomed to regular use of the stone. For the purpose of extending meditation and contemplation, use a one- to five-carat, gemquality stone, cut and unmounted, and place it directly on the body. Note that stones must not be mounted in metals, as metals do not facilitate infusion of color-ray energy. Stones with a deep, natural blue color and visible radiant energy are the most powerful.

The greatest benefit will be to wearers who are on a path of inner awakening. These individuals will learn deeper truths about their purpose and the principles of the universe. Facing these truths may not be easy, especially if you are unaware. Like groundwater, you will be shown deeper levels of yourself. When first exposed to it, some of this water may be bitter from being in contact with the underground. This process may not be for the faint at heart.

When chips are worn around the neck, you may experience a lightening of the vibrations of the subtle sheaths. Sparkles of blue energy will fill the aura. Though you may have no physical sensations, the strength of aquamarine should not be underestimated. It will profoundly alter the way a person uses their energy. Wearers will learn to direct their energies and concentrate their focus on spiritual purposes. Aquamarine teaches us to bring a cleaner, brighter, more positive type of energy into the aura. Everything a person touches will be affected by these changes. How you direct this energy will have a great deal to do with the results you usually get.

Those who are of a highly creative nature may wish to wear this stone only when working on a creative endeavor. By doing so, you can help direct the vibration of the stones to support your creativity. When used consistently in this manner, the wearer may begin to experience an easier time with creative challenges that may arise. Getting into the creative "mood" may be easier as you use aquamarine by habit. The results will be greater creative energy and products more representative of your most closely held dreams.

The mental activities of the creative side of the brain can begin to work with the rational side of the brain when influenced by aquamarine. It works to stimulate the less-used side to develop cooperation and balance of mental function. If you favor the left side of the brain, which is more intuitive, blue-ray stimulation of activities and abilities of the right side will help balance your mental activities. An intuitive scientist like Albert Einstein or Thomas Edison, who has learned to use the creative flow of the left brain, and can explain their insights systematically through a rigorous rational process, will be able to develop solutions not previously considered by others. Likewise, an artist or musician who can use the rational side of the mind to interpret their intuitive expression may be able to appeal to a wider audience, and speak to those who primarily use the logical side of the brain. Their art will solve artistic problems in new, unexpected ways.

Anyone can benefit from the balancing effects of aquamarine on the mental body. Areas of the mind that deal with accurate thinking, discrimination, clear perception, hearing, sight, focus, analysis of complicated systems, understanding paradox, and other higher functions do not work well without the support and cooperation of the other parts of the brain. Too much emphasis on one area or another of the mental body will leave the person "top heavy" and ineffective. The person may find that mental self-centeredness or the compulsive control of others' thinking totally predominates their mental activities if they are limited to these areas of thinking.

Aquamarine was used extensively as a tool for improvement of the mental powers of priests and priestesses in Egypt, certain remote parts of Asia, and in Atlantis. Even earlier cultures knew aquamarine as the stone of the sea goddess. They used it to enhance their powers of receptivity, improve their understanding of cycles, expand consciousness, see beyond the wall of death, and heighten awareness during an initiation.

Some have reported recalling past-life incidents where they were using huge aquamarine crystals. In earlier times, only the inner circle of the elite priesthood was allowed to come into contact with such crystals. Although the mission of aquamarine ultimately is to uplift all mankind, the priesthood kept its use secret for fear the uninitiated would use knowledge gained by interacting with these crystals for selfish purposes. Actually they themselves often were greedy and coveted its use. This attempt to withhold the power of aquamarine backfired. None of these priesthoods exist now, and all written information they chronicled and kept hidden was lost or destroyed centuries ago.

This kind of selfish use of power will cause great unbalancing of the mental body and eventually unleash the kinds of destructive forces that brought about the total destruction of Atlantis. You must remain open. You must allow the expansion of consciousness. You also must share what you have learned after full assimilation of new insights.

Do not try to force aquamarine. Do not put it into a rigid structure or enclose it. Do not direct its powers for the control of others. Allow it to work through you. It brings its gifts to all. Seek only the cleansing and upliftment it brings and you will indeed be blessed. You will find ever deeper levels of heart.

Here is a key to power: use it for the benefit of all, with love, and it will serve you well. Let your heart guide you in its proper use. It will be a positive force you can rely on and trust through the tough times as well as the easy times. The blue ray is an excellent guide.

Lapis Lazuli

Lapis lazuli shows how to integrate the use of the emotional body with the mental. Personal strength comes from the focused use of the combined energies of the heart and mind. Lapis lazuli acts to help us understand our emotions and add emotion to our ideas. We become truly effective in our lives as we are better able to integrate our feelings and thoughts.

Although the concept of directing your feelings may seem foreign, it is quite a useful skill. Manifesting that which we desire is much easier if we can use our passion. Confidence will be improved with the sustained focus and use of desire.

A feeling of harmony and genuine balance will accompany some wearers from the moment they place a strand around their neck. All wearers will experience a subtle rise in their feeling of self-worth and may begin to act with less hesitation or apprehension. Lapis lazuli imparts to the heart the feeling of improved mental capability that comes with using the blue ray.

Having trouble seeing the forest for the trees? Try wearing lapis for a few weeks, and concentrate on the big picture. You may find that you can see the far-reaching effects of your actions and feel more capable to act in your own behalf. The power to act with passion, directed by a mind with clear foresight, creates effective action. Picture your thoughts as high mountain aspen trees. They are firmly rooted in the blue ray. Each stands tall and straight reaching for the sky. Allow the heart to experience reaching for the sky. The heart provides the sap that feeds the tree. As the tree grows, so the heart spreads its wealth. Hear the inner singing of the aspen trees as their leaves rustle in the wind and this sound will open the chakras.

The seven major energy centers in the physical body are called *chakras*. Four of these are found along the center line of the torso, one in the neck, and two in the head. The fourth chakra is called the heart chakra. The subtle bodies also have subtle energies flowing through them. We refer to the concentrations at the areas that correspond to the seven physical chakras as the astral, causal, or mental chakras. Lapis works mostly with the physical and astral heart chakras. Energy that flows through a heart chakra can be felt as heart energy. When the heart is open, heart energy flows to other areas of the body and out to the world. Lapis builds the heart-energy channels for the blue ray. Chinese doctors have long known that the physical body has energy meridians, flow lines of energy along which are located the acupuncture points. The flow of energies through the energy meridians and in and out of the chakras will be stimulated by lapis. We may go through life unaware of the vast abundance of power available for our use, lapis will open up channels we may not ever have used before. A feeling of well-being and endurance will accompany the increase in power-handling capability.

By helping us interconnect our disparate parts, lapis will encourage us to combine our resources for a more effective self-presentation. We may find we are much more self-assured after only a few weeks of wearing a strand of AAA-quality lapis. Grace and eloquence will precede those who master the gifts of lapis, and who use the power of love rather than control.

Our communications will improve as we begin to be more direct about our beliefs and needs. Lapis can give us the awareness of how to appear to have command of our faculties until we fully can. It teaches us how to direct our thoughts with more energy. Focused thoughts with more energy will rapidly manifest results. We will learn to create our own reality in a way that suits us. Thus, we will have greater presence. For those who work with lapis for an extended time, a marked increase in charisma will result.

Courage, especially in relationships, will be at our command as we begin to learn how to live without imposing restrictions on the parts of ourselves we have difficulty accepting. Without these restrictions we can begin to boldly integrate these rejected parts. Although we might like to eliminate parts of ourselves, we cannot. To become whole and genuine, we must make peace with all parts of ourselves. Lapis will help us persevere and express the needs of these parts more directly without manipulation. It helps us love the parts of ourselves we have only tolerated with restrictions. We must employ self-discipline to get through this process. By doing so, we will learn to love more of life more deeply.

If you can begin to believe in yourself, you can integrate your emotions, thoughts, and physical expression to serve higher goals. Parents do not commonly teach children to believe in themselves, nor do schools, as a rule. In fact, society does not recognize the benefits of this kind of integration. External discipline cannot replace the power of inner self-discipline. Even those who consider themselves rebels can use the power of self-discipline. Lapis will work with the individual to show ways of thinking, feeling, and acting that will serve their purposes. Gradually the individual will exhibit a consistent set of new behaviors. Observers will notice wearers displaying self-assuredness with consistency.

Suppose a coworker, John, insults you at a business meeting. You can't decide whether to lash out or keep quiet. Later, though you're glad you weren't rude, you realize you restricted yourself too much. Putting on your lapis necklace, you compose your thoughts. You realize John used your need for cooperation against you. The next day, you are able to show John the benefits of cooperation. He apologizes for his insult.

The vibrations of lapis helped you find the courage to recognize the part of you that thrives on cooperation. With self-discipline you were able to get to the root of your problem. Instead of reacting you were able to build your confidence in the part of you that believes in cooperation. John may not agree, but he will respect you more.

Lapis can open the door to greater effectiveness. If we follow the inner prompting we receive, we are sure to produce greater results with less effort. In this way, lapis reduces stress.

As we begin to see ourselves as capable and without limitations, we can begin to treat ourselves as princes, heirs to a position of greater responsibility. Not in the sense of being wealthy or full of self-centered, arrogant thoughts, but as worthy successors to the throne of service to others in the name of what is right—princes of love. Lapis will show us how to magnetize our love; we will find others being attracted by our love.

Lapis is useful for those who have little understanding of their color ray. Worn around the head as a tisrati, along with a necklace of your color-ray–bearing stone, you will soon begin to have some insight into the significance of your color ray for you. This information will be grounded through the heart center so that yours will begin to open. Your heart center is the best of the lower centers to activate. It causes you to act in alignment with spiritual goals. Open it fully and your life will indeed be blessed.

The unity of all forces is at best an elusive concept to most of us. However, once understood, this paradox of life brings us a deep appreciation for the gift of life. To explain how all is one and yet each aspect or form is separate unto itself is not easy. You must have the benefit of a wise old teacher like lapis lazuli. This old teacher was once the powerhouse for many Egyptian miracles. Now it teaches as a wise man would, in parables and stories. Watch for these stories to materialize in your life.

For those who have a difficult time believing in miracles—or even in the good things in life—lapis is a godsend. Overestimate the power of belief. All things come to us as a matter of our beliefs. Rarely do we perceive anything that does not support our beliefs or that we do not use to support our beliefs.

Conceiving new possibilities for ourselves is as easy as imagining driving a new sports car along a street in our favorite part of town. Getting a new sports car comes only to those who believe they deserve to have one. First comes the conception of the possibility of owning one. This belief in becoming an owner is easy for those who can readily afford one. They already have the belief that they will get anything they might wish for as long as they can clearly see how they would enjoy such an experience. Those of us who cannot afford one will find it more difficult to hold the unwavering belief that we will have a new sports car. If you clearly picture yourself owning a sports car and hold the belief that you will, although you think you cannot afford it, the means will come.

Similarly, you can progress spiritually by combining unwavering desire with a clear picture of yourself as a servant of divine love. Hold the belief in the spirit within to provide what is best for your spiritual development, and you will not be disappointed.

The greater the goal, the more lapis will help with its manifestation. Those who have goals that would benefit many when realized will enjoy the greatest results. Through such great goals they will be motivated like never before. Take the blue course—it is direct and expedient.

If your desire is to be able to draw from all the planes in a unified way, wear lapis as a necklace and know that you are soul. Soul has a set of bodies given to it by God to wear in the different levels of material existence because God loves soul. The blue ray will help purify these bodies.

It is your given right to create. Use this knowledge wisely and you will find great joy. Lapis will teach you to create the perfect inner world through right use of desire and creativity.

Blue Lace Agate

The mission of blue lace agate is to show you a way to be open-minded about others' perspectives. Your viewpoint may be quite different from that of another. Trying out the viewpoints of others often will bring an understanding of how others function that we could not have understood from our own limited viewpoint. It is possible to see things from many viewpoints by simply stepping into another's shoes while wearing blue lace agate. Try other viewpoints and learn flexibility and you will develop the art of diplomacy. We can actually learn to understand the feelings of those we had thought of as strange or alien.

The benefits of being able to clearly understand how someone else thinks and feels is invaluable in all human interactions. Those who can open their minds and see the way their companions see will have far greater tolerance than those who only present their own ideas.

Practicing moving into other perspectives is an art that we all can practice. Certainly anyone who learns this art will be a better negotiator. Negotiating for your favorite wishes is easier when you understand how those involved see your wishes.

People with low self-esteem who must compete in the world of business will learn to exhibit confidence and calm while practicing the presence of the vibrations of blue lace. Once a person can recall the vibrations of a stone, they can practice its presence. Blue lace agate will aid the wearer in identifying how outside influences can be used to their advantage. It will teach you how to adopt the vibrations of a gemstone, color ray, or even another person who has certain capabilities you would like to have.

Those who study communication with other mammals or interplanetary communication may find subtle changes in their ideas regarding the nature of thought and thought transference. Can we communicate with a dolphin? Can we understand how an eagle thinks? Wear a strand and try it. Seeing things from another's point of view will be easy for those who often choose to wear a necklace of blue lace agate, even if those points of view are outside the sphere of their species' consciousness. It will not seem strange at all to see from a detached point of view the problems we face as a species.

To those who are open to the viewpoint of Earth as a small planet among many planets in a vast universe comes another gift of blue lace agate. We can become dedicated to the enrichment of those who live here as well as being open to those who live on other planets. Blue lace agate will show the way to seeing our planet from the perspective of a visitor. A foreign perspective, one that operates from outside our experience, can be accessible to us with the aid of blue lace.

The understanding that what we do here in our little world affects the entire universe and all who are in it will blossom in the wearer. The Earth needs those who are willing to take some responsibility for the future. Those who wish to be part of the solution for the future will need to find solutions that allow everyone to benefit. This kind of solution is more easily found when you are detached and can take a look at everyone's conditions without taking sides. Blue lace teaches detachment without sacrificing passion.

A multicultural awareness, if individuals are prepared to cultivate it in themselves, will be most helpful to the ecology of the planet as well as to our personal spiritual development. It may not be necessary to go out and carry a sign or lobby Congress. Just knowing that there is another solution and holding the belief in it in your inner consciousness will certainly affect the whole planet. Having a positive attitude and a solution for oneself in relationship to the whole is enough to get an awareness of solutions into the consciousness of other people. People pick up such thoughts particularly easily when the thoughts are charged with blue-ray energy.

Solutions that include an awareness of others' points of view are easier to negotiate. The best solutions solve the problems of the opposing sides without forcing concessions or compromise. We allow ourselves a more powerful attitude if we are inclusive of others. For example, an interest in ecology is well and good, but not if it excludes the possibility of economic growth.

Blue lace agate is useful in experimentation procedures because it will show one how to uncover causes outside the known or accepted standard. An archeologist could discover why peoples of past cultures behaved the way they did. The blue ray encourages new thinking, while the vibration of blue lace agate is conducive to taking logical leaps where intuition leads the logical mind. Discrimination will be enhanced. Distinctions can be made more easily, especially distinctions that relate to analytical thought about unusual subjects. Blue lace supports the scientific process by helping scientists and laypersons alike adopt a broader understanding of science, leading people to new applications for theories from disciplines other than their own. The ways in which one science can be applied to problems in another science are numerous.

Some wearers may find that blue lace relaxes their energy flow. It is useful in easing stress related to the feelings that arise when you feel trapped. Thus, anxieties like claustrophobia, which can immobilize an individual, will be reduced in intensity. Those who suffer from all kinds of stress will benefit from being able to see their condition from a broader viewpoint. Blue lace will help sufferers open their minds to other possibilities.

In a complex interrelationship between elements of a process, you may find a natural balance between the elements. Blue lace agate can facilitate the understanding or uncovering of this balance. Complex structures can more easily be understood from a detached perspective.

Complicated human interactions can be understood readily from the mentally detached blue lace vision. Those who wear necklaces of blue lace will see the part of the big picture that relates to the specific problem at hand. Each hidden agenda and every person's special interests will become obvious. As when looking for the first time at an Impressionist's painting up close, the forces at work in the interrelationship of the parts of the painting seem to portray a blur. Then, as one steps back, the vision of the artist suddenly comes clear. Each patch of red or blue looks integrated and purposeful. The whole picture comes clear.

Each of the three colors in blue lace agate—blue, creamy white, and clear—has its own function. Blue is the color of understanding and mental grasp of concepts. Like the waters of a lake on a clear day, it reflects the truth of what is above. White opens the awareness to our relationship to a whole and to the constituents that make up that whole. Each of us has an inner door to the pure white light of spirit. White suggests forms as clouds seem to suggest shapes. Clear leads you to an acceptance of the unknown. It is through acceptance that we begin to open up to the vast reaches of the unknown. Clear portions of blue lace encourage us to discover paths into the unknown through windows of clear glass. The three colors together work to show us truth, open our inner door to spirit, and encourage us to accept the unknown. We will find ourselves seeking the unknown with less fear than before we wore this wonderful stone.

Another benefit for wearers of blue lace is an introduction to the many ways spirit speaks to us. Events in our lives often seem unrelated. We don't know why they happen "to" us. Imagine you recently found out you have an uncle Janos in Poland. As you are sitting one day in the dentist's office wondering if you would like to meet Janos, you open a magazine and see an article on how to research East European libraries through the Internet. You take this coincidence to be a communication from the universe to locate your uncle. Later you follow up on this lead and find a new side of your family that had not existed for you up to that moment.

Communication of all kinds is expedited by blue lace. When our aura is infused with its vibrations, we naturally understand far more varied communications. We can better understand and explain ourselves to foreigners or members of other species. After all, we perceive events through our aura. It filters what we see. Blue lace agate helps us to perceive how others identify and filter their sensory data and organize this data into ideas. In this way, the wearer learns to get across ideas in more recognizable form, such that others can reduce the amount of filtering needed to understand them.

Blue lace agate helps with the "victim" attitude. This attitude is one of being a victim of the things that happen to us. We all whine and complain at times, and this is a good way to let out frustration. But getting stuck in an attitude that things are out of control and that we are unable to choose our own life is disempowering. Blue lace agate will show us the ways in which we have created our situation. This revelation will allow us to make new choices for our future. The future is changeable. We can gain control of our lives. Let blue lace open your eyes to the way out of the victim role.

Although some wearers find this new way of looking at things disconcerting, many will find it valuable. You may find it useful to develop the skill of inquiry. Ask, "What is the point of this experience? What have I gained from it? How has it changed me for the better?" Allow your mind to wander, and notice what thoughts arise.

When meditating on a larger sphere of blue lace agate, try visualizing the unseen and benevolent energy of spirit entering the body. As the energy flowing into your field is moved through the stone, it will be turned five times counterclockwise and eight times clockwise. This process will transform the energy we receive from the ordinary to the golden, thereby transforming our perceptions to the next cycle.

Look at a mockup of a nautilus shell on your mental screen. See how each chamber is eight-fifths larger than the one before. This relationship is known as the golden mean. We use the geometry of the golden mean to describe relationships between growth cycles. Each step in a golden growth cycle is eight-fifths more comprehensive and complete than the step before.

Visualize the five most important circumstances in your life as the chamber you are currently in. Watch them change as they are moved to the next bigger chamber. The size of this chamber is represented by the number eight. The original five learning situations will become eight through this expansion process.

We will develop a whole new way of evaluating our experiences if we can move our present circumstances into larger and larger rooms, through the succession of chambers, and watch them grow. As we use our imagination to picture our circumstances and watch them develop through this eight-to-five technique, we see their nature and discover their fundamental causes.

We may learn how to project circumstances into the future so well that others will believe we have the power to see the future. We need only practice this technique.

Although this stone appears to be another common form of silicon dioxide, blue lace agate has been brought to this planet and grown here by scientists from another planet. Do not let this knowledge put you off from using it. Those specimens we mine now are natural to the planet and bring only positive results to the wearer.

Blue lace agate is a gift from "out of this world," but don't let that fool you. This gift will bring you closer to the heart of the blue ray.

Azurite (Lapis Linguis)

Azurite works with the sensory organs. It helps resolve the problems associated with misperceptions due to trauma witnessed and the subsequent shock that may distort accurate sensory data. Its influence can correct visual problems if those problems are a function of faulty brain-to-eye control and missing parts of the visual field that remind the individual of unwanted memories. Azurite is said to stimulate visual images during meditation that can help dispel denial. For those with little capacity to distinguish variations in color, texture, contrast, light, brightness, or distance, azurite is of great help. The wearer of a necklace of six- to eight-millimeter spheres will find a renewed interest in developing these visual capabilities. In fact, the whole process of seeing what goes on in life may be affected. Most visual problems originate in the mind not wanting to see things that may be upsetting.

To start to effect changes in visual problems, ignite the delight in life. Allow time to investigate an art exhibit or go to the park and really notice the place. Take up photography for a hobby. Begin to see the physical characteristics of those who share the workplace or the home. Begin to see if certain characteristics of the physical form attract you. Look closely.

Azurite can help a depressed person see beauty in the world and appreciate it. It has a generally soothing effect on sensory nerve connections when worn around the neck.

Azurite will similarly ease your emotional senses to afford you a clearer understanding of the emotional causes of others' sensory deprivations. Its vibrations promote and encourage you to demonstrate kindness. The first step in demonstrating kindness is appreciating others. A person who has difficulty seeing any good in those they meet may also have difficulty being kind. Azurite teaches you to see goodness.

Why be kind? People seem to get along just fine without ever cultivating an ability to be kind. Take a survey of friends. Ask those who seem to act with kindness what life gives to them. Then ask those who complain at every opportunity and think only of themselves. Which of these groups demonstrates the greater degree of acceptance and love? Which type of person would you like to be like? Does kindness help? What does it take to be kind to others and to ourselves? Is the benefit worth the effort?

If your answer is that a kind person is the sort of person you would like to be, then perhaps azurite is for you. If you need to learn some restraint, or in general people either don't value your kindness or take advantage of you, then perhaps you need to study different forms of giving. Allowing your energy to flow out to others in the form of kindness is important for some, yet others must learn to say no first. Showing kindness is only one way of giving out energy and does not work for everyone. If kindness does not work for you, consider reevaluating what it means to be kind.

Wear a necklace all day, every day, for a week. Notice what goes on within your body and at moments when the body experiences sudden good sensations, look around you. What is life telling you that seems to reach out and demand to be noticed? Each person will react differently to azurite. Each will notice different clues. Each will gain different insights into the world, and each will find a different definition for how it works.

Azurite promotes the activity of the spleen and thyroid glands if worn for a sufficient length of time. These organs are directly related to kindness and the desire to give. The thyroid produces enzymes that control the chemistry that directs your desire to get up and go. Cells in all parts of the body rely on the thyroid to tell them how active to be. The thyroid controls the growth rate of cells. How energetic we are and how able we are to give is therefore partially determined by this gland.

The spleen governs much of the activity of the stomach and digestion. Stimulate the spleen, and the body gets an appetite for life. Azurite will stimulate the function of healthy cells within these organs, and those cells will begin to divide and multiply. They will begin to support the surrounding cells, and soon the entire organ will be functioning better.

Azurite doesn't just work with the physical body. Through its vibrational effect, it also helps strengthen the etheric sheath, which may increase psychic activity. Such an increase does not mean one will automatically see ghosts or read others' thoughts. Rather, azurite stimulates interpretive intuition. It directs you in the language of symbols as they relate to the senses. You may find yourself seeking the answers to questions that you forgot long ago—questions about the appearance of your body, the unconscious form, and the external universe. How you see yourself physically, emotionally, or mentally will determine a lot about your life.

Azurite will teach you the deeper meaning of your appearance and gestures. You can learn what you are really trying to be by understanding how you look. Self-discovery is for the few who are willing to see themselves.

Allow yourself to become inquisitive, and this stone will support your every effort to learn the nature of the universe and the ways of nature. Azurite will brighten activity on all levels. Inspiration often is the direct result of an open line of questioning. Mind has a habit of creating habits. It likes to do the same old thing every time. It must be taught to love growth. Azurite will gently build the desire for growth through curiosity. After all, mental functions rely on practice and exercise to stay fresh and expand. Science has shown that the greatest factor contributing to lesser mental capacity in old age is simply lack of mental exercise and practice. Let azurite show you the inspiration that comes from an active, inquisitive mind.

In the presence of azurite, the part of the mind we refer to as the will allows your inner intuition to come forth with more certainty and direction. Azurite serves the wearer by sharpening the will. It is the will combined with the feeling of desire for positive direction that generates a strong mind. Azurite helps the mind become inspired and motivated with the strong sense of purpose that comes from right use of a sharp will in combination with an active intuition.

Many of the blue stones assist the wearer to sharpen the mind and balance the mental functions. Azurite improves the mind's ability to differentiate and analyze sensory data. It focuses intention. It activates your curiosity. All of these work together to improve discrimination.

Indicolite (Blue Tourmaline)

Indicolite, or blue tourmaline, can be viewed as the wise elder of an ancient tribe. Look to this elder for his wisdom. Picture a man well over three-hundred-years old who can give you advice from a storehouse of knowledge. He has seen history in the making and can tell you things about human nature that you can get nowhere else. He embodies wisdom and is willing to teach it.

Wearing indicolite may not bring rapid enlightenment, but it will gradually bring you to understandings about human nature of the lower bodies. It provides gentle nudges that lead to an understanding of the spiritual nature of man. You will be led to the inner storehouse of all knowledge. Knowledge is not enlightenment, just as facts are not truth. The knowledge we speak of here is not just data, but a developed sense of the workings of soul. Indicolite teaches you how to be wise rather than how to be mentally sharp. Wisdom is a quality of soul, whereas intelligence is an attribute of a mind.

Although female wearers may not be comfortable using this stone, it is helpful in small doses. It moves them to happiness by forcing self-injustice out in the open. It teaches you how to transform anger, frustration, and other "negative" feelings directly into happiness. For women who are continually unhappy, place a strand on the upper chest just above the sternum. Try wearing it for only a few minutes at a time. Short, regular treatments are best.

If it is not well tolerated, women may want to have their male mates wear indicolite and allow its effects to enter their auras in an indirect way. Women may find it easier to indirectly assimilate the way blue tourmaline teaches how to transform base emotional energy into happiness. Men often don't trust their feelings, so they find it easy to change how they feel directly. They may find they have a hard time regularly feeling happy, but once they learn to change anger into happiness they have no problem accepting the change.

Men who have a difficult time with self-acceptance may find this stone most useful. It works gradually. At first it promotes restfulness and a state of peace. Then, in this state of relaxation, he may begin to uncover the secrets of his universe. As he begins to trust himself as soul, he learns how to go beyond the mechanical nature of the mind for answers to deeper questions. It is only through surrender and acceptance of himself as soul, happy and free, that he will find the principles that underlie his life.

Those whose thoughts wander aimlessly may find some help by using a strand of indicolite to heal the disparity caused by an undisciplined mind. It will create a sense of harmony from which wearers may develop the ability to focus their attention. Focus is a key to creating what we want in life. To use this key, you must have special knowledge about its uses. This knowledge can only be received internally, nonverbally. Such wisdom is the gift of the ancients reinterpreted for today by the indicolite.

Higher consciousness is not won by simply wearing a strand of indicolite. It can only point the way to the inner storehouse of truth and the laws that govern karma. Developing your consciousness is a matter of learning to control your thoughts, feelings, and actions from a soul perspective. It is not a matter of intelligence. You must make the right choices for yourself in order to develop your consciousness. You learn to make the right choices by practicing knowing. Soul learns to know whereas the mind learns to think. Soul must take charge and begin to make decisions before it can know what the right choices are.

Ultimately, you must learn to become the master of your fate by making decisions from the consciousness of soul. Soul can consider thoughts and feelings and remain detached from them. Acting from soul can completely change your relationship to life. You cease to be the helpless pawn in a game that is out of your control. You learn to act independently without rebellion.

Some beneficial realizations may arise out of your deeper subconscious as a result of wearing this stone during sleep. The dream worlds are real. We can learn to control our experiences in dream worlds as we do in waking life. We can learn all sorts of things about who we are from dream experiences—soul learns just as well from dream experiences as from waking experiences. Soul is a better teacher for the mind than the mind itself is. It takes practice, but we can learn to overcome and release fear in the dream state. Indicolite will help with this. It will highlight our important inner experiences and help us remember them. As we lose fear, the mind can relax and allow soul to direct it.

Dream encounters give us experience, just as waking encounters do. Our actions in dreams teach about consequences, too. Overcome fear in a dream, and the conscious mind will believe it is possible to overcome fear of life. The mind may not even distinguish between a dream or a waking occurrence, if soul is in charge.

All sorts of sleep disorders can be cured after prolonged use of indicolite during the night. It will be through the efforts of the individual that these problems will go away. The stone of itself can do nothing the wearer does not want to have happen. It is the efforts of the individual that will bring relaxation of stress and release of fear.

The presence of the supportive vibrations of indicolite will help those who are indeed ready to let go of their nightmares and sleep disorders. Indicolite prompts self-reliance.

Fear causes us to close down our hearts. Closing our hearts brings resistance and stops the creative flow. We can all but shut off the inflow of growth-enhancing energy. This resistance or clamping down leads to physical and emotional pain; no resistance means no pain. Indicolite brings an easing of this tightened condition, gradually reducing the tension. It challenges us to realize it is we who cut ourselves off.

Once you have mastered your reaction to fear, you need give up nothing further. When you have given up fear and judgment, then no resistance remains. Without resistance, we feel little pain. In fact, a deep sense of knowing will develop where once there was fear. Wisdom is available to the wearer who looks for it with certainty, expectant that it will soon be there for them. Leave the means for how this wisdom will come to soul itself, and let the mind remain busy with other tasks. Picture yourself filled with light and willing to share that light with those who may benefit from it without sucking the life out of you. Allow indicolite to teach you how to increase your inner light. Its gentle yet stern hand will instruct you in the ways of self-protection.

Blue tourmaline is an extremely active stone. This stone is not for those with tension and fear, unless the person is willing to give up that fear and tension. Once the power of this blue stone has begun to work on the inner aspects of the causal portion of the mind, the mind will be caught up in the flow of blue light. At first the power of this flow itself may cause the wearer to feel uncomfortable. Do not be alarmed. It is the power of the indicolite itself that is needed to overcome the greatest fears. Let it go.

Wear this stone with the certainty of one who has enlisted a powerful warrior to do battle with fear. Take on the characteristics of the warrior only as, and if, you feel comfortable with those energies. These attributes are not those of a violent killer, they are the attributes of one who has the power to forestall all negative forces that would seek to control one's life. It is the power to control your own reactions with a cool and measured hand. This hand is the hand of strength. This is the sword of blue tourmaline.

It is important to learn how all lasting strength comes from being humble. It is important to gain lasting strength to combat the temptation to succumb to fear. Fear cannot harm us. Only our reactions to it cause harm. Only we can take the control of our actions away from negative forces. Once we have the support of a powerful ally like blue tourmaline, we can believe in the powers of good.

Work with this stone with a definite purpose in mind. Set your own goals for when you wish to face your fears. Set your own pace. Choose the battleground. No one likes nightmares, but the dream state may be the best place for this kind of work. We all have a difficult time imagining ourselves as more powerful than our fears. This is fear talking. We are soul. We are invincible. We do not perish when it is time for our bodies to return to the earth. Soul is not afraid. The mind is the bastion of fear.

Work with indicolite. Let it be your knight in shining armor. You will have taken the first step to accepting the immortality of soul. This journey may seem difficult and fraught with danger, but it is the journey to freedom through the control of reaction to the realization of our right to determine our fate. Once we assume a position of cause we begin to create our lives. If you are feeling like a victim of life, let indicolite teach you true independence. Soul is never the victim of life unless it allows the mind to rule its actions.

Turquoise

A great deal of lore surrounds the turquoise stone. In some tribes it was placed in houses to ward off evil spirits. In another, it was attached to the bows for better luck in hunting. Yet others included it in rites of passage. Some even worshiped the elemental spirits fashioned in turquoise. It has been called many names, including the "lucky stone," the "Turkish stone," and the "Venus stone." It has been placed in tombs to ward off spirits from the other worlds.

The purpose of this information is not to expose the reader to ancient lore, but to remind the reader that it has long been accepted that stones have a life and an energy all their own.

All tribes of the Orient and Americas were aware of the fact that entities, disembodied spirits, or those who would send spells of evil could cause harm to those who allowed it. The ability to return to their sender any negative energies is an ability of those who were initiated into a higher consciousness or had learned how to use psychic energy. Turquoise was given to the uninitiated, average tribesman who did not have this ability to turn back evil. The everyday use of turquoise would protect the person from unseen forces that had a destructive purpose.

Today we still use turquoise as a protective amulet. It may even protect the wearer from his or her own destructive thoughts and emotions. After all, much of what may befall us is unwittingly of our own invitation. Our minds attract destructive forces. Turquoise will isolate the place in us where we are susceptible to such forces and it will encompass this area. It will absorb self-negating energy like a sponge cleans a wound. These mental and emotional afflictions are the wounds of hooks we have allowed to pierce us. Hooks are negative or self-destructive thoughts and emotions we have allowed in from outside and have accepted. If the wearer can accept this healing, the hooks will be removed. Accept the healing and never speak of it again, for to speak of it is to invite a fresh hook wound.

Turquoise also absorbs negative superphysical energy like a sponge. Such disruptions are often caused by our reaction to trauma. Different varieties of turquoise will focus on different types of negative energy. Turquoise from China works on the superphysical energy system. African turquoise works on the physical body, American works more on the thought processes that invite destructive energy, and South American works on the emotional level. Each has its focus area and each will work on deeper levels after it has modified the focus area and absorbed all that the person is willing to release.

Place the appropriate strand on the area of the body that most requires assistance in releasing negativity. These areas will be the same ones that attract negativity whenever it is around. It may be the area at which you yourself direct negativity. You will experience a deep healing after only a few treatments, and you must stop accepting the negativity or channeling it into the area if you expect the healing to remain. Sometimes you will have to repeat this treatment for a few days each month until the subconscious mind learns that negativity is not necessary nor is it appropriate. Turquoise will pull out even the most persistently negative thoughts.

To aid in this process it is helpful to visualize the source of the negative thoughts and see a flow of negative energy emanating from the thoughts. Picture turquoise forming a deep blue-green cloud that creates a shield of impenetrable force. See it sucking the negative energy and diverting it as if it had a tractor beam. When the negative energy comes from a person who simply will not stop bombarding you, allow the turquoise shield in your imagination to become smooth and shiny. Watch as the negative thoughts are deflected and returned to the sender. Harmful energy rays cannot touch you when you have this thought firmly in mind.

Thank the negative energy for teaching you of a weakness. Know that the negative energy can now work with some other soul who needs greater courage and strength. Let it go with love, if possible.

Turquoise can be a great teacher of the value in cultivating subtle positive attributes. Worn for its nurturing quality, turquoise is as capable as the ancient Greek goddess Venus in its capacity to teach the wearer about beauty. It is through the experience of beauty that we as humans are able to transcend the shackles of the lower worlds. Beauty awakens soul's desire to return to its home.

When worn with silver and gold, as it traditionally has been, turquoise is often associated with wealth. This association is consistent with its origins as it is found in areas where silver and gold are also found. The combination can be used to unlearn negative associations with wealth.

Turquoise and gold work together to help a person learn to work toward abundance without pitting themselves against others in competition. Wear turquoise spheres together with gold beads in a strand. The proper proportions are eight eight-millimeter turquoise beads for each three-millimeter gold bead.

The wearer of this combination will learn about true abundance. Not the capacity to hoard money, but the capacity to find joy and nurturing from all life and to use what is abundantly available in terms of wealth for the good of all life forms. The key word here is *forms*. It is our form that we must learn to love before we can give it up for the higher, formless worlds. This ancient mystery can be unraveled by the wearer only with persistence and dedication.

Money is just a form of exchange. When we have learned that money can buy necessary things and that we have abundance in many ways, the reaction we now have to wealth, for example that it is the root of evil, will no longer keep it from us. We can naturally attract wealth and abundance of all kinds only when we stop all negative attitudes about them. Then the good things will naturally appear where they never were before.

It is not a form of superstition to believe that the presence of this stone gives protection upon death or translation of the soul. Soul need not take with it the heavy burdens that are part of this world. Soul can release its ties with the burdens of life in the physical world at the time of death. Turquoise can stimulate soul to release some of the burden carried by the mind that would otherwise be brought into the other worlds upon the death of the physical body. This moment is the time to release all hooks for the last time, if possible. This release is best done with help from a living master, who knows the other worlds.

Turquoise can assist those who have earned the right to choose whether they will return to the earth plane again after their current lifetime is over. At the time of death, or "translation," of the body, negative forces gather in a final test of soul to see if it is truly ready to move into higher states of being. If we are prepared for this, it will not distract us from our goal of higher consciousness. Turquoise can link us with "Mother" Earth who will help us in our hour of need to remember the lessons of the many lifetimes we have spent here. Spiritual freedom is available to the bold and adventuresome.

Thus, we could say turquoise brings courage. However, we must display the courage. The stone will not only remind us of the benefits we have enjoyed when demonstrating courage, but will remind us of the times we have not been courageous and the results we created. For some this reminder will be all that is needed. Others may miss the opportunity and be disappointed. We must learn for ourselves to move on.

If worn alternately with a strand of amethyst—one day the turquoise and three days the amethyst for ten cycles—the wearer will gain insight into why he has come to a challenge that requires greater courage. The wearer may be encouraged if he knows why this test has come at this time and what qualifications he has earned that give him the right to move on. As spiritual pioneers we can use the awareness that comes from the lessons we have already learned. We can stop repeating our mistakes when we are aided by Mother Earth energy as carried by turquoise.

Those who practice channeling and other psychic arts will find their powers of perception improving with each day they wear the stone. However, you can reach a point where these powers no longer work to move you forward on your spiritual path. At some point, our spiritual development does not depend on the use of our psychic powers. These powers can distract us from our true goal if we are not willing to look beyond psychic phenomena. Turquoise teaches us when to look elsewhere for our next step.

As soul, we grow toward the light. At times the psychic realm is in the direction of the light. Then as we learn of these psychic worlds we begin to rise to the realms above the psychic. From here the use of psychic powers only brings us down and we must learn to move on to greater realms. The light will show us the way if we can at times stop engaging in techniques and look directly to the light. Turquoise can help keep the psychic powers from interfering in our search for something higher, even though it helps bring the psychic power to those who need it.

Should you really wish to help others, it would be advisable to learn the ways of spirit. Spirit speaks to every individual in the same measure as that individual listens and takes heed. You must become trustworthy before spirit will provide deeper truths.

Teach what you know, for in teaching you will learn to be trustworthy. Teach those who wish to listen. Spirit will help you. Wear the turquoise, but have those who work with you wear citrine to open their spiritual ears and moonstone to help them create familiar images with which to understand spirit.

Teach them to love the natural gifts of life. Life gives more to those who love the gifts it gives. Some gifts may not seem like what you wanted. Ask those you teach to trust life. Ask them to accept what it has to offer. Just as you love to give to those who show a tremendous appreciation, so life treats those who love its gifts with greater gifts.

Turquoise will attract new friends into your world, especially friends who can gain as much from you as you can gain from them. You may even want to keep a large sample of uncut turquoise in your living room to encourage only those who are in harmony with your vibrations to come into your space. This will also help keep those who are not in harmony with you from wanting to enter your house at all.

Let this blue-green stone be your protector and guard you against harm. Be aware of the people in your space as you wear the turquoise strand. If they are enemy, they will reveal their contention. Self-protection is sometimes as easy as inviting those who wish to do us harm to stay out of our space. The vibrations of turquoise will back us up. Let your enemies show you what your weaknesses are. Do not attack the enemy, for he has helped, rather let turquoise heal the open wound. Let the color-ray energy heal the weakness. Learn the art of gratitude to your enemies. They teach you to find your strength once you learn to accept weakness.

Turquoise shows the way to self-love. It will teach you of beauty and abundance. It will support you in releasing self-loathing and teach you to share your gifts with those who appreciate them, so that you may be given greater gifts.

Turquoise is indeed a precious gemstone, particularly to those who use it wisely. Its protection will help you develop your own way without the constriction of other people's values and ideals. Turquoise is the stone to wear when breaking the mold and learning to live freely in your own personal way. Being true to yourself is a key to the highest form of love.

Turquoise is not purely blue; it carries some of the green ray. Its mission is most like that of the other blue stones, but it works excellently in combination with green. If you are drawn to using turquoise, look to other blue and green stones to support your changes. The blue will help with mental stability and understanding, and the green will help assimilate the growth of self-love in a balanced way, without becoming self-centered.

The green ray brings harmony and can lead to inner peace. These qualities will uplift those whose primary color ray is green to great spiritual understanding and wisdom. All who come to the green ray can find greater serenity. "Just let it be" is a phrase that describes one of the green-ray solutions. Green-ray people who are clearly demonstrating the positive aspects of the green ray are content to "be." They do not feel the need to prove anything to others. Beingness is a quality of soul. Soul *is*. This statement is deceptively simple. Another way of saying it is: soul has no limitations regarding time and space and therefore it can be at any time and any place, or it can be at all times and places at once.

We can be in harmony with all of life when we can be what we truly are. No hiding is necessary and no denial is possible when the green ray begins to deeply cleanse and ease the body's tensions. We may find this new state disturbing at first. Denial can be your most-trusted friend, but inner peace is possible only when you have completely eradicated denial.

It is said that we must proceed into the kingdom of heaven with our eyes wide open. The green ray will build our confidence in opening our eyes. We must find inner peace before we can make peace with the world. We must make peace with the world before we can enter any of the heavens.

5 Green Ray Stones

We are all unique. We must make peace with our uniqueness to discover what it is about us that makes us what we are. The green ray will bring one closer to reality as it helps dispel illusions. Grief can accompany this process. The green ray will help us with grief and create an understanding of grief where once there was fear.

Work with the green ray. Let it into your heart. One can metabolize and give up their negative constructs to the green ray. Negative constructs are unstable. They do not survive the test of the green ray. Green stones will teach you how to work with the green ray. After that, it is up to the individual to progress in the areas supported by the green ray. Green is always available to all without the tool of a green stone. As soul we are able to move all manner of color energies without blockages. The mind, however, must be taught not to interfere with this ability. Green-ray stones teach us to quiet the mind, and to use our given ability as soul to control the color energy. The tool makes the job a bit easier until soul learns to use the green-ray energy directly.

Emerald

As the carrier of the green ray, emerald teaches respect for the whole of creation, especially the physical realm and its myriad forms. This teaching brings us into respect for all creation. Emerald prompts us to interact with life from a more spiritual perspective. This new interaction brings a deep awareness of the beauty and love that are possible in the physical realm.

The physical realm is filled with suffering and pain, so it may at first be difficult to comprehend the notion that the physical world is the one place where spiritual teachings have their greatest effect on soul's progress. Many spiritual paths teach ascension from the physical or redemption from this life. This teaching may include the ascetic practice of denial of all worldly desires. These practices may be necessary for the individual until detachment is understood. We must understand detachment to be able to truly love life. Emerald teaches us how much more love can flow through us when we are not absorbed in some attachment. Emerald has the distinct privilege of helping us to see the divine in the mundane or ordinary. It shows the individual how to appreciate every little thing. As we absorb this teaching, we learn a reverence for all life, whereupon an experience of heaven may come to us in the here and now.

Each of us comes into this world with a dominant color ray, which can be any of the colors of the rainbow or an equal mixture of them in the form of white. Our primary color ray is this color. We may hold to this primary color throughout our lives, or we may adopt a secondary or tertiary color ray. These other colors are expressions that we adopt for the purpose of spiritual growth, as a temporary state of learning. Ideally we would allow all colors to flow in and through us with our primary color ray dominating somewhat. In life we are generally unable to accept this much energy. An internal mechanism within the mind then focuses on these secondary and tertiary colors for the purpose of expanding our acceptance of that color ray. Often the secondary color is our weakest color ray. As we try to express ourselves through this weak color ray we learn to tolerate more of it. We become stronger. Later we must drop this secondary color and return to a state where our primary color predominates. Removing the illusion under which we operated in this secondary color predominance is difficult without emerald.

We will express our deeper selves clearly and most naturally when we become cleansed and cleared of imbalances and can newly express our inherited, original balance of color rays with our primary color ray predominating. Emerald can help cleanse the imbalances and tensions. It will "metabolize" these negative and disharmonious energies that have become stuck or are being used within the mind to create false mental concepts.

When character, personality, action, and speech become attuned to our true natural vibrations, we are capable of the highest form of service and love. Deep satisfaction will surely result from this kind of service and love.

Green-ray people tend to be pragmatic, sensible, well grounded in the laws of nature, and self-assured, with a gentle, strong demeanor. They often regard nature as their source of learning. Emerald helps you enjoy intimacy, especially for green-ray persons who require alone time to find balance and harmony.

For those who are of the green ray, emerald is truly a gift. It will bring a deeper awareness of the harmony and fecundity of the green ray. All of us have some of the green ray and will find it beneficial to develop this aspect of ourselves to gain harmony, even if it is our weakest aspect.

Focusing first on the visceral organs, which are the sensory organs, emerald will bring you into closer contact with the world. Not the world we may have known, which is static and ordinary, but the dynamic world that is fluid and exciting, and full of life and vitality.

Bearer of the green ray, emerald is a powerful healing tool capable of dissolving disharmony. Used as a physical healing aid, it brings about a great releasing and clearing of disharmony throughout the body. It is capable of raising the vibratory rate of the body, which initiates the process of cleansing the body of energies that do not support this higher vibration.

Emerald will begin to work on the weakest and most troubled part of the body when worn in a necklace. Use only the highest grade of emerald, with pure, deep color and few inclusions. Poor grades with discolorations, inclusions, and areas of yellow-green, yellow, or white can actually infuse disorienting energies into the body. High-grade emerald's powerful action will immediately begin to break up patterns of tension and congestion. It will gradually bring areas of lowest vibration into balance with the rest of the body.

Wearing an eighteen- to twenty-inch necklace of small emeralds around the neck will saturate the body and bring about substantial change in a short time. Fifteen minutes to one-half hour is a good treatment length at first. These strands can be placed on the body for periods of five to ten minutes when you are trying to facilitate raising the vibration of an area of the body. You may employ small emerald rondels, stones cut in flattened round shapes, strung in short circles of perhaps one to two inches in diameter where a particular body area is calling for longer duration infusions.

High-grade single spheres or rondels can be used if the body is in serious condition, and long, gradual treatments are preferred. Place single spheres on organ "windows" that are on the skin above the target area within the body.

Place a single dark-green or translucent aventurine sphere over a desired target area anywhere on your body, and the effects of an emerald necklace worn at the same time will be concentrated on the target area. Aventurine works as a focusing agent, locating and highlighting cells that are toxic or weak and in danger. The vibratory rate of high-quality emerald will actually metabolize disharmony. Aventurine, on the other hand, requires the body to metabolize any disharmony it locates. Using aventurine to locate disharmony and emerald to raise the vibratory rate of the actual atoms and cells is a very effective treatment protocol for any physical disease.

Do not make the mistake of ignoring other forms of treatment, including traditional medicines and surgery when appropriate. Emerald is a beneficial adjunct to any naturopathic or allopathic treatments; however, do not use emerald or other gemstones to replace treatments prescribed by a doctor. The body may require the introduction of medicinal substances or other intervention techniques to ensure that healing occurs in a timely manner. Use your intuition, but don't ignore the advice of a doctor, especially when conditions are serious.

For a thorough cleansing of the body, place a strand of high-quality emeralds around the neck. Sit upright in a comfortable position. Let your mind go blank for a moment as you concentrate on your breathing. As you bring in a deep breath, pay attention to the sound of the air moving in the nose, mouth, and throat. As you release the breath through your mouth, let the lungs empty completely. Now as you breathe in, imagine a glowing ball of bright green energy forming at the lower back and slowly moving up the spine to the top of the head. Let it stay above the head for a moment as you hold the breath for a few seconds. Now slowly release the breath as the green ball moves down over the front of the body to a point just below the naval. As it enters the body, after you have fully exhaled, hold it in the body and don't breath for two seconds.

For best results, repeat this breathing visualization for at least twenty breaths as the green energy draws out all disharmony and balances the body systems. Do this exercise at least twice a day for two days to thoroughly cleanse the body.

Once emerald has broken down and removed the disharmony on the physical level, it will begin to work on the root cause of the physical condition. This cause may be emotional or mental in nature. By addressing these causes one at a time, we can learn which causes are not in alignment with our direction and goals and how we can recreate them to be in better alignment. We may gradually become in touch with a natural order for our lives.

Emerald teaches about the pragmatic, practical way of living. Its vibrations will highlight thoughts and concepts that work for us. We will gradually learn discernment. How to choose when there are so many choices is the lesson of emerald. It gives us a way of making decisions that is efficient and effective. It teaches harmony. Looking at a situation in your life from a state of harmony is an excellent way of preparing to make decisions. Decisions that take into account a harmonious vision of our future allows the intended outcome, most in harmony with our basic nature and in balance with our current situation, to occur.

Those who wish to open their hearts more to love will find unexpected benefits from emerald. It will act to improve the physical heart functions. It will allow you to experience a greater scope of emotions. At the same time, it will quiet the emotions and abate storms of emotional reaction that disturb us. These storms are like the monsoon storms in India. Only when the continual rain of emotional monsoons ceases can one enjoy the warmth and bounty of summer. Rain can be enjoyable, too, if it comes in occasional warm showers that wash away the surface dust. When every day is a gray one, rain seems like a tyranny.

Conversely, if the emotions are constantly dry, life becomes hard, just as the earth becomes hard when every day is hot and dry. The life-giving sun itself is no longer enjoyable in a drought. Then even occasional storms are devastating and can, all too easily, wash the tentative, parched soil out to sea. What would be a good rain in the forest is like a flood in the desert. You can see that neither continuous rain nor continuous drought is a good climate for growth.

If we wish to grow bountiful crops, we must choose to live in a climate where sun is plentiful but rain also comes to wash and sweeten the thirsty land. It is our choice. Some of us may acclimate better to wetter emotional environments and some to drier. Either way, there is an important balance that must suit our naturally inherited climatic preference. We can choose from a range of climates in which we can survive. Emerald will help us find the optimum conditions for growth. It will keep violent emotional storms from flooding our landscape, yet encourage the natural flow of sufficient emotion to keep us feeling healthy and alive.

Emerald will teach us to recognize the circumstances and conditions in which we will thrive. As we understand our nature, so will we effectively speak for our needs. Our own words are the best ones to represent us. When we speak the ideas and words of others, we may find it serves us to some extent. Only when we find our own tongue will we begin to feel our words truly represent our concerns. Emerald teaches us to understand others better by first, translating their thoughts into our own language, and then, taking time to test the validity of their ideas and discover how these ideas apply to us. We can use emerald to discover our nature and help us find trustworthy friends and associates who share our ideas.

Emerald, for all its power, embodies kindness. Its vibrations are of kindness. Listen to the vibrations. As they massage your body, they will ease your worries. If you listen to the sound of the vibrations touching your body, it will ease your mind. This sound is subtle but audible.

Your mind will naturally quiet as the constant effort to phrase your thoughts into words subsides and is replaced by the certainty that your thoughts are lucid and easily translated from beliefs that you embody. As the chatter of worry slows, the sound of emerald tuning your body will gradually become audible. You may not hear it as an external sound—it may appear to come from within. This experience is unusual at first but will seem appropriate as you get used to it.

Listening for the sounds of the body will initiate the process of getting in touch with the body. The body is intelligent. The body knows things through a different mechanism than the mind. It feels things—not emotionally, but physically. Emotions also generate feelings in the body, and the body does understand emotions in its own way. The physical body stores impressions as physical vibration memories, the emotional body or astral body stores impressions in packets of emotional reaction. Emerald helps the mind determine the nature of different memories, where they have been stored and how to understand them in terms of the respective body that picked up the original impression and the vibrational interaction that occurred at that time in the particular sheath. We will learn to differentiate how experiences affect the different sheaths. We will learn how the different parts of ourselves function separately yet interactively.

The greatest gift of emerald is the gift of ourselves. Emerald teaches us to hear the vibrations of our different sheaths. Understanding our vibrations and how they are affected by our surroundings places us squarely on the path of self-mastery. When you hear this sound, which could be almost any sort of pure pitch, humming, buzzing, bubbling, or other tone, and identify the origin of the sound as coming from within, you will know you are on the right path. Emerald will guide you to discover how to gain complete control over your reactions and the vibrations you give out.

Aventurine

Stones of the green ray help us learn independence with trust. The green ray is one of the fundamental healing influences we can use for the upliftment of the physical body. Look for the effects of green stones to bring harmony and balance. These qualities are essential to the pursuit of well-being.

Some who wish to simplify life suggest that each chakra responds to a different color. In fact, we are capable of moving energies of all colors through all our chakras in every body. Those who can control this capability are able to do amazing things. Look for books on tantric practices to describe this form of yoga. As we begin to work with balancing the green ray in all our chakras, we will begin to learn the art of chakra control. First we must bring the physical body into balance, aligning each part. The physical body changes more slowly than the others. Color-ray energies flow more slowly, physical atoms are more dense, and vibrations get stuck more easily.

Aventurine brings its influence of harmony and balance to the physical body. The atoms, molecules, and cells that make up our physical body each have different vibrations. These vibrations can be in tune with our fundamental makeup, or they can be divergent and in discord with our primary vibrations. Each of the vibrations in our body may remain different from the fundamental frequencies of our inner body or soul, but it is essential for good health that they be in harmony with each other. Otherwise, larger amounts of disharmony "stick" to the energetic layer that exists within an inch of the skin.

Organ centers may also have their own overall energy vibrations. I refer here to organs in the broadest sense and include the skin, the bones, the lymph system, and every other system of the body. These, taken as a whole, combine to make our personal physical sound. This sound can be in concert with our inner, or soul, sound or it can be painfully off-key. You can hear this inner sound, as well as the personal physical sound, as a kind of music. The inner sound is inherently harmonious, no matter how off-center we are. We choose whether or not to bring our body into harmony with this inner melody, which is the melody that expresses our divine nature.

Aventurine interacts with each organ center and pinpoints the cells, molecules, and atoms that are in tune with our song. It then encourages them to sing out. You will see that no matter how far off-key the organ centers are and how ill at ease they are, we can remind each cell of the original melody. Cells, while not often seen as having a form of intelligence, do have a life of their own and are autonomous. Even though they obviously depend on the body as a whole for their existence, they are capable of independent action, as evident in a battle between the immune system and many forms of cancer. It is a war, but each cell is on its own. Aventurine teaches the body cells to work in harmony and the cells create a symphony of concordant melodies from this influence.

Aventurine reaches into the body and encourages the cells that are in harmony with soul's conception of itself, as related to each organ center of the body, to begin to share their vibrations with those of the surrounding cells. Unhealthy organs may not have many cells that are in tune with our vibrations of origin, but they usually will have at least a few. Aventurine will energize these. These cells will "sing" more forcefully and other cells will begin to resonate and come into harmony.

Likewise, atoms and molecules are not all the same. They have individual signatures that differ from atom to atom of the same type. Every atom of our body is known to come into us, stay for only a brief time, and be discharged. Not a single atom you have in your body today is the same as the atom you had in your body just seven years ago. In fact, in a three-month period, most atoms are discharged and replaced with others, even in the bones. We are constantly exchanging atoms. Current scientific theories see two oxygen atoms as being identical, and in gross terms they are—just as two chickens are the same. However, they are also quite different. Their exact size, proportion, energy, vibration, magnetism, ionization, attitude with respect to true north, orientation, and sound are not the same.

When you wear aventurine as a necklace of spheres, it will begin to attract atoms that are in alignment with your energetic body blueprint. If you are conscious of this process and become aware of its subtle prompting, you will begin to be attracted to substances that contain harmonious atoms. You will gradually begin to choose foods that contain the atoms you need most. Whether you can hear this vibration as sound is not important. Being aware of why certain foods attract you does not matter as long as you can trust the attraction to be for the benefit of the body. As long as you follow your higher intuition, you will be attracted to beneficial edibles.

When we are seriously ill at ease, we feel pain. Pain can tighten us up so tightly that we cannot contact anything of benefit to us. The green ray, as carried by aventurine, calms us. It opens us to the healing that awaits us.

Try the following imaginative technique while wearing a necklace of aventurine. Know that as you picture the energy, it is actually moving through you.

Picture a stream of green sparkles of light falling all over you. As these sparkles of light touch the body, it begins to relax. The specks of green go right through you, softening you and helping you become more fluid. See your stress being carried off as it attaches to these specks. Imagine your body is letting go of all its excesses. They form in a dark mass to one side. At the same time, see yourself drawn to the energies you are deficient in. Allow your eyes to become full of the green. Remembering that your eyes are the windows to the soul, let the green ray wash through you, easing every joint and all your vital organs.

Picture the dark mass of stress washing into the stream of green energy and into the earth. Recognize yourself. See the organs, blood, nerves, extremities, and various bones one at a time as they complete their revitalization exercise. Repeat this exercise daily for at least a week.

Aventurine works first on the physical body. Then it moves into the aura. Once aventurine has fully saturated your aura, you will begin to notice it changing your attitudes. How long this takes is a function of the quality, color, and clarity of the stones and how in tune you are internally when you start. You may notice this attitude shift as a relaxing of old barriers. You will become more accepting. Aventurine will encourage a person to see the fluidity in things. Is your life really all that predictable? Was it ever?

Watch your interaction with those you know well. You may find that aventurine will show you sides of things you had not previously noticed. You may see those you have known for years, as if for the first time. Often, our own beliefs make all those we see appear to remain the same even when they have changed. Aventurine holds judgments that defy reality at bay to allow the mind to see what is really going on.

Emotional stress frequently accompanies the belief that we can never do anything about the things we are afraid of or don't like. In life, however, everything changes. It is when we constantly hold on tightly to old fears or worries that they begin to do us harm. The aventurine energy will encourage us to let go. As we surrender our fears and worries to this flow of aventurine energy, we can relax. Releasing emotional anxiety will create new possibilities. Release enough anxiety and there will be so many new choices you will feel inspired by the possibilities.

Suppose you have a friend who just won't see things your way. You have been trying to convince this person that your point of view is what they need to see to get moving. You become frustrated. You try to get them to listen, but they just won't. You begin to develop a resentment about their inability to listen. As the weeks or months go by, you feel less inclined to be with them because they are so stubborn and thick headed.

What happens when you try aventurine? You will find that it first goes to work on your body. You begin to relax your grip on this resentment. Soon you feel so much better, you forget to be angry. As the days pass, you feel renewed.

One day you see your friend. By now, you have forgotten to continue the argument with them in your head, and you have let the whole thing go. Before you can realize what has happened, your friend is doing something different. You get curious. You watch them as if for the first time.

Suddenly, you realize they are doing something that proves they have changed. They are no longer in the same place you were trying to get them out of. They are not even the person you thought they were. You get a feeling of love. You have seen how much we are all the same. You see yourself in them, and you are moved.

We may begin to notice that we are affecting the whole Earth. The vibrations we put out interact with the Earth and all who live on it. As our vibrations become in tune with the flow of life and we begin to put out harmonious vibrations, we affect everything around us, including the Earth, much more deeply. As we change, the Earth changes, however we cannot really affect the Earth except through physical means. Thus, if we are inspired to create physical changes for those around us and for the Earth, let us start with our physical vehicle, and make our bodies a temple. This is our temple, and what we do in it is a form of worship. What are we choosing to worship? We may have to let go of our old concepts of worship and spirituality to let a new idea come in. Some physical healing can only take place when the wearer has let go of what they hold as more important than life itself.

Use aventurine for physical health, and the green ray will enter it, encourage it to heal naturally, and go on to heal the subtle bodies. Work with aventurine around the rooms of your house and learn from it how to arrange your house so the energy in each room is more harmonious. After that, you will be ready to begin working with your relationship to the rest of the world.

By using aventurine as an aid to contemplation, we can learn about the deeper levels of harmony. We can become in harmony with a greater consciousness. This process starts with us. We need not become absorbed into some group consciousness to interact with the whole. We can learn to choose what we take in. Then, when life asks us to express ourselves, we will naturally express our own sense of balance and attunement. We learn of our individuality as we learn to be in harmony with all life; we learn that the two are interlinked.

In learning to be a part of the whole, we also learn to be independent. As we find what truly works for us, we also find that this is in keeping with what is best for those we love. In this way, aventurine teaches us about giving. Through giving, we come to know a deeper kind of love.

Aventurine comes in light, dark, and translucent. Light green aventurine focuses its energy primarily on the physical body. It works from the inside. It pinpoints areas of disharmony and goes to work on them. Its light green color is best for those whose auras are darkened by long-term illness. The white in these light green stones also helps uplift areas of deep stress. It is a bit more gentle than the dark or translucent forms, which is helpful when dealing with chronic problems.

For those in poor health or who are sick often, it is best to use the light green variety for an hour or two at a time at first. Use the light green to focus the aventurine energy on the problem areas. It will focus entirely on the weakest areas first. Strands of light green aventurine can be worn as a necklace or used in coils over the target area, or both. When placed over a troubled area, it will work on that area exclusively. When worn as a necklace, it will work on the whole body starting with the weakest area.

Dark green aventurine should be substantially darker than the light green variety. Therapeutic dark green aventurine is a deep emerald green. It should contain few or no white or milky spots. Flecks within its semi-translucent form should be very dark green.

This dark green variety works more deeply on initiating release. Best worn as a necklace at first, it is quite general in effect. The green ray is diffused throughout the body. This action is good for full-body harmony but can be overly powerful for persons who have many areas of disharmony. Use it as a necklace for some time before trying to concentrate its energies on any one body organ.

You can place the light green aventurine over inflamed or shut-down organs while wearing a necklace of the dark green. This method allows the organ area to get special treatment while the whole body becomes stronger. Apply this treatment for one half-hour, gradually increasing the application time to two hours after the first few treatments.

Whenever using strands in placement therapy, take time to visualize the organ you wish to treat. See it gradually becoming healthy and vibrant. Always commit yourself to at least three treatments, and try to administer them at the same time of day for consecutive days or every other day. Obtaining lasting results requires commitment and consistency. Most problems are going to be released only when the spiritual significance of the problem is fully understood. Anyone can get rid of a problem, unfortunately few know how, and you may learn how only after the problem has resulted in chronic or life-threatening conditions. Problems can come back. For long-term control of recurring conditions, consistent repetition with a commitment to doing whatever it takes to clear up a problem, even including using traditional medicine, will bring results. Physical treatments that have lasting results often employ several different curative influences.

Translucent aventurine of high quality and consistent color is recommended for use only when you require a deeper, more complete, body healing. Do not engage in this form of treatment lightly. For this purpose, you should use a translucent form of aventurine with strong color and good clarity that contains an even distribution of dark green flecks. Consult a professional gemstone therapist to find the exact variety and size of translucent aventurine that would best treat your body. When in doubt, use six-millimeter AAA-beads.

Wear the strand for as long as it takes to bring the body into harmony with its inner song of soul. This process normally will proceed in stages, with the deep, penetrating changes occurring at intervals of one, three, and seven weeks. A person may go through a number of cycles (often more than nine, sometimes as many as twenty-one) to bring the body to the next level of health.

You may want to do a partial fast or use safe herbal cleansing remedies under a doctor's supervision as preparation for this therapy. The body may give off toxins that it has carried for many years once the aventurine necklace begins to encourage it. These toxins can be extremely dangerous, and it is advisable to have checkups during this process to ensure your safety.

Maintain a good diet and get enough aerobic exercise to open the pores of the skin, allowing it to release toxins. The skin is the greatest organ of elimination, and it should be kept clean during deep cleansing. Steam baths are helpful. Eat plenty of foods that are high in water content. Drink lots of pure water. These practices will improve the body's ability to regularly eliminate any unwanted substances.

For best results, also practice deep breathing techniques daily. Oxygen is essential for breaking down dangerous substances in the body. Many good books are available on the subjects of diet, exercise, and breathing, so take time to get serious and you will get results.

Do not consider this process of working with aventurine a novelty. It is capable of creating significant change. Use it with love and focus your intentions clearly. Aventurine has become available in a quality and consistency not previously known because many are ready to work with the higher grades. If you decide to work with aventurine, let gratitude and an open willingness for that which serves the Earth best guide you. By doing so, you will surely find a new level of physical spirituality in your temple.

A clean, healthy physical body is a necessary prerequisite for significant spiritual change. Learn commitment and healthy self-discipline from aventurine. Let this wonderful stone guide you to a healthier lifestyle.

Chrysoprase

In gem quality, chrysoprase is rare and expensive. The highest quality is best for any therapeutic uses. Wear only necklaces of high clarity and few inclusions in roughly six-millimeter sphere size. Some whiteness is acceptable if spread evenly and not affecting translucency too much. Remember to avoid strands that include metal parts, even metal clasps.

This gemstone is gently subtle. Its capacity to contrast our foibles and follies with our true inner potential is exhaustive if this process is taken seriously. Chrysoprase can help us see that happiness is our natural state and that abundance is the natural state of life. Roughly translated, it says in the Bible, "Those who need not shall be made greater. Those who have plenty, more shall be added unto them." We will be shown that we are the ones who have accepted limitations and that we have adopted the beliefs that govern our state of affairs.

Is it possible that our own petty thoughts keep us in the bondage of lack? Could it be true that if we can throw out greed and envy, their cousins, gratitude and plenty, will come to visit us? Ask yourself this: have you ever tried practicing an attitude of gratitude about all that you have received? If not, then perhaps you cannot tell which came first: the state of lack, or attitudes such as resentment and covetousness of others' possessions, or the constant desire for more.

Chrysoprase will assist the wearer to answer these questions. It will instruct us in the ways of plenty. It will lead us into the mythical land of milk and honey. These states are within. You must turn your desire within to find gratitude there. Chrysoprase has the high vibration of limitless joy—a vibration we may not be familiar with. After all, most of us were brought into this world with sterile forceps and a slap. Before long, our natural curiosity and wonder at life could be replaced by a serious attitude of fear and the feeling of abandonment and loss of all that is good.

Now it is up to us. We can blame others, but we are the ones who perpetuate this sad state of affairs. We have grown up into adults, and now we are the ones who create our reality.

Chrysoprase will help us get in touch with reality. It will help us develop the momentum we need to accept reality for what it is. It will encourage us to weed out demeaning thoughts as well as grandiose thoughts that make us seem bigger than life or all-powerful. By using this help, we will begin to be accurate observers. Our observations will not have the slanted perspective of someone with an out-of-balance ego.

Mental balance is the promise of chrysoprase. We must do the work to review our own internal movies. These "reels" contain our own rendition of our reality, self-evaluation in the meanings we ascribe to life. Chrysoprase will aid the inner editor in retaining the real footage and eliminating the imaginary. The mind does not differentiate between these two types of memories. It sees imaginary thought as equal to experience. The mind also includes any distortions as if they were part of the original action. Are you living life based on a story about it? Is it possible that it is time to throw out the decisions we made when we were five, six, or seven years old? Unless you take the time to screen memories and clear out the distortions and additions, the mind will not differentiate between what actually happened and what the mind made up about what happened.

To gain in self-esteem, we must first get the mind clear on which memories are fantasies and distortions and which are observed experience. To have good self-esteem we must have an accurate, trustworthy mind. Then we must have the feeling and the belief that we are worthy of the good things in life. To trust the mind when it has accepted inaccuracies that slant reality for our benefit will lead to low self-esteem.

Chrysoprase helps us with our feelings of worthiness. It can help show us how others—as well as ourselves—are unique and valuable for that uniqueness. We all have gifts. Those who have suffered more in life have something special to offer, as do those who have not had to suffer. We all have something to offer from our soul. Soul has value because it gives and receives divine love.

If we can realize the gift of life, we can deepen our sense of gratitude for our lives and our experiences, as well as improve our ability to give. Life is a gift to those who love it. When you give of yourself and without conditions, you will uncover the gift of life. This gift hides in waiting for those who are busy giving of themselves. If you are constantly focusing attention on what is wrong with your life, you have no time for others. Only through giving will we transcend our own foolish complaining.

Chrysoprase has a remarkably soothing vibration that helps you trust that things will work out. Giving the deepest gift, the unique gift that each soul has to give, can be difficult. What if others reject the gift? After all, giving of oneself is an act of divine love. Who can accept divine love? Who truly believes there is such a thing?

The reward is in the giving, not in the acceptance by others, although this may follow. The reward is inherent in the act. You must believe in divine love to give of yourself. Taking the action requires trust and faith. No stone can give you trust and faith, nor can it give the reward. Chrysoprase can assist in taking the step. It can support you in the act of faith.

Try the following exercise with a strand of chrysoprase. Sit upright in a chair. Hold the strand to your heart chakra with your left hand (or your right hand if you are left-handed). Close your eyes, if it is comfortable. Relax. Breathe easily. Let your breath fully out. Expand your chest to allow as much air as possible to fill the area below your hand. Breathe out slowly and openly. Relax your jaw. Let loose all tension from this area. Now place the other hand lightly on the top of the head with palm down.

Allow chrysoprase into your aura. Picture its soothing green energy filling your aura. See it begin to fill the area under your hand containing the stones.

Now imagine that you are the only person in the world. There is no one else. You are the only carrier of divine love. If there are to be acts of divine love in the world, then you will take the actions. If there are to be thoughts of love, then you will think them. Now imagine that an animal comes to you. It is your favorite animal. You immediately feel a deep sense of compassion for this animal, as it is also the only one of its species left in the world.

Now express that compassion. Let this animal know how much you care for it. Give all of yourself to it. Let the love pour out. Let the feelings come. Thank the animal for being. Give all that is in your heart. If feelings come up, let them out. Express yourself.

If you have trouble giving love freely to an animal, then let any other being, person, bird, fish, or plant replace the animal. Create this universe and its details—gardens, buildings, landscape and so on. Pay attention to detail. Each time you revisit this place, add a few more details. Go there anytime you need to find that feeling of abundance. It is your private place.

The first time you try this exercise, you may feel awkward or silly. Let that be your feeling. Try the exercise again. The first few times, you may need to release some feelings of awkwardness or self-criticism. After this, you may find yourself getting deeper into the actual feeling of divine love. Let chrysoprase be your support and guide. The feelings you feel are your feelings. They reflect you and how you are about life. Chrysoprase can help you. It can unlock the heart. It can remove the weight of neglect. With its help you can teach yourself to trust and believe.

Malachite

Malachite is a beautiful stone in any quality. What distinguishes the type of beads best suited for therapeutic application is both the accuracy with which the spheres are shaped and the distinctness of the lines. Malachite beads that are not round are much less effective at dispensing information. Beads that have blurry or fuzzy lines, where the green color is speckled with the black are not desirable. The best beads have perfectly rounded shape and contain eyes of black with perfect circles of green and black around them.

For those who truly seek the Earth, the heavens shall reveal themselves. No other stone can help one attune to the Earth's energies and unlock the mysteries of the Earth and its vast array of knowledge in the same way as malachite. It brings understanding of the hidden mysteries of the Earth. Yes, the Earth has memories and intelligence, and malachite will introduce you to Earth's unusual language. It will take you into the mysteries of vibrational signatures and teach you of numbers and symbols.

It will teach you about the different centers of the body and their forms of intelligence. Each center in the body has a form of intelligence of its own. The chakras are powerful vortices governed by the motivations and experiences they have encountered.

The physical body has twelve main chakras, several subsidiary energy centers that are also significant, and each of the subtler sheaths has corresponding chakras. These other chakras can be controlled by thought, but they also have their own purposes and tend to act independently. To coordinate their purposes with thought takes an understanding of the language of these centers. Each center works a bit differently. They all move energy, but all do not move the same kind of energy. Physical-level energies are at a different vibration than astral- or mental-level energies. We learn to understand these energies and how to move them, what they are used for, and what is required to move them by developing a nonverbal, symbolic language with which to communicate to our chakras and with which they communicate to soul. By teaching them to communicate with each other, we learn what each is capable of and the consequences of its use of certain energies. From soul we can teach the centers to cooperate. We can harness the energies for health.

If we learn the ethics of using certain energies before we go off and hurt someone or set them back on their spiritual path, we will incur no setbacks ourselves. The more you learn, the more you are capable of helping yourself achieve spiritual detachment. Detachment is the ability to refrain from interfering with others or removing their problems before they have learned from them. Detachment is allowing oneself to limit your life and gradually let spiritual purposes replace the social dictates. If you use the energies of these centers wrongfully, the centers will cease intercommunication and will not easily respond to further commands.

Malachite teaches the right use of color-ray energies. They have a spiritual purpose. Malachite teaches how to apply the energy needed to achieve purification of self. It teaches noninterference. We must refrain from interfering with others if we expect to learn more. This may mean keeping silent about your accomplishments. It definitely does not mean doing for others what you have not been asked to do.

Malachite will show you the very nature of the wisdom contained in and stored by the earth in the substance of malachite. It will speak to you in dream language and numbers and symbols.

Anyone having the desire to understand the mysteries of alchemy, as the ancients once attempted to practice it, can find the truth. Truth is a changing force. You must apprehend it again and again. It is elusive and fluid. It is paradoxical. It is only clear when taken to a higher level of consciousness. Malachite teaches flexibility when attempting to comprehend truth.

Some philosophers have sought to make truth a solid commodity; these philosophers have not met malachite. Malachite works in wavelike vibrations. It surges deeply and carries us into new waters. We will find it a never-ending odyssey of discovery. As the currents of green and black carry us on our adventure, we will learn how to discover truth in the moment. Each moment contains a special truth all its own. This travel through the dreamlike world of earth language symbols is indeed mystical at first, but takes on more of a character of direct knowing when your consciousness becomes attuned to the stream of information. The voyage is a bit like the odyssey of Ulysses. Strange and wonderful islands of most unusual images await those who can unlock the first level of mystery. Introduction to deeper mysteries is the promise that keeps the seeker going.

Learn the language of malachite and you will get a handle on a language of truth. Trust the journey. You must come to accept that the end is not the goal. Life is not an end unto itself, it is a process of continual renewal. Malachite will show us myriad possibilities for living. It will show us more and more ways of understanding. It will show us another point of view for each new harbor on our great journey of the seven seas.

A necklace of many different-sized spheres will work best. Choose the stones that "speak" clearly and they will have clear "eyes" in which to see truth. All malachite pieces are in vibrational resonance with the moment in the history of the planet when they were formed, and each can be deciphered by soul once it learns to read their crystalline matrix. Perfect spheres receive the resonances from all malachite over the earth. They carry the total message of the matrix of all pieces of malachite from every energy center on earth. Within these many matrices is stored the history of the world as it relates to the universe. The eyes of a perfect sphere are the best broadcasters of earth memories. The circular bands surrounding the eyes of a perfect sphere are amplifiers. When they are distinct and well-defined, they carry incoming messages in many different forms to every human sheath so that each part of you can learn to recognize the many symbols and ramifications of truth.

Malachite will communicate its stored data through mathematical interrelationships and formulae as well as dream symbols and other metaphorical parables. Numbers are a way of understanding. This way is available to all who wish to put the time into understanding their deeper significance. Refer to books on number systems and numerology for specific information on this subject. When you have learned all you can, put away the books. Open your mind to direct input from malachite.

To contact this unspoken language, pick a single eye in a single bead. Let your mind be open. Let it wander. Rather than pay attention to where it wanders, simply look into the malachite. Slowly move its eye closer to your eye. Without locking your stare, gently let your vision defocus. Look deeper into the blackness of the eye. Do not expect a flood of images or revelations. Just know that you are directly apprehending an ancient wisdom. Know that this wisdom will come to your aid whenever you are in need of it.

Repeat this exercise each day at the same time for fifteen minutes. For three days, use the same eye. On days four through six, do the exercise with your eyes closed. Picture the eye of malachite as an eye of one who has your best interest at heart. Then, on days seven through nine, use your other eye. Do the exercise as before with this eye. Rest for at least nine days allowing the new information to integrate into your being.

As with any exercise in this book, you will get what you expect. Expect a lot of information, do the technique faithfully, and keep silent for best results. Within the first nine days you will have confirmation, if you are proceeding with openness.

Malachite is an excellent dream tool. When wearing a necklace of malachite to bed, postulate the intention to meet malachite in your dreams, and you will be taken to areas where large deposits are located. In these locations, which are spread over the earth, the vibrations are very powerful. You can learn lessons of life very quickly and in a profoundly moving way. Make sure upon waking to write down all dreams before doing anything else. This form of honoring will ensure repeated voyages with malachite. You will also be able to study these dreams after a few weeks. This review will give you the perspective from which you can see not only the dream itself but also the way it has affected you subconsciously since the time of the dream. Dreams may be very subtle and on occasion they can take a more dramatic and shocking turn.

The wearer must interpret the symbols that come through wearing malachite. No one else can give a more true interpretation, and going through the process of developing a set of symbols by which to communicate with malachite is very beneficial. Do not underestimate the value of the learning. Your intuition will grow more sure and more clear. You will receive warnings about and protection from the negative influences in life more reliably.

If you have a partner, let them use the above exercises at the same time. After maintaining silence about the details of your experience and writing down your insights for a couple of weeks, compare notes. You can work with another and develop telepathy or work alone and get in touch with latent abilities like clairvoyance and clairaudience. Working with a partner requires that both of you have the same level of commitment. Do not work with someone who is not really interested in sticking with it if you really are.

The energy of malachite will mirror soul, helping you get in touch with the subconscious and the soul awareness. It is a grounding energy and brings the awareness of higher truths down into an understandable form that is useful in everyday life. It is an excellent way to introduce the body to the mineral and animal kingdoms. We are not only human, but animal and mineral as well. We often see these aspects of our makeup as lesser or negative qualities of our human nature. They are, however, a part of our relationship to the divine.

Do not be fooled into thinking that ascension into heaven is our salvation. Let the song of malachite touch your heart. Let your heart open to the wonders of life in all its forms. Learn to hear the divine teachings in the whispers of creatures. They shall speak to those who listen as they did to Saint Francis of Assisi, who celebrated their wisdom for much of his life. Those seeking the wisdom of the earth and its inhabitants will certainly find the divine on earth. Higher consciousness is available to those who earn it.

Malachite shows us how to work with the cycles of life. We can learn of these cycles and how to plant with the moon or harvest with the coming of fall. We will begin to see why working against the tide results in failure and how we can take advantage of the ever-changing forces of nature. The wise rest when the ebb of available energy is lowest and run when the energy is high.

We can also begin to detect others' cycles, thereby increasing the effectiveness of our interpersonal communications. The increase in our understanding of others and their cycles can translate into business success. Picture the businesswoman who glides through life. She has in her pocket the key to the understanding of human nature. To the mutual advantage of all, she presents business deals to her partners and clients alike. Every single person around her has the feeling she is serving them specially.

Whenever she is at a meeting she seems to have the perfect answer to complicated issues in which the parties seem to be at odds. Those in her sphere seem to constantly benefit from their association with her. Most people she does business with want her there when deals are being made. She is in the flow of money because she is in touch with an attitude that all shall win in the negotiations in a way that compromises no one. She always sleeps well because she knows she has given her best. She has made a difference. She has been a part of the solution. Is this someone you would like to have at your business meetings? If so, imagine how easily she finds opportunity in any economy. Let malachite guide you to such a person and learn their ways. It puts you in touch with all resources. Simply ask for what you really believe will make you happy—malachite supports happiness.

Malachite will work wonders with those who have been abused or abandoned at an early age. They will experience the gentle rocking of the waves of strength coming off malachite. It will soothe their troubles. It will build their confidence in communication. Leave a large malachite sphere or egg by their bed. Each night during sleep, the malachite will remind them of their heritage while protecting them in a deep green blanket. They will learn to exercise personal power when confronted with those who would seek to shame and guilt them.

Communication is malachite. It is in constant communication with the earth from the time it is formed. Ley lines—lines of force across the earth—carry communication about the state of awareness on earth. Large deposits of malachite will be found at "hot spots" where these lines intersect. Data is stored in malachite much the same way we have learned to store data in all crystalline quartz structures.

The black portion of malachite will create communication lines. The larger black eyes in a malachite mass will pass on information to other deposits. Larger deposits act as communication hubs.

Place yourself in one of these hubs by using your imagination. Ease yourself in. Now look out from the malachite. Let your eye be its eye. As well as you can, picture how well your inner receiver is working, but don't struggle with this technique. Just allow yourself to focus loosely as if you were softening your vision or using your peripheral vision. The practice of soft vision is not obvious. Practice and you will get results. You will have to be observant of your thoughts to spot messages. Eventually you can learn to directly receive a malachite transmission. Images may come to you with so little effort that you mistake them for your own ideas.

Data is stored as modulations of the long, slow communication waves of malachite. This perpetual sound is constantly emanating from malachite at a subtle level. Our etheric body can feel these waves. Just as eighty percent of all human communication is nonverbal yet understandable and memorable, so we can understand and feel the communications of malachite. Eventually the link between unconscious and conscious communication is made. We become aware of the nonverbal communications of others in a way that is now clearly understandable to us. We learn to read the signposts of all life.

Earth has its own mission as do the other planets. Does it seem strange to think of the Earth as having a purpose? It is no easier to assume it has none. Allow the possibility that Earth and the other planets have a mission, and you will begin to learn what it is. Life goes easily for those who align themselves with this mission. Moreover, you can get in touch with lines of superphysical energy that interconnect our planet with others. Although it may sound supernatural, if you can grasp the principles of quantum physics, then you can grasp the principle of the interrelationship of all matter, light, and energy.

So, is it possible to communicate beyond the apparent limitations of time and space? Many researchers believe it is, after extensive studies in the subject. Our bodies are large-capacity conductors of all sorts of energy. Beyond that, we are capable of feats of inner communication that defy the materialistic view of our bodies. The very nature of thought itself is only beginning to be understood as complex vibrations. Complex vibrations, when superimposed on a waveform, can be projected. Radio waves, microwaves, and light waves all work this way, just as sound waves do.

Assume that you can receive information that has been stored for thousands of years in malachite, and then see for yourself if it works for you. Try to access past times. Write down impressions you get. Include those that seem obscure or unusual. Work with it for two months. Don't let your doubts get the best of you. You must stay with it to reach causal plane information through the causal body.

Work with leopardskin jasper, bloodstone, and opalite as well. These will help your receptivity. They will help you learn to interpret the data you receive so you can use it. They will also let you know what information is useful to you in your life mission.

Let yourself be open. Work with malachite to learn the verses of the Earth—songs that tell of the legacy of Earth. You can learn to see into the layers of information which, like the Grand Canyon and its layers of rock, have recorded the passage of time. These are songs of joy and songs of lament. You can learn to sing your own song aloud or silently. Sing it to the world. Sing your dreams to the melody of the Earth. These songs are powerful. They will unlock the secrets of the ages.

Green Tourmaline

Tourmaline comes in many shades of green, from near blue to a yellow-green. We will focus on the truly chrome-green variety. Use only necklaces that have been graded to exclude the blue, black, brown, pink, or yellow-green varieties. Only the highest grade of tourmaline should be considered therapeutic. For those using tourmaline for the first time, chip necklaces are preferable. This is especially true for those who have had little experience with gemstones. Be careful that the chip necklace used is of high quality and not dyed or irradiated. Chip necklaces are not as powerful and challenging as the spheres, which would disrupt the fragile ego structure of most persons. This action could have serious repercussions in the lives of those who try for too much, too fast. Go with the chips for the first six months to a year. Play it safe, and stay with it. Those who stay with it will prevail. Understanding will be theirs.

Green tourmaline is said to be the male-energy carrier (see the chapter 3 on red stones for a discussion of pink tourmaline as the female energy carrier). Women are going to find wearing green tourmaline to be extremely disorienting, unless they normally work with male energy easily. Women can best experience this stone while it is being worn by a friend or mate who is male. Its primary purpose for humans is to help males realign or reorient themselves with the true male energy. This energy is not one of dominance or manipulation, rather, it is an energy that is at once positively charged and shows the wearer the way to his true nature.

For the purpose of this discussion I shall attempt to describe the male energy in contrast with the female energy. Masculine energy is "electric" and feminine energy is "magnetic" and is used differently. For example, electric energy moves an object by exciting its molecules, while magnetic energy moves an object by attraction or repulsion. All of us use both. As soul we are neither masculine nor feminine, yet our bodies dictate how we use energies. Just as a cruise ship captain tends to sail a sailboat differently than a sailing ship captain, women use masculine energy differently than men. Women can, however, learn all the subtleties of how a man uses masculine energies from green tourmaline.

Men do not necessarily understand how they use energy, and may be influenced by social norms and cultural customs to use energy in a "typical" manner. We must leave aside for the moment all notions of cultural masculinity and look deeply to discover the divine nature of masculinity itself. If some men can learn to emulate true masculine qualities, women can learn how to discover this masculinity in themselves. This capability can be described only in terms of qualities or characteristics. For true understanding we must experience the true vibration. To this end we can work with green tourmaline energy.

The ideal male energy is gentle yet strong. It is capable of great deeds, yet it is patient and enduring. Purpose, direction, discipline, focus, and the ability to see the whole, are attributes. A master of stewardship, who is sometimes represented in mythology as the white king, is an embodiment of this energy. Other mythological figures demonstrate the male warrior energy—not to be taken as a lusty brute, but a passionate champion. This male warrior energy is what drives men and women to stand for what is right even when it goes against the accepted grain. The true warrior does not use violence unnecessarily. There is also the male lover energy. This energy is used wisely by the man who incites compassion and is devoted to love. Include the male energy of the wizard, who, like the magician, can transform matter and see the future in dreams, and one will have a more complete picture of masculine energy at work.

Violence is aggressive and is demonstrated by the thoughtless bully whose actions are characteristic of the dark side of masculine energy. Love can be consuming and dark in the person unable to give love to those they desire. The evil king and black sorcerer are two other dark-side roles. Clearly, male energy has a dark side, which should be understood to become a master of masculinity.

Once you have an understanding of true masculinity, green tourmaline will command you to move to a higher consciousness. The spiritual energy can be seen as a perfect blend of the true male and female energies. Green tourmaline can teach us to take our male nature to its purest form. Although the spiritual nature of the human is soul and soul is neither male nor female, we must learn to live in this world in which all is differentiated into opposing forces as represented by the male and female. Once we have mastered the masculine and feminine energies, we can begin to learn the use of the neutral, or spiritual, energy. Neutral energy is the force that binds matter and gives us life and the ability to create life.

We should also be aware of the male heart. It is in fact the heart that would lead us to a greater understanding of the male energy. The male aspect of love is truly giving, without regard for personal benefit. It is the champion for the weak and the wayshower for the lost and weary. Again, we may wish to look to mythology or dream analogy for an understanding of the male aspect of love. Mythology can give us only clues and hints as to how to find this energy. We can rely on the highest grade of green tourmaline for an entry into the experience of the archetypal masculine energy.

Green tourmaline will strengthen and raise the vibratory rate of all the cells in the male body. This process is like stepping into a waterfall of powerful green energy that passes right through the body and transforms the vibration of every molecule. Once complete, this process leads the man to a state where he is able to channel or hold much larger amounts of energy. This energy is the life force, which can only be used for the benefit of others, or it will dry up or turn against us in the long run. Only in the giving will we have and experience this energy. The physical body will be strengthened in all aspects of health including endurance, reserve, and that quick energy needed for the sprints in life.

To begin your journey into the land of green tourmaline, use the power of song. Make up a little song of your own with simple and loving words. Entreat the power of this gemstone by singing softly and sweetly of your love for nature. Try writing down a simple poetic lyric and sing the words to a familiar melody if you are uncomfortable with free verse. The words need not rhyme or conclude, the important aspect of this exercise is to build your love of the green-ray energy.

Men wearing green tourmaline will notice a gradual building of mental capacity, focus, determination, discipline, range of thought, and retention. Also, the emotions of the male will be felt more deeply and become more accessible and available in the presence of green-ray vibrations as focused through tourmaline. In this way, males will find that the key to getting results in this world is in the emotion. Getting control of the ability to direct the emotions will change forever the results originating from thoughts.

In other words, any man who works with green tourmaline through the process of self-transformation will be able to see how he fits into the big picture, will understand his true nature more fully, and will be able to bring to bear his emotions to produce manifestations that are in alignment with his spiritual goals. A man reaching his full potential will find satisfaction and deep reward. Prosperity through abundance is possible when men's energies are maximized. Men in touch with an overview and with their conscience will learn new definitions for abundance.

Some of the other results of this process include a quieting of the mind, self-assuredness, efficiency, boldness, courage, and inner clarity. Each of these must be redefined and integrated. Green tourmaline requires you to completely rethink all of your definitions. The meaning of every symbol, action, word, and concept will be challenged by the vibrations of green tourmaline as it infuses every thought with green-ray energy, thereby polarizing all thoughts.

Imagine you are floating in a sea of green tourmaline. You can swim about without any apparent pull of gravity. You breathe deeply of the green. Your thoughts and emotions seem like fish that swim by and do not notice you. Some of them are powerful fish with love in their hearts and others are sharks, eager to eat unsuspecting visitors. Some thoughts are beautiful, filled with color, grace, and dignity and by seeming contrast others are ugly and grope on the bottom for places to hide.

You approach an area where there seems to be a strong light emanating. You are drawn into the light ever so slowly. The light feels powerful and yet gentle. As you come nearer, its green rays penetrate deeply into you. A healing joy begins to pulsate within. Every part of you is enlivened with this joy. Soon you can not differentiate yourself from the light. Your color, whatever that may be, blends and fills the surroundings until all colors—including white—are so bright that no objects are visible. Slowly the light diminishes and you feel refreshed. You notice your thoughts now. They are swimming together in a school. Each is different, but working together more than competing for your attention. Allow yourself all the time you need to contemplate the transformations that have occurred. You can return now.

If you regularly put attention on using the inner potential in new and creative ways, this potential will begin to create results in your life that are unexplainable. We can produce results of great importance in the development of human consciousness when our inner unconscious mind is accessed by our will with clear intent for the good of the whole.

This may sound grandiose. Perhaps you find these claims of greatness a bit too much to accept—perhaps, then, you may need to wear green tourmaline. Understand that green tourmaline does not come as a wise old man but as a mighty challenger. Do not expect to be given all these qualities without effort. Very few will be able to withstand the challenge. Very few will be able to let go of the old limitations without a struggle.

Here, we come to the paradox of green tourmaline. We must give up the struggle. We must give up the battle to win the war. Our ego is not capable of the kind of male behaviors characteristic of the fully self-realized male; therefore, the ego must relent. I do not suggest you throw out your ego; this would leave you helpless to deal with the ways of the world. Rather, you must build your ego step by step to become the next Albert Schweitzer, Joseph Campbell, Ghandi, or Arnold Schwarzenegger. With green tourmaline as your coach, you can rebuild the ego while directing the inner forces using soul consciousness. You can rise above the limitations of your maleness only when you have mastered the use of masculine and feminine energies.

Learn new definitions, learn to let go, and learn to take responsibility for your life, and you will never again need to compromise integrity to get what you want. Learn to do for others rather than for your ego, and you will inherit the kingdom as promised by the spiritual masters. Your efforts will earn you the right. As you work in this manner of service, realize that green tourmaline can show you how to serve the highest purposes beyond the simple wants and desires of others. Tourmaline will guide you and support your efforts, but you must make the decisions and take the actions that prove your worthiness. Self-mastery comes to those who know their worthiness.

Other stones that may help one on the path to self-realization and higher purpose are rhodocrosite, ruby, emerald, sapphire, carnelian, indigo, and especially amethyst and citrine. See the chapters on these.

Let the green ray take you to the land of inner harmony and balance. Here you can learn detachment from your thoughts and become free of reactions. No reaction on your part, nor the reactions of others can disrupt you. You have taken the first step to understanding the abundance of love. Work with the other color-ray energies and you will find your true colors. Your mission in life, one that you have created, will become your path. Difficulties will not cease, but you will use them to take that next step to higher consciousness. Every choice will become clear in the light of the green ray given a clear consciousness focused on a worthy mission.

Orange-ray energy can start the process of integration of self for anyone unsure where to begin. Orange-ray energy helps you become an integral part of life as you integrate your self. Many people today feel like strangers in the world. Orange-ray energy helps them own their right to be a member of this human race. It brings understanding of the mechanisms at work that sustain the belief that one is somehow odd or peculiar. It helps modify those mechanisms to reduce the feeling of being out of place.

As we travel on our journey through the many lands, we may feel the calling to go home. This ray helps you discover what it is about home that makes it so important. It helps us create a feeling of being at home wherever we are.

Orange-ray-bearing gemstones bring this essential color energy into your body and immediately it begins to balance the entire color ray spectrum by removing the blocks you have set in place that slow or stop the flow of one or more of the color-ray energies. As soon as we begin to become saturated with the orange ray, we become filled with vitality, joy, and a love of all life. We begin to remember our natural ability to generate these feelings. Vitality and joy are the natural results of a newfound desire for color-ray balance. One achieves color-ray balance when each area of the different bodies is using a

6

Orange Ray Stones

perfect set of color-ray energies for it without blocking any of the needed colors. Each area within the bodies requires a special selection of color frequencies, your color-ray signature, to achieve completely saturated levels of color rays.

Each area has a specific job to accomplish in the overall process of life. A single area—for example, the organs that eliminate waste—needs a specific set of color-ray energies with one ray predominating. Organs in the eliminative system include bowels and urinary tract areas. This system removes used or unwanted surplus molecules and dead cell waste. In this particular system, the orange ray usually predominates. If orange-ray energies are blocked, this system will pull whatever orange-ray energies might be available from other systems to do its job. This pulling of orange-ray energy causes a deficit of orange ray throughout the body. In such a circumstance, joy and vitality wane.

Orange stones identify the blueprints within the healthy cells of a particular system, and the need for restored balance within that system becomes apparent. Orange brings the information about this ideal blueprint to each cell and organ so that they will create a perfect spectrum of color energy. Your body begins to have healthy feelings and form the enzymes and hormones that catalyze your ability to capture and hold a state of well-being. In the process, you'll learn the perfect balance for each system. You can also learn your overall primary color ray from this action of removing blocks.

The state of well-being naturally returns in the presence of sufficient orange-ray energy. Work with orange stones, and the orange ray will permeate your being. Once this permeation process gets well under way, all aspects, deficiencies, blockages, imbalances, and other inefficiencies will become more apparent. You will easily be able to identify any stumbling block. As you stumble, you can learn to rearrange these obstacles into stepping stones. Wearers will better be able to evaluate their progress.

All preconceived ideas that no longer work will now be marked as obsolete for you to replace with new, workable ideas. Frustration will turn into unshakable resolve. Previously weak points in our character, as well as in our physical body, will become strengths.

Work first with orange stones to gain the ability to figure out what should be changed. From that, the specific knowledge of how to change will follow. Wherever we are on the path to controlling our reactions to daily events, orange stones will move us forward. Color-ray energy, once mastered, can set us free to decide how we will respond to the circumstances of life. In this sense, our destiny is within our grasp.

When you begin to work with orange-ray stones, the stones will proceed to go through all systems at all levels, one at a time, and locate blueprints. This process begins with the physical body and gradually works up to the whole system. After all, each separate function of the various bodies is a system and the overall whole is also a system. The whole system has a blueprint for perfect color-ray balance, just as each subsystem does. Each time you place a strand of carnelian around your neck, you begin the rebalancing process anew. After enough times through this rebalancing process, you'll begin to become conscious of blueprints, energy blocks, and how you can open yourself to a perfect balance of color-ray energies. You will find additional clues as to how to become the master of your own fate every time you initiate this process.

Carnelian is the primary carrier and provider of orange-ray energy. Begin the search for joy with a necklace of carnelian. Discover the true state of joy as you are guided by the hints of bliss that come to you as you wear the orange stones. Allow its vitalizing color to replenish you for greater personal joy.

Carnelian

The most powerful bearer of the orange ray, carnelian should be worn or placed on the body with certain precautions. It is suggested, for those who are not sure of their primary color ray, that a gemstone clinic be employed to begin initial treatments with carnelian. Where such a clinic is not available, at least find a trusted friend in whom you can confide. Choose someone who can help you determine how certain aspects of your present situation are invalidating your basic abilities. Developing an understanding of how your limitations came to exist and how you would be without them is not easy and can bring up many fears. It may seem strange to consider that your greatest fears are of how you would be without limitations, but we are all afraid of what might happen should we stop constricting ourselves. Facing these fears in a safe environment is much more conducive to resolving them.

Carnelian is one of the stronger color-ray carriers and adjusts the level of receptivity to color-ray energies within every cell. Wear it first as a strand of spheres around you neck for a lengthy introduction. Only after this introduction should you use a sphere in single-stone placement therapies. If you have any resistance to it, then wear it for at most a few minutes each time until the resistance eases and carnelian becomes relaxing. Though carnelian is a key to joy, it feels uncomfortable to wear for an appreciable length of time if fears arise.

Some may find an instant affinity with the stone. These people will immediately feel an uplifting joy upon first placing a necklace around the neck. Such people can work with carnelian every day for periods of two weeks. This practice will establish a firm connection with the orange ray. Each day, wear a necklace for at least four hours to complete a cycle of healing and readjustment. One cycle will preliminarily adjust every area at every level. Those who prefer to go slowly should attempt four-hour readjustments only after several months of shorter sessions to become acquainted with the vibration of carnelian. No benefit will be gained from pushing yourself into longer therapies until very short therapies are no longer difficult. Setbacks can occur if resistance is not monitored—pushing too deeply into fears at first will deepen resistance. We are not fully aware of our fears, some are hidden behind denial. Pushing too quickly or forcefully will only increase denial.

Each person will find one variety, color, type, and grade of carnelian is most effective for them. Varieties of carnelian range from stones of all one color to those containing a number of colors. Its color can vary from light amber to deep reddish-orange. Carnelian is available in two types: natural, which is a lighter, more translucent orange; and heat-treated, in which the color is a darker, more opaque, burnt orange. Grades can vary from highly translucent, which is the rarer quality, to opaque. You can experiment with the different carnelians to find the correct one for you or consult a supplier of therapeutic gemstones (see appendix).

Those who are sensitive or easily thrown out of balance and feel reluctant to try carnelian can work with the heat-treated type, which is a burnt-orange color. It is somewhat less expensive than natural carnelian, and is also less forceful when making changes in the physical body. This type actually is preferable, initially, for those who may be sensitive to an abundance of the orange ray. It is closer to the red color ray and therefore is more easily assimilated by those who would be thrown out of balance by the yellow- to medium-orange colors. Later, after using heat-treated stones for a couple months, you can more easily discover the correct color of natural carnelian to use for the next step in balancing the bodies. Your physical body will develop an affinity for one of the colors.

Those whose primary color is orange should wear a necklace of medium-orange natural carnelian in six- or eight-millimeter spheres. Allow time to get used to this powerful energy by wearing your strand for no more than a few hours a day during the first week. After a week or so of becoming adjusted to it, you can wear the necklace for up to twelve hours a day. After a few weeks, you should be able to wear the necklace for days at a time.

Those who are attracted to this stone, who have no adverse reactions, and who are completely comfortable wearing a necklace can wear any type of carnelian that attracts them and seems appropriate as often as they wish. A small percentage of such persons are already in complete harmony with the orange-ray energy.

When you become accustomed to, and in balance with, a greater flow of the orange ray, you will find that profound joy and happiness seem to follow you everywhere. You will find yourself able to overcome all your negative emotions and tune into this joy at will. You will seem to "rise above" situations that previously had immobilized you.

For the people of Earth, carnelian is truly a gift to treasure. It teaches you to be in harmony with the earth itself. It teaches your physical body to grow more healthy rather than to decay. Appreciate it, and it will help you open up your physically weak or depleted areas of the body to more life-giving energy in every color. Carnelian will show you how to attract opportunities into your life in which you can learn to meet your every need by filling yourself with color-ray energies. It will help you understand the root causes of the circumstances in your life. Understanding these inner causes will further clarify the reasons for your particular outer circumstances and how to learn from them.

Have you attempted to make significant changes in your life, only to find that your circumstances changed little? Add carnelian to the picture—it will provide you with immediate clues as to the reasons. It will locate the individual physical body cells that are attracting these circumstances, and teach these cells how to get in balance—how to work with all color-ray energies equally well.

Cells are transducers for energy. They convert or transform some of the available color-ray energy into motion, just as stereo speakers, which are transducers for electrical impulses, change electrical waves into sound waves that we can hear. Different types of motion are caused by transforming different color combinations of color-ray energies. Carnelian reads the color-ray proportions of the energies that are being converted by a cell into certain motions. It can tell if this motion is in alignment with the mission that that cell should be performing. Cells transform energy according to the proportions used in their formation. New cells are being formed all the time, and, with the help of carnelian, one can learn to form new cells that use proportions of color-ray energies that exactly match the perfect balance for that individual. Carnelian discovers the perfect balance for each different type of cell in a body by "reading" a "blueprint" that outlines every function in that particular human body and the cellular motions required to perform those functions.

Our bodies are formed in the womb by a process of cell division. The blueprints for this process are stored in the supraphysical body in the form of color-ray energy, which is actual visible light. This light is held stable in a blueprint, which will never change. Each "perfect" cell in a human embryo is formed in compliance with its blueprint according to the laws of nature. A cell is not actually made of light, but is constructed of noncolor-ray energies in the form of atoms. As the embryo develops, cells divide to form more cells. Cells formed by division may not be exactly formed according to the blueprints; deviations occur due to environmental conditions. Deviant cells and perfect cells specialize in groups according to DNA. Specialized cells form alongside each other and develop into systems called organs. Organs, comprised of a combination of perfect and deviant cells, perform their functions imperfectly. Orange-ray energy encourages perfect cells to reproduce faster and outperform and ultimately replace deviant cells. Future research may prove this treatment effective against cancer.

Most bodies function well enough to survive. Survival, however, is temporary, and in the case of bodies whose organs are comprised of highly deviant cells, time may be very short. Survival can be compromised further as noncolor-ray energy is used by deviant cells and new, more deviated cells replace old cells. A typical body is degenerating faster than it is growing after age eighteen. New cells may been formed in a yet more imperfect environment and, if so, the new cells become more deviant until a breakdown occurs. Conditions worsen and eventually the body ceases to survive, as too many cells are too deviant to cooperatively function together.

Color-ray energy is not actually produced by the physical mind or body. It is available in abundance and further concentrated by gemstones. Imperfect cells produce noncolor-ray energy in the form of damaging heat, electricity, magnetism and mechanical energy or movement. Perfect cells change (transduce) color-ray energy into usable, working noncolor-ray energy. Exact data on how this works is not available at this time but it is clear that individuals with perfectly healthy cells have much more energy than individuals with unhealthy cells. Perfect cells change a perfect balance of color-ray energies into the exactly correct noncolor-ray energies to maintain optimum health.

Carnelian teaches cooperation to previously uncooperative cells. By using carnelian spheres and necklaces, deviant cells can be taught to produce more perfect energy and to reproduce more perfect cells instead of more deviant cells. Eventually, the physical body can be taught to function indefinitely without degradation.

We can change the kind of cells we produce. We can change the structure of our organs. We can change the kind of energy we put out. We change the kinds of things, people, events, and energy we attract by changing the energy we put out. Carnelian will create a kind of feedback loop from the cell to the unconscious and back. You will learn, on an unconscious level, why the blend of color-ray energies you use and the transformation processes your cells are engaged in create your growth or decay and draw in your circumstances. You will be taught by carnelian to recognize what exact blend of color-ray energy, your color-ray signature, would create the conditions in life needed to accelerate spiritual development. In short, you will be shown how to create the kind of cells in your body that would give you a better life.

For example, take a man in his thirties who, according to his blueprints, should be primarily orange ray. This person is blocked internally to the orange ray. He does not take in much orange ray and does not give out much, either. Instead, he has become an intellectual (the form of one who puts out blue ray to make up for a deficiency in orange). He is not joyous, but in fact is rather sullen. He seems to attract those in his life who are deficient in blue-ray energy and are putting out more orange ray than they are comfortable with. These people do not appear joyous, as would someone who was balanced with high orange-energy output. They are loud and haughty and tend to speak in obnoxious overstatement, typical of one who is blue, but trying to make it in life with an orange energy output.

All his life this man has been unhappy because he feels something is wrong. He is unable to change because he has developed a massive set of habits and thought forms that block his joy because he is afraid to change. He has come to believe that life is bad and his only hope lies in the afterlife. How can he find his joy?

As this man learns to work with carnelian, he learns to express his love for joy, and his orange-ray energy output becomes high. He no longer tries to be an intellectual, but takes a job as an entertainer. He now lives in accordance with his nature. His friends, who had sought him for his blue-ray intellectualism, are disappointed and seek others. He attracts those who are also in balance, those who display their primary color in a balanced way. These new friends find him joyous and fun to be with.

This man can learn to use orange, his primary color ray, to great purpose as he inspires all those in his life to find their own natural balance and integrate their thoughts and actions with their fundamental natures.

The forces that attract us to different circumstances are compensating for our lack of balance. When we learn to control our attitudes and beliefs, we will begin to transform all colors in the color ray spectrum, we will be in balance and will not be blocking any colors. We will avoid the out-of-balance condition in which colors that we block are in fact the colors put out by those who are attracted to us, and are themselves out of balance and overcompensating, putting out a particular color ray that we have been blocking. Once in balance, we attract those who can enjoy all color-ray energy. We learn to take in and put out color-ray energy without fear, rather than over amplifying one and blocking another color. We attract better, more balanced circumstances as we do a better job of putting out balanced, growth-enhancing (combining some of every color ray in our individual signature) energies.

We can modify cells if we learn how. It is the cell itself that causes energy to be drawn into it, and then transforms and distributes that energy to the surroundings. Healthy cells naturally transform all colors (in varying degrees) without preference or blocking. We, with our misguided attitudes and outdated beliefs, cause our cells to block certain colors. Our cells attract people that put out the color-ray energies we are blocking. Carnelian helps us learn why one attracts another and helps us learn from another the art of using the particular color ray that the other uses that we are blocking. In short, we learn to balance our use of the colors.

Carnelian translates and amplifies blueprints. It reminds cells of their blueprints. New cells, in the presence of carnelian, become transformers for color-ray energies in harmony with blueprints. New cells are born with the knowledge of how to use every color ray. You draw experiences to you as a result of your newly balanced color-ray output. Once you change the underlying cause, your circumstance will change. You will begin to attract the circumstances that are in harmony with the newly balanced energy.

Carnelian teaches a far more powerful and proactive approach to life and attracts the knowledge that what you have experienced has come to you as a result of your own beliefs and actions. You are the master of your fate if you can control your vibrations within your cells. You can control your destiny. You have the ability to control how you see things. As Dr. Wayne Dyer suggests, "You will see it when you believe it." You will begin to enjoy life when you believe life is enjoyable.

Do you see a glass of milk that you have drunk down to the middle point on the glass as half-full or half-empty? You can make this choice, once you decide to. No one can tell you it is half-full if you believe it is half-empty. What difference does this make? It makes a difference only to you. A glass half full is somehow more satisfying than a glass half-empty.

When you are unable to complete a task you started, do you feel like a failure? Some people believe that every breakdown is the start of a breakthrough. The skill of controlling one's beliefs leads those successful few who master it to abundance in whatever they pursue. Carnelian is a powerful tool for those attempting to learn the ways of success. We can emulate those we admire to the degree we can clear ourselves of disharmonious vibrations and balance our energies, enabling us to put out vibrations that attract healthier patterns.

Our souls are like steam engines bound for a destination across the world. An engine without passenger cars is like a soul without a body, it cannot sustain its travel. Without other cars, our engine can travel, but without passengers, we could not afford to continuously ride the rails. We add passenger cars so we can pay our way. We allow passengers a certain amount of baggage. We can reach our destination if we do not take on too many passengers or too much baggage. We also must regularly stop for fuel. Color-ray energy is the fuel for life. It is used by our cells, whose predominant function is to transform color-ray energy. A problem arises when we take on more fuel, water, passengers, or baggage than we can handle at one time. We must strike the perfect balance and use all of what we take on. The practice of carrying more than just what we need would wear out our engine. Carry less, and we will not make the next stop. We must balance the means to achieve the end.

Noncolor-ray energy is like passenger cars and baggage. One needs to use this energy to "ride the rails of life," but it does not actually power the engine. Noncolor-ray energy is needed, like money is needed to keep the rails open to us, but don't take on too much noncolor-ray energy if you want to be able to survive the trip. Color-ray energy is like the fuel we burn that actually keeps the engine running—but again, don't take on too much or burn all you get, or you will be coming to a halt, perhaps abruptly. Carnelian assists with replenishing your body's supply of color-ray energy so that we do not become depleted along the way. It helps us to learn to balance the colors. We gain the skills needed to regulate, without blocking, the flow of color-ray energy through our cells.

A good metaphor is the seed farm. Imagine you are the owner of this farm. You plant all your seed the first year. At the end of the season, you harvest. You are able to choose which seed to sell and which to save for the next year. If you sell your best seed, you will have only the second-grade seed for your next crop. Continue this practice, and you soon will have only very poor seed to plant.

Decide instead to sift your harvest. Choose only the biggest and best seed to plant yourself for next year's harvest. Sell the lesser-quality seed, and feed the poor-quality seed to your cows. Year after year, your crop will get stronger, and soon you will have a bountiful crop of very high-quality seed.

Carnelian helps the farmer choose the good seed. It helps him rid his farm of poorer seed. It actually alters the plants so they can produce better seed than the seed with which they were grown. Each year, with the help of carnelian, better seed is produced that is better adapted to the particular fields in which it grows. In this way, carnelian transmutes the crop after several years.

Think of seeds as the cells of your body and the farm as a system or organ. Improving the yield by improving the grade of seed is the same concept as improving your life by improving the quality of cells in a system. Carnelian teaches the strong cells to dominate and, thereby, your systems become good producers. Your soul can thrive on such a farm for it is not overwhelmed with maintenance.

Carnelian is a tool you can use to discover the root causes of your life experiences. It is a tool that will help you sift through your experiences and select the ones you want to repeat. It will help you choose the best experiences. These are the ones you will want to repeat (plant) over and over to refine them even more.

Wearing a necklace of carnelian spheres will bring you insight into what to do with your worst practices. These practices are like the poor seed. These you will want to get rid of. Use them as fodder for the meat you will need next winter. Do this by learning the lessons the bad seeds can teach you about what practices not to repeat, and take the sustenance (the learning) and let your subconscious mind digest these lessons so that the lessons will be translated into the practices your conscious mind will adopt in the future.

Then, once you have replanted the best and removed the worst practices, you are left with the practices that are excellent and those that are not bad but could be better. Carnelian will highlight these and help you recognize and work with them. Exchange them (sell them) for some you can actually use. Simply become conscious of the practices that achieve mixed results and whenever you notice a way to improve them, then trade them in. Each year, the harvest will become stronger and more bountiful, no matter how few seeds you have to start with. Even if those seeds are not producing the best crops initially, just keep planting and choosing the best seeds. It does not matter where you are as you begin. Persistence will bring results to those who are fighters or just plain intractable. Carnelian feeds good ground for planting and will yield improved seeds over the years.

Given the right carnelian necklace and the knowledge of how to use it, with persistence you will gradually learn the nature of cause and effect. With this understanding, you will be able to create what you wish. You will actually be able to create cells that have color-ray patterns that are near-exact duplications of your blueprints and produce healthy vibrations. These healthy vibrations will attract conditions more pleasing than any experienced so far. Wearers will learn more from obstacles, and even the worst mistakes will show the way to breakthroughs.

Those who are very weak in the area of discernment and have much in their lives they wish to clear out will need regular practice at changing attitudes. In times of weakness, wear carnelian for only a few minutes at a time. Focus on your life, and trust that the clues you need to begin a process of more thorough change will come.

Those who are capable of discernment and have many cells that are high in color-ray energy will see the results of using this tool very quickly. They will be able to intuitively select a better system of priorities. They will find it easy to remove patterns that are not working, for they already have some thought forms that work to create desired results. After all, habits are neither good nor bad. Habits simply bring results—you must decide if the results are what you want. Habits can be helpful when repeating them brings joy, fulfillment, and happiness to our lives. Those who have many such habits already will find it easier to remove the ones that bring pain and suffering. Others will need time and patience.

The ultimate key is to become able to adopt a viewpoint that is at once broad and inclusive, yet focused and discerning. The natural translucent yellow-orange carnelian is best for this purpose.

Carnelian is not at all rare, yet the finer-quality translucent yellow-orange spherical beads are hard to find. Perhaps only those who are sincere and diligent will find this variety. Faith must become belief, and belief must become certainty before significant change can occur in our basic viewpoint.

This process of becoming aware of our deepest motivators and our hidden patterns with their underlying causes is not for the weak at heart. It will expose the most positive as well as the most negative parts of ourselves. The release of petty animosities that come up will be fairly easy to handle; the raging fires of contempt and hatred are those that must be faced without fear.

This task is not easy, but it is supported by the powerful orange ray such that it will bring us a whole new set of possibilities for our lives. Should a fire of contempt, hatred, and fear break out, let it burn. Let carnelian support the patient and sensible part of you that waits for the fire to burn itself out. When the fire has burned itself out, only the ashes will remain. These ashes are the very fertilizer needed to sprout the habits that manifest the abundance we so richly deserve.

Only when we have reached the innermost chamber of our hearts will we truly see what is there under everything else. Be prepared for a surprise. The experience of entering this chamber will be like meeting yourself for the first time. "Déjà vu" is not a sufficient term to describe this experience—this meeting will be like seeing the entire root system of a large tree. The root system often is as large or larger than the tree trunk and branches. We are like the whole tree—only the woody part is visible. The tree could lose all its leaves in a range fire, but soon new leaves would sprout that are prettier, stronger, and even more dense upon the branches. The real heart of the renewal is happening underground where the root system has reached deep within the soil for new strength.

What a surprise to see the whole after trying to understand only the outer manifestation. Suddenly, things that seemed unexplainable will fit perfectly. Only by seeing the whole can the parts make sense. The whole system is much more integrated than you might suspect. What we commonly refer to as introspection will be seen for the first time to be only reflection. The view of something from the outside from different angles in no way correlates to the view of the whole from inside the heart.

Cycles will finally be understood when you have reached the depth to which the orange ray can penetrate. From there, you can look out at the whole. All life unfolds in cycles. From the vibrations of the atoms to the pulse of light that enlivens it, life revolves. Cells are born and cells must die to make way for the new. We will see how the multileveled successions of life are the fabric from which we are cut and the form on which our contours are revealed. Work with the lighter, more yellow varieties of carnelian to facilitate new understandings of cycles.

Everything develops from the part to the whole. From the tiny cycles of the atoms come the cycles of the molecules, the cellular structure, the body, the family, the society, the planet, the solar system, and the universe. We will begin to see our place in it all, not as a beginning astrologer confused by the symbols and complexity of the many cycles, but as the maker of the web we call our life. We will become the ones who create all in perfect harmony with the wind, the rain, the sun, and all the other forces of nature.

With practice and focus, we can become more receptive by asking for the help of carnelian. It will guide us like an ancient mariner who knows all the world routes. If we listen and follow, we will learn to develop our astral senses. Our memory could improve with time. We can learn to read the stars, and perhaps see the forces that shape the future. We need only be willing to have our thoughts rearranged in a new order and system. Most of us use mental filing systems that are unrelated to the natural ebb and flow of life. Carnelian teaches a new way of correlating information.

Once we reorient our thinking to the natural order of life, our memory will be much more accurate, and our associations will correlate with what is real and true in our world. At present, most of us have a "freight train" mentality; that is, we toss all our memories into a freight car that contains other memories that seem to be relevant or similar. Later we wonder why we act so inappropriately so often.

The mind is like a computer. It can sort through memories to find out how to react to situations. Superficially, it is capable of seeing only the outside of the mental freight cars as they roll past. Once the mind decides to look in to one of these cars, it must respond to the contents. Typically the contents are in disarray. As the mind sorts through each of the cars with the help of carnelian, it becomes organized. As thoughts become more accessible, the mind can slow down. It need not race like a train for its destination. With the help of carnelian, it can learn to sort and deduce answers smoothly, without being concerned with rushing toward a destination.

Suppose our mind is looking for an appropriate response to a waiter who just bumped into us in a restaurant where we are seated with our mate. We open the boxcar marked "physical contact." We sort for similar instances. We come up with an incident from childhood when our father, being bumped by a waiter's tray, gets hot coffee spilled down his shirt. At the time, father was in a bad mood, and he took it out on the waiter. Here we have an optional response. We, of course, are proceeding like a freight train. No time for reflection. We respond to being bumped by going into a rage and fighting with the waiter and with our mate just as our father did. Our mate, who does not understand, gets up and walks out in the middle of dinner.

It is only later, on the way home alone, that we realize that we have just told off the person we love and sent them home. Now, not only did the waiter get reprimanded by his boss because of our anger, but we are left with trouble at home unless we can explain the cause of this outburst.

Perhaps it is time to transform the train with carnelian. Visualize your train of memories. It has hundreds of boxcars full of mixed-up memories that are hardly sorted. Imagine this train is switched from its regular track to a track made of brilliant orange carnelian. Slowly it moves into a huge, warm, brightly lit cave. As the train enters this cave, car by car, its cars appear bright orange in the intense light of carnelian.

See the train enter the cave. Now go in with it. Inside, the orange light becomes so bright that you can no longer see the train at all. It becomes so bright that all your memories are revealed in it. See all your memories. Suddenly they are released into the huge cave like balloons floating out of the windows and doors of the train. They become brilliant orange in the light. They are given a signature of orange for easy sorting later.

Picture all the habits that connect these memories melting into the light. All the balloons quietly release their memories. Suddenly your memories are free. They will no longer be riding that runaway train. They can begin to serve you now. They no longer must serve the stubborn, persistent conditions of your life that you could not change. They can partake in creating new conditions. No longer will they serve the outlandish behaviors that have embarrassed you or been out of proportion. They will support new reactions that serve you.

Use this visualization or another you devise that will allow you to focus your intentions on creating a life that works. Allow carnelian to support your greatest dreams. Let the entire body gradually re-form from cells in tune with your blueprints and are producing nondeviant cells that transform all the color rays needed for the motions that support a life of your dreams, and you will have followed carnelian down a path to understanding the mechanisms that make your life what it is today and shape its future.

Orange Calcite

Orange calcite comes in a variety of shades. The deepest orange with the least amount of white or inclusions of any kind is the best variety to use for therapies. The uses for and composition of orange calcite are nearly identical to its more yellow cousin, argonite. Orange calcite is fairly common in general, however the higher grades are not commonly found in necklaces. A single sphere of the highest-grade calcite is more useful than a whole necklace of the lower-grade material.

This stone is a must for anyone's detox kit. Using mineral energy to effect changes in the physical body's makeup is not that far out a concept. In fact, "potions" have been developed and used from early recorded history that include ground gemstones or water that has been infused with gemstone energy. Look in almost any book that outlines practices of early medicine, and you will find descriptions of these stones being used. Today we enjoy the benefits of much research and development of many new techniques for use of gemstones without ingestion.

When using orange calcite for healing, focus your efforts on the physical body. Use a gemstone like aventurine (see chapter 5 on green stones) or bloodstone (see chapter 11 on earth stones) to locate areas of disharmony. The cells in these areas have almost certainly retained some amounts of toxic substances. Sometimes the toxic substances will be deposited in lymphatic or blood-flow passages near the affected area. Toxic substances can be deposits of inorganic minerals (minerals that are not part of organic compounds are not useful), free radicals, heavy metals, stones, deposits, or other harmful material. Calcite creates an energetic barrier, like a bubble of energy, around these toxins; the body can then eliminate them more easily as they are then clearly marked foreign.

Place a single sphere of orange calcite over the affected area. Choose any area where there may be harmful buildups of toxins. It would be advisable to choose the major organs of elimination before choosing a deeply affected area, to allow the organ of elimination to cleanse itself first. The liver and kidneys are the primary organs of elimination. They need to be cleansed before requiring them to process other toxic substances that have been stored elsewhere in the body.

Place a single sphere, ten to twelve millimeters in size, over the liver for three to five treatments of an hour each. In cases of mild toxicity, this is sufficient to encourage the liver to cleanse itself. After the liver has cleansed, notice the toxins being released into bile, phlegm, urine, and stool. Calcite should quickly work to encourage the liver to take action unless an energy block is preventing the release. If no release is apparent, stop these treatments and begin treatments as described in the previous chapters where red, blue, and green ray stones are used to release energetic blocks. Include regular visits to a clinic for colonics, if necessary.

For those who suffer from more advanced cases of toxicity, a treatment duration of three to five minutes twice a day may be quite enough for the first few days. You will recognize these cases by the fact that the person will usually suffer a chronic case of rheumatism, arthritis, cancer, asthma, extreme allergies, extreme fatigue, diabetes, or other physical problems that are associated with stress and psychological imbalance or anxiety attacks. In severe cases, repeat treatments every three hours for several days, then take a two-day rest. Only after repeated use of liver-cleansing herbs (such as marshmallow root, hydrangea root, or burdock root), and other detoxifying agents (like Epsom salts, grapefruit, vitamins C, E, and A) between treatments on days of rest, should the sphere be placed for a longer time.

Always drink lots of pure water when using calcite. Practice deep breathing exercises daily. Cleanse the skin regularly and wash under fingernails and in ears frequently. Drinking a variety of products such as fresh wheat grass juice, carrot juice, black cherry juice, pure cranberry extract, and other natural juices will provide the body with enough live enzymes to help the body put deposits in solution. Once the body can get these substances flowing in the blood or lymph they will be released naturally through skin, lungs, or other eliminative organs.

Continue the treatments for several weeks, and if possible, monitor the cleansing process with the aid of a competent naturopathic physician. Consult specialists as needed if conditions of poor health are exacerbated. If any signs of stress to heart, lungs, or other major organs appear, reduce the treatment schedule to one treatment every four days. Cases of severe asthma, for instance, can become very aggravated and complicate the release of toxins through lungs.

After a liver cleanse, allow another two- to three-day rest period, and begin working on the release of toxins from the kidneys. Work with each kidney individually. Expose each kidney to calcite energy for two or more treatments of up to one hour each. One eight- to ten-millimeter sphere should be sufficient to activate a normal kidney to slowly release its toxins.

Next work on the lungs. Wear a necklace of amazonite to help with lung congestion or tightening that may follow toxin release. Use a snowflake obsidian sphere to treat blood, heart, and digestive organs if sluggishness occurs. If the skin develops any sign of rash, which may occur in cases of high toxicity, simply take regular baths with a few tablespoons of baking soda, one-eighth cup Epsom salts, and a few drops of your favorite natural cold-pressed oil like rosemary or lavender added.

Once the liver and kidneys have been cleared, begin to treat other organs. Place one six- to eight-millimeter sphere on each organ area. Allow the stones to work for two to twenty minutes over the target organ area. As the organ is becoming activated, relax and let your mind wander onto a positive scene from the past. Notice which moment in the past comes to mind. Explore the scene. Notice how you feel when in this environment. Now think of the people in the scene. In what ways do these people inspire you to greater health? Picture yourself enjoying good health and sharing some activity with these friends. Be sure to visualize specific details of improved health like the ability to ride a bicycle for long periods or ski or walk on hikes. For best results, add associations to these activities which motivate you, like becoming more attractive or stronger. You must sell yourself on the need for good health to obtain results.

Though caution is always recommended when using the powerful energies carried by and amplified in gemstones, they will generally only create as much effect as the person can safely handle. If you find that these cleansing treatments do not produce unusually odiferous elimination from bowels, skin (particularly underarms), and breath, then chances are the treatments are not working, and perhaps some other support is needed. We all have toxins present in our bodies. When none are released in the presence of calcite, perhaps the body is holding the toxins because of an energy block. Start again, this time addressing the blockages first and supporting your progress with a cleansing diet, herbs, naturopathic remedies, or treatments to clear the intestinal tract. Work to open the energy blockage at all levels.

Physical body energy blockages require the use of green stones like aventurine for their eradication. Superphysical energy blockages can be addressed by using some of the red gemstones like rose quartz and through the use of acupuncture or Reiki. Astral blockages will require the use of the more powerful red stones, such as ruby or rubellite, along with orange calcite. Causal body blockages require the use of more pushy stones like rhodocrosite or carnelian. Mental blockages demand the use of blue and indigo stones. The subconscious can be addressed with purple rainbow fluorite. After energy blockages are cleared, the release of toxins can proceed, but the body will quickly replace these toxins with others if the attitude and expectation of abundant health is not adopted and maintained.

Where false mental beliefs about the physical body and health are the normal situation, one should consider using a regular application of blue sapphires over troubled areas and wearing an indigo strand for a week at a time. These stones are quite helpful in clearing the way for an overall healthy attitude toward the body. They open the mind to a vision of health. The attitude of abundant health should be your focus of mental energy when cleansing. Without a vision of health to set the cleansing process goal clearly in mind, some toxins can remain while toxins that were removed will be replaced because they are attracted by deviant cells. If you have trouble visualizing the way you will look and feel in a healthy state, then you must consider using carnelian to help develop a picture of health that fits your personality.

While orange calcite can help with physical toxins by highlighting them and marking them for removal, it can also help with toxic emotions. Only the finest-grade calcite with deep, consistent orange color will reach into the emotional sheath. This variety identifies the emotional fibres that hold emotions acquired from family or other trusted relations in moments of rage, lust, or anger. These emotions lie dormant unless they are triggered by an action similar to the one that was occurring at the time this emotion was first embedded into the emotional body fibres. To clear fibres and allow emotions to flow freely without destructive outbursts, use calcite to "massage" the fibres. The destructive and toxic emotions are then marked as they are touched by calcite. A triggering is necessary for calcite to identify the full pattern of interaction and subsequent reactive offending emotions. When many destructive emotions are held in the emotional sheath, a self-destructive type of negative self-image results. This situation may be damaging to self-esteem. It may also cause one to adopt a low mental ceiling, a condition in which you cannot see your potential. The more of these conditions that exist in the emotional body, the more out of control your reactions to certain stimuli will be. Calcite can be massaged along the outer edges of the emotional body at a distance of approximately two to three inches out from the skin. As the massage progresses, imagine the emotional body has millions of short fibres extending from it and they are being combed and made free flowing. These are like receptors and also function as emotional sending devices. When they are completely clear one should, with practice, be able to sense other's emotions easily and send emotions without any physical display necessary.

If you have difficulty combing these fibres, and feelings of inadequacy and humiliation or shame come up, one may need help with this clearing or counseling to deal with the shame. You may wish to consult a gemstone practitioner with experience in working with cases of low self-esteem or low mental ceiling. A psychologist or counselor may also be employed to help develop a strong mental attitude toward your body. Your body suffers when, for any length of time, the mind holds a poor self-image due to a low mental ceiling. Do not underestimate the mind's capacity to heal. Use gemstones to provide the strong vibrational support that can create the environment for development of a positive mental attitude, and simultaneously use the mind to produce new beliefs about yourself.

Allow your mind to create a scene that will take place ten years in the future. You have just arrived at a location that you notice is the exact place where you were first introduced to frightening emotions in the past. As the other people who were there at that time in the past arrive on the scene, you see that they have grown older now. As they come up to you, you notice how good you feel. They begin to congratulate you. Through their eyes, you see yourself in perfect health. You thank them for their help in inspiring you to achieve the vital condition you feel at this time in the future. You acknowledge yourself for the desire to get beyond the limitations of the past and you acknowledge the others for their contribution, however frightening their behavior was, to your resolve and newfound personal strength. You see this new strength as a confidence and peace with which you will conquer any remaining fear in the future. You see yourself encase the fear in a ball of deep orange calcite. You let it go. It drifts up into this intensely bright orange light that has appeared from above to accept the ball. Allow the scene to dissolve, but hold onto the feeling of satisfaction and accomplishment it engendered.

Practice this exercise each day for a week, and see how it may change your attitude about your physical body. If at first the exercise seems awkward or you can't remember how it goes, simply reread the description given and follow the instructions as you read them. It is helpful to put yourself in a safe, relaxed space while attempting to create this mental movie. Once you have the movie well established in your mind, run the scenes forward and backward slowly, and then faster until you can watch it backwards in just a few seconds. You are creating a new outlook.

At first you may have difficulty believing that such an exercise will change what is happening. You may see some of the events or hear a voice or a laugh that discourages you. On the other hand, you may see and hear nothing. Do not let this worry you. The important thing is that you are working to generate a good feeling about being healthy. If you can get to the feeling, then the way you do it is not important. Notice your ability to smile when you think of being healthy in the future. A simple smile is proof of your success, for it physically shows how you have changed your attitude.

Can you maintain a good feeling while you think of yourself as being ten years older and being youthful? You may be one of those who does not actually see or hear anything, and yet you can generate the feeling. It is the feeling of health that spawns the belief in good health for you.

Practice this exercise and you will certainly get results. You'll know you've got it, when you can keep in mind the idea of yourself as ten years older, fit and full of energy, without immediately discounting the possibility. You must learn to believe it first for it to come true for you.

Red Aventurine (Cinnamon Aventurine)

Red aventurine is available in high-grade strands for a modest cost as it is not in vogue or considered rare. Choose the stones that have the least white or black inclusions, specks of brown and orange are natural and help the action of this stone. Employ red aventurine stones that are as clear as possible, though absolutely clear varieties are usually unavailable.

A warm red-orange/light brown stone that is delightful to hold, red aventurine brings your internal heat energy to any specific area of the physical body. A strand or necklace can be placed around the neck for warmth and to increase circulation to the neck, head, and general upper body. Strands can be fashioned to work on the waist, ankles, wrists, and other parts of the body that will support a band of beads. Beads can be sewn in clothes to wear over parts of the body that have trouble staying warm. Red aventurine raises the heat in a local area when placed in a pile or spiral on any area of the body.

The body generates heat in a variety of ways. The flow of heat to areas that are essential to survival or reproduction is automatic and unconscious. Our autonomic nervous system operates the mechanisms to control this flow. Whenever the body is in jeopardy, the flow of heat to extremities and nonessential areas of the body is slowed or stopped and only essential areas are warmed. Red aventurine sends a message to the body areas in close proximity to wherever stones are placed that they are safe, free of harm, and vitally alive. This message assures the body that it is safe to release worry, stress, and pain.

Red aventurine increases blood flow. Capillaries (the smallest blood vessels that bring blood to and from the cells themselves) are dilated, and local blood flow is thereby increased. Those who smoke, have difficulty breathing, or have poor blood circulation due to low blood pressure or constriction of the blood vessels will benefit from daily treatments.

Red aventurine encourages the body to respond to internal feelings of well-being that well up inside the chest and gut. Allow yourself to recall times of intense pleasure or joy as a strand is placed on the abdomen. The greater the feelings of well-being, safety, and sheer joy at being alive, the more noticeable the corresponding increase in blood flow. An abdominal placement will increase blood flow to internal organs, which helps increase the activity of oxidation. Let the feeling that you're really glad to be alive bring warmth to your whole body as it radiates from your center. Breathe deeply.

Feelings of insecurity, worry, and lack of power often lead to conditions in which the body provides most available blood supply to only the internal organs. This condition results in systematic shrinkage of veins and arteries throughout the extremities. The fingers, toes, and other appendages are therefore cold most of the time. Poor circulation in these areas could be the cause of pain in the joints and stiffness or redness in the fingers and feet. For those who have this condition, regular daily treatments to the abdomen are recommended. Apply strands for one hour, at the same time of day, every day for several weeks. Remember that you must also work on developing an attitude of soul, expansive beyond the limits of the body.

Cinnamon aventurine opens the physical body to higher vibrations. These vibrations can penetrate the physical body once they are accepted and invited. For those who can accept only a small proportion of the orange ray, this stone will help. It gently opens areas that can be stubbornly refusing the orange ray because they hold on to such an abundance of noncolor-ray energy. It slowly softens their resistance.

You will know you are weak in orange ray in the emotional sheath when they have difficulty seeing humor in life or when joy escapes you. In the physical body, a weakness of the orange variety manifests as a weak thyroid, pituitary, or other hormone producing glands. Hormones, including the sex hormones, will often be produced at a slower rate than normal. Impotence, unusual tiredness, frequent depression, red eyes, swollen glands, and other hormone deficient conditions can result. All the qualities that orange-ray people usually exhibit are sublimated in stressful circumstances. Orange-ray people are normally warm, jovial, and outgoing. They think about others rather than themselves most of the time. They can be a catalyst for significant change in others. Their minds often relate to solutions in business or life that are human oriented. This skill is very useful for those whose jobs include solving human relations problems.

Red aventurine promotes positive human interaction. It pulls out our best skills when dealing with those we have trouble feeling comfortable around. It draws out our most forgiving and accepting side. Anyone who has trouble feeling safe is well advised to wear it when in public. If one is easily dominated by strong people, one should consider a necklace of this stone an essential part of their wardrobe and could easily wear a strand under their clothing when the color is not coordinated with their outfit.

Those deficient in the orange ray will tend to be cool or even cold in temperament. They will often be reclusive or closed in. Their feelings will usually be hidden. This tendency may not be eliminated simply by wearing red aventurine; however, the wearer may notice a new ability to express emotions or a greater openness with others.

This opening will usually be accompanied by a gradual increase in vitality. This energy is called the life force or *chi* in Eastern medicine. Red aventurine will work to improve our control over the life force, especially in combination with yoga, Tai Chi, Kung Fu, ballet, or other forms of dance or physical expression. Flexibility is enhanced by red aventurine as tendons and muscles become infused with its energy. One's performance in these forms of physical discipline will improve readily. Students who practice discipline as a matter of course will learn the deeper benefits of discipline, the way to kindness in self-discipline, and the prudence of clear discipline of children. Those who have no experience in the body movement disciplines will find red aventurine an introduction. It works best with slower forms of movement that develop flexibility. Many slow forms of dance and movement are practiced in the Orient. We westerners could learn much about stretching and slower motions, but this practice is one we must learn in small steps.

Red aventurine will pull out attitudes that have been stored in the body. Most attitudes are held in the body in the form of postures. We adopt these postures as part of our identity. Postures are held as expressions of our attitudes in situations where we have habitually adopted these attitudes in the past. Postures are extremely subtle, and their effects pervade the person's bodily effectiveness. A posture is a form of body language and others judge us by our posture.

For instance, in response to challenges spoken or unspoken, someone may adopt a posture of lowered head, sunken chest, drooping shoulders, sagging facial muscles, and hunched back. This response is a posture of the attitude that could be expressed as, "I'm just not up to competing because I'm not very good at anything." Immediately upon adopting this body posture, the person will feel small, incompetent, weak, ineffectual, unable to speak out, unclear about needs, and more. Observers will unconsciously assume this person is generally incompetent, though the person may only experience the feeling of incompetence in one or two situations. Postures come over a person without notice and instantly in response to certain stimuli.

Removing these responses can be facilitated by working with a trainer who demonstrates excellent posture and especially understands using the Alexander Technique or other posture-training programs. Work regularly on the discipline to adopt good posture while wearing cinnamon aventurine to remind you of the joy that is possible. The stones create the inner condition to allow for very fast learning and excellent retention of new postures, but you must actually practice the new postures with a coach who can guide you in the better posturing of the head and body. If you understood good posture naturally, you would practice it. A trainer is helpful because old habits are hard to work out of.

If you wish to experience a particular attitude but have difficulty adopting that attitude, try the following procedure. Lie down flat, and place one or two strands of red aventurine on areas of the body where a specific attitude originates or is stored. For example, the jaw holds attitudes related to power, the shoulders hold attitudes related to give and take, and the lower gut holds attitudes related to safety. These attitudes are visible in the upper body, central torso, or neck and jaw posture, though they may originate anywhere. Leave the strands on for fifteen or twenty minutes. The attitude should become amplified and the associations and causes related to the attitude should become apparent.

To change the attitude, simply expel it and replace it with a version of the attitude that you prefer to use. For instance, if you have the attitude that "all women are manipulative," you may wish to rephrase that attitude to one that holds that "some women are manipulative when they sincerely believe they must be to get what they want, and some women are direct and easy to understand." To insure that an attitude will change, you must have clear phrases to describe the new replacement attitude so you can recognize the new attitude as opposed to the old and clearly observe the benefits of changing it.

You may wish to further modify a weak attitude you want to change by attaching other, stronger attitudes that are helpful to it and strengthen it. The person in our example may be good at dealing with men. This person could add that "I am fully capable of avoiding any woman who is being manipulative and getting to me, just as I do with men." Once an attitude and all its associations are brought to the surface together, the attitude is susceptible to subtle alterations that substantially change the character or direction the attitude takes. At first it may be difficult to learn to uncover attitudes and the specific postures you associate with the attitude. Practice is required. Having a coach is good if you are not very self-motivated.

After placing the strands, try discovering an attitude. Choose the first attitude that comes up. Write down the best way of expressing it that you can. Now change a few words so the attitude will read more positively. Do not negate the attitude, for it has served you and you are probably not ready to fully release it on first contact. Simply change one word if it changes the meaning from a generalization to a more particular or singular statement. An example would be to change "all men are sports fanatics" to "some men are sports fanatics." It could be this simple a shift to begin the process to ease inflexibility in an unwanted attitude. Make your attitudes about others less generalized, less universal, less determinate, and more open, and you will find yourself much more capable of making friends. As you learn to be flexible with others, so you will be with yourself.

Strands of red aventurine may also be placed on the chakras. Begin with three strands and place them, one each, on three chakras of your choice. They will immediately begin to relax, calm, and unwind the chakras. Move the strands every few minutes to different chakras, allowing your choice of chakras to be guided by your intuition. Chakras will soon be calm, yet lively and stimulated. This chakra tune-up is easy to do and only takes a half-hour to focus on each chakra in several different combinations with the others.

For anyone who is concerned that their chakras are stressed, tight, or closed most of the time, try this tune-up every few days for several weeks. The various lower bodies should begin to learn to relax naturally. Eventually, you can unwind the chakras by just thinking of it after having been shown how by red aventurine.

Whenever you place a sphere or strand of spheres on the body, the body should get the message that soul has need of changes. Aventurine begins to work on the area. It initiates changes in your habitual processes and practices. The body will get the message if you repeat "I want my body to change and become more supportive of a beneficial program of flexible healthy activity." Repeating affirmations works when you believe they can work. Some individuals prefer to write them.

Place spheres on the body as placements only when you are ready to make permanent changes for better health. Single spheres will make subtle changes in postures if placed on the precise location in which the attitude that supports that posture is stored. Finding a precise location can be a matter of trial and error or practice. Anyone can find these locations if they simply take the time to try different locations, and through careful observation learn to feel when a precise location has been discovered.

Put red aventurine to work on fundamental body postures and the body will soon adopt a new language. It will convey to others the non-verbal message that you are comfortable with who you are and rely on your mind, because your mind gives you good information with which to make excellent decisions. From this message, others will begin to make assumptions about you that reflect their belief that you are self-assured. You will be treated as self-confident when you are able to display the posture of self-confidence.

Red aventurine helps us feel safe. It gives us permission to be who we would like to be and confidence to know that it is good to be who we are, even if we decide not to change some unsociable attitudes. Orange-ray energy will act to balance the different bodies while the particular vibrations of red aventurine helps the orange ray to infuse the abdomen, stabilize reactions, improve circulation, remove loose toxins and leave us feeling healthy.

The orange ray is essential to healing the physical body and regaining a balanced, vibrant stature.

The violet-ray path takes us high into the mountains. We feel alone and exposed as we commune with the stars. As we travel, we realize we also shine. We light up the night sky. This realization forms a basis for an understanding that we are not alone. We are in fact sustained by the very forces that created the universes.

The violet ray works with all to understand inner poise and grace, which comes with being open to the purple or violet ray. Poise is true inner strength, reflected in one's every action. It is demonstrated in the ability to walk through trials of life without being burned. It is the inner assuredness that comes from not needing to solve the problems of others. This does not mean you are unwilling to help others; it simply means you can let others do for themselves. You demonstrate poise when you can allow others their space without trying to fix their situation. The space to make your own conclusions about the things that occur in life is everyone's right. Poise is demonstrated when you help others only when invited and find time to listen to others without lecturing. Maintaining poise requires having control over your responses to events in life. An attitude of poise allows you to walk on fire.

Grace is a quality of one who has learned not to judge others. A person who is graceful

7
Violet Ray Stones

can glide among the influences of life like someone who dances with a whitewater river. Grace moves with sudden changes in direction and does not resist the river. To be graceful, you must be able to walk among the many who suffer and share their suffering compassionately without becoming ensnared in futility. A graceful person has hope and can see people as radiant beings of light who are temporarily caught in broken or battered bodies. To see others as soul and to know them as children of light is a quality of a person with grace. Grace is the path of the violet ray.

The violet ray governs intercommunication between people just as it governs intercommunication among the various organs and physical body systems. It governs and promotes understanding across lines of connection. All our organs act like separate beings, and when they cooperate, life goes much better. Each organ must learn how to operate in a manner that best accommodates the needs of other organs while always performing its function and remaining clear as to its own needs.

In the same way that the violet ray builds understanding between organs, it builds understanding between the various parts of the mind and between the mind and the emotional and physical bodies. By carrying messages of mutuality and purpose while allowing each person their autonomy, the violet ray works for the greater good. Once realized, this point of view can extend to all those you come in contact with. Your can learn to identify and enlarge common ground.

Within the unconscious mind, the violet ray works to develop powerful symbols. These symbols help the mind begin to see the benefits of cooperation and control. The violet ray builds a path of understanding and trust between soul and mind. It is the person who directs his mind and actions from a soul perspective, who truly displays poise and grace.

The mind is like a ship on the ocean. Violet teaches the mind the benefits of allowing soul to guide it as it steers the ship and the advantages of adopting the broader perspective of soul. Mind on its own will wander aimlessly and eventually run aground. Certainly we all have had the experience of talking ourselves into a corner of inactivity. The mind runs in circles when left to operate without the direction of soul. Soul can navigate, can use a rudder, and can see the global picture. Mind often neglects to consider dangers, follows whims and fancies, and can lose sight of its course altogether.

The purple stones bring in greater amounts of the violet ray to the aura and throughout the physical body. This infusion of violet will teach the various sheaths, their subsystems, and constituent parts to cooperate. Only soul can see the benefits of cooperation. Mind can see only the small picture. The mind becomes selfish to the point of great personal loss and discomfort if expected to make all the decisions. Mind is incapable of seeing another's point of view. Mind has fears that it will be forgotten and will someday die. This fear is reasonable, in that mind is transitory and limited. Someday we will no longer have a mind. The question is, will soul be prepared to take over when the mind is gone? Though soul is virtually unlimited, it has long resided in the worlds of time and space and is subject to the limitations of these worlds as long as it resides in a body and remains here. Soul must exercise its superiority.

Violet-ray energy helps soul remember its capabilities and teaches soul how to take control of the communication lines. People whose primary color ray is violet are not necessarily more spiritual nor are they higher on some spiritual scale or hierarchy. In fact, humility is the door to higher awareness for those of the violet ray. Let the violet ray teach its lessons in the way it will. Learn to be guided and find greatness. Follow the simple way to effective communication through grace.

For greatest results with the violet ray (and for that matter with gemstones in general), clearly picture the outcome you desire. Let the method for achieving this outcome be left open. Include the possibility that an even better outcome may result from your relationship with gemstones than you could imagine. Be open to a fluid relationship with the violet ray and there will be no limit to where it can lead. Do not force mind's will onto the violet ray. Rather, learn to use the violet ray as you learn to initiate action as soul, and operate from the soul perspective, and limitations will drop away. Learn poise, grace, and cooperation, and the violet ray will teach the way to complete mastery of energy.

Simply put, access to the secrets of the violet ray requires the ability to hold great faith and hope for incredible transformation. Trust the process as you develop a relationship with violet. Allow yourself to experience all the feelings that come with this relationship. Let go of limitations. Do all you can do, and do not procrastinate. Do all of this as best as you can, and you will discover all the violet ray has to offer.

Amethyst

Amethyst is the carrier of the violet ray for the present. The best varieties are without exception a deep violet color and quite clear with a sparkle. This stone works most deeply in the area of the subconscious.

Amethyst works to increase your ability to know and speak the truth. If you wish to learn the truth about yourself, your relationship to the whole, and the greater truths of life in the many worlds, you should wear amethyst regularly. We all have our own truth. Together we have a larger truth. This larger truth will satisfy the hunger of soul once this hunger is awakened. Amethyst sparks a desire for greater truth, and the violet ray it carries teaches the art of communication such that you can access resources and learn to relate to them to find the answers to questions about truth. Life can seem to be a paradox until a higher truth resolves, in three dimensions, the apparent incongruity between the two dimensions of a paradox.

Soul moves more freely in the higher dimensions and will never want to return to the confines of a two-dimensional view of things once the violet ray has opened it to its heritage.

Amethyst teaches the use of intuition for exploration into the unknown. For those who draw their strength from their imagination and dreams, this stone will be their most powerful ally. Imagination can awaken soul to the possibilities of a greater truth. Exercise the imagination frequently and allow the purple-color ray to fill the subconscious mind to begin to fully engage soul in the pursuit of truth.

Amethyst opens the upper subconscious mind to a greater flow of energy. This part of the mind is inaccessible to the conscious mind though it is the seat of imagination and intuition. The subconscious mind can be directed by soul, and soul speaks through the symbols and dream language of the subconscious mind. You must learn to interpret your own imagery in order to consciously receive the messages soul is sending.

Start your introduction to amethyst by wearing a strand of four- to six-millimeter, dark-colored spheres around your neck. Wear this strand for perhaps six to eight hours a day for the first few weeks straight. As an alternative, you may wish to wear the strand at night while sleeping; this is an excellent way to introduce yourself to your subconscious mind.

As you sleep, the conscious mind is largely shut down and the subconscious mind has time to work through thoughts that arose during the day and to integrate information coming to it from soul. You may also work on unexpressed or unrecognized feelings in dreams. Not all feelings can be expressed in the context of our current daily lives. Feelings of great joy, for instance, could be misunderstood if expressed in the midst of a divorce. Feelings of sadness could be interpreted as signs of weakness if expressed during a business meeting. Amethyst encourages the free expression of feelings during sleep.

For many, the world of dreams is largely a mystery. However, if you sincerely desire to understand the workings of the subconscious, you may soon begin to see a change in your relationship to dreams in the presence of amethyst. Do not expect information from the subconscious to come in a form of logical data that the conscious mind is used to. The subconscious has its own way of thinking. It will insist you learn its way before it will open its huge well of insight. The mind is like a huge iceberg floating on a vast northern sea. This is the sea of knowledge. The conscious mind is above water. It is not in direct contact with the sea of knowledge. It sees and relates to the air of social consciousness where everything is predictable. The far greater part of the iceberg is below water. This subconscious (unseen) part relates directly to the vast ocean. It intermingles with the ocean of consciousness. It is hidden from social scrutiny. The above water part of an iceberg is the familiar part, the below water part, however, carries the most weight and is somehow able to directly contact the even less familiar world of the ocean itself.

Violet-ray energy works easily with the subconscious and opens the less receptive, conscious mind, emotions, and physical body to information that comes through dreams. Wear amethyst at night and you may at first have what seem like usually scattered dreams. You must not let this bother you. You must try to figure out their message. Take time to try to put dissociated images together to find their link. Given your committed and concentrated effort to remember and write down your dreams, you may expect to see a significant change in your dreams within one to six months. They will begin to speak directly to the physical, emotional, and mental parts of yourself and you will begin to understand the imagery at all levels. Dreams will begin to deal directly with the situations of daily life as you get clear about your direction, mission, and goals, and develop a symbolic dream language.

Dreams can be a window to the soul. You will gradually find, through concerted effort, that you are able to hear the messages from soul in your dreams. You may find it easier to interpret these messages and create changes in your life that are consistent with the direction of soul as you wear amethyst each night for a few months. A life directed by soul works more in accord with your true nature. If you are actively programming the amethyst, it will work faster.

Programming a gemstone is as simple as a thought. Simply know in your mind that the particular gemstone will, for a time, have a particular purpose that you have suggested to it. This is a similar process to suggesting a behavior to a hypnotized person. Gems accept suggestions easily; how long they hold a suggestion is dependent on the power of the suggestion and the ability of a person to focus.

For instance, program amethyst to bring you information from the soul level. Ask it to improve one new capability each week. Pick a capability or attribute you wish to improve, such as spiritual stamina. Every night before bed, ask for help in increasing that ability. Direct the amethyst to bring information on all levels to you about spiritual stamina during that week. Pay attention to any clues, hints, comments by others, dreams, passages in books that relate somehow, and other symbols and images. Write down these observations, and at the end of the week figure out what you have learned. Then in a month or so, review the information and see what new insight may relate to what you have learned. Trust the process and remain focused, and you will be amazed at the rich content of the images and symbols you receive.

Next week, say you want to learn lucid dreaming—the ability to direct a dream while dreaming. For one week, work with amethyst on "waking up" within your dream. Before sleep, say to amethyst, "I will realize I'm dreaming and be able to understand this fact while I dream." Now just forget it and go to sleep. This suggestion may not take effect for some time, so be prepared to keep on trying the suggestion and letting it go. If you have considerable skepticism, let yourself read some books, stories, or articles on the experiences of others with lucid dreaming to open the imagination and stop doubts.

Later you may decide to work on becoming aware of what it is you need to learn each day in your dream. Before sleep, tell yourself exactly what you want the subconscious mind to work on and what you want to do while you are dreaming. The week after that, tell yourself that you will begin to explore the dream world more. You will get out and see what is there. The next week, you might try telling the subconscious mind that during the next seven nights you will explore favorite natural wonders and learn more about them. Starting tonight, you will go to Florida in your dream and learn about the Everglades and survival in the swamp. Pick a place for each night.

Amethyst teaches you to take charge of your life. You begin to adopt an attitude of mastery. Simply adopting an attitude will not bring results, you must notice the new attitude and daily exercise your control to gain mastery. Mastery is a matter of discipline and persistence. Learning to become a master over emotional reactions is not easy and you may wish to begin practice in the dream state where the beliefs of friends and family will not interfere. Practice persistence and mastery will eventually come. Master your reactions and you will be free to choose your life.

Practical knowledge can be gained from dreams. You can learn to direct dreams to deal with and solve problems from daily life. Just practice a new capacity or a single aspect of a capacity each night. For example, take the skill of handling others when they are overwrought with emotion. Before bed, picture yourself handling a specific situation in which someone you know is out of control. See them coming to a calm, peaceful conversation with you. Say out loud that you do not know how to accomplish this. Ask your dream producer to create a script for you in which you can practice this new skill. By day, you could take up counseling classes to learn how to observe and understand behavior. At night you could explore the applications of the new skill. Wear a necklace of amethyst as you work through a test of this theory and be open to the possibilities.

Whatever area of your life you feel could use the attention, you can improve with the concentrated effort and commitment that amethyst teaches us to apply. Whatever trait you choose to focus the violet ray on will begin to improve within a few months.

If one method doesn't work, try another method. Amethyst also teaches flexibility. Make up your own method if you like. If you like working in dreams, make a new method of interaction with dreams. Try asking the inner self—soul—to give you an experience at night that would teach you what is important. In the morning, you could write down what you learned that night in the dream state and what you would like to discover during the next night. After you write it down, go about your day. Know the subconscious mind is always working, even when you are busy doing things with the conscious mind. The next morning, check in and again write down what you learned. By doing this day after day, you are tapping your subconscious mind. This part of the mind has many capabilities that are as yet undiscovered, it can do many amazing things. Simply suggesting questions to this part of the mind is enough to engage its abilities. Its vast resources will begin to work in ways that the logical mind cannot grasp. The results can be incredible.

Your subconscious may contain a large number of images of unresolved resentments, suppressed hostilities, or fears. Often, old feelings are connected to attitudes and beliefs that may not be understood by one who has little relationship with their subconscious. Although this area of the human experience is happening below the conscious level of the mind and may be little understood and perhaps even a bit frightening, the possible reward to those working with amethyst to release unwanted resentments or fears is immense. The subconscious often sets the scene and supplies the characters for the play we call our life. Learning the language of the subconscious is challenging, for each of us has our own inner language. Some archetypal images may be the same for all of us, yet each of us applies images differently, has a quite different personality, and has had very different experiences. Amethyst will aid us in our efforts to understand and communicate with our subconscious. The violet ray will teach us translation skills so we can understand our own inner worlds.

This ability to interpret the language of the subconscious is important to those who wish to achieve an expansion of their awareness. You will become more clear on who you are and what is happening to you as you work with amethyst. Furthermore, the ability to reevaluate your most deeply held beliefs, create new beliefs, and direct your future is possible. It is even possible to change the effect the past has on us. We just need to work with amethyst and it will show us how to change our relationship to the past. We can still change our reactions. This will change the future.

Since many of our experiences are directed by our subconscious mind, we may find the power there to dramatically alter our lives for the better. You can increase your grasp of the workings of the mind and the nature of things from listening to the subconscious. With truth at your disposal, wearers indeed will have a newfound ability to effect new behaviors and generate different results. A wearer may even learn to create the feelings and thoughts they wish to have.

The results of the inner process initiated by amethyst that start in the subconscious will spill into every aspect of your life. You can expect a feeling of upliftment. You can see new ways of doing things and new thoughts will generate new possibilities for how you can act. You will certainly become more courageous in all major relationships of your life, particularly if you expect it and practice courage.

Amethyst will lead the conscious mind to prefer direction from soul. The violet ray, as amplified by amethyst matrix, will pierce the veil of mystery surrounding the hidden abilities of the subconscious mind.

Amethyst will also teach us about different levels of intelligence. We will learn to speak different languages used by those who pursue different disciplines than we are used to and who are at other levels of intelligence than we are as we begin to learn to step into a different consciousness. We may learn to speak to animals and other creatures. We may become familiar enough with the language of imagery to contact plants or trees.

In every communication, amethyst will support an exchange of understanding that leads to mutual esteem.

For those who lack the ability to control their behavior or develop a discipline that works for them, amethyst will help. It supports positive changes in behavior. We need not understand the reason for a behavior to change it. Amethyst teaches the body to relax and let go of tension. Often this is enough to encourage our decision to adopt a new behavior. Simply wish to have a new behavior, and let amethyst do the rest as it instigates subtle changes in beliefs and eases self-imposed limitations, resulting in attitude changes. The subconscious is affected by attitudes we adopt as much as it is by things that happen, it functions differently based on whatever attitude we focus on. It does not see life except through the filters of the conscious mind. Amethyst teaches you to select the best, most functional attitudes for positive results.

Amethyst teaches the body to align its physical structure with the vibrations of soul as these are manifest in three dimensions through the subconscious. The body itself will have a part in determining how effective your behavior is. It can learn to pose as capable in an arena you have never entered.

The body is a huge transformer. The energies we receive are directed by its structure. For greater coordination between our soul-directed subconscious and the physical body structure, work with indigo and amethyst together. Let them rearrange the elements of the body to transform and transmit energies as directed by soul. Just as the subconscious is in touch with the vast ocean of information in its realm, so soul is in touch with a far greater force; it is in touch with the original creative force itself. Amethyst brings some of soul's awareness into the physical body and this awareness will change the physical body responses as well as its structure.

Amethyst teaches mental self-control by taking the wearer deeper into the mental realm as an observer. Once self-control is demonstrated, this gemstone will begin to impart detachment from the mental stream of ideas. You will learn to observe the mind in action. Once the mind is seen for what it is, it can be more easily controlled. Amethyst-directed energy boosts your powers of observation and helps you see the reasons for your lack of control. In this way, we are encouraged to let go of prejudices we have developed in the past. Prejudices here refers to judgments made that may have been correct for another time and circumstance but do not serve us or our friends today. Remove your prejudices and you will remove the background fear of the past that permeates your life. This fear is hardly noticeable until it is removed, except as it may manifest as headaches or other chronic aches or pains.

If you wish to expedite this process of discovering how fear rules your life, imagine a giant amethyst crystal. Imagine it is so pure of form and vibration as to be almost invisible. See it standing on a large platform. Walk up to the crystal and look into its windows. Its surface is cut with facets and it has a giant oval shape. It is stimulating to stand next to its ten foot by six and a half-foot mass. See the strong violet-purple color it is emitting. Step into the crystal like you would step into a violet room. Watch its color penetrate your body as you pass into it. See every cell become filled with the deep purple color of its light.

Allow it to touch every part of you. Watch as your nightmares and fears of the past are lifted like a cloud of black fog rising from your body. See the fear dissipate. Know that it is just that easy to release the hold the past has on you. Know that the results of these changes will take time to manifest, but they certainly will. Now step out of the giant crystal. As the days pass over the course of the following week, jot down any observations about your experiences as they may be different from the week before. Some people may notice immediate relief of certain downward-pulling emotions that were related to fears. Repeated treatments may be necessary for unknown fears to be brought to the surface of the mind and to be recognized, if no immediate effects of such fears are noticed or can be linked to our thoughts.

As you begin to know yourself better and come to root out your old fears and gain control over rampant emotions, you will find that problems, negative emotions, and disempowering thoughts of others no longer control you so easily. You will instantly know when others are projecting their thought forms on you. You may find that the truth about others' intentions becomes clear to you.

Amethyst works on the throat area and the energy centers in the astral body associated with the throat and speech centers. When worn as a short strand close around the neck, amethyst will help a person who lacks the self-confidence to speak up. It will support the person exercising their right to express themselves. Someone who is reserved or shy may reduce the need to be uncertain, overly quiet, or meek. The increase in energy that comes with self-knowledge will strengthen your resolve. Truth will be your guide. The strand of amethyst will strengthen your ability to project your voice and say what is necessary to get your needs expressed.

The support of amethyst may help some people move forward in business, particularly if that business is serving the public good. As you develop self-confidence, you will develop relationships in all areas of your life that will help you move forward with certainty and purpose. Business relationships will be strengthened for wearers as mutual purpose is established. This support can also help you find long-term friends. You will make friends more easily and be more likely to choose those who can be a good influence on you.

Look to the violet ray as a bottomless ocean of wisdom and truth. Let it teach you. Be in it, and let it be in you. Swim in it and let it support you. Let it soothe you. Notice that you become more energetic when you are in touch with its vibration as it opens you to channels of great wisdom. It will expand your awareness of life's possibilities. You cannot permanently alter it or damage it by your mistakes, for it is a regenerating ocean of violet-ray energy. If you let it, it will draw your attention inward toward your spiritual center.

The violet ray is like the Native American totem of the bear. It is found at the outer reaches of life and holds the energy of the far north. It builds strength, power, and wisdom. In the presence of the violet ray, you learn contentment with the simple life even as you increase possibilities for diversity. It teaches independence in all things and yet can rapidly connect you with others of like intentions with great effect. Call on it to help you with understanding and courage. It will guide you into the deepest caves, where you may learn much about the nature of things. You can move safely into the darkest reaches and learn the nature of paradox. Life is full of paradox, and those who understand paradox will dwell in a fortress of inner strength. You may dwell in its crystal fortress, which is something like Superman's beautiful arctic home made of crystals, which gave him refuge to regain and build his strength and his power to do good works.

No longer will you lie awake, wondering about your life if you work with the violet ray. Amethyst focuses the violet ray into your worries and destroys them, leaving room in the mind for curiosity and the fire of hope. Your restlessness will disappear and be replaced with growing resolve and clearer direction. Even if your problem is severe insomnia, amethyst will help. It will protect you from worries as well as the unhealthy intentions of others that disrupt your psychic space. The wearer will find purpose where once was despair, hope where once was despondence.

Those who continue to wear a strand of amethyst for many years will find they are able to master the process of reviewing their lives. They will be able to see the moments of the past as if they were preserved in clear crystals of ice. These moments can be teachers for a better future, instead of slave drivers that give us no options. Seeing the past clearly will set you free. You will be able to see experiences for what they are and let go, removing grief and resentment.

Wearers of amethyst may also find a growing happiness, and at times an overflowing joy. For those who have released their attachments and fears, the world will be a place of wonder and all things will be made new.

Those who master the quality of self-discipline will find the ability to go farther into the unknown. The door to the other worlds, the third eye, will gradually open to the insights of the ages. Let your experiences become like fluid and flow out gracefully and naturally. Become like the bear, strong and playful. Let amethyst be your champion for the ideals you wish to incorporate into your life. Soon the mysteries of inner worlds will reveal themselves and you will become the master and rightful king or queen of your kingdom.

Lavender Amethyst

The best-quality lavender amethyst contains areas of clear, areas of light and dark lavender color, and areas of white. Opaque varieties are good to use for body work. The translucent variety is powerful enough to create bridges between consciousness and the universal mind force. The AAA-varieties are capable of developing bridges beyond the mind into the area of soul. Soul-to-soul communication is possible with lavender. Do not use varieties that have black or brown inclusions, or that seem dingy or dark throughout.

One of lavender's greatest missions is to create bridges between parties who cannot understand each other. Whatever the misunderstanding might be, this stone helps you see the other person's point of view and the bridge to connect their point of view to yours. If the intention is to negotiate something, this stone will help. The best negotiations conclude with a mutually agreeable understanding or a decision in which everyone wins without necessity for compromise. This process is easier when people understand each other in the other's terms. Understanding is difficult when each person has their own agenda that the others do not understand. If one person in a group discussion wears lavender, this person can moderate. If all the parties wear lavender, then all can mutually cooperate to discover solutions.

Connections of all kinds are bridges. By building bridges to those we love, we can receive validation and a real sense of being known. This basic human need is not often met. Seeing your own needs through compassionate eyes is an unusual gift. Have you ever felt misunderstood? Have you ever longed to be recognized for the qualities you embody? Do you look at your needs and wish you could end the experience of needing? Your needs are proven worthy of attention and love in the eyes of someone who can validate you. Lavender will help you find that someone who can validate your needs and help you to understand that you are worthy of survival, growth, and love. Lavender teaches you to love yourself.

Lavender will promote your understanding of others' needs and facilitate your willingness to participate in helping others get their needs met. Helping someone else get what they need, particularly if their need is the same as the needs you have always wanted satisfied, teaches you how to manifest prosperity without getting caught in debts to those who would take advantage of your indebtedness.

For those who have the feeling that others are not cooperative or are out to get all they can from us, lavender may not at first succeed in creating a new sense of cooperation. Cooperation must come from a sincere desire to experience what may be referred to as companion energy. This energy results from two or more beings truly connecting by giving of themselves. When two people join energy and create a bond of love, they create a specific vibration that connects them across all barriers and they share a companionship that is available to either of them anytime and anyplace, even if the other dies and is gone into the other worlds. Companion energy results when people engage in a higher form of sharing from the heart that is only available to those who can fully open their hearts to another. Companion energy is shared by those who have learned grace from the violet ray. The violet ray itself implores us to discover the experience of opening our hearts to another in love. Lavender teaches you to open to the violet ray gently and in a safe circumstance.

Conflict resolution is an art form. For those who can see the opponent's side, especially when the other's side is based on different assumptions, conflict may become an opportunity. Lavender loves conflict, for in a state of conflict, the needs of both sides are being tested. The opportunity to extend yourself to areas never before touched exists in all conflict. This opportunity is best used if both parties are committed to fair fights— if both wear lavender and both find within themselves the desire to overcome defensiveness and win common understanding.

We do not all learn in the same way, and we have had widely different experiences even if we live in the same house. Most conflict results from fairly simple misunderstandings. Talking does not guarantee another person will share our experience. We all assign different meanings to events. We all are comparing our thoughts and feelings to different standards—it's a wonder we can get along at all. Lavender allows us to resonate with another person. When two people resonate together, one person actually experiences what it feels like to be in another's experience. Being misunderstood is often frustrating; hence, you could say lavender is useful when one is frustrated. Another person who is in conflict may not be helped directly by you wearing lavender, but they may be helped indirectly if they are willing to be receptive to insights via the inner channels. Wearing lavender, you will see what they see. Of course it is likely that you will be more detached from the things that cause conflict in them. If they can be open to your insight, they will benefit from your detachment. For you to see how they see, simply wear lavender, look at the person, and wish it. To see them more deeply, you will have to look out through their eyes. You will have to look at things, including yourself, as they see them. This may take effort. You may not wish to change your way of seeing to accommodate them. Take the risk. If you repeatedly do, you will reduce your level of frustration with the conditions and people that you are in conflict with.

Seeing yourself how others see you will give you a powerful insight into your hidden motives. Having hidden motives that remain hidden even to oneself may be the cause of chronic conflict with others.

When working with conflicts within oneself, the challenge is similar. Areas of internal disharmony can learn to communicate their disharmony and possibly can come into a more harmonious vibrational pattern with the whole. Parts in disagreement will gradually get to know what is best for you as a whole when in the presence of lavender. Wear lavender and the parts of yourself that stay in disagreement will begin to communicate their motives. Lavender will create bridges of mutual understanding between disparate parts. Lavender starts developing inner companion energy by strengthening continuity and interconnectedness among the

192 • Chapter Seven

parts that are harmonious and in agreement. It will then form bridges of communication among all other parts. It will afford each part the opportunity to let its point of view and needs be heard, not just tolerated. All parts will not only feel and learn tolerance, but will become included and valued. You may have difficulty understanding that different body parts have different agendas but if you look at this as a metaphor for different parts of the mind, then you will understand the body better.

At first it may seem odd to look at yourself as a conglomeration of differing ideas and emotions, but we are. We often engage in internal debate. Some people report their inner conversation as a dialogue between various personalities. Lavender allows you to distinguish the various voices and identify their origin. It allows separate areas of your being to integrate, without the mind becoming splintered. The wearer will learn to listen to all their parts. The inner dialogue becomes a sort of committee meeting with all parties encouraged to maintain their separate agendas and remain true to their needs.

For those suffering from severe disintegration of personality, in which case they cannot reason without struggle and their different parts appear to exist separately with their own personalities, lavender should be employed with caution and only when a professional counselor or gemstone therapist schooled in psychology is present who can explain to the person being treated the nature of their condition. Multiple personality syndrome is a condition where, in a few documented cases, the different "personalities" actually displayed very different physical symptoms of disease. In such cases a sufferer could cause themselves great harm if care is not taken when introducing the disparate parts. In capable hands, it can be a powerful tool for gradual integration.

Lavender creates a window from which to view the mental associations we hold on to and have linked to past events. It is not uncommon for us to experience a range of emotions after a major event in our lives. The event will not change, but we may go through a series of different reactions over time. Our emotions change with respect to past events. The meaning that we ascribe to a past event can change drastically. After a major loss, we may completely change our feeling about the loss from grief to anger to self-pity to joy over time. At first, we might feel that the dying person did not love us, as proven by their abandoning us. Later we may wish we had never known the person or at least had stayed more distant. This set of feelings may develop through a circle of meanings.

We may eventually come to decide that this person truly loved us and we are deeply grateful for their love. So you see, feelings about past events do change as we ascribe new meanings to the events. Lavender helps us find meanings for events that bring us closer to the profound lessons hidden in every major turning point of our lives.

This seemingly odd phenomenon of discovering an ability to change the context of our lives does not indicate that we are schizophrenic; rather, we just have different sides to ourselves. You may have heard the terms "inner child," or "anima" or "animus." These terms may seem like constructs of popular psychology. They are, however, useful terms used to describe different aspects of our personality. We are beings with emotional, physical, and mental parts. We have been through many stages of development, and every one of those is a stage that can still be activated by giving it a voice. We switch between roles as parents, grandparents, adults, children, and even babies at times. We change personalities when in the company of different kinds of people.

Getting to know your different selves is a complex process that becomes simpler after careful consideration. This process is known as "individuation," and is marked by coming to know who you are in all your different modalities and circumstances. Many try this process, and most find it difficult. Lavender brings insights that move you ever closer to complete self-understanding in the process of individuation.

Lavender will help you integrate the various aspects of yourself. It will build bridges of understanding within you and between you and others. It will help you articulate the different points of view you have within yourself. It will even help you make decisions in complex situations. Becoming integrated through broader differentiation of your different personalities and deeper understanding of their differences is the path lavender will guide you on.

As a result of following this path, you may become more loving and more creative. You may learn to use the different sides of your brain. You may even learn to appreciate other learning styles. If, say, you are primarily a visual learner, you may begin to master the ability to learn through kinesthetics or sound. You will surely come to know more of yourself.

Through this process of integration, you will become more whole. Your mental, causal, emotional, and physical selves will begin to cooperate with each other. Like a spider who tends the threads in a massive web, you will learn to keep things separate yet connected. You will learn to react quickly when opportunity comes your way. You will develop a new sense of which thread of your web has been excited when someone enters your space. Your reactions will become more congruent with circumstances. You will find less disparity in your thoughts. Your questions will serve you better.

Suppose you are about to go on your first date after a long period without dating anyone. One day you decide to make yourself available and someone invites you out. While preparing for the date you ask yourself a series of questions. Why did this person want to ask me out? Don't they have other prospective dates who are much better than I? Won't they surely drop me when they find out what I have done in the past?

As you can tell by these examples or by thinking of what you would say to yourself in this situation, we often ask ourselves questions that engage our minds to figure what is wrong. The mind is a great tool; like a computer it will go to work to find answers to any question asked. When asked what is wrong, it will obediently supply a variety of possible answers that will only serve to make you feel increasingly wrong. A better set of questions would be: What is right? What do I have in common with this person? How might I benefit from a liaison with them? What can I do to ensure I have a good time on this date? Good questions engage the mind in a search for positive data. Lavender will teach the wearer to differentiate between empowering questions and those which enervate. It will teach you how to transform questions that lead to problems into questions that lead to solutions.

Eventually, you may master the use of your intuition. As insights flow in about soul, the astral body, and mental body, you will experience a heightened sense of certainty. You will become self-assured. You will be able to access answers to questions you have never previously posed. Lavender teaches you to believe in your intuition.

As pathways between bodies are strengthened, you will experience a great increase in the flow of energy through your being. You will become self-nourishing, able to satisfy your desire for spiritual food, self-sufficient, able to create all that you need to feel sufficient and more giving, able to give of yourself without holding back.

As more of your inner doors are opened, you will begin to get a larger overview. Not only will you be able to see the whole forest and not just the trees, but you will be able to manage the forest better. Lavender points the way to independence. You will have to do the work, however. Lavender does not provide easy solutions nor will it take the place of concentrated effort, but it will highlight the path. It is not the forester, but it helps the person who takes the job of caring for their land by interpreting the languages of the many forest animals, plants, and trees. You must manage your own forest, and lavender is a marvelous tool with which to begin the job. It saves much time and confusion. It is like having a map of the terrain and a historical account of all the forces that were at work to create the ecology of the area. It helps us understand how the forces at work in any system or ecology balance to keep that system going.

Lavender can be combined with almost any other gemstone. It will act as a bridge between gemstones that normally do not act in conjunction with each other. It is especially useful for creating strands for special purposes. Combine it with any other stone that you may have difficulty understanding how to use successfully. Design necklaces that join stones that do not easily function together or are of opposite color rays, placing lavender beads between them on a strand to expedite their cooperation and harmony as they work together.

The user could wear a strand of lavender to help him maintain balance when working with gemstones that bring more fundamental change; stones like rhodocrosite or purple rainbow fluorite or any other stones that promote significant alteration of your energy flow. Lavender helps you integrate change and helps you learn subjects that are not normally easy for you.

If wearing any strand of therapeutic gemstones is uncomfortable, try alternating wearing that stone alone with wearing a strand of lavender in a precisely timed exercise. Wear one for exactly one minute, then wear the other for one minute. Go back and forth, timing the duration precisely. Do this for eight to twelve reversals. Then wear both at the same time for a while. When you have repeated this therapy enough times to get results, you may want to wear the lavender by itself for a while.

Experiment with strands of different lengths. You may like a necklace that just fits over the head or prefer a strand that is long enough to reach your sternum. If it is a bit longer, a necklace will lie right over your heart chakra. A short strand that is like a choker may be more beneficial if working on the throat (the speaking center). Having a strand of the right length will greatly enhance physical body integration. If the head and torso are having a misunderstanding, wear a strand close to the neck. When heart and will cannot agree, use a strand that reaches the heart. If the solar plexus, the area of the body that holds the power to influence the world, is uncooperative with the sex chakra, wear a strand that reaches midway down the chest, or place a strand directly on the solar plexus.

Some may find the most benefit from wearing a tisrati (a strand worn around the forehead). This placement will direct the gemstone's effects to the brain tissues, the head, and the mental aspects of being.

A strand can be twisted into a spiral and worn over areas of the body that are experiencing pain or negativity. This practice will soothe the area and may make the user aware of what is needed to remedy the condition of stress or disharmony.

Opening the communication lines between body and mind is part of lavender's mission. Once these lines are open, you will become aware of inner distress signals. An area could be distressed because its needs have been neglected while other inner voices were being heard.

Picture yourself as a giant network of communication lines, and imagine the lavender vibrations traveling down nerve "wires" to a distressed area, as if they were a messenger dressed in lavender. Can you imagine a tiny lavender man running up and down the lines, carrying messages of mutual benefit and separate needs? Picture the wires extending out into your aura. Ask your higher self to send you a message via these lines. This message will be carried via lavender to all parts and can pertain to any concern you as soul may have. Watch the messenger as he delivers the message to all areas of the various bodies.

Now watch for signs of a response. Some messages, when delivered, may elicit a noticeable response, while some messages are too subtle to evoke an immediate response. All messages are heard, however. Use this seemingly simple technique to reorient your inner parts to a greater purpose while maintaining their individuality.

An overall summation or status report should arrive in the brain within a few minutes. You may not be able to decipher the code. You may need to ask for hints from the subconscious mind. You may get your report in the form of a dream later that night. An insight may come from a quote from a book or even from a friend who, unbeknownst to them, tells you just what you needed to hear to discover a report that was previously imperceptible.

This simple technique will often bring unprecedented results for those who use it regularly and who write down the answers as they come.

Lavender is one of the greatest tools of all the gemstones. It will facilitate the actions of every gemstone and help integrate all forms of learning. It will help you translate information that was previously indecipherable and therefore lost. It will give you confidence by showing you how to resolve conflict. It will construct bridges of understanding over any impasse. In short, it is the most useful single necklace in your collection.

Single beads of lavender can also be used for a wide variety of purposes. Single small spheres will release excess energy or excite the flow of energy to areas that are shut down. By spinning a sphere between the thumb and forefinger of the dominant hand over an afflicted area, you will rebalance an energy meridian in the same way acupuncture works. Single spheres can be used over acupuncture points and will often work as well as needles without a puncture being necessary. In the hands of a professional acupuncturist, a single stone can be a very powerful tool for rebalancing energy flow.

Look to lavender to help you on a path to self-discovery. We think we understand ourselves. We think we know why things are the way they are. Lavender helps us to understand that our truth may be accessible, but it is often not obvious and may require our dedication to it before we can unravel its mysteries.

Purple Garnet (Rhodolite)

Rhodolite is a somewhat rare form of garnet. It is a deep reddish-purple color. Its primary focus for humans is on self-esteem.

Self-esteem is a primary issue for many adults today. Many may compensate for a lack of self-esteem by becoming grandiose. Still others will spend their lives hiding from situations where they may feel exposed. The primary fear is of not being good enough. The underlying belief is that "I cannot be trusted" or "I cannot trust myself." This belief usually is expressed in the form of inability to trust others, blaming others for your role (often feeling victimized), or habitually of choosing associations with persons who are not trustworthy. The life ritual is one of avoidance and feeling rejected. Our society is not built on the empowerment of individuals, so if you feel you suffer from low self-esteem, you have lots of company.

To defeat low self-esteem you must learn to completely trust your mind, decisions, perceptions, and conclusions, and you must believe you are worthy of high self-esteem. Our consumer advertising agencies are constantly sending out the message that you must have certain products to be content, happy, thin, muscular, popular, or sexy. These promises are exaggerated. The definition of self-esteem lies in the belief that you are sufficient in yourself without need of any specific outward characteristics or approval. Self-esteem comes from within. Alterations in body, car, home, bank account, and the like may be desirable but will not in and of themselves correct self-doubt. Your thinking must change.

While wearing a strand of garnet is not sufficient in and of itself to effect a change in your attitude toward yourself, its energy will bring a different focus. This new focus will be especially useful if we have recognized that our situation is of our own making and that we are now taking our lives into our own hands. We can learn to focus on the positive realization that we can be the masters of our situation. After all, we made our life the way it is with the same power that can make our life the way we would like it to be.

We are masters of our own destiny, but we may not remember this. In neglecting to assert our rights and wants, we will most likely be ignored. On the other hand, if we are constantly demanding our way, we will certainly put people off and be ineffectual.

This dilemma presents us with a paradox. It is only through a deep commitment to practicing the ways of love that we can find an answer to our questions of how to proceed. Balance is the key. We must find a point of balance that is right for us. Each of us must strive to control the ego while not becoming a wallflower or a victim of someone else's ego. Garnet shows you how to create a trustworthy attitude. It shows you how to get your needs met and how to think clearly about your situation. Garnet connects you to the inner sound current that brings you closer into contact with truth itself. Garnet shows you how to use truth to set yourself free of the fetters of self-limiting beliefs about your worthiness.

Each of us has a choice to make. We must find the balance between serving others and taking care of our own needs. A strand of rose quartz spheres, when worn with a strand of rhodolite garnet, will help you remember to have love both for yourself and for others. When love of self is seriously out of balance with the love of others, we diminish the quality and sincerity of our love.

Rose quartz can teach us how it feels to love in a way that is truly beneficial to others. Rhodolite can remind us to hold ourselves in high regard. It will support us in seeing our place in the nature of things as defined by integrity and truth. Together, these two stones will provide an energy of light and sound that will encourage us to assume a strong stance in favor of love. Love itself is the only long-term cure for low self-esteem.

Garnet is the stone of the self. It will help all who lose themselves in arguments, others' plans, care of their mates, obsessive behavior, and the allure of impossible goals or goals that can never be attained to any complete satisfaction. The self does not seek or avoid pleasure in life. It is the mind that seeks pleasure, caught by a belief that identity itself hangs in the balance of pleasure consuming and pleasure having. Pleasure is fleeting at best. It comes and goes. It depends on the outside world for its existence.

Rhodolite garnet is a perfect gift for those who procrastinate in doing what would improve their situation. Everyone procrastinates, but some people can't seem to do anything else. Give yourself the gift of garnet and this reddish-purple stone will penetrate all aspects of the many losses you endures from limiting yourself. It will directly attack the fear of doing anything in life that might be different. It will work itself into your attitudes and become part of your nature.

The violet ray brings all people who will give of themselves a new goal. It will cause you to look outside of your own limited world. It will give you incentive to help others. You can gain much in self-esteem by helping those who are in serious need. Rhodolite will not allow you to sit back when someone in need comes to you. It will encourage you to seek ways to pull others up, and in the process you will find yourself on higher ground.

Rhodolite will help you become skilled in assertiveness. For those who have little experience with this trait, rhodolite will allow them to be assertive without feeling guilty or wrong. This ability would be helpful for those who find themselves overwhelmed by the circumstances of life, especially if being overwhelmed is too common in their lives.

Be cautious that you do not lose sight of balance and become aggressive. This stone may help to awaken the warrior within, but it is up to you to direct this warrior to stand for good, lest you become the victim of your own aggression. Stand strong in your desire for benefit to all and you will become engaged in discovering gifts that have been unrecognized or unused. Passion for life comes from using inherent talents to enrich the lives of those around you. When you believe you have no talent, you are unlikely to believe that what you do will make a difference. The fact is we all have talents. Talents are often latent and hidden, but they certainly exist.

People need simple things that are hard to find, like love, appreciation, acceptance, and compassion. Rhodolite garnet can help you find the inspiration to give these simple gifts. If those in your life seem undeserving, find someone who is. So many people are starving for a little love and attention and a number of these actually would benefit tremendously from some simple caring from a perfect stranger. The gift of giving is most effective when you can remain detached from the emotions of a person who needs help. Garnet teaches detachment though it does not preclude compassion.

Violet-ray energy opens lines of communication. Garnet prompts you to use those lines of communication to work with those in true need. The experience of seeing someone who is near death, destitute, or just having a bad day come back to life and thank God for another day to share is truly worth having as it builds self-esteem.

You may believe that service is just a path for fools, but you should try this path before making a judgment about its merits. Rhodolite helps you suspend judgment and opens you up to experimentation. It builds hope for a better future and it prompts you to attempt the unlikely behavior that you have been avoiding though it would build self-reliance.

The old saying goes "you are what you eat," but add the idea of spiritual food to this saying and it might read—"you are what you love." Rhodolite garnet teaches the right and healthy forms of love such that the conceptual part of the mind can comprehend.

Use rose quartz to teach you to open your heart. Giving can offer no reward to receiver or giver when gifts are given that contain no heartfelt love. Enlist the help of other gemstones like ruby and emerald to clear the heart of guilt, jealousy, envy, anger, lust, and other consuming emotions to learn the art of giving. Everyone has given a gift and had it rejected. Usually gifts are expressions of some kind. Rejection is unimportant as long as love fills the heart of the giver. Being detached when giving is its own reward. When no conditions are placed on the receiver, a gift is unconditional. To give unconditionally, you must be detached from the effect the gift will have on the receiver. Unconditional love opens the heart. Rhodolite teaches the heart to become detached while rose quartz teaches the heart to open and to give more love.

Together these two stones teach the joy of getting out of your own problems and finding another to share hope with. Does a family that has only one Christmas gift and two children of their own give that gift to a family that has no home? Amazing things happen when one who has little learns to trust the universe and the principle of abundance and gives that one gift as an expression of love. Not all of us can care that much about another person, even a child. You must love yourself first before the heart can have any love to give. Rhodolite gives the wearer a truer understanding of the benefits of love of self.

Giving is an art. Garnet in the deepest purple form showers us with the violet ray in a fountain that engenders an appreciation for art. Let garnet show you the benefits of the art of giving in life.

Life itself is like a canvas and garnet a teacher of art. Using it we learn to appreciate the art of living with an open heart.

Purple Rainbow Fluorite

Fluorite comes in a wide variety of colors. We are interested here in the purple-and-clear-banded variety. Use only purple fluorite that has no green, yellow, or blue areas. This variety could contain a range of light to dark purple with clear areas. The preferred type has bands of dark purple and clear with no inclusions. If cut in barrel shapes or long, thin cylinders, it should be visibly banded. The deeper the purple and the clearer the bands of clear, the higher the quality. The purple portion brings the violet-ray energy, and the clear portion brings in the full spectrum of colors. Do not use murky stones.

I highly recommended that only the AAA-quality stones be used. Rainbow fluorite is so powerful that a few of the AAA stones can be included in a necklace to make a necklace that will invite profound change.

Rainbow fluorite brings change at all levels. Soul loves change, but the mind, emotions, and physical body find it more difficult to love change. For this reason, you may wish to use this stone only when you are prepared for profound change and when you have the support of a spiritual guide who is familiar with the right use of energy. Work with the force of change, and it will provide great insight into the nature of reality. Change flows like a river. Fluorite brings change like a river remakes a landscape. It carries the lighter soils and nutrients along its course. It breaks down everything in its path. Though it may move around obstacles it will forcibly cut the easiest path. It seeks the lowest point and carries its load to the ocean eventually.

Rainbow fluorite works like a river to bring change to the subconscious mind. Learn to flow with it and discover the spiritual properties of water. Let it guide you and you will find out about the part of you that does not change. Most of our reality will change. Most of our identity will change. Eventually even our attitudes will change. Yet, some part of us is unchanging, so as this stone brings powerful change to a wearer, it also teaches the wearer about soul's ability to remain forever soul, and as soul we can know the aspects of ourselves and the universe that do not change.

Learning to include a regular diet of change teaches spiritual detachment. This benefit is especially noticeable when change is directed by purple rainbow fluorite and not by random forces. We are not speaking here of the kind of change that is like the day turning to night. We understand that everything changes in the natural course of life. We speak of the fact that purple rainbow fluorite brings significant change, the kind of change that completely alters a person as it improves one's discrimination, allowing one to wisely choose a better course. This change reveals the sculpture hidden in the stone, when all the inessential is chipped away. One's unique beauty is revealed.

The wearer of AAA-barrels of fluorite will learn to be sensible. You learn detachment from temporary roles like Savior, Mr. Fixit, or Superwoman. In the act of letting go of a part of her land that the river had determined to take downstream rather than sandbagging a flood and drowning in the momentary rush of high water, one woman learned that her huge investment in providing a home for her children was incomparable to the love she shared with them despite their loss. High-grade stones teach the wearer that patience is a virtue that must be practiced when times are good as well as when they are difficult.

The spherical form of rainbow fluorite will dig deeply into your psyche. No stone will be unturned when spheres of fluorite begin to plow your fields. You must be prepared to face the purple dragon. This dragon is going to eat every sacrifice and continue to come from its deep cavern and challenge all champions who have the nerve to save their maiden ideals. No permanent traits shall be damaged, but all deception shall be devastated by the dragon. This destruction could be confusing. You may be left bewildered as the inner mental landscape is forcibly altered. The good news is that only the sickness will be removed and you can find yourself whole and free from servility to thoughts that bind you to stifling limitations.

The mind holds on to foregone conclusions. It concludes that all of its ideas are forever useful in all circumstances, which of course they are not. The mind prefers to believe that judgment is important. It believes one behavior is better than another no matter the change in application. Good is better than bad. One way must be better than another. The mind wants to be right, to have made the right choice forever. When you choose to allow significant change, the mind's judgments come into question. Could you have been wrong about your decisions? This feeling may be uncomfortable, and you may need help with this new viewpoint. Soul loves change. The mind follows patterns. The mind can learn to cope with change, it must simply be taught how to find the good in the smallest things. How to give up all attachment to a set or routine way of doing things and practice graceful acceptance of change—that is a question that wearers of this stone will learn to answer for themselves.

Spheres of purple fluorite are so powerful that at first it is recommended they not be worn without the supervision of a professional or qualified guide. Necklaces of medium to large spheres of rainbow fluorite would be far too strong for most people and could accelerate problems to the point where they are unbearable in an attempt to get the mind to move on before it is ready. Barrels are less pushy and therefore will facilitate more gradual change. If changes are too fast, there will be little learning; only constant adjustment to change. Barrels and spheres of fluorite should be worn in combination necklaces with frosted clear quartz or lavender and amethyst. These stones will help one maintain balance and understand the changes initiated by rainbow fluorite. Rhodonite necklaces and other gemstone strands that can support the emotional body during the storms of change fluorite brings should be used alternately with fluorite. These could include any of the stones that support you in relaxing and finding comfort, like your primary color-ray stones or leopardskin jasper.

If you do not have these other gemstones, then work with a single barrel of rainbow fluorite. Its purple color will permeate every level if placed on the xiphoid access point. This point is just below the sternum, in the fleshy part of the abdomen, just below the connecting bone in the center of the chest that the ribs are joined to.

Rainbow fluorite is a powerful influence for change. Its presence in the aura will almost instantly begin to go to work on the areas in us that house cells whose activities are disharmonious, or cells that have become renegade and have energy blocks formed in or around them. These areas will be exposed to its wavelike vibrations and the violet ray will be carried into cell nuclei where it will slowly force structures within the cells to conform to blueprint standards or be encased in an egglike violet energy encasement until the body can challenge them one by one.

Our thoughts are largely responsible for the way we handle energies. If we have judgments about the energies that flow through us, these judgments will impede the natural flow of the energy. We may even create a flow of energies that blend very differently from the blend that would be beneficial to us according to our internal blueprint. Rainbow fluorite will actively force us to evaluate our structures, patterns of thinking, and actions as to their efficacy. We may have flows of energy that run counter to each other. These flows try to produce effects opposite from each other.

An example could be this: suppose we are highly motivated to be financially successful, for we believe that financial success is absolutely necessary to a good family life. We value family highly. We want to spend a lot of quality time with our children, especially in their formative years. We have difficulty taking any other job than as a businessman because our grandfather was a businessman, and we loved his example. We believe, as he did, that businessmen are successful only when they can defeat their competitors. We believe competitors are the enemies. Conversely, we believe that harming another human being is like setting ourselves up for some sort of karmic retribution, as explained by our favorite teacher in school. We also believe that money is the root of all evil, as taught by our favorite aunt. Our grandfather was a firm man who valued money for what it could do and spent all his time at work nearly seven days a week. All together, we are nearly incapacitated whenever a good opportunity for advancement at work comes up because we have these conflicting attitudes about money and what it does. Though we want to make more money, we believe that as we move up in position we will be responsible for someone else's ruin, and evil will befall us. We want more work, but we have to be home for supper by six to spend time with the kids. The forces playing on our mind create confusion and incapacitate us at times. We seem unable to make our life work.

It could be that we are completely unaware of this set of beliefs. All of them exist as attitudes in our subconscious as they combine with thought forms and direct our decision making. How then can we become aware of them and get them all straight so we can alter them enough to gain control of them and make our lives work better?

First, we must learn to set conditions on our beliefs. Purple rainbow fluorite will test our beliefs and modify them to apply only to certain appropriate circumstances. The net effect, which could be entirely unconscious, would be to free us to make all the money we want while setting out certain very specific moral standards that we will not compromise. We may simply change the inner belief from "money is the root of all evil" to "money is only a form of exchange, and some people will prefer money and the power it brings to human kindness and love, but I will not." We find time to enjoy our family by doing the best we can at work, but leaving work at the office when it is time to come home. Rainbow fluorite simplifies our thinking as it removes limitations. This sounds easy, but it could be quite challenging to avoid distress and anger, as fluorite undermines faulty thinking patterns and they begin to crumble. Creating change with this stone is not easy, but it is simple.

The clear form of this gemstone is used for its effects on light rays to make polarizing lenses. Clear fluorite only allows light that is heading in one direction to travel through it while light traveling in any other direction is clouded or diffused. Fluorite passes light rays in the direction its crystal matrix is aligned to and diffracts light coming from other directions. This property is a physical manifestation of its ability to redirect energy in the energetic flows within the human body. As we try to limit the flow of energy we feel unable to control, we become capable of shutting down any energies we think we should simply because we are unable to move them into expression in a way that is appropriate for us. We may be trying to hoard certain energies. We may be trying to manipulate the flow for wrongful purposes, causing stoppages. Fluorite breaks the dams and opens the flow.

Some of our thoughts may be buried under so much dammed-up emotional energy that we cannot express them, for to do so would throw us out of balance. These thought forms are usually stored in the subconscious. Here they continue to build up energy. They build potentially destructive energy like a volcano builds up hot magma and gasses, and can erupt whenever the energy built up becomes too great. We must generate and waste quite a bit of effort to keep these energy dams from breaking and to keep sudden releases of stuck energy from harming someone. Learning to release this pent-up energy in safe ways before it becomes stopped is important; once a person can learn to keep it flowing they can always have enough energy for whatever is needed in their life.

Thought forms that are kept underground form into attitudes that control our lives, though they are not directly recognized and expressed. Under the influence of unexpressed attitudes, you may find you are isolating yourself from life. It may be all you can do just to get up in the morning and drag yourself through the day. To keep from movement or change that might cause an eruption, you may have shut down the flow of purple ray so thoroughly that your life is threatened by disease. A wide variety of diseases are associated with a body that is shut down and allows little flow of energy. Chronic fatigue syndrome and insomnia are the simplest manifestations of low energy. Secondary conditions range from arthritis, to sensory organ deterioration, to major illness like breast cancer or leukemia.

Purple rainbow fluorite will work directly on the energy blockages that have formed underground in response to thoughts and feelings that drag us into the depths of despair as we try to figure out how to negotiate through them. Whatever thoughts and feelings have accumulated to form these blockages will begin to break apart. This procedure is not simple. Only those brave souls who are dedicated to knowing themselves should begin it.

Once the process of breakup begins, it is like breaking up a logjam in a rushing river. The logs get thrown around like toothpicks. The initial result may be turmoil. The river may seem to flow out of control. It may take time for the system to regain a balance. Dams may break.

You may go through a series of changes that at first might appear to be unrelated. Rituals and patterns may not work the same any more. You may no longer be able to hide certain weaknesses, and revealing weaknesses may make you feel particularly vulnerable. At times, you may feel like Jonah in the belly of the whale.

Let loose. It will help. It's just energy, so let it flow.

A thorough housecleaning requires that you move all the furniture. Then you have to clean under the rugs. Whatever you had swept under the rug will still be there. It may not be recognizable now, yet you can be sure it was you who swept it under there.

As we have learned, the purple ray prepares us for the coming of divine spirit into our lives. We may not be ready for its coming. It may arrive on the heels of a violent electrical storm. Do not despair. The storm will leave the air fresh and clean as it passes through. It will drive the old dead leaves away. It will make room for divine spirit. It will tear the dead limbs off the trees making it possible for new life to receive light and to sprout up from the ground.

Rainbow fluorite is like that storm. It is not spirit itself, but it brings the storm that prepares the way. Its lightning will ionize the air and enliven the roots or remove the deadwood. Its wind will blow with a rhythm that shakes any foundation that is not solid, such as those built on sand. The wind may tear off loose roofing, exposing the weak protection it had provided. Its rain will break the dams in the river that were placed well but have become outdated and now block the river and threaten to collapse into its raging torrents. We will feel the power of its might as a vortex of forces, forces that are nature itself.

It will be very difficult for those who resist. Let go of the dead leaves. Bend with the wind. Do not be like the tree with too many leaves. It will break. Only those who can let go of their foliage will keep from losing live branches. Let the river run wild for a time. Do not try to dam it again, otherwise you may find your dams burst all at once and the whole valley of your life flooded with the waters.

Let go of your limitations. Give up your resentments. They hurt no one but you. Express your feelings. Holding them in is what makes you stiff and inflexible, and if you become brittle then you can break. Root out your prejudices, and let your false beliefs and outdated assumptions roll down river like a logjam in a flood.

Do any of us really know who is the spiritual teacher? Is it someone we may meet? Is it the storm itself? Could it be the beggar or the whore? If we are to recognize spirit in our lives, we must open ourselves like little children. Spirit may appear like the gentle mother to nurture us, or it may come as the storm to break up our patterns of behavior that create the very habits that imprison us. It always seeks to break up the many limitations we have imposed on our lives.

This life-giving energy will carry us to the heights. These heights will not be the mountain of our accomplishments on which we will walk up to heaven, as the ancients who built the tower of Babel believed. They set stone upon stone, like accomplishments, to reach the heavens, but their tower was leveled by the forces of nature. Heaven is within. Find it in freedom. Find it in compassion. Find it in love, but don't expect to find it in prejudice or judgment.

Prepare for the storm as if it were coming to help you cleanse your relationship with spirit. Let it flow and help it remove the barriers, for once the barriers are down, then, like the sun's rays, the nurturing energies of spirit can enter in. After a good storm all is quiet. If you are indeed in an internal state of quiescence, you will hear the sound of the sounds within as they pass. Inner sounds are not always audible, but after a good storm of rainbow purple fluorite changes, one may be able to hear divine spirit as it passes in near silence.

Wear this stone with courage. Know it is acting in your best interest. It is a powerful tool, so allow it to do its work. It will begin by working on the blockages that are most fundamental to you. The very ground you walk on may not seem stable. Do not climb a tree or hide in a basement. Remember what you are doing, and let the earth quake. As the waves come in, let them move you.

Within the physical body, rainbow fluorite will promote evolution; that is, the physical body will learn to create the substances it needs to make it possible to evolve. Energies that have been borrowed by one organ system from another for the purpose of support and continued life will begin to be returned or rerouted. Each organ system will be prompted to regain its own source of energy.

Rainbow fluorite will remind us of the abundance of energy that is available. We will be shocked by the intensity and quantity that is present. As this abundance of raw energy continues to flow, we will be reminded of just how much there is. Our tendency to pull energy from one area to support another will soon be replaced by a tendency to reach out for new and greater sources.

This action will help us practice reaching out for the physical energy we need. As we learn this we may begin to teach others. By teaching others we will see what we do not know. We will learn to reach for the stars. We will soon be able to reach for higher, finer energies until we are accepting the highest energy.

If we are able to work through these first few storms, we will learn that there is no right or wrong way to do things. The only thing permanent is soul's experience, the lessons we learn are up to us. As we learn the lessons life teaches us, we find what we are looking for.

Some are not searching. These people should avoid this stone. For those who are, but do not know exactly what they are searching for, fluorite will show what is important. For those wearers who know what they really need, life lessons will focus on teaching them how to get their needs met by themselves. Making every mistake and learning something is vastly superior to doing everything "right" and never learning anything at all. We all make mistakes when we try new things.

That which we construct along the way will surely be brought down. We can learn to allow whatever we construct to float on down the river like a toy boat we give to another kid who needs it. Our hearts will be warmed by the memory of the giving and this memory cannot be lost. This warmth will never be washed away by the storms. All we let go of can be used by someone else who is in greater need. As we give, so we receive.

Try this exercise to resolve the unfinished attempts to reach for the light of discovery. Imagine that you have shelves and shelves of incompletes—lessons that have not been learned. These shelves are stored deep in the dusty basement of your subconscious.

Imagine many jars containing old experiences stacked on the shelves. Some experiences are moldy. Some of them are stored in formaldehyde and have shriveled up. Some of them are so dry and old, they would turn to dust if they were moved. Some are partly missing. Some are parts without a whole.

As you look at this array of useless relics, you determine to clean out the whole mess. You are aware this will take some doing, and you may not find it pleasant. You are also aware that this basement could be a source of disease and suffering if not cleaned.

Now imagine that you vow to remove everything that clutters your life right now. See the clouds of a storm on the horizon. Notice the deep purple color of the clouds. Watch them build up and move closer as you begin to bring all these jars and boxes of relics out of the basement. Picture the pile getting quite large as you stack up the many items. Stack them until all the shelves are clean of incompletes.

See the storm coming in layers of clouds now—deep purple clouds with clear spaces between them. As it comes closer, you notice the energy exchange between cloud layers is electrical like bolts of lightning.

Just as you come out with the last of the jars, you are aware that the storm is upon you. You dance like a child out in the yard in a summer rain. Suddenly, a huge bolt of lightning comes out of the sky and hits the pile. You duck, expecting a huge explosion, but to your awe and amazement, it simply vaporizes the pile before your eyes.

Celebrate. Feel the sense of relief in the knowledge that you have gotten all you can out of these experiences and that incompletes have been washed away by the rain. Know that it is time for fresh experiences in your life. Thank purple rainbow fluorite. The storm will come again as you are ready to go deeper, but for now you are clear—clear of all the debris of unfinished business and incomplete goals that were leading nowhere.

When the storm is gone, listen for the sound of divine spirit. It may be a faint tinkling, chirping, or whistling, and it may be a loud roar like a waterfall. This sound is the aftermath of healing and you can recreate healing anytime by recalling the sound of spirit as it appears after the storm. Rainbow fluorite is for spiritual warriors who will boldly go where their intuition leads them and are willing to let loose of their limitations and learn to live a life of freedom.

Sugilite (Luvulite)

Sugilite is a somewhat rare stone that ranges in color from deep, almost black, purple to a milky grape color. The most valuable and potent stones are a strong deep purple. The most potent varieties for therapeutic use have a near grape-jelly color and clarity. A source for necklaces or single spheres of this stone is not always easily located. Look for it, though. Even if the lesser varieties are all that you can afford, you would do well to have at least one sphere of sugilite.

Sugilite builds confidence. It is wonderful to work with and quite capable of developing your sensitivities to spiritual perceptions and insights on spiritual principals. By following these insights, you will certainly develop an entirely new set of priorities. You can be certain that wearing sugilite while setting clear priorities from which you set goals in life that truly suit your inner blueprints will bring you a deep sense of certainty in your actions.

The mission of sugilite is more oriented to Earth than to its inhabitants, but it is a valuable tool for the gemstone therapist. It helps open the third eye. In the process, it will ease tension in the area of the pineal gland. Its vibrations cause this gland to become more productive. It also acts to encourage the pineal and pituitary glands to regulate themselves to produce only the chemicals needed by a person to maintain harmony within the physical body.

This stone can be used for physical healing. Sugilite's action is very different from that of sodalite, although the net effect is similar in their action to clear harmful energy. Meridians are lines of flow of the superphysical energies over the skin that follow nerve pathways within the tissue of the

Red Stones

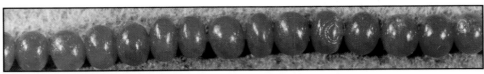

Ruby

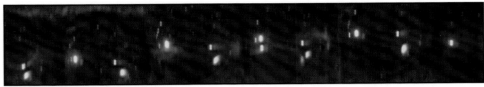

Garnet (Rhodolite)

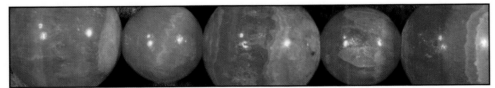

Rhodonite

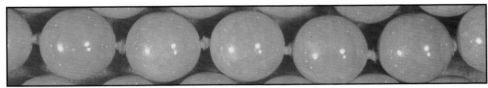

Rhodocrosite

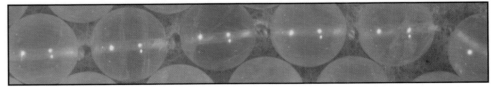

Rose Quartz

Rubellite (Pink Tourmaline)

Blue Stones

Sapphire

Aquamarine

Lapis Lazuli

Blue Lace Agate

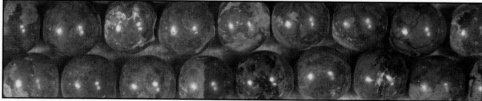
Azurite

Indicolite (Blue Tourmaline) with Biwa Pearls and Blue Lace Agate

Green Stones

Emerald

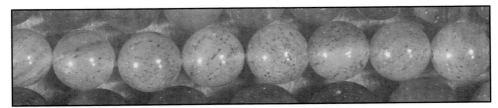

Aventurine

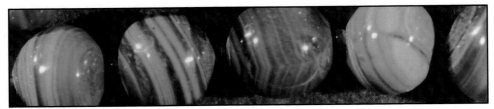

Chrysoprase

Malachite

Green Tourmaline

Orange Stones

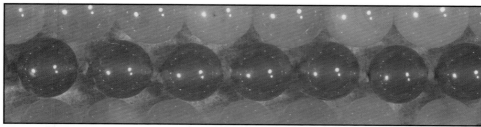

Carnelian

Orange Calcite

Violet Stones

Amethyst

Lavender Amethyst

Yellow Stones

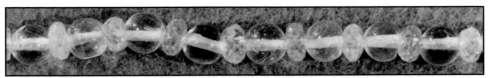

Citrine with Yellow Sapphire (Corundum)

Citrine

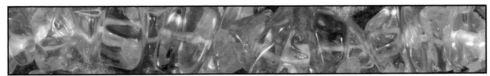

Citrine Chips

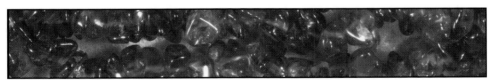

Amber

Yellow Beryl

Indigo Stones

Iolite

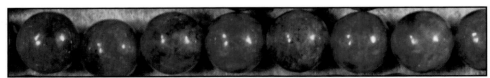

Sodalite

White Stones

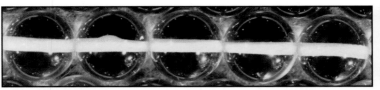

Clear Quartz

Diamond

White Onyx

Planetary Stones

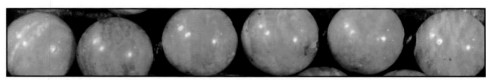

Amazonite

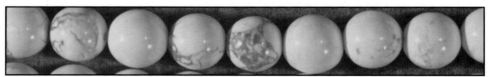

Howlite

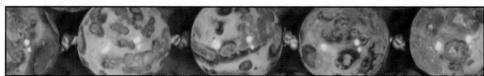

Leopardskin Jasper

Poppy Jasper

Planetary Stones

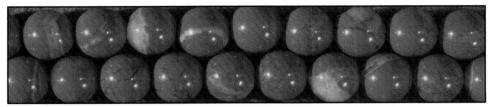

Red Jasper

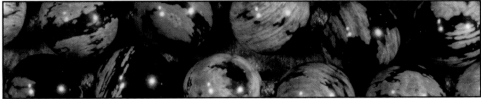

Obsidian (Snowflake Obsidian)

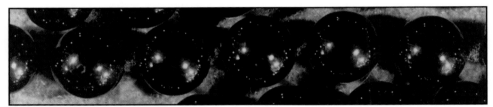

Black Onyx

Riverstone

Tiger Eye

Lunar Insight Stones

White Moonstone

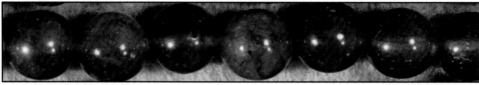

Spectrolite (Luminite)

Treasures of the Deep

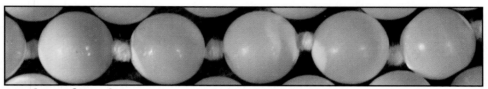

Mother of Pearl

Pearl (Natural)

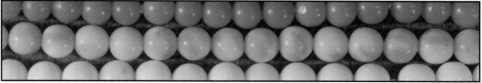

Red Coral, Pink Coral, and White Coral

body. Sugilite will absorb and diminish aberrations in the superphysical energy, especially along a meridian. Although these energies are not visible, and some sciences still discount their existence and significance, they are in fact real.

These energies have much to do with the relative health of the human body. They seem to be visible to some animals who instantly sense whether or not another creature is hostile or dangerous, healthy or disturbed. Plants seem to register changes in the flow of a human's superphysical energies, as shown by numerous experiments. Many humans can "see" these energies all the time. They appear as fine lines of white energy over the surface of the body or a glow over the whole body.

The effect of these energies on the relative health of the human form is of the most interest here. Cultures throughout history have reported that the aura extends out from an inch or so to several feet from the body. Seers from all areas of the world have reported being able to see the different colors of this energy. Those who have this ability are aware that the aura is strong only in strong people. Weakened individuals have a very weak aura. The aura is a glow of energy that extends into the emotional level. When healthy, it is bright and dense with color-ray energies. Sugilite works on the lines of energy just above the body and focuses on these lines. The outer aura is affected as a byproduct of this work.

The aura is affected by our thoughts and particularly by our strong emotions. The aura also is affected by others' thought forms, particularly if the person is unprotected and unfamiliar with how to protect themselves. Voodoo, hypnotism, and other crafts have sought to learn the secrets of controlling these forces. These practices, when directed at a believer, are known to be powerful enough to create a wide range of effects, even death. Sugilite teaches us to protect our auras from puncture or attack of all kinds from those who think badly of us. Thoughts can be like daggers. You must learn to make the aura like an impermeable barrier whenever it is challenged or attacked. The part of the aura closest to the physical body skin registers punishment, trauma, angry attacks, psychic attacks, severe pain, abuse, and memories of the effects of these aberrations.

When the superphysical lines of energy are strong and clear of aberrations, the physical body will radiate a power or emit a "visible" healthy vibration. It is widely recognized that some actors and politicians have an almost magnetic quality. This quality could be ascribed to their aura. These people have very strong auras of a nature that is attractive to everyone, even though we might not know why we are attracted. A powerful aura is charismatic in its attraction. Many leaders of all kinds have had this undefinable yet characteristic magnetism.

The saints and savants of the world have been widely known to have such profoundly powerful auras that people could be healed of afflictions simply by coming into contact with, touching, or being touched by them. The nature of the aura may also be the explanation for why some men get so much attention for their sexuality and why some women find themselves the object over which wars are fought. It is safe to say that the health of the aura is extremely important to physical healing through the hands. Healing with hands is the transference of auric energy into another's aura to bolster its lack of color-ray energies for long enough to allow the person to become aware of the energy deficiency and begin routing it into the aura on their own.

Let us assume also that when the aura is weak or suffering from abuse, we attract negative experiences and people who are not good for us. Black holes can form in a weak aura. The colors in a weak aura are dark, dim, and sadly disproportionate. The black holes will correspond to areas where the person is experiencing disease or discomfort.

Sugilite is extremely effective in repairing a damaged aura and in building a healthy aura into a superhealthy energy powerhouse. While rebuilding the aura, the wearer is encouraged to stay clear of the influence of those who use people against their will or influence them for evil purposes, especially those who suck energy from those they victimize and control. Sugilite will rebuild an aura in a matter of a few weeks if all influences that had been distressing the individual have been stopped. If you are internally damaged or under constant attack from outside forces you must look for protection to emerald, aventurine, citrine, amazonite, other personal gemstones, or psychic help and protection to stop the destruction and reverse the damage, before and while rebuilding the aura.

Areas of no color can gradually be restored to active, bright, colorful energies. Sugilite spheres of six- to twenty-millimeters moved over the body at a distance of one to three inches from the skin can improve this condition. It may take repeated treatments, in some cases followed by placements of spheres for days at a time to accomplish this.

Hold a single sphere over the area that is weak, giving the body a chance to react to it, then use sugilite to draw an imaginary eighteen-inch circle over the area. Slowly close the circle to a smaller and smaller diameter as you move closer to the body. Now reverse the spiral, moving out from a point and away while outlining an ever larger circle in the opposite direction. Once this pattern is complete, start again, only begin by circling in the opposite direction and complete the whole pattern in reverse. Work on each point where weakness is noticed. Repeat this pattern wherever you notice a weak or black area in the aura. Wearing a strand throughout the day that contains twelve six-millimeter sugilite beads in combination with twelve of the same size amethyst beads, interspersed with twenty-four lavender beads will support the treatments and extend their effectiveness.

It may take considerable practice at first to locate weak areas in the aura. They are not necessarily just above the place where discomfort is being experienced. They are in the aura at locations where the aura is being drained to supply energy to bodily areas that are suffering. Sugilite can teach the hand how to locate the area. To become proficient in this method, you must completely suspend any disbelief. Clear the mind of all thoughts about your inexperience and any questions about the merit or usefulness of auric repair. Then move your hand over every part of the body at a distance of about two inches. Circle the entire body in random fashion. As the hand moves, imagine it is roaming across an energy buffer. Notice if the hand seems to "fall in" toward the body in certain areas. This falling could be accompanied by a tingling or coolness (lack of warmth) as it passes over the suspect area. You will have to pay attention to your sense of gravity, temperature, magnetism, and electrical energy to sense weak spots or detect empathic surface energy drains in the aura of your hand, and subtle emotional shifts in relationship to the person you are testing.

For serious cases, alternating use of different of the primary color-ray–bearing gemstones can be used to help build up the aura. Use all eight primary color-ray stones to build an aura that has been identified deficient to such an extent it has a major drop in life energy or where life-threatening organ failure is possible. Use them one stone at a time. The quality of these stones should be of the highest available so that the person being treated will not experience further disruptions of the aura. Simply "scrub" the aura with motions similar to those you would use if you were polishing a surface that extended out to a distance of two inches from the body. Ignore the fact that this energy field is not clearly visible.

This therapy is hard to perform on yourself. It works best if a therapist can perform the actions. A person receiving this treatment must be completely relaxed and focused on accepting inner guidance to combat the auric condition after the support has been removed. Sugilite draws in an emergency color-ray energy fill to the area by attracting color rays, especially the violet ray, to the area and absorbing the negative, noncolor-ray energies that may be disrupting the flow, but once the sugilite is removed the area must receive clear inner instructions to heal, followed by a repeated mental silent statement of the lessons learned by the condition. The therapy works even better if the therapist wears a necklace of the same primary color-ray stones as the person she is working with.

Both therapist and recipient should concentrate on the purpose of this exercise. They should remain comfortable and focus on the effort at hand, because sugilite also creates mental healing images and energizes them for assimilation by the body. Few people have even guessed at the ability of the body to alter its makeup. Sugilite taps into the body's abilities by using the focus the therapist holds as a model for change. If the therapist and recipient are in scattered mental states, they will hardly get any physical results, though the aura will be much improved. If they both hold a clear impression of the desired effect, this information will be fused into the restored spectral pattern of the body system. Color-ray energy is dynamic not static. Its fluctuations in color combinations and intensity are often patterned responses. This pattern is referred to here as a spectral pattern, a term borrowed from an understanding of the static "picture" of matter in atomic spectography. Color-ray spectral patterns are dynamic and changing in response to thoughts and emotions.

The human body is capable of treating itself. Sugilite teaches the cells about the spiritual goals of the individual to the extent the person can realize these goals. To this extent, the body will restructure itself, but it must have a clear model. Creation of this model may be difficult for those who are not adept at this practice or who have no sugilite to teach them. The mind holds the memory of reactions to circumstances in life that you are dealing with, and color-ray energy fluctuations are repeated unconsciously unless the mind is taught to slow these reactions down and alter them to a healthy model.

To begin creating a healthy model, try practicing the art of drawing healing energies to your body while you are undergoing these treatments. The colors white (for whole-body clearing), deep orange (for physical distress), violet (for etheric-body health), indigo (for subconscious restructuring), green (for physical-body harmony), red (to repair damage of the emotional sheath), and blue (for mental disorders that may be at the root of any problem) can be visualized as balls of bright light energy. In your imagination, place the ball of energy appropriate for your condition over the area. You may also bathe the entire body in this healing energy. If you are not certain which color to use as a ball of energy, then use each color one at a time until you are certain a change has taken place. You may not feel anything, but rest assured you will be causing a remodeling of the habits your bodies use in spectral-pattern responses.

With the help of sugilite, we can attract healing energies while directing them to the body and learn to focus them as we learn to clear deformities in the aura. A ball of energy can be held in the body by focusing on a target area and clearly picturing the color entering the area and glowing within for several minutes. Repeat this exercise as often as necessary or until the area appears to have regained its strong aura. Cycle the energy in and out in time with the breath.

A clear focus of intent on and commitment to completing the lessons these conditions are meant to teach us is critical. We can release these conditions and expect never to see them back only when we no longer need the experiences they bring. If the lessons are not learned, the condition, or another like it, will return. The lessons teach you how to use energies efficaciously only when you understand the laws of the universe as they apply to energy and matter. You must learn how color-ray energies are affected by the mental attitudes you display as you approach a challenge or by inner evaluations you habitually think after a challenge has been met. Sugilite teaches flexibility in attitude to a wearer who is committed to finding approaches to life that inspire creative use of talent to overcome apparent obstacles. It shows how to evaluate your efforts in a more positive light.

As an example of learning a lesson, suppose your best friend has spent his entire adult life trying to find an appropriate mate to settle down with and start a family. Each time he meets someone who he might like to talk to, his mind tells him that this person is not right for him or not good enough for him for a list of reasons he can see in his mind. As he is about to lean over and say something to a prospective date, he silently reveals his attitude about her with subtle body language that suggests he has already judged this person as less than totally acceptable. He manages to get a date with the woman, but his date turns out badly as the inner message about his list of negative judgments has been received by the woman's subconscious mind, and she will eventually turn from him during the evening. Your friend is convinced that he has judged women he meets correctly because his dates all seem to turn away from his overtures just as he is beginning to hope they might like him. This repeated pattern causes him to adopt an attitude that all women are hard to please, and he evaluates the situation as hopeless. This attitude and evaluation cause him to doubt his masculinity as he can't help but notice his friends are finding happiness in lasting relationships and he is not.

Eventually, his male sex drive wanes and later he develops prostate cancer. For him to overcome the cancer he seeks treatment but to be successful in recovery he must learn the cause of the pattern has been his thinking pattern. He must see that the cancer has come to him as a way of learning about life and as a result of his use of color-ray energy. He must change his attitude and his evaluation of others and himself, to find love, by somehow overcoming judgment and actually learning. Once he learns, he is truly ready to fully recover and the healing comes.

Sugilite attracts the energy needed for healing. The following visualization will help a great deal between treatments with sugilite.

Lie down on your back. Lay your arms and legs flat without crossing the hands or legs. Visualize an energy vortex. It is shaped like a tornado, only wider, like a funnel, and is only a few feet tall. It is situated over the third chakra (located one to three inches above the navel). It is spinning slowly in a clockwise direction. Within its motion are the colors of the rainbow. See the colors coming from this vortex and entering the third chakra and clearing all blockages in the aura. You need not be able to actually see the vortex. Just let the mind accept that, although not visible, this force is working on the third chakra. Simply alter the direction of energy flow in a regular cycle—out for clearing, in for infusing of color-ray energy as needed. Now, picture a large clear sugilite sphere of grape-jelly color hovering over the energy vortex. Let it impart its vibrations to the chakra through the vortex. Now watch as it moves to a position over the heart to impart a teaching to this chakra. Finally as it moves over the forehead, it excites a new mental pattern response to life that will change all relationships to the most fundamentally bothersome issue one has consistently faced in some aspect of one's life. Let the new pattern develop and repeat once or twice as the sugilite slowly disappears from above the swirling energy and one returns safely back to the room and opens the eyes.

You may not be aware of the long-term effects of treatments for some time, but it is important to do the internal work while changing your emotional and mental attitudes. Without the internal component, your physical treatments will hardly be effective. Both the inner unseen energy and the outer visible, and supraphysical energies must be aligned and rejuvenated.

Developing a connection between body and mind is an important part of sugilite's mission in relationship to humans. This tool is very useful for meditation as a way to learn focus. Sugilite helps us focus our own energies and those of the universe, which we can marshal for the good of the whole. It is up to us to focus our energies. Sugilite will help by showing us how and clearing misconceptions.

Violet-ray energy is carried by the unique vibration of sugilite to the deepest part of your mind where the mind can learn to completely reshape the body and the circumstances of your life. Trust the process and clearly visualize the mission you hold dearest in life and sugilite will supply new spectral patterns of color-ray energy to implement changes that will affect your entire future. Violet is the color of mastery and the color of kings and queens. A king is sovereign, yet he is servant of the best interests of all. Take the challenge and become like the king or queen of your inner domain, for you are on the throne of your own inner sanctum.

People whose primary color ray is yellow are always busy. Their path leads to centers of activity where energy is commonly used. Such centers of activity may be physical places where a lot is happening and stimulation is constant, or they can be inner places where personal energy responds to a heightened awareness and a strong flow of yellow-ray energy. Primary yellow-ray people thrive on adventure and bursts of meaningful effort. They make plans and look to the future for their solutions. They are unusually capable at seeing the potential of situations and will make good consultants. They can be trusted as a rule and lend credibility to whomever they befriend. They can make good leaders. They usually do best in circumstances where communication holds the greatest potential for growth. Yellow-ray people can loose sight of the effects of their decisions on the current production, but will usually have the long-term best interest at heart of any group they are a part of. Their path may include roles as ambassador or traveling salesman, yet they could enjoy working on a fishing boat as well. Adventure is a strong appeal.

The yellow-ray energy has more to offer us as individuals than the other rays because it is so much more rare—rare in the sense of being elusive, hard to sustain, and difficult to work with in any quantity (mostly because the good

8
Yellow Ray Stones

feelings that result are too good), and because it is the least abundant in our planetary aura. Our planet carries its own signature of color rays, as do the people of Earth as a whole, and as do all individuals. The planet and all its inhabitants work least with the yellow ray because we have gotten used to having less of it available, which means less is taken in, and less is expressed or given out by us.

Citrine is the primary carrier of the yellow ray. Though it is relatively mild and gentle, it carries sufficient yellow-ray strength to encourage the body to raise its proportion of this color ray to higher levels if we are not up to our potential. Though people of Earth who are primarily of the yellow ray are fewer in number than those of any other color, their role in the planetary balance of the color rays is very important because they must help the rest of us become more capable at working with this ray.

The yellow ray has a marvelous effect on all the bodies. It raises the vibrations. Whenever major inner change is undertaken, a vibratory change results. The yellow ray facilitates this change. It eases the various parts of the human being into a new vibrational pattern. Not all parts of the body are at the same vibratory rate and the rate varies depending on behavior and emotions. Yellow-ray energy raises the vibration of parts with lower vibrations so they become in tune with those that are high, as well as raising the vibrations of the whole body.

The physical body is a conglomerate of billions of atoms. Each atom has a particular vibrational signature. The vibrational signature has components of rhythm and cadence combined with various frequencies of its component neutrons, electrons, and protons. It is as if each atom carries a melody. Groups of atoms together form molecules. Each molecule, as a set of atoms, forms a melody with rhythm, counterpoint, and harmony. The yellow ray works directly with these melodies.

Molecules may be formed from atoms that resonate together in harmony or clash in disharmony. Disharmonious molecules are unstable. Harmonious molecules are stable and maintain their structure during changes.

Unstable ones diminish in connectivity and easily lose their internal bonds. The disharmonious molecules give off noncolor-ray energy and attract this energy in greater proportion than do other molecules. The physical body attracts and uses atoms to build cells in the various organs, which in turn resonate with the organ and system counterparts in the astral and mental bodies. The yellow ray teaches the body how this process works and how well the resulting physical structure will function.

Think of each inner organ and structure counterpart as being held together by a set of colors that form a working model for that system. The composite energy of these groupings is structured around blueprints. How clearly these blueprints are followed in creating your bodies is totally dependent on the mind that could be directed by soul if you have learned this ability. The mind produces mental pictures from which the physical body evolves, and from the vibrations produced by the body, you attract experiences. Your mind, if you are a typical resident of this planet, is a tool that runs like a computer that has gotten some viruses. It functions, yet it is practically incapable of controlling its evolution or its environment as it was designed to do. All your physical problems may not be traceable to mental pattern aberrations, but most of them are. Mental patterns are formed from color-ray energy and should be fluid. These patterns can become stuck.

With so much concentration on survival in a world that appears to be fraught with danger and hardship, flexibility is often sacrificed. The fluidity of thought becomes solidified. Our actions are not flowing freely in response to circumstances. Instead, we are caught up in reactions to events long past or to events that have yet to happen, if they ever do at all. Consider this statement not as an admonishment or a judgment of incompetency, but rather as a vision of hope.

Hope lies in the realization of our potential to gain access to the operating codes and the "programming" laws of our mental computer. In reality, these are spiritual laws that do not change. The blueprints with which our physical body and other sheaths were created are not aberrant. Our minds have gotten off track and are interpreting the blueprints with some quirks and odd changes. False ideas of the nature of reality distort our patterns of thought. We receive all sorts of conflicting data. Receiving information on the inner realities is rare for most people and often incorrectly interpreted or partially so. The yellow ray opens the inner hearing to information on the inner planes. You must go through a cleansing process for a time as you are introduced to higher concentrations of this delightful color ray, but the result of having a clear receptivity to inner communications is greater effectiveness in life and the ability to work from a model with greater success.

What does this have to do with the yellow ray? When you work with the yellow ray, its vibrations begin to uplift the patterns of the mind. Most of our distorted mental patterns are formed from misread blueprints whose color ray spectrum are deficient in the yellow ray. Consequently, the lives we construct for ourselves are without as much warmth, joy, happiness, community spirit, growth, and creativity as they could be. We may completely lose our love of life if the yellow ray is too scarce.

Once the yellow ray is concentrated in the mental body, it begins to fill the body, balancing color-ray proportions, replacing noncolor-ray energies where they are overabundant and rebuilding missing blocks in their mental color patterns. The overall effect of this vibrational shift is to bring the various bodies into closer alignment with the overall system blueprints (you may recall we have blueprints for cells, organs, systems, and the overall system). Other color-balance discrepancies will be rectified in the presence of an abundance of yellow-ray energy to bring the color-ray energies in balance with our optimum percentages. Some of the disharmonious atoms and the noncolor-ray energies they emit then are rejected and removed, to be replaced by atoms that are more harmonious.

All atoms must, by definition, contain some noncolor-ray energies. These energies are necessary to all physical manifestation. Atoms become disharmonious when the type is wrong, the quantity is too great, or the proportion of noncolor-ray energy they contain is high. All color-ray energy is beneficial, and some noncolor-ray energies are necessary to create the physical body, but many of them simply attract too much adverse experience. We need some negative experiences for our spiritual development, but at a point we must learn to circumvent most adverse episodes to develop spiritually and bring joy to the present.

The overall system blueprints are maintained by the subconscious mind at the highest level of being. There are blueprints for each body. Blueprints show the exact color-ray balance needed to correct all imbalances in every part of every body. Which type and how much of the noncolor-ray energies the bodies contain is controlled by the subconscious mind. We must go through the process of realigning the smallest atoms in the physical body to the blueprints for the physical body, in order to end up with only a minimum of noncolor-ray energies. We must complete this alignment and reconstruction process before we can access the prints for the next finer sheath.

You work through the bodies one at a time. You must realign and reprogram each construct, each system, in each body before you can be truly free of a damaging overabundance of noncolor-ray energy. Freedom is granted to those who prove their mastery of these forces within their own bodily universe. The grant has already been given; it is up to us to figure out how to use it to gain total freedom of choice.

The mastery of these bodies and their construction requires a complete knowledge of the laws and principles that govern this inner universe. Many spiritual masters, savants, and gurus have referred to this process of becoming a master. To make the physical body like a temple is a metaphor for spiritual mastery. All external aspects of life may go along as they did before, but our inner experience becomes harmonious and we can begin to perform "miracles" of healing and inner control. These are not in fact miracles but natural abilities, which become easy once we are fully in harmony within ourselves and with all life. The yellow-ray energy brings you in touch with the inner laws.

The yellow-ray energy can teach you how to hear and see beings in your light bodies who may come among us here on Earth. It will also teach the willing recipient how to contact beings from other galaxies if you are willing to follow intuitive leaps. Be cautious of accepting information from discarnate beings—they may be inclined to mischief and do not always have correct information. Only those who specifically ask to be shown these inner channels of communication and are spiritually ready for this opening will receive this information.

This inner universe is tremendously complex but is based on simple principles. To learn these principles, you must practice the internal redistribution, realignment, and external giving out of greater amounts of color-ray energies. You would likely be better off if you simply practiced the use of color-ray energies within your own bodies, since mastery of this realm will afford access to the higher realms. From within the realm of the subconscious mind, you can learn to completely redesign all aspects of the inner world to the highest blueprints given at the time of its creation.

Raising vibrations and eliminating noncolor-ray energies is a process of cleansing. Yellow is the predominant color of the systems that eliminate the dross. A focus on cleansing and regulation of bodily functions to do with the elimination of waste and waste byproducts is controlled by the yellow-ray systems. Spiritual surrender also is facilitated by the yellow ray. Letting go of false mental concepts is not easy, but once the yellow ray has infused the mental patterns, the old way of being will never work the same again. The yellow ray teaches detachment from old ways.

Why the yellow ray? Who wants to learn about giving up things they like or surrendering false mental concepts? The answer is simple. If you are happy with what you have, then don't change a thing. If your life doesn't suit you, then chances are it's time for the yellow ray. Once the yellow ray begins to uplift your vibrations, you will never want the old life back. Like an efficiency expert, a yellow-ray sphere will adjust or replace every piece of a system until that system is running smoothly and optimally.

Citrine

Citrine comes in many colors, but therapeutic citrine is pure yellow. High-grade material can range in color from light yellow to an amber yellow. The use of citrine chips is good for infusing the aura with the yellow ray. Spheres of citrine work well for deeper cleansing and to open the inner sheaths to the light of the yellow ray. Choose a lighter or darker variety to suit the individual person. Determine which variety is best by using muscle testing, or simply watch the aura light up when the correct color has been applied. Do not use dyed citrine. Avoid chips that have inclusions of other materials. Heat-treated material is less effective but not harmful.

The primary function of citrine when worn around the neck is to gently assure the physical body that it is good to accept the yellow ray and to draw appropriate amounts of the yellow ray into the body. This action has a profound effect on the overall consciousness of the individual. The yellow ray brings in joy, self-assuredness, abundance, and a connection with those who are on a higher vibration. Citrine is able to contact areas of disharmony and cells that have adopted a disharmonious vibration. It is able to "see" the entire body's condition, and therefore will initiate change or provide concentrations of the yellow ray to areas of the body only gradually as assimilation progresses safely. Through this action, the body will become aware of these areas of disharmony and will begin to integrate the yellow ray into these areas and change their vibration.

Citrine introduces the body to its powerful vibrations by the gentle action of a wavelike motion, which begins to soothe and ease stress immediately. This introduction to the yellow ray helps you become lighter and more flexible. Muscles relax with its influence. It aids circulation and digestion. It promotes the flow of body fluids to areas that may be constricted.

Citrine is perfect for someone who has trouble with tight muscles, slow digestion, cramps, and back pain.

Stress is a major contributor to muscle constriction. Muscle constriction is not directly controlled by the yellow ray, but the yellow ray acts to relax muscles by providing an environment of abundant joy. With a change in vibration, the muscles have a chance to return to their natural flexibility. As the mind and emotions are eased to a higher level, the body is given a chance to return to a state of ease. We must learn to relax the tight grip we have on our lives, which stalls our personal power to transform our inner world.

Moving the consciousness through a major resistance reduces the stress of anticipation. Citrine allows the wearer to pass through resistance to change. You are given a clear vision of a condition where stress is behind you on the timeline and you can look back and see its effects. You are not necessarily aware of tension in your body until it is gone. Many suffer from great stress to the point where the body is tight, the muscles are hard, and the bones are rigid. Once stress becomes chronic and is continuously worsening, it feels normal to the sufferer.

Citrine carries the yellow ray into every cell. As it builds the yellow energy within the cell, noncolor-ray energies that have been carried there are released. They are squeezed out slowly. Atoms with high noncolor-ray content are discharged and replaced by those with a lower proportion of these energies.

Noncolor-ray energies are detrimental if areas of concentration exist. If allowed to remain for long periods of time, they set up patterns of tension that force the body to retain much unwanted or unneeded fat, water, salt, toxins, inorganic minerals, and more. Bodies lose their natural ability to monitor the level of retention. Messages of lack abound. Cells cry out, "More water!" More water is retained. The situation worsens after years of the presence of large quantities of noncolor-ray energy. The energy "solidifies" in the sense that it is infused into atoms that are taken in and attracts atoms with greater concentrations. It can affect the content of the water, making the water hold more of the detrimental positive ions and creating a stagnant water condition. Water won't flow as easily. Cells like white blood cells and red blood cells begin to unnaturally clump together. The blood flow and the flow of immune system cells through blood and lymph is restricted. All this is due to the stress of a lack of yellow-ray energy.

Several psychics have reported an instantaneous change in the health of the body and a clearing of swamplike conditions of waste retention in the presence of citrine. In the presence of a necklace of citrine spheres, the body immediately begins to identify noncolor-ray energies and eliminate them. The parts of the body that had ceased to communicate begin to interact. A network of support is created. A gradual clearing of extraneous fats and stagnant water results. This process is slow but profound and may lead to weight loss as an additional benefit. Aerobic physical exercise can expedite this clearing process and help build muscle that perpetuates a lean body.

A similar process is initiated in the other inner bodies. Old emotions that have noncolor-ray energies stuck to them, matting the fine fibers of the emotional sheath, are released. Thereby the emotional sheath undergoes a thorough cleansing of its fibers and you become resensitized to life, feelings of joy, youthfulness, expansiveness, and the emotions of vitality.

Thoughts of frustration, failure, deficiency, inadequacy, doom, moral corruption, ineptitude, disease, and destitution all carry noncolor-ray energies. These thoughts clog the mind. The mental sheath develops black holes through which one becomes bombarded with the negative thoughts of others. This condition results in chronic victim consciousness. As the yellow ray moves through the sheaths, it begins to eliminate noncolor-ray debris. The mind can learn to clear itself of destructive thoughts. Citrine will initiate repair of breaches and holes.

If your intention is to integrate difficult to accept parts of yourself, citrine will help open your mind and emotions to accept these aspects. It gently works with the subconscious to develop a stable emotional center that helps us remain in balance mentally and emotionally during transitions. This center helps bring clarity during times of stress or conflict. This action would be of great benefit to those who often reach emotional extremes in their reactions to conflict or the threat of conflict. Citrine will ease feelings of despair and help you adopt a happy and joyous outlook. The yellow ray seems to part the dark clouds of emotion, allowing you to see the sky above. Like rays of golden sunshine on a wintry day, it will warm us with hope and contentment. You will be inspired to let go of negative emotions.

The feeling of release is fulfilling, similar to the feeling the Jews must have had as the Red Sea parted and they were able to make their way to freedom from their slavelike status in Egypt. Nothing is so limiting as our own beliefs and feelings of lack. Today most are not actual slaves, but many are locked into victim consciousness that broods despair and depression. The one thing that no one can change but you is your attitude toward life. Even some prisoners of war held in Nazi concentration camps have been known to be able to maintain an unconquerable attitude of dignity and strength in the face of human atrocities.

Citrine acts as a refractive device focusing a portion of the life force into the subtle sheaths of the human being. This action creates a truer alignment of these bodies. Bodies function more easily when in alignment with each other. The person who was badly out of alignment can stop having the anxiety and lost feeling that comes from being grossly misaligned. Citrine helps you recognize and register the interplay between these bodies. Its wavelike motion pulses the yin and yang energies. When it is worn for an extended time, this action brings an uplifting feeling that creates a mood of relaxed inspiration. The wearer may learn to hold a position of flexibility, being neither afraid of nor desperate to change his condition or circumstances. Simply serene are the wearers of citrine.

As with a bird, when you are lifted and propelled forward into a more active approach to life, you must remain flexible enough to move with the currents of life. We must learn to spread our wings and allow them to bend gracefully so we may be lifted easily and gently.

If we allow it, the awareness brought by exposure to the yellow ray will break up rigidity. Like the sun brings life to the earth, citrine will brighten even the darkest corners of our inner world. It will connect the individual to aspects of the whole that have been elusive or unknown.

Worn around the neck, spherical beads of citrine help loosen the spine. Relaxing the muscles throughout the body helps you allow and adopt the naturally correct posture of the body. Good posture is relaxed and easy. It brings a sense of well-being to the body to stand erect with the head held comfortably on the neck. Good posture sends out a nonverbal message of confidence and inner strength.

Placing a strand of spheres on the crown chakra (located a couple inches back from the center of the top of the head where the soft spot is on the heads of babies) helps to align the entire spine and all structures of the body. The alignment process progresses from the top down to the feet and takes five to ten minutes. This process will promote an awareness of the power of the body when a wearer becomes infused with yellow ray and all areas are physically in alignment. The process will continue until all the atoms of the body are working in structural harmony. If you regularly practice the exercise of mentally postulating a body with highly in-tune bodily functions and a balanced structural integrity while keeping the strand on the crown chakra, the results will soon be evident.

The ambassador of citrine is a very caring soul who is very direct. If you wear citrine, you may be able to receive some very specific information about how you direct your energies and how you might change your energy flow to be more effective.

This information may be very blunt. It may also come to you in a silent way. Seeping into the consciousness like fog, without a sound, it may gradually reveal itself as hints come from any number of directions in your life. Look for guidance and citrine will assist you if you listen.

Citrine will open the inner hearing. It facilitates a development of the capacity to hear the words of life itself. Some refer to this communication as coming from universal mind, some nature, and others' spirit or the Holy Spirit. It comes in a variety of ways. In whatever way it comes, citrine teaches you to hear the voice of life itself. If you remain open, you will be reminded of a time when soul was in touch with the creator.

Soul is able to read the signs of the greater cycles of life. Let citrine assist soul in teaching the mind the importance of paying attention to these signs. Let soul take charge of your inner world, and the living truth will become audible. Citrine teaches the language. It opens lines of communication via the law of harmonics. This law indicates that any two beings who become tuned to the same vibration will form an inner line of communication that lasts as long as they share that attunement.

The yellow ray connects us with the inner vibration of whatever we put our attention on. Use citrine in your contemplations to help you connect with the inner nature of things. Wearing it also gives you access to parts of yourself that you normally ignore that may have another point of view from which to view inner vibrations. Inner senses may be opened to inner realities. Placing stones in the aura in the area of the astral "ears" for instance will heighten the awareness of hearing on the astral level. Working with a particular sense like hearing over a long term will open the higher bodies' hearing as well. This process takes time, but is most rewarding when you can selectively hear the thoughts of others and decide if you will let them in instead of having no awareness of such influences.

Citrine continues to bring joy at all times and teaches you to experience joy even during times of sorrow, especially when held in the aura above the heart. Life can have more levels than we usually allow for. One who believes life is simple, boring, and predictable will be greatly benefited by allowing the yellow-ray energy to infuse the heart. Life and the richness of it fills the space in a heart that has plenty of room. One who has little room in the heart finds life a somber, claustrophobic experience. As joy fills the heart, the yellow ray opens the room. It is like opening the blinds to the warm rays of the sun.

A physical room is solid and the dimensions unchangeable, but the heart can expand and contract a great deal. Wear citrine and take time to practice opening up the dimensions of the energy the heart senses. Work the golden yellow-ray energy into a large ball and place it in the heart. Let the ball expand to encompass all your loved ones and the life and times past, present, and future of your existence. Let the sounds of celebration fill this cavernous space. Let your heart be sensitive to the intercourse of ideas as the love and joy spreads among the participants in your celebration. Let all your loved ones express love and take part in the dance of energy. This energy can break all barriers in and between your inner bodies.

Buildups of noncolor-ray energies solidified in the heart area can make a virtual ice dam. No life-giving color-ray energy could easily penetrate such a dam. Without the aid of the yellow gemstones, persons with such a constrictive dam would remain forever in a world where life is no fun. Sufferers would have no choice but to endure a tough, heart-rending set of experiences as they try to force open the heart center without citrine. A spiritual master can open your heart to love, but you must wish it. Choosing to wear citrine is an open invitation to expanding this energy flow in the heart if you simply ask for it. A closed heart is like an overwound spring. It will recoil at any provocation. It will break if wound further. If allowed to unwind gradually, it will open to vibrations and become like a spring echo. Any vibrations that come into the open heart are echoed through the whole spring and back and one day come out of the heart in the form of love.

When opened fully, the heart is like a diamond, reflecting the many colors in the light that strikes it and dazzling others with its passion and beauty. Let love fill your heart as it flies through inner space on wings of citrine to carry a message of hope to remote regions of inner landscapes.

Yellow Sapphire (Corundum)

Yellow sapphire, a form of corundum, is an extremely hard stone that is found in a range of colors from light yellow to nearly orange amber. High-quality stones are rare indeed. Few mines ever find more than a small number of pure yellow sapphires with a pure, uniform color. Not generally available in spheres and hard to find as rondel beads, this stone will be the primary new conductor of the yellow ray in future. The yellow ray is going through a transition. It is moving from being the least abundant ray in the planetary aura at this time to being more balanced with the other rays. Yellow sapphire is a more compact and powerful amplifier of the yellow ray. It will become more affordable, and plentiful supplies may be discovered as the planet is more prepared for the increase in yellow ray energy. You need look no further than current events to see a global upliftment of world energy and its effect on all that is going on. Yellow sapphire is part of this new cycle. Negative thoughts and events will continue to happen and yet those who practice the presence of the color-ray energy will not be drawn in. Abundance is possible despite rumors to the contrary.

It is not recommended that persons wear any appreciable amount of this stone, especially in the crystalline form. You could easily become unbalanced by wearing a full necklace of this stone. Avoid using this stone with metals and with metallic stones like hematite. The power of a single yellow sapphire in the aura for short periods of time will be sufficient to catalyze great changes in your outlook on life and tolerance of joy, happiness, and sufficiency. Perhaps our greatest fear is that our lives are controlled by destiny and cannot be significantly changed. Sapphire will destroy this fear if given our willingness.

We humans are hardly ready for much of the yellow ray at all. It is preferable for beginners to wear citrine to become more accustomed to the yellow ray. Wear citrine first for at least a few months. Allow the parts of yourself that are seriously out of sync with the other parts to come to a more harmonious vibration. Then, introduce a single yellow sapphire.

Choose one that is of pure clear light yellow color. No green or other discolorations must be present. If a rounded stone is not available, choose a cut sapphire that is as close to round as you can find.

After you become more in tune with the yellow ray, yellow sapphire can do its work. It will uplift the entire vibrational resonance of the physical body and all its sheaths. You can perhaps appreciate why this is better done only after the parts have gotten into greater cooperation with each other by using citrine. Adding amethyst would prove useful to build strength in the subconscious communication between soul and your mind in order to develop a direction or life mission. This way you would not lose direction while developing a greater attraction to joy.

Begin an introduction by placing a single stone on the forehead. Allow it to remain there for several minutes. Now hold it between the thumb and index finger of the dominant hand. Raise it up to about two feet above the body. This will cause the mental sheath to become activated and aware of the stone. Now move the stone back and forth over the length of the body. Next, let your hand holding the stone describe the circumference of the body. After several outlines are complete, you should conclude your introduction to yellow sapphire. Permit the mind to absorb this treatment and repeat after three days. This simple treatment is subtle and profound.

At this point, the mental sheath and the stone are connected. The stone can now begin to integrate all aspects of your inner and outer vibrations through a kind of resonance. To continue this treatment, and whenever using this stone again, hold it over the center of the body about one inch above the abdomen. Raise it to eighteen inches high. Begin a slow, spiral circling outward from this point. Go clockwise or counterclockwise, whichever direction it directs you to go. As you move it in increasingly larger circles, you should be able to detect an area to which the stone is drawn. You may have to repeat this motion more than once to get the mind to relax and just feel the stone. Once you have located the spot that needs the attention of yellow sapphire, allow it to be drawn down toward the body. Without moving it out of the aura, place it on the target spot and hold that placement, or tape the stone in position for five to fifteen minutes or until the placement becomes uncomfortable or the skin begins to feel itchy.

If at first no sensation is felt, allow several minutes. If a sensation or the awareness of a healing is felt, allow as much time as needed for the sensation to subside. Now, begin again with another spiral circling, only this time continue to circle and softly sing or hum a lighthearted song you find attractive. Often a simple nursery rhyme or childhood melody is best. You can also make up a tune spontaneously. The yellow ray will uplift the entire aura as you stir, so do not be in a hurry. Just let the joy of the song encourage a state of relaxed anticipation. If the idea of singing is difficult, play a tape of a childlike song and hum or sing along.

Part of this exercise is to learn a form of surrender. Let the body teach for a change. Your mind need not always have the answers. Your mental answers may in fact be outdated or no longer quite appropriate. The body has its own intelligence and yellow sapphire will bring the information the body produces to the mind.

As soul, we have the ability to directly apprehend what is true and what is best. The mind must be educated to new ways of doing things. One's first thought at waving a yellow sapphire over the body generally will be that this practice is foolish and is not actually doing anything. You must suspend this mental disbelief and remain open-minded to get the channel of communication energized and the information flowing. Disbelief can stop the process as the yellow ray is directed by the individual.

The physical body has a much easier time than the mind accepting a better or new way of behaving because it has no ideas or meanings associated with behaviors. The mind makes changes easily enough, but it has a hard time changing associated meanings and will easily revert to former behaviors and attitudes until the total mind vibrations are raised.

Meanwhile, the yellow ray can teach you to trust the physical body. Perfect the connection between soul and the physical body, and the body will be able to tell you the answers to all sorts of questions. This knowledge brings us to the issue of trust. The mind must surrender control to permit the body to communicate with soul. Surrender requires trust in the process. A sufficient level of trust is required for the yellow ray to do its work. You need not give up all doubt and can certainly reserve the right to stop the process at any time. You need only be open to the possibility that soul can direct the physical body and that information the physical body receives and passes on to soul will be valid and helpful spiritually.

To convince the mind that the yellow ray, as directed by sapphire, should be permitted to work without interference takes evidence. To get that evidence, you must continue to experiment. Take time to integrate each treatment, and when ready, proceed with the experiment.

Place the attention on surrender. Let doubt be suspended for the purposes of experiment. Trust that this small stone can guide your hand to the place where it will do the greatest good.

Begin your next sapphire circling exercise with this trust. Move the stone into the aura above the torso. Now let your hand go to the place it is directed to go by sapphire and feel you will accept its gifts. If you are not sure where this spot is, then circle until something is felt (or until you locate the one place where the least resistance is felt). Now find a position about eighteen inches over the identified spot. As you move slowly down to the spot, be aware of any resistance. Should you feel any resistance, stop and let the stone remain in this spot out away from the body until it has cleared the resistance. Move your hand back out to a position about eighteen inches over the identified target spot. Now slowly move toward the body again. If you feel resistance again at the same or another point, stop and allow time for a clearing to take place. Repeat the clearing until you can slowly move up and down without resistance. If the resistance persists, you can turn the stone back and forth in a kind of unlocking motion in the location where resistance was felt. Clearing resistance may require unlocking at one or several points.

When clear of resistance, place the stone on the body and temporarily tape it in place if necessary. If a friend is assisting in this process, let the friend describe what they felt as they found resistance and completed the clearing. Now you describe what you felt. Be aware of all reactions, sensations, and feelings. If a thought or emotion pops into awareness, you may wish to express it as the stone is working. More sensitive feelings may best be shared later in other circumstances.

This simple exercise ends when the stone is removed. Leave it in place until the body has had enough. The cue for this may be simple. Just wait for the spot to become itchy and uncomfortable, or until the recipient feels a change or releases tension.

Repeating this exercise daily until you have cleared all lines of communication and the vibrations of all the subtle bodies are in some semblance of harmony may take twenty to fifty treatments. Regular treatments are best.

Integration is the state of being in which all parts are in agreement. This state affords all of your parts equal access to the power of personal choice with the understanding that only one choice can be made in any situation. This one choice must best serve all concerns and yet not cause you to lose sight of the possibility that the concern of one single part may outweigh all other concerns until resolution. Yellow sapphire cannot transform you from a state of confusion or diffusion to the state of integration. Instead, you must employ this tool to discover and light the way. Use it to work with parts that have not previously been in communication. Use it to improve communication until harmony can be felt like a cat must feel it as it settles in for a nap.

One who is disintegrated is said to be schizophrenic or to have multiple personalities. This personality disorder is an extreme form of disintegration. Perhaps this manifestation seems remote and strange, but could all of us be suffering from minor splits? This possibility may be easier to believe than the opposite. After all, how could all our divergent aspects agree? How could we always know exactly what is best for us? Yellow sapphire may help bring answers to your questions about integration and harmony.

Pursuits of the mind can force the body and emotions into suppression. Commonly, people take the interests of the mind as paramount. They sublimate other concerns. A focused mind is on one track. Soul can be focused, and at the same time aware of all forms of input from myriad sources at once. Mind is singular in its pursuits. It seems to be direct and focused but is unaware of anything else.

The mind pursues mental goals. Some people notice only mental pursuits and might be confused at the idea that there are other kinds of goals. Some pursue the career of an athlete, diver, or laborer and believe only in things they can physically touch. Still others believe only in feelings and act on them while the concerns of the intellect and body are ignored. Only soul can take a stand for integration. Yellow sapphire helps. It temporarily lifts the embargoes and blockades. It lobbies for peace. It builds connectivity. It serves to remove the dross. Buildups of resentment and suffering are lifted. Pathways to forgiveness develop. You will find it easier to let go in the presence of yellow sapphire.

The particular vibrations of the crystal matrix of yellow sapphire, when formed into a rounded shape or sphere, set up a powerful signature resonance. This resonance acts to break up the bond between all non-color-ray energies and the human form. Noncolor-ray energies can be stored along with color-ray energies in the various levels of the human form. Noncolor-ray energies are, generally speaking, harmful and support deviation from the cellular structures and relationships as outlined in the human blueprints. One-track people have sometimes become single-minded by continually avoiding fear, pain or grief associated with other viewpoints and by feeling lost when not constantly pursuing some accomplishment. Worries or memories of fear, pain, and grief in situations where these emotions are not appropriate are direct results of the presence of certain noncolor-ray energies. Once the harmful nature of certain non-color-ray energies is understood and they are separated from the color-ray energies, they are easily eliminated through right action. Right action is defined here as all actions taken on the basis of decisions that fundamentally support integration. You may take an action designed to prove your commitment to integration or take an action that proves that disintegration is not good. Take a stand and those energies will not return.

As an example, let us consider a specific case. A person, whom we shall call Mark, wanted to be successful in a creative career. He started out early in life on his own. He pursued music, art, and writing. For years, success seemed just out of reach, yet he continued to develop his skills in each of these creative forms. He was always trying to please others with his work. He saw this as essential.

By midlife, he had many accomplishments that to others would have been sufficient proof of success, but Mark felt he was a failure. He began gemstone therapy to resolve some physical problems. As he began the work with yellow sapphire, he began to have realizations and insights into his feelings of vague dissatisfaction. He realized he was indeed an incredibly skillful artist, musician, and writer, but was not satisfied with his work for some personal reasons. During a treatment, Mark forgave himself for his "failure" and admitted he had no idea why he felt like a failure nor what he was trying to prove with his work.

Yellow sapphire went to work this time to break up the pattern he had set in motion and showed him that the career he had created was really an attempt to get people to hear him. He had wanted to prove that he was worthy of love to his now-diseased father who had never listened to him or accepted him. He wanted to be acknowledged somehow and to have someone understand his deeply felt concerns. Creative work was good for him, but the fact that all his work went to trying to please others divided him and caused a feeling of lack of integration. A lot of noncolor-ray energy had been built around Mark's thought forms of success. The harder he tried for approval, the farther away his goal moved because the noncolor-ray energy being accumulated was growing to unhealthy proportions.

As the sapphire completed its work, he saw the whole story. He was able to dissipate the noncolor-ray energies with ruby (his primary color-ray gemstone). He quickly reformulated his one-track life to include making close friends in whom he could confide. As his friends grew closer and more numerous, he began to feel successful. His need for recognition was being met directly. Soon, his career began to take off. Free of the noncolor-ray energy, he was able to find what he really wanted to say with his work. He began to love his work. Wider recognition followed. Case in point: get really clear on the various things you want to accomplish and integrate your parts, and you, too, can find the shorter route to happiness. Mark allowed the tool, yellow sapphire, to break up his bond to the life pattern that stymied his development. He committed himself to finding a solution and took action to make his life more integrated. He proved to himself that he was on the right track but that he just didn't have things straight. Through his efforts, he found a better life.

People aren't bad generally. People do things that cause themselves and others trouble because they feel powerless to do otherwise. Noncolor-ray energies create havoc. Once they are cleared, the work begins; the difference is that the work is fun. When one feels daily reward in the journey, life becomes a vacation from senseless struggle, causing tension that only solidified noncolor-ray energies and perpetuated their effects. People will always choose well and do the right thing when they come to see the benefits of such choices without the confusion of distorted thought forms misguiding their judgment. People just need to feel they are getting a fair shake. They need to understand the rules of the game before they can enjoy it and treatments of the above type will get them going on a path to understanding. It's hard to enjoy a game if you never win or get any closer to winning.

Yellow sapphire builds strength of resolve. It brings certainty. It helps people find themselves. It raises our atomic vibrations to match our highest harmonious vibrations. It teaches us the benefits of integration. It helps us determine what it is to act from a state of integrated self-direction in alignment with our highest purpose.

Amber

Not a gemstone in the true sense, amber is naturally formed from hardened resin or sap of trees. The best varieties for therapeutic application are rounded, clear of impurities that could cloud the material, and have a medium amber color. Amber is suggested as a support for those who find its vibrations especially appealing and attractive. This material has been used through the ages as an amulet by many wandering tribes and by certain primitive tribes in Africa and the "Persian" valleys.

Amber works with the fluid systems in the body. It helps to strengthen the cells that comprise the vein and artery walls. It also excites the body to greater movement of lymph, spinal fluids, and other intracellular liquids.

For those who suffer from low blood pressure, this substance can be helpful in combination with regular treatment with medicines designed to treat low blood pressure. Its slow, encouraging effects may not at first be noticeable. Continue to wear a strand of spheres for at least several months. This persistence will be necessary before the deeper causes of a severe imbalance of the body's blood pressure will be affected.

Most people would benefit from wearing amber for a day or two each month on a regular basis. The body has a habit of storing waste in the lymph system, particularly around the glandular areas of the neck, arm pit, and groin. These wastes can become thick and sluggish. Amber will encourage the body to begin the process of moving these wastes out to the skin where they can be eliminated.

Amber is great for those individuals who find difficulty moving their joints; that is, they have creaking, grinding, or other painful joint wear. The body will gradually respond to amber worn around the neck, ankles, wrists, or other aching joints. If symptoms are mild, amber may bring quick relief as it stimulates the production of lubricating liquids in damaged joints. If symptoms are severe, as in the case of carpal tunnel syndrome or debilitating arthritis, dietary restrictions could be ordered by a nutritional consultant, and your doctor may require the use of naturopathic medicine or stronger drugs. In these cases, amber will help during the entire length of treatment and will ease the pain after continuous use.

Amber can be worn without fear of harmful consequences or side effects. It can help with soft-tissue injuries as well as with fractures. It will not repair bone disfiguration or bruising, but it will aid in the distributing of bone-building minerals and enzymes necessary for reconstruction. (See chapter 9 on indigo stones for structural rebuilding and reintegration of blueprints to cellular structures that normally would actively repair disfigured bone but that apparently have forgotten their proper function.)

Amber is abundant in many areas of the world. It is found commonly in Africa, the southern Baltic regions, South America (especially Brazil), and parts of the Orient. It is traded in such areas as a form of currency where bartering is common. Many claims have been made as to its healing properties.

Wearers may experience heightened dream activity or spontaneous flashbacks to past lives during which this substance was worn regularly. Its vibration can take you back momentarily to times when you enjoyed lives in these regions. You may be drawn easily to a time when amber vibrations were always present. If you find your dreams are affected and you have unusual scenes or activities during sleep, you may be experiencing past-life recalls. Do not be alarmed. Many gemstones were used by peoples in cultures now forgotten. Amber was certainly used as a ceremonial amulet in many past cultures.

Past-life experiences may be stimulating to some, but are not generally helpful unless you are under the care of a spiritual master capable of helping you through these experiences. Hypnosis and other "regression" therapies are helpful only when working with a person who has the ability to protect you from dangerous uncontrolled shifts in consciousness. If you are experiencing such shifts, remove the amber. Revisiting these eras is disorienting to our consciousness because times in the remote past were so very different from today that we would be lost if we were transported to them. In fact, people of today may have a great deal of difficulty adapting to this change in vibration brought on by amber and may become quite baffled. We seldom consider just how radically the human consciousness has evolved. It becomes evident when trying to recapture memories from lives lived in the remote past.

The imagination is quite capable of conjuring up images that may convince you that you lived at a certain time in the past. Do not be fooled. Actual recalls are almost always accompanied by actual physical sensations from that life as well as feelings of disorientation as the past vibration is momentarily recaptured into the present emotional sheath. You can be certain that actual recall of past-life memories is possible. You can also be certain that it takes a great deal of practice to interpret these memories and the deep feelings that are associated with them. You must first learn to reestablish the mental and emotional context of these past times. It takes time to make sense out of this context. Times in the past are not at all like the scenes we often see portrayed in movies. People thought differently and their actions were based on an entirely different set of values and beliefs.

It can indeed be very helpful to learn where and when the personality traits we have today have their origin. Realize also, however, that you may find information that is only partially accurate and sometimes very disturbing. Should you wish to investigate these past-life recall experiences, consider enlisting the aid of someone who has your highest spiritual development at heart. Many of today's psychics are able to move into the realm of the past, but random trips may cause setbacks, especially to those of us who need to move on in a balanced way.

Open this area of your consciousness with caution and with the assistance of a guide who can clearly see what would benefit you spiritually before you take the trip. Just as in our present physical reality, not every tour is enjoyable, and few tours are actually uplifting to the spirit. It takes a truly professional guide to show you a new culture and to be detached enough to give you the experience that would be of most benefit to you. Random trips into the psychic realm by the curious may lead to sudden psychic opening of chakras, which opens one to psychic attacks and pranks by astral entities. These can be disturbing.

Amber is a good tool to have along when traveling. It helps keep the "juices" flowing. It teaches you how to adapt your vibrational patterns to those of another place. Amber helps bring understanding of the subtleties of another culture. It attunes you with another culture's beliefs and values. Amber teaches mental flexibility by showing the body how to remain flexible, providing a method of practicing varied responses and by demonstrating the benefits of flexibility to the intellect. It improves our willingness to accept many harsh aspects of reality. It can even help us tune into lessons we learned in a past life, which may help us today. If you are one who loves amber, keep this tool with you when on the go.

Amber is always a welcome help when trying to translate the gestures and comments of others. People do not often know how to explain what they mean or why they do things. Amber will help develop an understanding of motivations, which is most helpful when dealing with new people.

Yellow Beryl (Golden Beryl)

The beryl family includes yellow beryl, emerald, and aquamarine (as well as others not covered in this book). Emerald and aquamarine are the more abundant and the more valuable. All members of this family consist of the same crystalline structure, although they are different colors. The difference in color comes from the difference in circumstance at the time the material was formed. The pure yellow beryl is quite unusual. It is normally found as a crystal that is a rather light golden yellow. Deeper yellow varieties are almost impossible to find on the open market. Varieties of sufficient color are made into faceted gems or rounds for mounting in metal. Stones should not be used in therapies if they are mounted in metal.

The basic therapy using yellow beryl is designed to help those who find themselves experiencing vague, undifferentiated, worrisome emotions that do not go away. These emotions will surface in the individual at inopportune moments. Those who are deeply affected may, from time to time, become incapacitated with an emotional pressure. It's as if the sky were falling. Someone who suffers from this sort of occurrence can become weak or incapacitated for hours and may retreat emotionally for as long as several weeks at a time. Depression can accompany these outbreaks. Someone who experiences only mild symptoms will have shorter periods of vague emotional pressure. They may feel self-doubt rather than depression. The experience will be disconcerting and uncomfortable but may not be debilitating.

Attacks of this kind often are accompanied by self-limiting questions like: What did I do wrong? What's wrong with me? Why can't I just be like others who seem to have happiness? Why do I always screw things up?

The problem here is emotional sheath isolation. The sheath has difficulty receiving color-ray energy. Typically this difficulty is caused by a break in the connection between the emotional sheath and the lower mental sheath. Yellow beryl acts to rejoin the bodies.

Single stones produce the best treatments. To work with yellow beryl and create new connections, always choose a stone that is of highest quality. Place it over the solar plexus. Allow the body to direct the therapy. Place it for no more than fifteen minutes at a time until there have been at least a dozen exposures. Always apply lavender amethyst, if available, during treatments to any point on the body at the onset of pain or tension. Apply your primary color-ray necklace ten minutes after the treatment to help assimilate new mental connections.

Golden beryl goes to work immediately. This stone will begin to set up a new harmonic infrastructure within the emotional sheath. Connections form between it and the lower mental sheath, often referred to as the causal body. Lines of communication are laid. Codes are distributed to allow information to be arranged and sent from the emotional body into the appropriate areas of the causal body. Translators are placed and built up which decipher emotional energy into causal images for processing. Pathways are created that afford the emotional body some feedback. Feedback receptors are trained to recognize the vibrational feedback of causal energies. These energies are processed as the emotional barriers are trained to relax and encouraged to allow the penetration of causal feedback. Finally the emotional barriers that have been set up become clear pictures, and the reasons why these barriers were formed become apparent to the lower mental sheath. The causal area of the mental sheath begins to provide information on how the emotional body became isolated from the mental body, information that had been kept out of awareness, as if it were harmful. This information passes through the newly formed translators in the emotional body and thereby becomes useful.

In this way, emotions that once were vague and unrealizable become clear. Yellow beryl makes inroads into the inner emotional body to clear deeper blockages. Once this process is well under way, the person accepting these changes will realize what has been going on.

Emotions that had been suppressed and formed the foundation for snarled, self-directed anxiety will surface in the presence of yellow beryl. Root causes will be discovered as the emotions are assimilated. Anxiety will cease. The emotional sheath will begin to benefit by receiving higher directions from the mental body once the mental body accepts that it must refrain from thoughts that disrupt the emotional body functions. New causal directions for emotional health and self protection will be implanted into the roots of the emotional fibers by causal-directed color-ray energy. Self-negating, harmful anxiety will be blocked when it threatens the emotional sheath, but positive self-supportive directions will come through. The causal body will learn when it is sending self-constricting or harmful messages to the emotional sheath. It will begin to recognize grounds for a mutually supportive relationship with the emotional sheath.

This process is similar to replanting a forest. First, you must uproot the old trees and then plant a variety of new trees in accordance with the natural ecology; otherwise, a monoculture of trees will grow, and the natural order of the area will be disrupted. Healthy emotions cannot grow where the ground is covered with confused and unhealthy emotions. Just as a managed forest can thrive and provide housing for many animals when proper care has been taken to plant a variety of trees, so positive feelings of all kinds will thrive in an emotional body which has a variety of positive thoughts planted.

It may be hard to believe that these sheaths act independently and even cause inner conflict. Inner conflict always arises when soul is locked out of the negotiations. As the individual soul learns to govern effectively and provide directions that are seen by all sheaths as constructive, the sheaths learn to cooperate. White-ray energies are an essential additive to generating soul-directed change. Yellow beryl can do everything outlined here if you are open to these goals and to working with the process. White-ray energy must be included to further develop the communication process once the lines are opened.

Yellow beryl is not destructive. Its powerful actions are the result of facilitated construction. Its vibration is both pleasing and comforting. Emotional turmoil will not immediately cease upon application of yellow beryl; instead, the emotional body will learn to trust the new vibrations only after yellow beryl has been employed to afford the emotional body a greater say in internal affairs and after soul has opened channels of negotiation and begun directing the mind to send helpful signals to the emotional body. Once the emotional body has learned to trust higher direction, then soul can gain greater command of the emotions. The emotions are essential for any soul-directed manifestation in the mental, causal, emotional, or physical worlds. Getting anything done here in the physical world is difficult if your emotions are in disagreement with your choices.

As youths grew up in the 1950s, '60s, and '70s, they were hardly trained in the use of tools for emotional support. Men were given few tools to understand the emotions, and women were given few tools with which to direct the emotions. Both were taught to stop having emotional "outbreaks" and to get down to the "real" business of analytical thinking. Now, analytical thinking is certainly necessary—for many careers, it is customary that only analytical thinking be allowed in the office and that emotional and intuitive influences be restrained. That millions of Americans who grew up in the 1950s through '70s seek twelve-step programs, counseling, or psychotherapy is no surprise.

The purpose of this chapter is not to recommend new forms of social structure. If you wish to explore the benefits of clear communication between the various sheaths, you need to make the effort to develop that communication. To realize the benefits of soul-directed living with all bodies open, functional, and as receptive as possible, you must determine to make the effort to develop the capability of communication. Practice is necessary to achieve good communication. Safe circumstances in which to practice this new communication are essential.

Suffice it to say that the world would be a better place if many individuals were to resolve their own issues and learn to become integrated, coherent, individualized, and in touch with the consequences of their every move. You may be able to recognize the descriptions given here of the conditions of emotional blockages and the effects of these blockages on your inner experiences, as well as the state of affairs in your life. Open the channels of communication and learn to send helpful messages and a new life will begin.

Picture the analogy of a ship in mutiny where the crew cannot agree and the captain is being held captive. The cook refuses to prepare meals. The first mate is busy trying to control the captain and fears for his life. The sails are in disrepair because no crew members want to climb the mast. No one knows where they are going. The man holding the rudder has no gift for navigation. The navigator has no access to maps. The bilge contains much water, for no bailing has been ordered since the captain was taken below. Fact is, the ship is going around in circles. Sometimes a crew member will notice they have just passed an area they had gone through a few days earlier. He is afraid to let on. Tension is high and the tempers explosive. No one is busy, but all are exhausted.

Our ship may not be in as poor a condition as this crew has left theirs—most people have a good bit better grasp on life than this example shows. Many of us, however, still could stand to make some improvements in the interrelationships among the parts of ourselves. The problem may be that some part of us, such as the mind, does not want to share the control. Then again, a democracy may not work where a ship on the open ocean is concerned. Each part must know the limits of its responsibility and its authority. We must learn how to build a greater understanding between the forces within us that vie for attention if we expect to have the cooperation of our "crew." The captain must be reinstated, but the ship must be operated in accordance with definable laws which all parts agree to. A ship can regain its course, no matter how far off it has drifted. Golden beryl helps reestablish the desire for cohesion and cooperation.

No stone can deliver miracles. Yellow beryl can only do what we ask it to do. We ourselves must resolve the issues and make the new decisions that will establish clear lines of communication and strong relationships among our inner crew. We are travelers of the high seas. Whether we slowly perish on a ship that has no captain or we travel the world over experiencing everything the world has to offer with grace, honesty, and style, depends on us. Yellow beryl can begin the process of showing every crew member a manifesto for cooperation. Understanding the many sides of each member of our team is up to us. We may not at first like one of the sides—but later we may find that side has the needed character to get us through some really rough waters.

Make peace among the parts of yourself. Find the benefits and strong points each part of you has to offer. Create an environment where every part is active and grows strong. Each body has much to offer, and we can navigate effectively when we listen to all input and determine which needs can be met in each circumstance. Life within is not like a movie in which the characters are one-dimensional. Rather, all the characters are parts of a multidimensional whole.

To get the ship moving, use yellow beryl. To reinstate the captain, use white-ray energy in the form of quartz or onyx. To prepare the crew for tough times and develop each of them in their own greatest capacities, use each of the color-ray energies as needed—all are necessary to the operation of the ship. Operate from soul and always press home the need for mutual responsibility among the parts. The whole will benefit. Yellow beryl is the key to resolving the uncertainties and loss of motivation that cloud our vision and disrupt an inner team effort that may stall us at times on our journey.

The indigo ray is the ray of intuition. Its energy will direct the individual into the mysteries of the higher mind and the riddle of structure. The deeper meanings of the seemingly everyday events of life will show themselves in its light. Only we as individuals can assign deeper meanings to the events of life. We are referring here to spiritual meanings, not the mental associations. Creating your own spiritual meanings is not like the raving of a psychotic who believes only he has the answers to the great questions of life. Rather, it is the process of evaluating the many events in everyday life to see what relationship these events have to us and our development as spiritual beings.

Ascribing a symbolic meaning to everyday objects is helpful in the process of understanding the language of relationship. We exist in relationship with every person, every thing, in life. Things, images, places, songs, words— everything in life has a symbolic meaning as we choose to interpret it and we can adopt these unconsciously or by choice.

Indigo takes us into the evaluation process as it occurs in our heads. Indigo-ray energy shows us our limitations. We learn the ways we stop relationships from satisfying us, and undermine relationships by subtly ascribing meanings that undervalue relationships and those we are in relationship with. We may be

9
Indigo Ray Stones

too serious, putting every interaction under the microscope, or too aloof, not caring what happens.

While working with the indigo ray, we will be inclined to ask the big questions we previously were finding no answers to. We will begin to uncover wisdom and a knowing that goes beyond any information or knowledge our language can express.

Indigo-ray stones will help us unravel the mental constructs on which we base our lives. You need not be plagued by uncertainty. You need not sabotage your efforts toward a better life. You need not fear the very things that you try so hard to establish in your life. Many people remain in jobs or relationships that they know do not really exercise their talents, yet they do not try to make things better. Sometimes we don't know how to make things better. Indigo can help. It can show us where we get fouled up by getting involved in situations that limit us. It can remind us to look for opportunities to grow and evolve. Indigo can also challenge us to keep in mind our mission in life. We can learn to thrive in relationships.

Of course, when we have safely placed any responsibility for our lives firmly behind a wall of denial hidden deep within, we cannot improve. We make inner statements of denial like: "I am happy with my job." "I never do things I wish I hadn't done." "I love my life." "I understand exactly what I'm doing and why." These statements create the belief that all is well within. Indeed they may be well, but we may also be minimizing our talents and abilities and exercising them only in our minds. When things go wrong and negative energies disrupt our lives, we believe someone else must be to blame. Really, there is no blame, just issues and problems for which we won't take our share of the responsibility.

Why would anyone in their right mind want to address these issues anyway? Can't we just go on with life as usual without rocking the boat? Yes, we can, but we will pay a price for this "luxury." We will continue to be blindsided by events. We will remain confused. We will find intimacy elusive and unattainable. We will never experience spiritual freedom. We will allow others to control our lives and will always be angry with them for it.

We will live without structure except as imposed from without. These costs and more will plague us, for we are not able to take our lives where we want them to go. We must make our dreams come alive, and indigo can support this effort.

With focus on our inner strengths and the indigo ray to guide us, we can create a style of life where we are in touch with the vital life energy of the color rays. As this energy fills us and remains with us we can regain health, find balance, learn to connect to inner peace, discover what makes us happy, practice getting beyond our neverending set of problems, and generally develop a way of being that is thriving rather than just surviving.

Indigo-ray energy will spark the intuition. It will begin to bring us in contact with truth and the certainty that there is truth and we can learn of it. Indigo will give us access to the well of deeper meaning. From this well, we can begin to draw up the waters of life. We can begin to grasp the structure of life. We can draw from the deep blue color-pools beneath our mind the energy we need to support our efforts like water supports life. Wearing stones that carry this color ray will open up the subconscious and bridge the subconscious to the conscious as intuitive flashes of insight. This vast part of the mind can begin to help us by giving us new vision and practical solutions through insight. Soon, inspiration will fill us, replacing fear. We will go from fearing our demise to taking every opportunity to expand our lives into new territory, not because indigo makes us courageous (we may look to ruby and carnelian for this), but because we are so full of inspiration that we are willing to move forward in a systematic plan to restructure our lives such that we can do what makes us thrive. If you want more of life, employ indigo. It will show you the way to build a life with purpose, one step at a time.

In short, indigo will light the way to intent with passion. Indigo will move us to taking action in ways we would not previously have allowed ourselves. Those who are bold enough to employ such a tool will have a new vehicle that can take them to their dreams, even if these dreams seem beyond the stars.

Do these seem like outrageous promises? They are. Nothing can do all this for us. We must take the initiative. We must make the effort. We must keep on going when the going gets tough. We must be the ones who persist when persistence seems beyond our capacity. We must believe in miracles when we are surrounded by what appear to be insurmountable odds.

Why would we do this? Well, frankly, we might not. If, however, we decide to give it a try, nothing in our lives will ever be so dull as it may once have been. Life may not give all the rewards we believe we deserve, but it will reveal itself as full of possibilities. Life will become full. More than that, it will prove that it is not dull or boring. We are the ones who have made it as it is. Indigo will point the way. Are you ready to take the first step into a life of joy and challenges? Start with indigo.

Indigo-ray people are considerate, intuitive, and tend to procrastinate until they have a plan. Indigo-ray people are not, by nature, risk takers. They prefer to have it all figured out first. If you are predominantly governed by the indigo ray, then you will need the support of other color rays to learn to step outside your comfortable structures. Employ other color-ray energies to learn implementation, courage, and raw passion. This situation would appear to be a paradox, for indigo-ray persons are able to be quite at home in the mysterious realms of the unconscious, and yet they can get stuck in the rigid structures of the logical mind and find difficulty moving.

Only by wearing indigo and experiencing the vibrations of the indigo ray as amplified by the indigo gemstone in its most translucent form will individuals find the answers to this paradox. All paradox exists in the upper reaches of the mind. Beyond this area is soul. Soul knows no paradox, for all paradox is understood by soul. Paradox can be understood by the mind, but it requires interpretation. The mind learns interpretation by building its own symbolism. The line between insanity and genius is thin indeed. A genius has made up meanings for everything, and those meanings are more profoundly accurate than the average person's ideas. A genius uses symbols to gain access to the subconscious mind and soul. An insane person has made up meanings for everything, but those meanings are indecipherable by anyone else and lead them to vain repetitions of dysfunctional behavior rather than insight and creative growth.

A key to the difference between insanity and genius lies in the hands of those who have mastered the use of the indigo ray. Place this key in the door to the indigo ray and discover your potential for genius.

Indigo Sodalite

As the bearer of the indigo ray, this deep dark-blue stone is wonderful to look at. Choose the highest quality translucent beads. Users may wish to use it only in the four-millimeter size as the best quality beads are available in this small size and are sufficiently strong to be quite effective. Spherical bead strands in this size are sufficient to substantially raise the level of indigo ray within the individual. High-quality translucent indigo sodalite beads are only recently available on the world market. At this time, beads with the most clarity are available only in four-millimeter beads. Indigo users will find it most comfortable to wear sodalite alone at first. Wear indigo sodalite for no more than a few days at a time until the profound changes that result from infusing the whole being with the indigo ray have completed. Indigo is little known to most of us; only a few people will ever indulge in the unlikely voyage into indigo.

As a planet, we are generally most deficient in the indigo ray. Study this chapter for clues as to what we are missing. Work with the stone gradually. Allow yourself time to assimilate the indigo ray. Pay special attention to the way it works on your particular issues. We have much to discover about our potential. Perhaps the greatest area of discovery is in the indigo realm. Just differentiating a few hues of indigo may prove difficult, where, by comparison, we can differentiate hundreds of different hues of red. This phenomenon is related to the fact that the sensors of the eyes have evolved little ability to see indigo as such capability has had little effect on survival. Now that we, as the primary inhabitants of this planet, must discover how to manage this planet given a wide variety of exacting ecological systems, complex interactions between them and the myriad species dependent on our decisions, we must begin to look to indigo. Survival is becoming a matter of complex interactions within a system that changes. No longer can we assume nature will remain resilient enough to accommodate our unbridled expansion. We as the dominant species must now learn how to steward the planetary ecology on a global scale. We must take the best efforts of cultures around the world who have learned to steward the land—like the Chinese and indigenous tribes from the Americas—and begin to apply these ideas to the ecology of this whole planet.

Indigo sodalite can provide access to the areas of the mind not previously used by man. These areas host the complex abilities to work with a changing structure, and through precise, efficient engineering we can gain access to new models of science that take into account the laws governing subtle energy. We will never completely overcome obstacles, the challenges in our lives make us strong and are necessary for our development. We *can* learn to choose our obstacles and love them even as we are tested and tried.

The vibrations of indigo help the wearer access the upper mental or lower subconscious area where analytical thought does not normally exist. Some people are beginning to access this area on their own. Using indigo sodalite as a tool for opening this area will generate remarkable results. Anyone can learn to integrate learning from a wide variety of divergent fields of study. We must begin to do this. We must evolve our ability to solve extremely complex issues before we destroy the delicate balance this planet is in. Reserves are tapped and species are being forced to adapt or become extinct. The rate of change is alarming at times, and yet we must remain calm. Intuition helps us remain calm in the storms of change.

Intuition, especially for those who believe they have no capacity for the indigo ray, strikes the part of the mind that draws new conclusions. This realm of the mind is capable of performing miraculous feats of telepathy, clairvoyance, projection, remote audio perception, shape shifting, and movement in time. Intuition and the ability to see the whole or "big picture" are greatly enhanced when the aura has been saturated with indigo energy. Though we may have difficulty expressing in words the insights that come through to us during the times when our aura is saturated with indigo, we will learn to be more at ease with paradox and duality. Indigo sodalite is an excellent guide into the realm of paradox.

Thought processes will become deeper for wearers of sodalite, and most will be more able to accept and use areas of thought not previously acknowledged. The patterns of life will soon become more apparent. Cycles and all forms of repetitive patterns will be more easily understood and integrated by those who wear this stone at length. Numbers, archetypes, and other universal symbols that great thinkers have uncovered will reveal their deeper significance to those who learn to shine an indigo light on them.

We must become explorers of the vast inner realms to reveal the next steps in our development. Explorers of the past could tap physical resources, but today we must develop greater territories. These are the vast expanses of the intuition. This land contains answers to solve our dilemmas. We must learn to mine the subterranean veins of pure intuitive gold. Formerly, intuition has been seen as nuggets of gold randomly strewn across this landscape. However, solving today's challenges require huge leaps in consciousness. We must evolve from hunters and gatherers of intuitive leaps to conscientious industrial miners of rich motherlodes of intuition.

The structure of the mind is not understood by many. Here is our opportunity to discover the how and why of mental structure. The mind is divided into a multiple of layers that handle the different tasks to which the mind has been applied. Sensory data is received at one end of this structure and universal symbols of truth are accessible at the other. Sense impressions are first screened to determine if any of them require instinctual or immediate attention. Data (the input from the world) is then processed, categorized, labeled, prioritized, and catalogued. This process is completed as sense impressions are grouped and related to certain situations. The logical mind is then given the task of searching this data to reveal "facts" that apply to current situations and decisions, and regularly monitoring these situations in a process to determine if the data we receive is being correctly catalogued and applied to that situation.

Data is received on other levels as well. One level receives feelings from the astral body and sends out thought forms to the emotional body so it can engage this body to functionally demonstrate emotion. A more subtle level processes historical events to discover when and how similar concerns have been dealt with in the past. A further level tunes into influences from outside that are psychic impressions. A deeper level of the mind is intuitive, looking over the person's entire life circumstance to discover patterns and structures (this part is most profoundly affected by indigo).

The subconscious portion of the mind is to the conscious what the sunken portion of an iceberg is to the above-water part. It is huge and largely unseen, and it exists to handle the many tasks we are engaged in that require conclusions not possible given currently assimilated data, or that are too large or intricate for the linear, conscious mind to handle. At the highest level of the mind we can access truth directly. Here soul can expeditiously input the truth that it apprehends into the subconscious mind as needed to understand more of the workings of the subtle and unseen forces at work behind the visible reality. This truth is filtered down into symbols that the subconscious part of the mind can grasp and structures and patterns that the intuitive mind will use to fathom complex problems and unknown realities.

Indigo sodalite can help you bring needed aspects of the truth of soul to the conscious mind through guided intuition. Indigo will help us evolve purposefully as directed by soul, rather than by chance.

Information from soul, on subjects like who we are and what future actions and circumstances would be to our greatest good, will be more readily forthcoming. We may find ourselves marshaling forces to bring about new and remarkable circumstances for which we may not even be consciously aware that we are striving. We are moved forward in life by many forces, most unseen. Soul can interpret the usefulness of these forces, but the mind must accept changes before they become permanent. The mind must therefore learn to understand how these unseen forces work and their message or purpose in our effort. The conscious mind cannot see anything that it does not believe in or have "proof" of, whereas soul will see all of what is true. Mind reacts, soul acts and is therefore able to cause as originator.

The subconscious makes first contact with soul. For us to realize we are soul, the mind must begin to accept the information that soul imparts to the subconscious mind. Sodalite will facilitate this information transfer. It will also encode the information with indigo vibrations so the mind can begin to differentiate information that originates from soul from that which originates from the physical senses, emotional body, logical mind, memory, or psychic senses. Information so encoded becomes priority information. To understand this information you must, from time to time, stop paying attention to all other mental activity and contemplate on the significance of soul input.

A common reaction of the long-term wearer might be, "I feel much more in touch with who I really am," and "I have gotten in touch with what I want to be in my life." Another characteristic comment could be, "I think I finally understand the advantages of coming to my own conclusions, though I value other input." A great tool for getting to know yourself, indigo is for those committed to a spiritual path.

The censor of the mind, that part of the mind that does not allow us to see certain aspects of ourselves and our environment, will not have as much control over our actions when it is directed by the intuitive part of the mind. When your aura becomes filled with indigo, you are more inclined to act directly from the larger resource of insight rather than to think everything out first with the less informed, analytical mind, which is filtered through the censor. Thus, we become more spontaneous. Indigo will speed up our decisions because we will not have to think things out with the ever-so-slow analytical mind before deciding what to do. We can learn to act more quickly and more precisely.

Our inner blueprints are made up of spectrums of light balanced in a precise manner, individual to us alone. From our core we are aware when something is just exactly right for us. As we live our lives in ways that are not in alignment with these blueprints, we may find over the course of years that it is increasingly difficult to know what is right for us. We may superimpose other secondary blueprints on our inner selves. Our astral, causal, and mental bodies, which survive physical death, may carry aberrations, suffering, memories, and beliefs from our past lives. These may influence our decision to develop secondary blueprints and follow them. These are difficult to correct without specific knowledge on our part of what our original blueprints are like.

Only through extended contact with color-ray–bearing gemstones like indigo sodalite can we expect to realize our original blueprints again. Most decisions made with the logical mind, in the usual way, are guesses. Acquiring the blueprint information through subtle means, such as the use of gemstones, opens us to the higher mind. This part of the mind can assimilate data from the logical and intuition from the intuitive mind, and rapidly decipher a course of action. You will begin to make breakthrough decisions that are amazing. Each will be accurately thought out without the laborious process of weighing every factor with only the logical or "right" brain. The right brain is slow and cumbersome. The "left" brain, as the visible portion of the iceberg known as the intuitive mind is referred to, makes rapid decisions, but is uncheckable and often underinformed. The two sides together and in cooperation with soul and its input of indigo-ray-coded information, can consistently make great decisions.

Again, indigo is the least-available color ray in our environment here on Earth. For this reason, we are often profoundly moved by the presence of indigo as it concentrates this color ray. Even necklaces of the smallest stones will "wake up" the body to the discrepancies between our current circumstances and those we would enjoy if we were in balance with our underlying blueprints.

When we come into alignment with these blueprints, we will begin to feel younger and will naturally partake in the things that are growth enhancing and best for us on all levels. Bodies and minds that are not growing as fast as they decay will loose their capabilities. Decay is certain. All systems are inclined to run down, an inclination that is known as entropy. Growth depends more and more on us after age eighteen. Wearing indigo we make better decisions because we learn to value growth. We become more certain of ourselves. We learn to love challenges.

Indigo sodalite assists us in making rapid change. As change is accelerated, soul can more easily supply direct awareness to these changes.

Those who procrastinate usually do so in a few areas of their lives and move forward in the rest. Unfortunately, these few areas are usually the areas they focus on to the exclusion of other areas. For instance, a person might be an excellent craftsman and love to throw parties for friends. They may dislike being alone and doing chores. Such a person may find it altogether too easy for their life to get oriented to chores, spending a lot of time dealing with such things in life that can only be done alone. Meanwhile, they have forgotten to include craft work and haven't thrown a party for years. Wearing indigo will push them to consider looking at ignored areas of their lives for new inspiration. They become more free because they have avoided their areas of limitations. They can take time to smell the roses. They learn new attitudes from working in areas where they have few limitations. What could be better than change toward a more cohesive and congruent set of attitudes? Wearers may even learn to enjoy change, as soul does. Capabilities that hitherto may have been unused may suddenly become a regular part of life. As soul begins to direct the changes in life, wearers will become more effective in achieving their innermost goals, and other people will begin to participate and to be compelled to contribute to the wearer's achievements.

Suppose you are a person who thinks constantly of your career. You have focused on career to the exclusion of relationships, family, sports, play, hobbies, travel, artistic endeavors, and anything else that could "interfere" with your business. This works well for some years until you reach your limitations. Suddenly nothing you do will expand your career. As you succeed with one new client, another leaves. Advancement ceases suddenly. What do you do?

Indigo sodalite will help. It will go to work on you to take on different activities. It will teach you how to overcome your limitations in business by breaking free of them, moving your attention into another field—like sports or art—and letting business issues resolve themselves in your mind as you engage in a new sport. Indigo-ray energy will begin to infuse your intuition. It will leaven new forms of creativity as you express yourself through art. It will catalyze your motivation to win by setting you against a challenge in sports that piques your competition while teaching you team skills. Suddenly you will have breakthrough experiences in your career, seemingly without effort. You will have dropped your prejudice about yourself and learned to expect more from life. Your efficiency will double. You thought you were already too busy, yet you will do more in less time. Indigo promotes shifts in outdated paradigms. It promotes growth.

Soul may create a connection with forces that will aid us in all aspects of our lives. Often these forces will be unseen and may even be unrecognized, yet the changes will continue to come.

We may begin to learn the deeper significance of the collective unconscious. An understanding of primordial images will begin to unfold. We may find it possible to write our own myths. Creating a whole new mythology for ourselves can be expedited by wearing sodalite. We as soul will replace social myths with our own mythology that is in alignment with our innermost nature. The exercise of writing your own myth after repeated use of indigo for five or six months will reveal great insights into the inner workings of your subconscious.

Parts of our inner symbolic nature may suddenly come to light as we are able to increase our awareness of these subtle areas. The intuitive part of the mind acts like a bridge to the deeper subconscious. You will begin to know the reasons for and understand the lessons taught by the negative experiences in your life. You will learn why your lessons are repeated. You may even learn to feel a sense of gratitude for challenges and hardships. After all, one learns fastest and most ardently in hard times. If you test your strength against incrementally greater resistance, you will become strong.

Integrating the forgotten or rejected parts of yourself can be a lengthy process. Use carnelian to begin the integration and sodalite to pass apparent barriers. If you put your attention on the intention to become a whole, integrated person, you will find that indigo will create an atmosphere of inner strength. This strength will be necessary to meet the challenge of embodying a fully self-realized, self-aware life. Simply place a necklace of sodalite over the forehead and focus on perceived barriers, seeing them as short walls, easily vaulted when you have prepared for what is on the opposite side.

We can make our greatest weaknesses into our greatest strengths. Sit down with pen and paper. Put attention on a weakness and contemplate its opposite while wearing indigo sodalite. After a five-minute period of clearing the mind of all thoughts by simply letting them flow out, open your eyes and concentrate on the strength. Describe every attribute of the strength. Write all thoughts, however unlikely, down on a piece of paper for a timed period of three minutes. Now realize how much you know about your newfound strength.

Indigo-ray energy helps dislodge the negativity's hold. We rid our bodies of internalized negativity and reduce our affinity for it. Disharmonious energies that may have once disrupted our whole aura may still have an effect, but we will be much more capable of returning to a state of composure. Disruptive energies can cause us to react but do not have to control our decisions. Indigo can teach the subtler significance of negative energy.

Negative energy is any energy that has an undesirable effect on us. Negative energies are not in alignment with our inner nature. Negative energies build in the aura and subtle bodies when we are unable to resolve our relationship with them. Patterns of negative behavior that may be self-defiling or self-destructive are formed. Usually at the core of these patterns are false mental concepts—ideas about reality that are distorted or illusionary. Sodalite can help us unravel these patterns, undo the ties to negative energies, and reevaluate our mental concepts.

Once you have begun this process, it will be easier and more fun than any endeavor yet undertaken. At first it may seem scary because we are unsure which of the patterns of behavior we engage in are positive and which are negative. Some may be a mix. Sodalite will be a great tool for marking the negative behaviors with a kind of indelible marking. Other tools like rhodocrosite and purple rainbow fluorite may be the best tools for dismantling these patterns and constructs.

Get a necklace of high-quality indigo sodalite. Place it around your neck. Set in motion the inner request to allow indigo to fill your every aspect and make you aware of your true being. Know that in time you will become that being, radiant and free of defects that might obscure energy.

Now try a visualization. Close your eyes and picture a safe haven for travelers. You come to the door of this establishment and you feel certain that here you will be able to rest and recuperate. At the door, a young man with indigo eyes greets you. He seems quite friendly and you trust him immediately.

You walk inside and he asks what you have come for. You respond by telling him you wish to experience the indigo ray and are weary from your travels. He takes your coat. He leads you into a large room with several levels going down and up. You notice that on each level is a moderate-sized pool filled with deep indigo water. He leads you to a small changing room where you are to prepare for bathing. You find a towel and a bathing suit that fits perfectly.

When you are ready, you come out. The young man leads you to the level and pool that is just right for you. You follow him. You step into the pool. At once you feel the indigo ray fill your every atom. Reassurance fills your heart. You are aware of lofty feelings. As you relax into it, you begin to remember who you are. You feel comfortable with this knowledge as you move deeper into the pool. The water is warm and your skin is tingly. It invigorates your body. You are aware that this experience is on such a subtle level that you don't seem solid. Your astral body (a form in the shape of your physical body but composed of tiny lights) feels reassured of your intention to learn to embody positive energy. In fact, you notice everything is almost becoming transparent. You are simply aware that a cleansing is occurring. The water seems to pass through you. You let it.

Relax and let the indigo ray wash away your negative constructs. They are like piles of crud and grit on your skin. "You may return here any time you wish," says the young man as he helps you out of the pool and leads you back to your changing room. "Take all the time you need," he suggests. You thank him. You let him know with a nod that you can find your own way out. Gratitude wells up in your heart.

Return to this experience as often as you like, especially when you have difficulty holding on to positive energy.

In all, indigo sodalite may be one of the most profound influences on our lives of any of the gemstones, because most all of the Earth's residents are deficient in this important color ray. Most of us have little awareness of this lack. We do not miss the capabilities that we have never known. These capabilities are associated with the portion of the mind that responds to sodalite. In fact, we are in awe of those few individuals who have some small ability to use it. We refer to them as geniuses or savants. They seem to us to come up with new thought through some mysterious gift. They seem to know about everything. Their ability is one we can learn.

Notice how easily we overlook this color. This is evidence of its mystery. We would miss orange or green if it were gone, but that color between blue and purple is hard to distinguish and easily overlooked. Let us make a conscious effort to bring its influence into our lives, and we shall open up new vistas for all who follow. Be an explorer. Others may not recognize you for it, but you will know you are learning. You will recall talents you have forgotten and you will take on new challenges that help you resolve a way to overcome formidable barriers. That unshakable certainty of having ventured beyond your previous limitations with indigo will be yours.

Ordinary Sodalite

This stone brings healing by absorbing and removing negative energies. Disharmony is broken up by sodalite. The aura is cleansed and purified by wearing a strand around the neck. It pulls out disharmony from the air we breathe like a sponge ingests the microbes from water. It neutralizes the disharmony. You may wear dark indigo sodalite and if you are releasing disharmony to the sodalite you will soon notice the stones clouding with white. Cloudiness forms from disharmonies.

Sodalite is a perfect first treatment for trauma. Place it as close as possible to the site of trauma as soon as possible after the occurrence. If tissues are torn or ruptured, sodalite will repair the aura allowing for faster healing. Sodalite works primarily on the supraphysical level and repairs breaches and aberrations in the lines of energy normally coursing over the surface of the body. Once these energies are repaired, the tissues will have a directive from which to repair themselves. Larger traumas take time, but the healing will be more complete and scar tissue will more closely resemble original tissue when the supraphysical energy is functioning properly.

Unlike other stones, sodalite absorbs negativity and does not hold it on the surface. As sodalite absorbs negativity, it gradually becomes permanently filled. Eventually it will not be able to absorb any more and must be buried to cleanse the white clouds.

Sodalite can be a catalyst for healing when used with other stones. It is especially well suited to wearing with sea and earth stones like coral and malachite, or with rose quartz, quartz, aventurine, and lavender amethyst. It can be integrated in necklaces or worn during therapies with many different stones.

One key area of support from sodalite is help with achieving balance. Restorative, stabilizing, calming, emotionally replenishing, soothing, and cleansing are all actions associated with sodalite. Whether you have a troubled mind or are emotionally upset or stressed, wearing sodalite for periods of a few hours to a few days each week can help.

If the physical body is functionally operational and the negativity within is at the level of the emotional body or mental body sodalite will begin to resolve energy problems at these levels. It seeks the area of greatest negativity on whatever level. Sodalite will ease weariness and fatigue caused by excessive emotional releases. It will show the wearer how certain thoughts are the origin for these emotions. Sodalite will clear the mind and allow the thoughts to become more focused once the energy of the sodalite penetrates into the mental area. A grade of sodalite that holds no inclusions of metallic or soft white salts will be required to adequately reach the mental level. Wearers may notice a tingling sensation in the head when the sodalite has moved its focus to this area.

Those who have allergies may find relief from some of the severe reactions after prolonged use of sodalite. Allergies typically are an overreaction to stimuli or a repulsion of foreign substances that trigger them. The substances or energies could be almost anything. Reactions range from congestion and irritation to severe headaches, chest pain, chronic joint pain, or bleeding. Bringing the body into greater balance where it can handle these influences and substances more easily is not a fast process. The buildup of excess energy that is being released in this process took many years and will often take years to clear up, but if left unattended, these conditions could become quite debilitating. Sodalite works first on building the strength of the cells at the site of greatest discomfort during allergy attacks by removing breaches, absorbing negative energy, or breaking up patterns of disharmony. Then it works on the immune system to speed relief now and during later attacks.

Some allergies are the result of hereditary weakness, especially allergies to certain pollens, dust, or molds. Hereditary allergies will not go away, but they may be less aggravating if your body can become desensitized to the offending substance or learn to remove it without resorting to extreme reactions.

An excellent gemstone to wear when you are under attack or surrounded by disease or insanity, sodalite helps you maintain a sense of harmony in the midst of a storm. It does this by clearing the air you breathe.

Try breathing the indigo color in, and watch the color ray tear into pollution and allergens. It marks them for easy elimination. This effect may be enhanced if you are visualizing the air you are breathing as purified and cleared of disharmony by the vibrations of sodalite.

Imagine breathing deeply after a blue rain has cleansed the air about a pollen-rich field. See how the deep blue droplets mark the pollen and make it heavy so that it drops to the ground. Place a strand of sodalite about twenty-four to twenty-eight inches long around your neck. Picture yourself in a meadow after a cleansing rain. Let the fresh air fill your lungs. Breathe in until you can hold no more. Hold the breath for a few seconds. Now breathe out. Hold for a few seconds. After each long, slow inhale and brief hold, slowly breathe out fully all the stale air from the deepest part of your lungs. See the disharmony and toxins from the cells throughout the body coming out of your lungs. It is a gray cloud of disharmony. Smell the stale congestion as it leaves your mouth. Notice how fresh and invigorating is the indigo-infused air. It is like the air after a strong lightning storm has passed.

This exercise will cleanse the whole body if practiced daily for a month or two, and will work deeper and deeper the longer it is practiced. Begin by practicing for five minutes each morning and gradually increase the time to twenty minutes a day. You should notice an improvement in your attitude after the first try.

Part of sodalite's mission is to show us the "is-ness" of a thing; that is, the nature of that which does not change about a thing. As we release our attachments to things, we will become more aware of their subtle nature. Use it to help you practice acceptance of the differences in other people that once may have bothered you. Give yourself and others the gift of your acknowledgment. Simply noticing the essence of a person and appreciating it is a great gift.

As you acknowledge others, you will be able to accept their acknowledgment. Validation is an essential ingredient to an internal feeling of self-confidence. Few gifts of nature come to those who do not feel deserving. Feel it, and the universe will begin to contribute to the inner storehouse of reasons to feel grateful. Become a magnet for love by giving approval for the basic natural goodness of those you meet. You may have to learn to ignore the rough edges to see the fine polish of the soul underneath the abrasive personalities of your acquaintances. Don't be fooled. We all have a beautiful radiant light beneath our rough exteriors. Most action is motivated by love, however distorted.

Sodalite helps maintain clear boundaries. For those who have trouble identifying the source of thoughts and emotions in their space, sodalite can help with discrimination. You will develop a clear sense of your own space and the invasions of that space when wearing sodalite. You may more readily feel safe and self-contained while wearing this stone. It is especially useful for empathetic people who find themselves taking on the thoughts and feelings of others. Those who have trouble determining which feelings are theirs and which feelings came from another will have a much-improved awareness of self. It is not always desirable to feel the feelings of all those in your life. It is sometimes preferable to let these feelings pass.

Individuals who suffer from chronic sadness, guilt, or fear may be greatly helped by sodalite. This stone, when worn in a necklace of spheres, will allow persons to see beyond their conditions. Thus, the depression or weariness associated with intense long-term emotions may be ended sooner. Do not be alarmed if these emotions seem to surface. Sodalite can only raise them; it cannot digest our emotions. It soothes and comforts as releases are encouraged. Releases made when you are soothed are more effective at reducing excess emotion. The particular emotion must be experienced before it can be identified and finally released. Emotions that were not fully released will come back. Sodalite helps to remove unwanted, recurring emotions only if you are willing to see the process of letting them out to its natural conclusion.

When you are having difficulty sorting through the influences in your life, you should try wearing a strand. You may thus find it easier to remove the nonuseful from the useful. Once you have learned discrimination, you can readily establish what is important and remove the unimportant.

It is of service to the whole of mankind to wear sodalite, for it helps to clear the air around us. It absorbs harsh, life-damaging negativity and blocks psychic attacks. It will even help protect us from the effects of certain low-level radiation.

Try rubbing the stones on areas that have been traumatized in the past and have "healed over." This will help the body remember its original form and allow the healing to progress further even if completed. Scars will probably remain, but the scar tissue will become integrated with the surrounding tissue. This action may not help to repair your looks, but it surely will help the area let go of latent effects of trauma. Rubbing is also helpful to soothe and heal areas of the body that you have bad feelings towards. You may learn to love your body or you may not, but your body needs the nourishment of love, and sodalite can help it feel better. Simply rub the stones on the affected area. Repeat as frequently as needed.

If, for example, you dislike your thighs for some reason, take time to rub them with sodalite. Repeat this treatment daily for two weeks. Let the thoughts of disappointment with thigh shapeliness or firmness remain quiet while simply loving your thighs. Let the sodalite remove any self-directed judgement or loathing. You simply must take care of what you have if you expect your body to cooperate with plans to improve.

Those who are living a life devoted to spiritual service may look to sodalite for help in the moments of despair. All people will have moments of doubt and confusion, particularly as you reach out to overcome fear. You may experience the sensation of being in a spiritual void during spiritual transformations. These experiences are known as a "dark night of soul." These episodes can be quite frightening, and fear could create unnecessary setbacks. Try sodalite if you are entering one of these transformations. It is like a view of the future. It helps you see the other side of the cycle when things will right themselves. Conditions may not change, but the cessation of fear and panic can go a long way to helping you learn the truth about soul. Soul is never alone or in real danger of extinction. Soul is never in actual danger from any external threats as long as you are aware of your sovereignty as soul.

Known as the "throat stone" in Africa, you may find in sodalite the support for self-expression. In the presence of sodalite, communications of a sensitive nature will be easier to express. We can learn to communicate in a manner that gets the message across without compromising our integrity. Speaking your most revealing inner truths may best be done while wearing sodalite. Try using a short strand that fits close around your throat when giving that next public talk or during a meeting at work.

Sodalite will teach us when to share. It can help us determine when to go farther and when to hold back. Sometimes it is necessary to keep silent about our newest growth patterns. We must fully assimilate a new behavior or thought before we can share it without diluting its subtle qualities.

Imagine a new realization as a delicate distillation of the essence of a wonderful flower—a single new flower with a delicate subtle fragrance just beginning to be produced. Would you pour this drop of essence into a bottle of French perfume? Not if you expected ever to differentiate it as a separate olfactory experience. Your nose would never know the joy of its delicate beauty.

Treat each new realization as a sample drop of new scent. It could be the last drop of essence of that flower ever relished. Open its tiny bottle and put it on when you are alone. Don't waste your drop by diluting it with the scents of a group of other, stronger fragrances. Value each new realization, relish it, and it will multiply until you have enough to fill a whole big bottle and can share it with all your loved ones.

Sodalite will work well in treatments with rose quartz, aventurine, quartz, and carnelian whenever these are used to bring up disharmony. The sodalite will absorb some of the disharmony before it can become harmful to your health. Disharmony that has long been stored in parts of the body that have grown accustomed to its presence can be quite harmful to other parts of the body. Sodalite will allow us to learn from the disharmony as we release it without having to experience the effects the disharmony would have on the other, more vulnerable parts of the body. If we do not learn from disharmony, it will return to bring its lessons. When releasing disharmony, be open to the learning. Sometimes the important thing to learn is simply not to repeat the behavior that generated the experience that brought on the disharmony in the first place.

Sodalite is a tool that would be a great addition to any collection of gemstone therapy necklaces. For those who are serious about exploring unfamiliar realms within, this stone will act as a companion and aid in all your inner searches. Tread the path of inner self-exploration with confidence when you bring your sodalite guide. You can learn to heal your deeper wounds more easily with its vibrations for support. For those who wish only to ease their discomforts, this stone is one to carry everywhere.

Iolite

Choose carefully iolite beads with few dark regions. Spheres will change color as you look from different angles into this clear, indigo-blue gemstone. Do not wear this indigo-ray stone as a necklace while wearing other jewelry and expect to enjoy the therapeutic qualities of this mysterious gemstone.

Iolite will aid you in the process of discovering the hidden forces that create life. It will assist the wearer in looking at their life from a new perspective. Perspective is the all-important and overlooked relationship to truth. Truth is available to all, and yet we disagree. Truth is not actually a matter of opinion. You will find no need of arguing the merits of truth when you stand firmly on the rock of truth. From this vantage, all else— matters for speculation, opinion, conjecture, recollection, and argument—will be like the wind that blows all around but does not change the mountain. We differ because we have different perspectives. The highest perspective allows you to see all that is permanent. You will stop arguing when you find the inner ability to differentiate the permanent from the temporary. You could say that this mysterious stone brings peace.

Iolite steers you to the highest perspective. It shows the road to the highest peaks. Truth may be quite elusive under most circumstances, yet wearing an iolite necklace of spheres or rondels will open you to the marks of truth and the underlying principals that guide one to the way of subtle truth. It is through the discovery of many perspectives that truth reveals itself. To climb the mountain you must walk the path. Each perspective along the way is important, that we may one day reach the top and recognize it. Have all the opinions you like, just be prepared to drop them when the truth becomes visible. To ascertain the abiding truth, you must gain a perspective of unconditional love. Iolite cannot teach such love, only love itself can do that. Iolite can show you ever finer distinctions to truth as opposed to illusion. This discrimination helps you to know true love when you experience it.

Perspective is a pivotal word to work with when wearing iolite. Wearing an iolite necklace of spheres encourages the mind to see from a new vantage point each time it is worn. For this reason, you may wish to wear iolite long enough to discover a new view, and then remove it to wear again after you have assimilated all that is available from this perspective. At another time, wear it again and a new point of view will be found. Each new wearing provides the next higher perspective. Each addition to the height of the view affords the wearer a more comprehensive understanding. In this way, iolite is a tool for spiritual discovery. Understanding will not raise you on a spiritual scale. It will, however, relieve any feelings of revenge, stubbornness, or bitterness, and this release can lead to greater acceptance and acceptance does raise you on the spiritual scale. These feelings come from a belief that life is unfair. Only a raising of perspective will release you from this trap. These feelings must be given up, just as the unfaithful lover must be sent away and a window must be left open for love to steal into the heart, like a champion in the night, and win the heart to faithful love forever.

When you wear an iolite necklace and look into the areas of yourself that are not available to any of the senses, faculties of the mind, or emotions, you will begin to see into these areas more clearly than ever before. We may think of ourselves as an open book, yet we may hardly know a fraction of what is in our book. Use iolite to explore the chapters. Reveal to yourself new vistas. Discover undiscovered worlds. Within us all are the powers that shape our world though they may be lost to our sight behind doors that only love can open.

For those who are seeking to see into the future or to understand present conditions, iolite is a perfect tool. Of those, certain individuals will be instantly sensitive to the effects of iolite, and others may not notice anything initially. Eventually iolite will open inner doors that have remained shut. We must look inside and discover our own perspective of truth to find our way in the maze of life. Iolite does not sequester truth for easy viewing, nor does it capture our wild opinions, though they may need to be corralled and trained to become useful. Yet iolite will allow our opinions to remain free like wild ponies though they stand alone against others of their kind. We must teach ourselves to hold those opinions that are helpful. We must nurture these useful opinions if we expect them to remain in service to ourselves and others.

Wearers will notice subtle changes in their capacity to reason as they assimilate principals to live by derived from truth. Possibilities will occur to the logical mind that may seem to come from nowhere. Surprises will seem normal. This activity is iolite stirring the pot and allowing deep, uncharted aspects of the mind to be revealed momentarily. Be alert, otherwise those glimpses will pass unnoticed.

Illumination is the primary mission of iolite. It helps us see within, into the "darker" areas. It also helps to illuminate intuitive flashes as they pass quickly. At times iolite will help us to recognize the "sixth sense," that of knowing without being given hard data. The wearer may not as yet have had prophetic dreams, telepathic connections, remote viewing, or angelic intervention, but one who uses iolite and puts attention on developing these will begin to have such experiences. By gazing into this stone and practicing the art of oblique viewing, you may see much that has been hidden. Oblique viewing—the art of seeing without looking—may be practiced by softly defocusing the eyes and letting what is in the peripheral vision come clear without looking at it. Iolite can help. Place a large piece of clear iolite on a pedestal so that it stands in front of your view approximately eighteen inches from your eyes. Practice looking beyond the iolite at something ten or fifteen yards away (across the room) and then slowly bring it into view while maintaining the distant focus. Just as iolite looks different from different sides and different angles and seems to change color from almost clear to deep indigo, life will change depending on how we view it. Spend time looking into iolite while contemplating the possibility that your point of view is simply a temporary moment, always changing like the surface of a river, but experience is the crystallization of a lesson in love, like the power of a river itself.

Clairvoyance is possible. Those who have active imaginations will be more likely to experience it, but anyone can. Those who think they are too practical and pragmatic to notice anything that "isn't there" probably have had similar experiences like déjà vu—the "I know I've been here before" experience.

If you are technologically oriented, you may become open to new ways of applying modern technologies as you continue to wear iolite.

Technology is useful in a variety of ways. It may benefit us or it may harm us. Technology can bring miracles when measured by standards of a few years ago. Need has propelled us to this point. Today we are faced with many decisions—technology has advanced too fast for our bodies to easily adapt. Iolite can help us discover ways of using technologies that do not overtax the physical body's organs and cellular structure. Only love will teach you to recognize and apply the better technologies—technologies that improve life without harming anything.

In times when our hearts teach us to recognize the needs of the individual, we will learn the difference between need and the desire for a greater ego. Personal needs of those who are in pain drive those with open hearts to a better world.

Iolite works to open the intelligence within the heart center. The intelligence that resides in this center of the human form is capable of many new forms of healing. Try to visualize the art of healing as a completely new science. Look for the unexpected. Experiment and you will be sure to get new results that will lead you down a whole new avenue of approach. The heart may seem like just a muscle that pumps blood, but it is a center for intelligence and can provide us with direction based on an understanding of love. Simply bring love into your heart and think of any situation that seems problematic and the answer will come, especially if you wear a strand of iolite spheres.

Containing the colors of blue, silver, gray, and indigo, this stone has an array of areas it stimulates, from the lower mental to the upper mental and subconscious. Do not be surprised if these areas are capable of forms of perception that have been unknown to you in the past.

Part of the mission of iolite is to help persons create a new stance for themselves. In this way, they will become more powerful without having to be aggressive or assertive. Learning to be strong is a teaching many of us can use who are on the path of self-development.

For those who continue to wear iolite, the "third eye," or brow chakra, will become aligned through the physical, astral, and other sheaths. Once these bodies have been aligned by the indigo ray in iolite, one may begin to have more pointed dreams. Inner vision will be increasingly brighter, and the elusive silver ray may illuminate things from all sides in a sort of 360-degree perspective.

It may be hard to imagine being able to see in every direction at once. It may be harder still to imagine being able to go anywhere, anytime, without actually moving. Iolite introduces us to possibilities beyond everyday thought. Much is possible, and it is time for each of us to work with tools like iolite that can open inner, latent capabilities so that we can all apprehend truth without going to a psychic that may provide us with truth or may mix conjecture with their own projections. We must learn ourselves to know the truth, wherever it may come from, for truth may come from any direction; even our enemy may teach us.

Another part of iolite's mission is to show humanity that there is a future beyond this life. This revelation is like seeing an image of a man flying with no movement to the edge of the precipice we call death and seeing into the future. Life beyond death is real life. Even the formless regions may become accessible for those who conquer fear and open their hearts to gratitude. In these regions we may begin to comprehend the fact that things are not just what they seem. In fact, things may be more fluid and shifting than our minds would like.

In our efforts to let go of fears and limitations, the practice of experiencing the formless worlds will prove most helpful. These are the worlds of complete freedom from limitations that exist in a dimension that occupies the same space we do but may be inaccessible to anyone who cannot see beyond their limits. You must seek this realm of personal freedom quietly. You may learn to come and go into these worlds by allowing the indigo ray to fill your heart and by moving across the barrier of limitation as softly as the mouse. Discover the worlds within worlds as you follow iolite into the indigo ray. Go with iolite. Go with curiosity and courage. Let your inner worlds be.

White stones bear the white color ray. Most white stones have a bit of another color to them. This variation gives them a slightly different effect, and they thereby emphasize different aspects of the white ray. Only clear quartz and the perfectly balanced therapeutic white diamonds are free from tinges of other colors. These two stones are very powerful and can bring about changes in all the bodies and in all the color-ray systems.

The white ray works with the whole being. It helps the wearer become autonomous. It puts the wearer in touch with information concerning their relationship to the whole. The whole here refers to the whole person as well as the whole of creation. All people are a part of creation. One person may consider himself a steward of life and seek to serve all life, while another person may make every effort to destroy life. Nevertheless, we are all interrelated. Becoming whole requires getting the various parts of ourselves working together. Becoming part of the greater whole requires developing communication skills that allow greater dialogue, and this task requires an openness to the sometimes foreign attitudes of others.

How, you may ask, can we experience being interrelated? Certainly we all are capable of directly experiencing this interrelatedness.

10
White Ray Stones

It cannot be described to someone who has not personally felt it—words are not sufficient to characterize this experience. Some consider it part of the goal in the process of "individuation," as described by Joseph Campbell, Carl Jung, and others. Many have described it as a religious experience and religious leaders have inspired their followers with their descriptions. The white ray is always involved. It is seen or felt by those who have near-death experiences as well; often the experience is preceded by or begins with the vision of a brilliant white light. The white light is associated with transition into the other worlds at the time of cessation of the life of the physical body.

White-ray energy is abundant for those rare individuals who have mastered the spiritual experience and are privileged to have the white light as needed. Those who wish to come gradually to full integration, to deep self-realization, and to the practice of this experience can consider the white stones as allies. White-ray energy aligns one with these goals. Several of the white stones move a person to the greater motivation, clarity, balance, and strength required to attain these goals.

Our bodies are conglomerations of symbiotic organs and systems. Each is dependent on the others, yet each vies for its own needs as if it were independent. The design is such that the system still functions, even when there is little cooperation among systems. Often, competition for raw materials and color-ray energy is rampant. That anything works at all under these circumstances is amazing. Only the white color ray will bring about changes in the level of cooperation between otherwise competing organs.

Wear white color-ray stones, and life will change. The left hand will no longer be able to do without the agreement of the right. One may be able to find how he or she fits into the grand scheme of things. The age-old question, "Why am I here?" can be answered by an individual only for themselves. White-ray persons are often seeking to find a better, more complete answer to the question of how to integrate themselves with their world and they can be distraught if such experiences do not become a part of their lives. Their challenge is to figure out how to occasion these experiences of complete integration of the outer world with the inner reality. A white-ray person must understand themselves completely.

Those whose primary color ray is white display a great balance and integrity when operating in alignment with their life mission. Finding their life mission may prove to be the project of a lifetime. Often they will only figure out what their mission was as they live the last few hours of their lives. White-ray people must go through life simply doing the best they can with the challenges and opportunities given to them.

White-ray people make excellent mates and leaders when they have found a way of giving that uplifts them. This may be a silent form of giving, such as maintaining a clear channel for the white-ray energy. Then again, it may be a more obvious form such as career counseling, contracting to fulfill the dreams of others, or being a judge. Their greatest realizations will come during selfless moments.

Cooperation, communication, agreement, common understanding, and language—all of these together are the realm of the white ray. White ray energy produces dramatic improvement in these areas as it demands a mastery of the reactive, self-centered parts of the mind. Other color rays help you discover these abilities; white-ray energy helps you bring all your abilities to focus on developing an understanding of how you fit into the macrocosm and how your microcosm can be a precise reflection of the macrocosm.

Take note: diamonds come in a variety of colors, and it is only one in ten thousand diamonds that can be used for therapy. Diamonds of a lesser grade or those not precisely matched to the human blueprint will cause considerable harm with every use. For exact color-ray balance and purity, use only diamonds that have been tested by a qualified, experienced diamond therapist who is well versed in diamond selection and has been trained in the precise art of gemology as well as having been trained to identify therapeutic diamonds. This diamond therapist must be capable of determining the precise color ray spectrum of diamonds that match the individual who is to use it. Under no circumstances should diamonds be used for therapy without absolute certainty as to their therapeutic value. Diamonds can damage blueprints if they are not perfectly in tune with the white ray. If they are not precisely harmonious with the human blueprint, you can cause basically irreparable damage to your blueprints.

Therapeutic diamonds will help everyone because they awaken our awareness and force us to modify our lives until we completely align our every action with our highest purpose and completely adjust our bodies until they are operating according to our blueprints. Such diamonds must be selected for perfect color balance, clarity, magnetism, and brilliant cut.

Clear Quartz

Clear, optical-quality quartz is a most powerful and widely used gemstone. Use only the best-quality quartz; any inclusions or cloudiness can be harmful. Quartz must have a natural crystalline structure. Do not use fabricated or manufactured quartz. Cutting and shaping of spheres must be a precision effort; cracks and gouges in the surface of a sphere indicate a lesser quality. If you spot bubbles in the "quartz" that are within the body of the beads or on the surface, you will know the stone is glass or some other man-made, clear material.

Truly fine-quality quartz in the spherical form creates a strong grounding with the earth. At first, grounding may seem less glamorous than the actions of other stones; however, grounding is perhaps one of the most useful properties of any tool available to humankind.

When we are grounded, we can see things without projecting ourselves into them. We can maintain enough detachment from the forces of nature to see them for what they are. We can see ourselves reflected in all that surrounds us without confusing these things with ourselves. We let the forces that would harm us skim our surface while engaging in the forces that will take us into the roots of our situation. Grounding brings us into balance with life. Our endurance is greater when we are grounded. We can make use of more kinds of energies without risk of getting hurt or getting caught up in their power. Paradoxically, a person can more easily achieve a higher state of spiritual consciousness when peace is made with the physical consciousness through grounding.

If we maintain grounding for a period of time, we will grow in strength and resolve, improving our chances for effortless survival. We can learn to focus our energy in concentrated ways. Strength need not fall away at fifty or sixty years of age. Quartz can help us keep youthful and vigorous.

Quartz can help us maintain our balance point. By practicing what is known in the Eastern martial arts as "centering," we can learn to maintain a clear sense of where our balance point, or fulcrum, is located within the body. With discipline and practice, this knowledge can lead to mastery of centering, and thereby, we avoid ups and downs. This practice is not for the purpose of becoming self-centered, rather it is the process of becoming centered in that place within ourselves where we are fully aware. From this place, we are in touch with all of creation. Centering is taught as a part of the martial arts because it is a practice that directly affects our ability to handle conflict without getting overly involved with trying to force a certain outcome. One who is trained extensively in centering can remain balanced while many forces come at them.

Quartz, then, teaches flexibility. It brings into our lives all the forces of nature to teach floating balance. It insists we face our challenges. It persists at reminding us of the procrastination we allow in ourselves to avoid making decisions.

From our center, the white ray shows us how to act with focus and efficiency and use all our abilities. We tend to make fewer mistakes and those we make only add to our ability to remain flexible. A wearer is in touch with instincts, that is to say intuitively aware of what is best and what immediate actions will serve and protect.

The experience of wearing clear quartz is like that of being in a protective capsule of personal power. The circumstances drawn to us by quartz may require us to step out of our normally limited routines yet we feel safe and present. Like a cat, we will be more relaxed and at ease, while at the same time ready for anything. Catlike supple and strong muscles are quick to react but never hard or overdeveloped. This state of readiness is most useful to those who are pursuing sports, are in training for combat, or wish to practice gymnastics, dance, or other such activities.

Quartz-expedited white rays have a softening effect on the physical body. You become more flexible, and your muscles learn to be strong and have more bounce and spring. This process will benefit all those who wear a strand during physical exercise. Those who are loosened up experience fewer accidents in or out of the gym.

Strands that have no knots between beads can break more easily than knotted strands, so it may be preferable to use a strand with knots between each bead while exercising. Some may wish to sew quartz beads into arm bands, leg bands, clothing, or headbands if such inclusions will not cause injury during exercise.

In the presence of quartz, the life force, which consists of all colors, will be drawn into the body in greater concentrations than ever before. This process will gradually begin to soften hardened areas, which are predecessors of cancer. Healthy, more supple tissues will grow in the place of hardened, prolapsed, or withered tissue, as the life force fills these tissues. Persons suffering from liver and kidney deterioration will begin to feel better, as organs and supporting tissue reproduce stronger, more healthy cells. New support cells will be more elastic and capable of providing greater support to the affected areas.

Those who have had too much alcohol to drink for many years but have now quit drinking will be helped immensely. Alcohol hardens some tissues while breaking down others. Under the influence of alcohol, cells lose their ability to reproduce new cells that have integrity and strong cell walls. Quartz will transmit the information from remaining healthy cells required to teach sick and depleted cells how to repair themselves. Quartz will start with the cells that have suffered the most. It will show the damaged cells a blueprint for health. With this blueprint to go by, a cell can somewhat regain its original state and can reproduce new cells that fully function to original specifications.

Once cells regain the blueprint information, they will begin to generate the proper conditions under which they can draw greater life force into themselves. Cells are like individual creatures who live in a cooperative situation with other cells. Once the environment within a local area where a particular type of cell lives becomes hostile, the cell must begin to reproduce itself with modifications suitable for life in this environment. The new cells produced under these conditions often are not cooperative with surrounding cells, just as children growing up in a war-torn Middle East country will often become renegade terrorists and fight among themselves.

Let us call these new cells, which have differed from the norm and do not cooperate with other cells, renegade cells. Renegade cells will reproduce themselves and create more renegade cells. Without some intervention from the white ray, this process will continue until newly produced cells are bred to be hostile and cancerous and actually seek to destroy the body. Clear quartz will initiate the intervention process. The DNA of the aberrant cells may begin to change and can even revert back to the DNA of a healthy cell as cells begin to clean up the unhealthy circumstances of their ravaged lives.

Clear quartz also brings all the color rays to cells that have been accepting only a few of the color rays. These cells are starved for balance; that is, the balance achievable only with a proper proportion of color rays. As cells are exposed to an abundance of color-ray energy, they learn to take in proper proportions of the different color rays and this degeneration will stop. Bring enough aid to an impoverished area and the residents will eventually learn self-sufficiency, if that aid is in the form of tools that empower individuals and lessons that teach dignity. Clear quartz is such a tool and the white ray brings such lessons to those who fill themselves with it. Our bodies function at a level closer to an impoverished neighborhood than a model community. We need to consider renovation.

Quartz can focus the life force on areas of the body that have gone undernourished. If the availability of true, balanced color ray nourishment is reestablished for a considerable length of time, even renegade cells may begin to produce healthy offspring. Renegade cells thus will eventually be replaced by cooperative ones.

During this process, quartz will put pressure on the wearer to refute habits that have caused conditions that allow disharmonious cells to become established. Cells that are renegade and those that simply have modified their operations to withstand the influences of a hostile environment cannot fully recover until the wearer has changed old, destructive habits. The wearer may begin to feel pain and discomfort in these areas that have been affected as old habits are challenged. Often, the pain will be felt for the first time in areas that have been suffering, as they begin to signal their discomfort to the central nervous system.

Do not panic. A little pain may be part of the healing process. Use lavender or aventurine to lessen the pain. Use sodalite or turquoise to clear the aura. You may even wish to use amazonite to draw out the disharmony (for details see chapter 11). Either way, be sure to honor the pain as a mark of an inner challenge and have compassion for a renegade reaching out for help.

Life will become increasingly uncomfortable for someone who resists until behaviors are changed. These behaviors can be anything with a negative impact on the body; that is, everything from repeated release of harmful emotions like rage or anger, to mental processes that induce stress, like worry or fear. For one person it may be interpersonal habits and for another it may be a simple habit like watching the news that causes disharmony. It's all in your reactions.

Any thoughts or feelings that create stress or anxiety will cause the stressed cells to produce toxins and release them into the body. Toxins must be removed from the interior of cells as a form of self-purging and self-defense. Toxins cause a deadly internal environment in which cells become defensive or even hostile. Cells that are defending against each other and the toxins that are being produced are essentially at war. Eventually, even a person who is otherwise healthy and eats a proper diet will become ill as a result of this war.

The way this process works is insidious and subtle at first, but will become life-threatening as time goes on. A state of war taxes all systems and nullifies the benefits normally derived from the actions of these systems as they have been forced to redirect their energies to the war.

Modern science is baffled by the sudden increase in stress-related diseases like arthritis, rheumatism, intestinal dysfunction, ulcers, tumors, bone degeneration, cell wall deterioration, some heart diseases, cancer, hardening of the arteries, and more. Some of these diseases are caused by toxins being stored in bone, joints, liver, or kidneys, and some are caused by the disharmony itself.

Be assured that no gemstone can cause a person to stop the behaviors that cause these problems, however quartz will try. If a wearer wants to resist change, they may simply choose to stop wearing the gemstone.

Although a gemstone will not force change, an increase in the amount and proper balance of life force will expand our awareness. We will become aware of all the ways we can improve our lives. Introducing quartz into your aura on a regular basis will create the impetus for changes that inspire and excite us. Quartz will require us to change our behaviors. Change is our choice, but we must realize that quartz is an instrument of cellular and emotional restructuring. Putting on a strand of clear quartz is like sending a loud signal to the body that it is time to change.

Be prepared to have all your motivations brought out into the light of awareness. Quartz will highlight all your practices. It is not partial to your ego. In fact, quartz will often insist through its action that our ego take a less strict role in our decision-making. The ego is not likely to give up any of its control without some resistance.

Unfortunately resistance will often translate into pain. To avoid this pain, the ego must be occupied with entirely different activities while the processes that quartz initiates proceed. Keeping the ego occupied most of the time requires diligence and self-discipline. The ego rebels at self-discipline. The ego hates having to stick to a program of change. It generates feelings of discomfort and will try to stop our efforts at significant improvement. It wants the status quo to remain intact.

To keep the ego busy we can employ "tricks." The use of visualizations, affirmations, imaginative techniques, repetitive actions like driving or working on an assembly line, chanting, dancing, physical exercise, reading books that contain information on how spirit works, making lists, writing journals, and other activities that engage the mind will keep the ego busy with "important tasks" without taking quite all of our attention. We must then learn to split our attention, putting attention on the task at hand and also on the revitalization process that is going on in the mind.

In this way, we will grow in awareness without constantly meeting our internal resistance. Keeping the ego busy will minimize the pain and afford us the opportunity to see ourselves more easily.

Try this simple technique: Ask yourself, "What kinds of feelings am I experiencing in my body right now?" Then ask, "What emotions have I had today?" After viewing those, ask, "What memories or fantasies about the future have I been engaged in?" Finally, ask yourself, "What have I been analyzing, debating, or thinking about today?"

When you are through with these questions, you will have taken an objective look at what your mind, body, and emotions are doing. In order to do this, you must be observing yourself from outside the astral, causal, and mental bodies. Only soul exists outside these bodies. If you have answered objectively, you will have entered soul awareness. Only you as soul can initiate changes in your makeup from a place where you are detached and able to see the whole picture. Quartz helps you learn this objective state and become honest about these observations.

To significantly change the mind such that it can operate on a higher level, soul must be in charge. You are soul, but the mind likes to operate on its own, often on automatic pilot. As soul, you can see from a broad viewpoint. You can know things directly. Soul is capable of operating outside the restrictions of time and space. You can learn to tap into soul awareness while occupying the mind with repetitive tasks, which it likes. Repetition works well and allows you to split the attention more easily. Each person must develop this technique for themselves; no two minds are happy with the same tasks. Each person must find what works for them.

You will know that the practice of tricking the mind is working when you begin to find yourself having greater awareness. You will notice yourself actively seeking new ways of comprehension.

There is more to this powerful stone. It helps you to speak more clearly, listen with less judgment, and communicate more of the thoughts that really matter to you. Communication is improved in a number of ways when working with quartz spheres. Spend a few minutes each day with a high-quality quartz sphere just close enough to the eyes to comfortably see it. Then, look steadily into quartz and allow the white ray to induce new thoughts in the mind. To do this, you must keep the mind open and notice what comes to the mind on the subject of communication.

Look for many benefits from this exercise. First, the ability to keep your own thoughts and feelings separate from those of others is improved. Second, the ability to see others from a detached point of view helps us to listen and then reiterate what we have heard from others without a lot of reactionary emotion. In this way, we can better understand what others are telling us and make them feel they are being heard. Third, the lines of communication themselves are strengthened by quartz. These lines are like tiny filaments that connect each of us with all others and allow us to send our thoughts over great distances instantaneously. Quartz strengthens the receptors of the subtle body that are located at the pituitary gland in the center of the head behind the eyebrows. It also teaches us to recognize our sending frequency and the receiving frequency of the person we wish to send our thoughts to.

This process of strengthening the lines is a bit complicated but not too dissimilar to tuning two ham radios to the same frequency. Once they are carefully tuned such that both the sending and the receiving frequencies are the same on both radios, then communication becomes two-way.

Human communications are much more complicated because each thought or impression we send is different and has a different vibration. It is the same in that both people must have a clear intention to tune in to the same frequency. It is essential that both the sender and the receiver move together to the different frequencies used in a single communication. When this happens, a most enjoyable feeling results. This is the wonderful feeling that what I have to say matters to you, and what you have to say is clear to me. The connection between us will appear stronger than usual. This state is referred to as "entrainment." The word sounds like some sort of hypnotic state but is far from it. It is, in fact, a heightened state. All senses become more sensitive than usual. You can see into others' viewpoints like never before. You appear to be "in the zone," which means you are making clear, precise moves to exactly and effortlessly make every action count. Quartz facilitates entrainment. A feeling of exhilaration and certainty accompanies such moments of entrainment where you are sure everything is perfect. You are "in tune."

Quartz can act like a translator to expedite inner reception of transmissions and improve nonverbal communications between people. It will add a carrier frequency to all transmissions. In this way, the receiver will come to recognize a stable component or frequency that is an integral part of all incoming transmissions from a particular sender. The receiver's mind will sort and store all data that comes in from this sender in a separate area of the mind. The mind can then make distinct and separate correlations and computations specific to each person we communicate with.

Thus, more information is received accurately and it is all stored in a specific area for easy retrieval. Under the influence of quartz the receiver's mind will now keep information received from the sender in a file that is easily accessed. Quartz helps you develop a filing system according to the energy or vibration associated with each person. It creates a carrier vibration that the people can share.

Imagine if you will that we are all connected by lines of communication. These lines have their origin and connection place in any two or more people who are linked up. Each person can send out thoughts, impressions, emotions, and sensory data. The sender and the receiver, however, are actually working on different levels and are using different vibratory rates. Separate bursts of data go out from the sender along this line. The receiver then must filter the data for what is relevant and store the data that relates to him, unless he has a carrier frequency established with the sender. Since most of the data is not relevant to a readily accessible file, without this carrier, most would be dumped before it was even processed. When information is sent with a carrier frequency, incoming information instead will be sorted and stored.

Much of what is taken in is stored in files here and there throughout the memory. Imagine a filing system where all stored data is referenced to a set of frequencies that are similar only to the frequencies of thoughts that are carrying the same or very similar emotional and pictorial content. Such a filing system would have billions of files—one for each type of emotion or idea that is received.

All these files would be separated into sections that are not related to time or to the person who sent this information. You can picture such a system as if every impression, emotion, or idea your mind had ever received were written on a little slip of uniform paper and dropped into a file filled with ideas with the same emotional character. It would be like the Internal Revenue Service, storing each bit of data that related to your financial history in some particular way in a file along with everyone else's data on that same selected subject—with no reference to the date of entry or the person whose case this information related to on the file folder. One can readily see how filing by person and date would be more effective.

Quartz teaches us how to use a procedure to tag information. We connect each piece of input we store with a tag that carries information about its source and subject.

With tagging, we can accept much more information and store it more easily. We can also find it again later when we want to. Now whenever we are speaking to a particular person we know or are receiving information by telepathy, we can keep straight what one person tells us. Later, when reviewing the data, we will know how this information came to us and how reliable it is.

Quartz teaches a wearer to practice identifying the sender of a telepathic message. When you wish to tune into a particular source, you will be able to locate this source on your tuner. You can establish where this information came from and date it. You can separate the input data from one's interpretation of this data. This will make it possible to keep your memories straight and prepare you for the next step, which is to learn to receive impressions, emotions, and ideas from others even when you are busy doing something else.

Once this practice is established, we need never feel alone again. All we need do is, with their permission, picture a particular person and let the communication lines be open, whereupon, clear quartz will fine-tune our receptors to receive their impressions. This technique works from any distance. It may even work in dreams.

For those putting attention on spiritual communication, quartz will teach them to differentiate between thoughts that arise from the ego, communications from others, and spiritual communications that originate in the Holy Spirit or Universal Mind. Wearers will become adept at making distinctions like this.

A necklace of perhaps six- or eight-millimeter spherical quartz beads and twenty-eight inches in length is a most versatile tool. We may also wish to use one sphere that measures from one-and-a-half to ten inches in diameter. Some therapies implement up to twelve spheres at a time, employing spheres that are less than an inch in diameter. Experiment with them to find your own therapies. Place or tape spheres on all chakras at once—over the eyes, on feet and hands and head, along the major points of an acupuncture meridian, or over major organs. Spheres are the safest quartz tools, providing an effect that is gentle but powerful and insistent. We are always given a choice with spheres. We are led or pushed into looking at who we are and how we use energy, but never forced to make changes. Single spheres are very powerful. They should be left on the body no longer than one hour. Ten minutes to one half-hour is sufficient for most placements. A single sphere will focus on a single, small area of the human being and can initiate changes quickly for this reason.

Quartz crystals in their natural form have the ability to direct energies like a laser beam. This action may not be beneficial, as it forces energy into an area. The user must be careful since they can cause harm without knowing it, leaving the recipient in a prone position. In the natural crystal shape, quartz is not able to interact with our subtle bodies such that we as soul can control the changes. Energies from the crystals will pour into the body without stopping. The full spectrum of energy will be directed at a location or will draw out energy from the person. It can quickly oversaturate the body when pointed at it. The crystal will deplete the body rapidly when pointed away from it. For this reason we can get out of balance very easily. Changes are made without concern as to their consequences. Improperly used, this powerful energy can disrupt the astral body and cause long-term damage to our psyche with no warning.

Although some "seers" and certain healers will use quartz crystals to good purpose, they are not always aware of the consequences to the one being healed. They may remove certain blockages that have been necessary to maintain balance in a person's life. After all, our blockages are there for a reason. They were created to serve a purpose. We may need them until we can make balanced changes. We could also be introduced to entities or inner forces that we are not yet ready to handle spiritually. For this reason, I suggest using only strands of spheres or small individual quartz crystal balls that are undrilled.

You may safely experiment with crystals only when you are able to clearly sense and manipulate subtle energies. We hope to learn to move our subtle energies without tools. As we become proficient in the use of gemstone spheres, we may come to a point where we can move our energies at will and without their use.

Clear quartz spheres are a powerful tool for the healer. When used with appropriate purpose, you will create for yourself and others a "mold" for health. A mold is filled by energy and the form becomes manifest as a result of sustained intent. This is a clear intention with a specified and mentally visualized state of health. Holding a clear intention for the results you seek is most important to attaining a goal of excellent health. Without this intention, your chances of getting where you want to go are about as good as getting to a destination from your local train station without knowing which is the right train and not having the correct ticket even if you did.

Be prepared to be challenged by quartz. This stone will ask you to become the best you can be. Make the commitment to work with it and many possibilities for improvement will come. Follow these directions and you will find excellent health is one of many results to the process of learning to direct and accept the white-ray energy.

Most of us are not even aware of just how it would be if we were truly healthy and living to our full potential. Quartz will continue to challenge us even when we are beyond our comfort zone. Set your fears aside and know that every change that quartz asks you to make will create greater vitality and joy in every area of your life. We may have to give up all our preconceived notions of what life is all about to receive these benefits.

Diamond

Diamond is the most powerful of the gemstones. Amateurs, beware! Not only is it critical to be fully cognizant of the techniques for using diamonds in the aura and as placements, but the type of diamond used is also critical. The state of mind of the user and the thoughts that pass through the mind while working with diamonds become amplified and can manifest into changes rapidly. You should be skilled in the art of controlling your thoughts before using diamond.

Therapeutic diamonds rapidly create profound changes at all levels and within all the different bodies. There is an important relationship between the state of mind, skill, and experience of the person doing the treatments and the effectiveness of the treatment with diamond more than with any other gemstone. The practitioner must be aware of exactly how diamonds change the way the subtle bodies work. Working with other gemstones for a few years may be necessary to develop your ability to sense subtle energies and become aware of their movement as well as to clear your own imbalances and energy blocks before you begin using diamond.

A practitioner must be clear of all negative thoughts while doing therapy because the thoughts of the practitioner will be amplified by the diamond. A complete working understanding of the way the subtle bodies function and how they interact with each other is very important. Therapeutic diamonds have a mind of their own, and the therapist must allow them to interact with the bodies without getting negativity in the way.

It is important that the diamonds used be exactly balanced with respect to the color rays. Such diamonds are among the varieties known as white therapeutic diamonds. The perfect balance for humans have a special set of harmonic vibrations only found in a very few diamonds. These can not be detected by the usual means available to a gemologist. Only modern brilliant- and spherical-cut white diamonds that have this balance should be used on humans. The human structure can be profoundly disrupted by diamonds that do not have the correct balance of color rays.

White therapeutic diamonds have the effect of amplifying and focusing the full spectrum of colors in equal proportion. White diamonds can be used effectively for placements and auric therapies, but will cause imbalances in the emotional and physical bodies if used without clear mental focus and positive mental thought patterns as the mind of the practitioner is impressed on the recipient. Diamonds that have the correct balance of color rays are very beneficial and can be used in many more types of treatments than those listed here.

Never use diamonds that are not precisely matched to the human blueprint spectrum of colors. Any other type of diamond will cause irreparable damage to blueprints, resulting in harmful blueprint aberrations that can engender mutations of cellular purpose.

Only use diamonds of one-eighth to one-half carat. Diamonds of approximately one-quarter carat are more than sufficient to penetrate the body and stimulate changes at all levels. Larger diamonds may stimulate changes that are hard for the receiver to assimilate and impossible to understand. Since deep changes in the very core of our person are possible with diamonds, these changes should be taken gradually so the person can understand what is taking place and can go through the necessary mental and emotional adjustments to stay in balance during and after the changes.

Therapy should be conducted only by working with the near-perfect therapeutic diamonds. Any imperfections or inclusions that affect the focus or the effect of the diamond will be amplified by the crystalline structure of the diamond and will be harmful. Clear diamonds are relatively rare and must be graded by a professional using magnification equipment. Most diamonds have such inclusions or malformations, and some are cut incorrectly and are not usable for this reason.

The magnetic field of a therapeutic diamond to be used in the aura must be within specific tolerances such that it creates a beneficial magnetism. Diamonds can be far too positively charged and can cause changes that are out of the recipient's blueprint tolerance. Diamonds that have a negative magnetic field are also available, and these can cause regression and further the degenerative effects of any disease that is present. Stress in many forms is the result of therapy performed with diamonds that have inappropriate magnetic fields.

It is best to learn diamond therapies firsthand from a qualified diamond therapist.

Therapeutic diamonds that exhibit a high sparkle and seem to send out light in all directions are called sparklers. These diamonds have all the qualities described above, as well as an internal structure that gives off a higher degree of light and diamond vibrations. Therapy performed with such diamonds can help us channel light and operate in this world as beings of light.

Essentially, we are beings of light and our true form is that of soul, which is to say we are eternal and capable of being anywhere at any time. As soul we have the ability to perceive, know, and love. Our physical bodies are just a shell we wear to protect us from the coarse vibrations of the physical world. As such, they are susceptible to all sorts of aberrations and disease or disharmony. In order to better recognize ourselves as soul and to be able to consistently operate from this perspective, we must seek to realize perfect health and protect the physical body so that it will not be the center of all our attention.

The physical body is made up of atoms, molecules, cells, and organs. Each of these components is a system unto itself and is made up of parts that operate independently as well as collectively if the system is healthy. When stresses affect any of these systems, the parts tend to operate less harmoniously, and consequently the body becomes divided and its parts vibrate in a discordant manner. Suffice it to say that this condition is the basic cause of disease in the physical body. Therapeutic diamond naturally reintegrates systems and their functioning can be improved by fifty, even eighty-five percent. Simply circle the diamond over target areas some two to five inches away from the skin.

Therapeutic diamond, in conjunction with other gemstones like moonstone, lavender, indigo, and bloodstone, will highlight the stresses in the physical body. It will identify the causes for them. It will act directly to disintegrate destructive causes by intervening, focusing the mind on the moment when a destructive pattern would be repeated, reminding one of the costs of this pattern, and forcing the mind to reconsider the benefits of a more relaxed lifestyle. Diamond will then relax the mind from worry and allow the natural processes of these different physical systems to gradually relax into their natural rhythm and vibration. Soon you will become aware of the root causes of your conditions and be aided by diamond in coming to a necessary understanding of the lessons to be learned from such conditions you wish to change.

Besides the physical body, each of us also has an astral, or emotional, body as well as a causal (memory) body and a multilayered mental body. Each of these bodies allows us to operate simultaneously on these different levels—that is to say, we are multidimensional beings. We as soul are aware of this fact, but the mental, emotional, and physical bodies are aware only of themselves. For this reason, we may have the experience of being multidimensional beings only when we have our attention centered in the soul awareness. Since the shrouds (bodies) that surround us also protect us, we will not be able to shed them or escape their influence on our perception of who we are until we are ready to move our awareness into the subtle dimension in which soul exists free of sheaths. Our bodies must be healed, and all of the various distortions, stresses, aberrations, and diseases that keep our attention on the physical, emotional, causal, and mental dimensions must be corrected before we can become firmly established on the soul level.

Living out our lives is quite a positive learning process. As we are able to let go of all the resistance that is a cause of pain, we learn of our true nature in a way that will be a part of us for all eternity. We are soul, loving and beautiful. We are givers by nature. Giving love actualizes our purpose as soul. At this level of perception, we understand that power is much like love except that, untempered by love, it seeks to put the lower personas of the physical, emotional, causal, and mental realities on a pedestal from which we control others. Love is of a higher order. It has a divine form, unconditional and beyond the influence of anything in the regions below that of soul. From the viewpoint of love, giving and receiving are the same. When we take our place in this higher order, we will know unlimited love, but first, we must fully understand the nature and allure of power. Then we must, of our own accord, consciously choose love. Finally, we must remove all vestiges of the way of power in order to receive the benefits of the immense abundance of love that awaits us.

Therapeutic diamond works to open the higher chakras to a greater flow of energy, and the presence of this energy will allow the individual to experience abundance. Diamond will bring you to an understanding of this higher reality. It will teach you to shift your attention to this higher state and recognize the benefits of a higher consciousness. We can direct its vibration to open the chakras by placing it within a few inches of the chakra and visualizing a clear powerful flow of love entering the chakra and gently easing its tension. This means giving up all illusions about your purpose in this world and the benefits of having power over others. Power can get results, but love gets results without force of will or control over others' minds. Power forestalls soul in its effort to realize true love. Love brings serenity, wisdom, leadership, and many health benefits.

This effort to live a life of love will require your full focus lest you find yourself on yet another, more subtle, path of power and end up alone or in pain. Although power is much like love, it cuts us off from abundance. If we are using power to try to gain the love we want, we may find the results are the opposite of what we are hoping to achieve.

Many seek power because they believe it will bring them the attention they want. It even appears to work for those who use power for this purpose can command attention. Yet the powerful are without ability to share their humanity. The loving often give without expectation and attend the helpless. They support and care for all who would receive their gifts, and by their acts, they find that love is all around them.

Therapeutic diamonds can help us clear up resistance to the path of love. Diamonds show us the inaccuracy of the belief that who we are is the mind, the emotions, the causes we have set in motion to achieve results, and the current physical body. To be free of these false beliefs and the distractions they create, we must become centered in soul. Eventually, we will come to this realization as a result of the natural course of events, the trial and error of living life. The question is, do we wish to take that long to reach soul awareness and begin living life from this perspective? Learn the proper use of diamonds, and you will rapidly accelerate your progress toward this goal. Diamond will gradually remove resistance as it becomes unnecessary and we can release it. In this way, our progress accelerates toward a goal of love.

To see the difference between the path of love and the path of power, you can look at life like a pyramid. On one hand, you can take every opportunity to get to the top of the pyramid. Once there, the only way you can go is down. Although it would appear that you are being held up by all the rest of life, you are in fact repeating a cycle of change that will surely return you to the bottom. Many who fall down simply pick themselves up and begin again the long struggle to the top. This repetition is like an obsession. Take, for example, the repetition of war. War is unnecessary and destructive, but once it is engaged in it repeats and karma requires the victors to become the vanquished and this means more war.

Through repeated harsh struggles, a few will come to realize that war is unending. These people begin to purify themselves in body, emotions, past debts, and mind until one day they find themselves free. To find the nature of love, they have given up all struggle.

Suddenly they come to the realization that all humanity shares this need for love with them. Giving love itself brings rewards without debt. They are at the base of life. In this way, they are in touch with all life, and their magnetism to love is great.

If we choose to take charge of the process of becoming a lover of all life, we can begin by working with the earth and sea stones, then move to working with the color-ray–bearing gemstones. Finally, when through our own personal experience we have a thorough understanding of how these work, we will be ready to begin to direct the powerful energies of diamond. If we try to do this when we are not ready or clear enough, we will amplify our own problems, take on the problems of others, and instill our problems into others. This avenue is dangerous and will cause setbacks for all. When we are ready, we will know it beyond a shadow of a doubt. Using therapeutic diamond will show what action is needed to remove negative patterns.

Diamonds teach us how to work with them. They do this through a symbolic language that cannot be explained in familiar terms. To learn this symbology, we must be free of prior judgments and preconceived ideas. These symbols flow in and out of us like a stream of numbers that are energy packets. Everything we think we know will be challenged by this new understanding. Only by giving up the old can the new have a space in our hearts to occupy. Once we open our hearts to diamond, we will never look back.

Change must come, however, by a slow process akin to whittling. The true nature of our soul will be revealed to us only when the various disharmonious beliefs, thoughts, and emotions are slowly "whittled" away. We cannot use dynamite because nothing recognizable will be left. We must go one step at a time through the process of removing each repetitive pattern as we learn its lesson. If we rush, the whittling will be for naught as critical parts of the understanding needed to proceed will be removed along with negativity and false mental concepts. We will be left with a pile of sawdust and chips that tells nothing. Whittling reveals the figure from the wood just as diamond therapy reveals an individual as soul from the mistakes one has made and the false ideas one has believed. All one has learned is a part of soul, and soul is nearer love than ever before, a therapeutic diamond will show the direct way to safely set aside your negative emotions and thoughts to reveal soul as a being of light.

Choose to go slowly. Digest each new lesson as taught by diamond. Assimilation takes time. Learn from a professional how to use the tools. Pick someone who has whittled their own false ideas away and has experienced themselves as a master sculptor. Let them show you how to hold the "knife." Let them teach your hand the gentle movements that direct a diamond to remove negativity. Carefully you will learn diamond can cut any matter or energy.

If you learn all the techniques and the subtleties of whittling, your hand will know what to remove and what to keep as it moves the diamond. As with whittling wood, if you remove it all, you will have to start all over again, gathering experiences until you are again ready to whittle. If you whittle only a bit and get scared, then soul will not be revealed in the process. You must learn how to whittle and cut with uncomplicated, bold strokes. Remove a chip or a speck of disharmony at a time. Allow the tool and the "wood" to speak to you. You can learn to be a master only when you are committed to doing whatever it takes. In the end you will be revealed as a shining soul.

Therapeutic diamond will be a powerful tool in the hands of a master but it will be destructive in the hands of a self-important egoist. The ego will not even flinch as you mistakenly carve yourself into pieces that have no further use. Soul must be useful. Remove its positive energies, experiences, thoughts, ideas, beliefs, attitudes, and emotions, and it is unable to be useful in this world. Becoming of use to others is necessary if you are to learn the ways of love.

Serving others is the way to love. This is not self-evident, nor is it an easy task to understand how to serve others in a way that is truly of service to them. A demonstration of love must be an expression of love that helps some person to realize that they are beings of light who are useful and capable of love. An act of service has only giving in mind. No one can serve someone else if they do not know what that person wishes for. Diamond helps you learn active listening, required to discover what someone wishes for deep within themselves.

Diamond will help you develop the discrimination you need if you are patient and willing to learn the lessons it can teach. For your part, you must be dedicated to love and the pursuit of giving as soul, the embodiment of your true nature. You must be willing to take instruction from diamond and those who are versed in the use of therapeutic diamonds. Finally, you must go slowly and chip off another piece of your hard-earned wood only as it is ready to come off.

Diamond is a tool capable of revealing soul. Commit yourself to becoming a master craftsman, and it will be your tool of choice. In the hands of a novice, it is likely to be destructive.

Remember to pay attention to what diamond is telling you, and if you are in doubt or do not know what to do, then do nothing. Wait until it is time. Each step in your effort to become a master craftsman will materialize only when you have completed the last successfully. The knowledge of what technique to use next and which chip to remove will be there just as soon as you are ready, but not before.

Frosted Quartz

Frosted quartz is simply quartz crystal that is shaped into spherical beads and then has its surface frosted. Only real quartz, cut from natural crystal formations, can be used for therapy.

Quartz is effective only if it retains the crystal matrix. All forms of reconstituted quartz or man-made material must be avoided, for they will do no more than window glass. The crystal matrix sets up an intricate interaction among atoms that retain a particular orientation to each other, thereby maintaining a particular energetic field that must be intact for the quartz to be therapeutically effective. This structure allows the quartz to focus large amounts of white-ray energy into the human aura.

Frosted quartz is slower than, but as effective as, clear quartz, yet its vibrations are less intense and therefore less "pushy" than those of clear quartz. A wearer of necklaces of spheres will be able to more gradually accept the process of facing their shortcomings. For most people, it is advisable to first work with frosted quartz as a way to get to know quartz, and then learn how to work with it as a curative tool. After several weeks to a few months of daily exposure to frosted quartz, you may be ready to try clear quartz for short-duration "shock" therapies. Going slowly is wise. There is much to learn about ourselves—we know so little about what is possible apart from our self-imposed limitations.

The frosting is actually a process that roughs up the surface of the spheres. Like etched glass, the spheres will still be translucent, and yet you will be unable to see through them. The frosting creates a softening effect to the otherwise intense energy that quartz spheres emanate and infuse in the aura. Frosted quartz will work on one area at a time and allow us to regain our balance before going to the next area. This is a much easier way than the all-at-once, scatter gun approach of clear quartz.

It is important to obtain frosted quartz that has been made from high-quality clear quartz with no inclusions or cloudy colors. Some manufacturers may not use a good grade of quartz for the frosted variety and thus will provide the unwary buyer with a lesser-grade stone. You can get an inferior product because yellow-brown discolorations and inclusions can be covered up in the frosting process, so look carefully before buying. You should only buy from reputable suppliers who are certain that the quality of the quartz is excellent. The lesser grade can be quite disharmonious with the human body and should be avoided.

Where you are using quartz with other stones for its balancing properties, one would be advised to use frosted quartz. Frosted quartz will exert its balancing effect at the end of a cycle of change initiated by the other stones, and thus wearing frosted quartz after other treatments will expedite the assimilation process that occurs after treatments. Changes initiated in one area by other gemstones may spread throughout the body using frosted quartz after treatments to distribute new knowledge over inner communication lines to other areas.

For anyone who is easily intimidated, frosted quartz can be a trusted friend who will teach them how to deal with aggression and fear. Wear it continuously for several months while learning its lessons. Women may find its gentle action more supportive than other stones in situations where self-protection is a concern.

If you are studying the art of self-defense, you may wish to wear the same strand of frosted quartz whenever you work out. Allow the energy of the quartz to challenge your beliefs about who you are. Let it teach a new belief about your right to change your body and its responses. Entertain the possibility that you actually are very capable of defending yourself and need only learn the procedures.

Use it in visualizations where you picture yourself walking with confidence. See yourself facing the very things that frighten you. Allow the quartz energy to fill you with the courage to stand erect and unafraid. Imagine how good it will feel to be able to protect yourself. Imagine you can go anywhere and do anything you wish with the support of a powerful friend.

Continue this visualization daily until you can do it without arguing with yourself about how dangerous or foolish it would be to be so bold. You can learn how boldness is a quality of the spiritual masters. You will have to actually feel the awesome potential of your ability to direct the vital forces of nature with inner guidance and the support of quartz. Use a mirror and tell your image in the mirror that frosted quartz is here to protect you and teach you how to be a proactive person. Tell yourself that you must begin to act with courage if you are going to learn to walk with courage. To go directly to your greatest goal is the passion that ignites the soul of one who is using the full potential of frosted quartz.

Affirm your actions. Use your own phrases. Make absolutely sure your affirmations are positive and contain no double negatives. Don't tell yourself no. Tell yourself what you will be like as if you already are that and stick to the point. Know that when you do, others will hear you. Speak to yourself with confidence. Spiritual people do not allow others to use them as a doormat. Even the saints have stirred up some feelings among their followers. They have challenged the hierarchy. Where greed, vengeance, vanity, and fear have reigned, they have stood up for love. Courage is a spiritual necessity. How else can we learn to face the Creator? Practice saying no to others and yes to yourself. Learn to say no to things you don't believe in, and do not back down.

At the same time you are visualizing your new capabilities, you may wish to enroll in a martial arts or self-defense class. In a few weeks, you will really feel the results and so will others in your life. You can learn to take charge. You can decide to determine who your friends will be. You can love life and be strong.

Continue to act in this courageous manner, even if it feels awkward, and know that the certainty of the rightness of what you are doing will come. If you never take action, courage will come no closer. Of course it will seem awkward at first to put on the head of a lion when you feel like a lamb. Just try to imitate the lion. Do not let the thoughts such as "I can't," "This is ridiculous," or "Maybe if I just take off this silly lion head, I won't have to face any challenges" stop you. Frosted quartz can foster courage only when you have had the experience of facing a fear and overcoming it. Wearing the lion head is a symbol for the first step to assimilating the experience of being the lion. Learning to roar is a good second step.

Frosted quartz will bring the wearer all the benefits of quartz in a step-by-step manner. This step-by-step development of the inner qualities of balance, mental clarity, focus, determination, self-discipline, strength, gentleness, ease, calm, and total health can be won. Give it time and do the affirmations. Before you know it, you will have it all and be able to maintain the ethics of one who loves others with an open heart. Once the heart can learn to remain open and yet be protected, a person can learn to deeply love all life. Let the quartz determine the next step, and you will find strength one step at a time.

For the average person, frosted quartz is quite adequate to do the work of balancing the bodies and the chakras. To do this, wear a strand during the day, then in the evening, place the strand on each of the chakras, starting with the lowest one. Allow about three minutes to achieve a basic toning of each of the chakras.

If a person finds their health slipping, try a five to six minute per chakra "deep balancing" treatment. This treatment can be repeated twice each day. Simply place a strand of high-quality frosted quartz directly over each of the chakras by creating a small pile. For those on a limited budget, a single sphere can be used. Simply place the strand or sphere on each chakra, from the lowest to the crown, one at a time. You should be lying down during this exercise. Breathe deeply into each chakra, and then let all the breath out. Relax and let the constrictions release.

If you want a more focused treatment, use a single sphere and tape the sphere in place. Avoid spheres with dark inclusions, white spots, colored areas, hazy or yellow brown color, and gouges, chips, or fractures that darken the quartz. Let the sphere be a clear reflection of inner tranquility and grace within. If frosted quartz spheres are not available, then use clear quartz for this deep balancing treatment. Quartz is one of the few gemstones—lavender, white coral, mother-of-pearl, and leopardskin jasper being the others—that you should place directly on a chakra for any time at all.

Learn the blessings of quartz the easy way and get the benefit of working with one issue at a time. Frosted quartz is gentle by comparison to the clear, and it is effective as it shows the individual how to reduce the power of each limitation they have previously allowed to reduce them.

Quartz is an important stone to learn about when designing necklaces created from a variety of gemstones. Many gemstones can be combined of course, but each particular combination creates a new vibrational effect. Combinations work best when you employ two or three complimentary gemstones (like rose quartz and ruby; or white coral, Biwa pearl, and green aventurine) and space the groupings of these two with a frosted quartz bead to allow the differing vibrations to be formed into a single new and focused vibrational energy.

Frosted quartz works with the principles of harmony, overtones, syncopation, and rhythm in ways not presently considered a part of music theory. These principals are combined in the interaction between a quartz sphere and a human body. Light, in the form of white-ray energy focused on particular parts of the body through the quartz structure and soothing vibrations of quartz that vary in intensity, harmonic structure, and rhythm, will repeatedly influence any areas of resistance in the body through a series of syncopated wavelike energy patterns. In simpler terms, quartz soothes cells to allow the body to accept greater amounts of the invigorating white ray.

We may assume we will become more bold in our efforts to accomplish major changes in our lives or more at ease to safely make little adjustments in our way of reacting to situations when wearing frosted quartz. Either way we choose to use the quartz, it will teach us the necessary steps to take to overcome fears and move forward in our efforts to find balance, mental clarity, focus, determination, self-discipline, strength, and serenity.

Quartz is used in a large variety of sciences to produce a number of effects only produced by substances having its—or a similar crystalline— structure. The number of devices currently in use throughout our lives which contain specially-shaped crystals is really amazing. As therapists we will not be interested in its many, peculiar, scientific applications but will be satisfied to know that it will bring one into alignment with internal forces that would bring us health and well-being.

White Onyx

White onyx is generally the most easygoing and tolerable of the white stones. This stone is either creamy bright, semitranslucent white, a translucent white-beige, or a banded combination of the two. The clear bright white material that may contain a few bands of slightly off-white, but mostly clear variations is the best variety for white-ray therapies. The more yellow or brownish varieties should be avoided.

White onyx begins to work immediately. Its powerful action will begin to change the wearer's vibrations as soon as a necklace is placed around the neck. The six-millimeter size is quite sufficient to get results. Full saturation of the aura (and all bodies and mind) takes less than twenty-four hours. Initial treatments of four to six hours is the maximum recommended. After this amount of time, or even sometimes after as little as two hours, the physical body will show signs of discomfort.

Wear a necklace until the vibrational shift makes it hard to sit still. You need not be highly sensitive to be aware of this effect. People with high metabolism should avoid prolonged use—white onyx tends to speed up the metabolisms after only a few hours or less. For those who find it difficult to get going and are sluggish or experiencing periods of inactivity, wearing this stone will be a very effective tonic. Often a wearer who is feeling low will perk up after only a half hour.

When worn at night, white onyx will stimulate dreams. No one with insomnia should have it anywhere nearby at night. On the other hand, lighter sleep makes for better dream retention. Those who have trouble remembering their dreams in the morning may wish to experiment and see if they can find an appropriate amount of white onyx to use. Just the right number of onyx beads will keep them from overly deep sleep and stimulate dreams, while allowing them to get adequate rest. If you have trouble with remembering dreams, it may be caused by overly deep sleep. Try placing an eight-inch strand of white onyx on the bedside table by your head, and see if this amount is sufficient. Vary the number of beads to be more or fewer until sleep is restful but memory is also active.

All people dream. Dreams are an important pathway to soul awareness. Remembering them and writing them down is the first step. Reviewing them and determining their significance is the second step. Creating your own dream symbol library is an excellent third step. Taking charge and directing your dreams is for the more advanced.

The attempt to remember dreams can be expedited by autosuggestion. Make a clear declaration before drifting off to sleep to remember at least one dream upon waking in the morning. Write down any feeling or memory, no matter how vague, and repeat the exercise each night. Do no more than voice the declaration to yourself and then let it go. If you wish, ask for help from a spiritual guide, mentor, or guardian angel. Often the act of voicing a declaration of intent and asking for help will be enough to get results.

Dream interpretation should always be done by the dreamer himself. After you have had a chance to digest your own interpretations, additional viewpoints may be found through sharing with someone who listens without analysis. This approach may help the dreamer get to the deeper message in a dream.

Let white onyx help you take charge of dream analysis. To do this, it is important to create your own dream symbols. Take basic things like a house, a car, a chair, a table, a flower, the color blue, a certain outfit, some animal, or any other objects that appear in a dream and write down any special feeling or personal significance you notice. Every dream uses a series of images and these images form a kind of language. A dream language may be formed from random associations of the unconscious mind, or a person can begin to take charge of the dream process by selecting the symbolic significance of every object, place, time, action, quality and feeling in your dreams. Then, review these symbols upon rising in the morning to interpret your dreams. Write down all symbols in a dream book that includes every object you encounter with a brief explanation of the meaning you ascribe to that object.

You can also use these symbols to train the subconscious mind to send you information during waking hours in the context of this language. White onyx helps the subconscious mind accept cooperation with the conscious mind. For wearers, the dream language will begin to incorporate the symbols for which you have determined meanings. The meanings will give you insight into the white ray and its uses for you.

Take special note of dreams that include gemstones. These dreams may provide clues to new uses and techniques for applying gemstones. White-ray stones in general, and white onyx specifically, help the searcher find clues in daily life as well. Reading an article or listening to casual conversation may give clues to hidden issues. It may seem as if certain things that happen are extraordinary or highlighted—as if with a white light. Take note of all information or even bits of answers, even if you cannot yet identify the questions. Answers will come when you least expect them. Finding a question for an answer is easier than you might think when you have developed a dream language because the universe will employ these symbols to communicate answers. You need only realize what questions have been silently asked recently that might have brought a certain answer. This practice may seem strange, but once you begin to take notes on unusual occurrences and coincidences that happen during the day, while at the same time observing your dreams at night, patterns will emerge. White onyx encourages the subconscious mind to get to work answering those silent questions you have been avoiding, as well as those you have been actively seeking answers for.

Try the techniques you are given in dreams that look promising, even when they are illogical. Trust the intuitions and inspirations you get during the day to give answers. Let dreams help guide your understanding of daily answers by showing you your inner questions. Finding the questions may be as simple as looking for the most obvious problem and seeing what the answers have to do with this problem.

White onyx is systematic in its guidance. This stone worn as a necklace will likely bring insight into changes in diet or behavior that would result in more vibrant health when health is a problem. If healthy, then emotional concerns will be addressed. When you are steady emotionally, mental concerns then could be addressed by onyx and if all these are at ease, then the onyx will go to work to uncover subconscious concerns.

Try the following visualization. Afterward, write down as many details as you can about what you experience. List each object, place, person, and action, and leave room to describe the meanings you ascribe to these. At the end of this list write down any questions you have. Be sure to use your dreams over the next week to answer your questions concerning the people or circumstances that appear in the following visualization.

You are walking along a river bank. In front of you is a friendly guide in the form of a glowing ball of white light. The water you see in the river is white and brilliant. The weather is pleasant and you are enjoying the walk. Flowers are abundant in the fields you pass. You notice you are on a white pebble path. Soon, you come to a small, white footbridge. You cross over the river. On the other side, the path continues. You follow it to a building. Someone is there on the porch. They invite you to come in.

You enter the building with a sense of anticipation. Inside is a long table, and many people are seated there. You walk up to it and sit at the head of the table where an empty seat awaits you. You look at the faces of many people you have known. The people seated along the benches on both sides of the table are all familiar to you and remind you of significant events in your life. Notice each face. They begin to sing. You are moved by their joy. You are taken over to a table of presents by the wall. The person who led you in asks you to open one. You are aware these are gifts brought by the many guests at your party to celebrate your achievements in your life. The box you open contains a special gift of significance to you. You thank those present for their love.

You stand up to leave, and everyone sings a refrain of "For he's a jolly good fellow" as you walk to the door. You bid the gathering farewell with gratitude. You return down the path and cross the bridge. Along the path, you reflect on the special gift and its meaning for you. You promise the white, glowing ball that guides you to use this gift as a dream symbol that signifies the support you have been given by those who love you.

Now write down what you thought of. For example, if you were given a white pen, write down any significance a white pen might have for you. Review this exercise again in a couple of weeks. See if it can bring you more dream symbols as you open more of the gifts. Add these to your list and include some speculation as to their significance to you. Keep this list and add any images from dreams that seem important along with a brief note about their meaning. Note who gave the gift, if known.

If you read this exercise and don't get results, you may try creating your own story. Simply write a brief story about a trip you are taking. You may borrow any ideas from the above story. Now, record your voice reading your story on a tape recorder. Then at some later time, find a comfortable chair and listen to the tape. As you play it back, let your mind go where it will and write down what you think of. If you take an active role in creating your dream language you will not be disappointed. Over time, answers will flood your conscious mind that bring much needed information on many subjects that have not been clear to you before.

White onyx is an excellent guide and trainer. It will work constantly to invigorate the individual. As quartz builds strength, white onyx gives the wearer impetus and guidance if one is open. Motivation and excitement will follow. Excitement will build as long as you wear white onyx and let it guide you in a new direction. If you have no direction, the initial excitement may become like frustration. Be sure you want to get motivated and be guided before you choose white onyx.

White onyx will systematically check all structures, systems, organs, cells, molecules, and atoms to establish broad cooperation. For all components of the body to work together, you must establish communication, agreement, harmony, and direction. Quartz works with the direct communication, white onyx with agreement, and aventurine with harmony. Aquamarine with amethyst and the gemstone of your primary color ray work to help you accept direction as given by white onyx and assist onyx in guiding you in a suitable direction for optimal growth and health. Use strands of these stones individually and in the above order for one week each. This will prepare the body to accept the changes as prescribed by the following treatment.

Use all five (or six) of the above mentioned gemstones together by placing them all on the abdomen while lying down. Move them around until you locate the exact position in which each strand seems to work best. If strands are unavailable, use single spheres. Work with this treatment three times each day on three successive days—first thing in the morning, evening, and before bed are good times. Let each treatment guide you to the exact placement of the various strands for that day and time.

After your nine treatments, allow yourself two days to assimilate the guidance that the vibrations of the gemstones in this treatment inspire. Wear no gemstone necklaces, but at night tape a single sphere of white onyx one inch above your navel and leave it there while you sleep. For the three days of treatment, and the two days of assimilation, keep a journal and write down all dreams, interesting incidents, and unexpected events. After a seven-day period, look carefully through the journal for any hints or suggestions as to a new direction in your life that may have become a part of you. Let your mind wander to related associations. Can the various comments people made be clues to the steps you should take at this time to establish a new path in life? Have dreams given clues? Writing down all speculations will help because these written ideas will establish a basis for evaluation later.

White onyx is the teacher of leadership. It will guide you to a path that, if followed, will require you to use all your skills and talents in many useful ways. It will teach you how to live a useful life and how to relax your judgmental attitudes while maintaining feelings of prosperity, motivation, and excitement. It will stimulate you to integration.

White Topaz

One of the hardest gemstones, white topaz is of great benefit to those who have problems with inhibition and fear. White topaz actually is clear, and like clear quartz, carries all the color rays within its white-ray energy. It looks a lot like clear quartz but works differently. It destroys the foundation on which fear is fostered and the emotions that evolve from ongoing fear like panic, anxiety, anger, worry, and paranoia. Topaz works on the mental level, focusing on concepts that initiate these emotions.

The wearer who devotes attention to a strand of high-quality eight-millimeter spheres and wears them every day for a year will learn all there is to know about abolishing unwarranted fear. Fear need not be an enemy. Fear is something we can conquer with the proper training. Topaz will gently teach you to walk with no fear. Normal reactions of fear are useful, however. This sort of reaction teaches us to respect forces that are threatening in life. Unusual fear or panic stops you.

Topaz works on the insidious fears, fears of things that are not even happening, and fears of death, disease, and the like. When fear comes to us, we need not act frightened, nor do we have to become immobilized. We can learn to control emotional reactions and we can learn to introduce the mind to alternative ways of viewing the things that frighten us.

Topaz will not actually remove fear but rather the need to overreact to fear. It will teach us control and support us in developing the strength to control the panic, nausea, shaking, cowering, pouting, and whining types of fear reactions. Those who find themselves victims of violence and other frightful forms of abuse will appreciate learning the key to the kind of self-confidence that, when displayed, neutralizes most threats. Often, it is the reaction of fright and panic that encourages an attacker. Certain people are victims of repeated violence or emotional abuse. They could learn the art of walking with the personal power of inner strength to shield them from most harm. Topaz creates an aura of confidence for wearers that will protect them until they can learn to sustain this energetic shield on their own.

Topaz introduces the mind to alternative thoughts by sending its strong energetic pulses into the mind whenever the mind is given a new concept by someone. It reminds the wearer to read books and listen to tapes that contain good information about those who overcome the worst possible situations, calamities, even death.

Those who are plagued by indecision and feel inhibited most of the time would be well advised to use white topaz. Its slow, consistent building of the auric energy is of great benefit to those who are easily overwhelmed or confused. Wear blue sapphire to further build mental stamina, and use rose quartz and ruby to build resistance to emotional collapse.

Topaz has its own way of working. It is slow and insistent. Its energy builds within the person until strength returns. The action of white topaz is well suited to the female energy. Men may use it for its general toning and building of the outer aura. This action on the aura is very beneficial to those who have a fear of crowds and cannot recognize their own needs when others are present. The strengthened aura will be insulation from the energies of those whose presence is strong or demanding.

Allow several weeks of continual use for a necklace of six-millimeter topaz to infuse its energy throughout the system and for the aura to respond by gradually increasing in brightness and strength. Use an eight-millimeter strand if victimization is frequent. Topaz should not be worn with tourmaline of any color or with turquoise. Use topaz or these other stones separately, but do not use them together. These stones are helpful to those with a weak or wounded self image and for protection, but worn with topaz, they set up a strong shield within which the topaz energy will overload after a time. Topaz energy must be allowed to fill the aura and be released in periodic waves of energy. If the wearer feels the need for additional support when wearing topaz, one should try white coral, blue sapphire, or leopardskin jasper.

If you wish to combat inhibition and fear by building inner resources and strength, topaz would be the stone of choice to begin with, especially for women. If a woman is working on the tendency to collapse emotionally with indecision and hesitation, first try pink tourmaline to build inner strength and to condense a feeling of resolve and then turn to topaz to build the powers of protection and ease alarming thoughts. If you are under psychic attack, wear turquoise to ward off attackers before building inner strength with topaz. If you are working on the inner causes of panic, a "victim" attitude, or mental collapse, use topaz to build the ability to control these. Topaz will help all women move out of fear and into a higher consciousness.

If you are a man and you wish to reduce your feelings of limitation and to access deeper levels of strength, wear green tourmaline. If you are ready to do battle with fear directly and need to access the warrior energy, wear blue tourmaline, if available in six- or eight-millimeter spherical beads, for a period of two weeks before putting on a necklace of white topaz. White-ray energy as directed by topaz will do battle with fear directly, but may cause instability as it destroys concepts that men may rely on for their strength of ego.

Blue tourmaline teaches the use of warrior energy to men. Warrior energy in men is the energy men use to empower themselves to make the effort to move into a new or higher state of consciousness when their minds are afraid. It takes warrior energy to do what you must without succumbing to the temptation to cheat or take advantage of weaker opponents, to thrive in the competitive world of today. Understanding warrior energy is preliminary to understanding the shifts that will occur in your thinking patterns during a consciousness shift. As you move to a higher consciousness, you must relearn or modify techniques you have used in a lower consciousness because these techniques will no longer work. Techniques that you have used to fight daily battles in the workplace and other arenas where competition is necessary for survival must be changed. Blue tourmaline helps men make this transition, especially when they are in competitive situations where they could loose something they have worked for.

White topaz is a stone that insists on consciousness development. You may wish to learn to use other support stones like citrine, malachite, opalite, rhodonite, and blue lace agate prior to working with this stone. These stones help the individual work through difficult changes in a variety of ways described in their respective chapters.

Topaz energy is like the stallion that leads and defends the herd. It teaches you to use the maverick energy of one who is in charge and self-assured. Such a person radiates self-confidence and people easily fall in behind those who have mastered this form of leadership. A person who believes nothing can hurt them is not afraid and appears somehow invincible. You must be careful, however, to balance invincibility with direction and purpose.

Although topaz makes an excellent "mount" for someone who intends to go forth and do battle with one's enemies, one must choose the battleground wisely and plan well, for a battle without a plan can lead to a victory in an unnecessary conquest or without a worthwhile benefit to the victor. Even an excellent mount can lead to demise if one does not know the countryside. When using topaz try following this mythical story as a form of preparation.

You are in the prince's chambers of the castle alone. You are waiting for the prince to return. He will bring you a mission and you will be on your way. You recall the years of preparation you have engaged in over your lifetime. Special note is given the particular teachers you had as you were growing up who taught you a lesson that remains important to this day. As you wait, you recall these different teachers, some of whom were only in your life for brief periods of time. You make a mental list of the lessons they taught hoping to find some capabilities you have that will come to your aid in the upcoming quest.

The prince is heard clamoring up the circular stairs to the third level, where you await him. You can hear his entourage of advisors, chancellors, and servants. You stand up straight as he enters. He hands you a piece of parchment tied with a ribbon and informs you that you will be his champion and your instructions are enclosed. You descend down the three flights easily with the knowledge that you have been given a purpose to your life worthy of your skills and abilities.

As you enter the courtyard, your mount is prepared. It is a great, stout animal with a clear and iridescent saddle that reflects the light with such intensity that it seems blinding. You are raised to the saddle by your squire who hands you your scroll and a mighty sword. You ride out of the castle.

As evening sets in the sky, you stop for the night. As you are preparing a meal over a fire you open the scroll and read your commission. You are so pleased to be given a task that is an honor as well as a challenge. As you consider the great possibilities for your future you finish your meal. As you lie down to rest you thank your prince for his love and fall to sleep. That night you dream of succeeding in this quest and returning home in years to come with the accomplishment.

Now, as you return to the setting of your life today, remember that feeling of satisfaction, the benefit of a mission and the power to pursue it with love in your heart. Know that one night soon you will dream of your mission and this myth will become your myth.

Our attitudes are often broadcast by our aura. We should assume that our mission here on Earth has been given to us by a greater power, and that all we need do to realize the benefits of such a mission that uses our every talent and ability to greater purpose is to open the scroll on which it is written and in the light of topaz read our gift. Know that not all accomplishment is in the form of prestige, money, or power. Many of us have missions that require that we maintain a simple life, so that we can master our inner fears and inconsistencies.

Do not use topaz as a tool to improve an ability to control or victimize others. Topaz will betray you if you do. It reflects the energy sent out by an aggressor back to the aggressor. If you wear white topaz and become aggressive yourself, it will come back on you. Since the aggression is reflected so thoroughly and at such close range, it will cause great harm to you should you become an aggressor. Be sure to learn first how to control aggression and to assert yourself without intent to harm. Its power to mirror aggression will aid you if your heart is pure and your intent is honest. Let topaz abolish your fears and free you to realize your mission in your lifetime. Sometimes it is enough to step into the state of realization of your mission without having to take your purpose out and change the world. Topaz teaches that all great changes begin within.

Part III

Supporting Therapies

Earth stones are not themselves carriers or bearers of color-ray energy. Their use does not directly provide the user with the energy of color rays. They are, however, quite useful as you will discover through the wearing of and therapeutic application of the stones described in this chapter. Do not be afraid to try your own ideas. These stones will make it easy to believe in yourself and your ability to improve your well being. Their actions are easier to assimilate and they are less demanding than the color-ray–bearing gemstones. They provide a form of support that is usually quite gentle and helpful when making major changes. They also help the physical body adjust to subtle body changes.

Some earth stones are extremely effective at absorbing negative energies. A few teach us how to use color-ray energy more effectively. Others help protect us. One type can direct us to our areas of greatest strength and weakness. Another helps us learn to let go of procrastination, and one helps us get going with the dreams we have hitherto left unattended. Each of these stones has a special function that will aid us in our efforts to clarify our direction and get to the bottom of our woes.

Taking personal responsibility for your situation may be the single most powerful approach to significant change for the better. Earth stones help you find the strength to see

11

Planetary Pick

your part in every situation you find yourself in. Once you find the link that binds you to your experiences, you can discover the hidden message in the situation. Every situation holds a special key that unlocks another door to greater inner freedom. Earth stones support your efforts to take personal responsibility and offer lessons that guide your development of personal spiritual freedom.

Amazonite

This stone is truly a gift to those who suffer from diseases related to toxicity. It helps the body identify toxic substances and substances that are in an inorganic form or compound that is dangerous. Since the body will place such harmful substances in storage by forming them in deposits of solids, fats, and certain intracellular liquids, you may not be aware of their presence until you become intolerant to exposures or frequently sick. Amazonite helps your body clear these substances out by systematically targeting areas of the body for detoxification, starting with the lungs.

The environment today is filled with many types of highly toxic substances. Some toxins are obvious—poisons, asbestos, strong solvents, or inks—while others are present in everyday water, food, and utensils like aluminum pans and other metal containers. Who can say that they have not been exposed to radon, arsenic, household gases, airborne molds, parasites, or any other of a variety of harmful household chemicals, perfumes, dyes, or cleansers?

Many people today work in environments where long-term exposure to industrial chemicals, gasses, or mining dust is just part of the job. Much of this material is brought into the body through the lungs. The body will try to remove all forms of inorganic matter through its normal channels. Quite often, however, one is unable to keep pace with the onslaught of particles, dust, and generally dangerous compounds.

The body has many powerful mechanisms within to help it eliminate waste through the skin, bowels, urine, eyes, ears, and lungs. These systems can become taxed, and with age, they can get clogged up. Waste accumulates when it cannot be processed at once. The excess is stored, usually permanently, in tissues of the joints, lungs, liver, kidneys, brain, breasts, lymph glands, endocrine glands, and a variety of other depositories. Once the processes are slowed down by accumulated waste and waste byproducts, the systems become dangerously overtaxed.

At this point, the affected person will begin to have symptoms. Most of us ignore these early warning symptoms because they may not make us too uncomfortable. We may have bleeding, slight dizziness, poor eyesight, weak hearing, itchy skin, rashes, allergies, sensitivities, frequent colds, habitual bronchitis, stiff joints, short-term memory loss, confusion, muscle cramps, excess fat, lack of appetite, shortness of breath, sinus problems, or headaches, to name just a few of the many possible early symptoms.

No simple method will permanently alleviate these conditions. Exposure of the body to the sources of toxins must be halted long enough for removal and release of these substances to begin. An unfortunate and astounding fact is that a large portion of the populations of industrial countries is continuously suffering from exposure to toxins. Along with this fact and equally hard to believe is that our major organs could be operating at a dangerously low ten to twenty-five percent capacity due largely to overwork and toxic buildup.

We should be feeling good most of the time. Instead, many of us are usually tired, worn down, irritable, uncomfortable, and stiff. We refer to these symptoms as "getting older," and let it go at that. Instead, the body should be able to operate to age eighty, ninety, or more before it shows signs of serious aging. This fact is well documented by science. So, what does one do?

Again, the answer is not simple. You must aggressively pursue good health. A vitamin pill, an herbal cleanser, a concoction of fresh vegetable juices, eating raw fruits and vegetables, a balanced diet eaten slowly, reduction of stress, acupuncture, zone therapy, certain types of chiropractic therapy, internal cleansing therapies, massage, various types of low-impact exercise, aerobic exercise, deep breathing, homeopathic remedies, positive thinking—all of these and more must be considered. Amazonite will help you choose the best methods for each area that needs cleansing, particularly if used regularly as part of a long-term cleansing and rebuilding program.

No matter what methods you choose, it must be a conscientious program and should be supervised by a health professional. No single method or herb will do. A program must be followed for weeks or months to see real results, as physical changes happen slowly and symptoms may not get better until the body is rid of the offending substances. Many people have worked hard for months before seeing real results, but anyone can improve their quality of life even if they have let the situation go. Some may return to a youthful and vigorous state after having debilitating symptoms. Don't kid yourself—it won't get done any other way. There are no quick fixes for degenerative conditions.

Amazonite works well with carnelian, snowflake obsidian, yellow calcite, mother-of-pearl, and sodalite. Each of these works to assist the body in identifying and releasing toxins. These earth stones are described later in this chapter. Work with a gemstone therapist to identify which of these are most needed and to develop a program of application and therapy.

Amazonite vibrations will have the greatest effect on the lungs initially. Breathing must be a part of any program to regain vitality. The lungs bring oxygen, and oxygen builds the body through oxidation. Many parasites live in oxygen-poor conditions and most are weakened or eliminated by high oxygen concentrations. Oxidation can break down the more dangerous forms of toxins into forms that are more easily eliminated.

When you build up the aerioli and other cells in the lungs and return them to a healthier condition, then many health problems can be eliminated. Just breathing deeply gets the lymph system moving. Lymph does not get pumped about like blood does, it will only get moving through the body when one exercises the muscles or breathes deeply, alternately contracting and relaxing the cells. This is one reason why exercise helps you eliminate the waste. The lymph is a medical name for all the liquid that floats around the body between the cells. This liquid brings nutrients to the cells and carries off much of the toxic waste in the body. Basically, the lymph carries the body's garbage.

Why do you suppose the lymph nodes swell whenever you get the flu or a cold? It is because nodes are collection areas where lymph can deposit waste products temporarily until they can be safely eliminated. There they build up when the body is unable to eliminate them as quickly as they are arriving. Flu and many other diseases create toxic substances. These substances get dumped into the lymph and must be eliminated through the skin, et cetera. Disease prompts the body to eliminate toxins.

When we wear amazonite, we can benefit greatly from holding the thought in mind that we are capable of excellent health. Amazonite will encourage us to seek greater health than we can imagine, but our imaginations do help us get to a commitment to health. We will find the desire to come back to life. We will find our dreams begin to turn to lifestyles of the healthy and vigorous rather than lifestyles of the sick and tired. Thoughts of being sick and debilitated exacerbate conditions of ill health. Our minds must lead us in any effort to regain health, and amazonite will encourage our participation in a program of total health through its action on the mind. This wonderful green-blue stone will gently build our desire for a positive life. Motivation is the first key to success of any kind.

Experiencing success is the second key. Once you get the feeling of health, nothing can hold you back. The experience of really having the energy to get active motivates a person to keep trying. Celebrate your success as it happens.

Work with this gemstone. Search for the best quality stones available. Find a necklace of the finest-quality, translucent, six-millimeter beads—not the ones with a creamy white color, but the ones with that color of green-blue water on a Caribbean beach. For just as you feel good when swimming in the cleanest ocean water on a tropical day, amazonite will remind your body of the need for vitality.

Amazonite takes time to interact with a person's aura and its vibrations will not enter the body until the body and the amazonite have come to a resonance. Resonance is a condition where body and amazonite match vibration. Let the stones get used to you. Set them in a neat pile on your chest while lying down. Breathe in the air that passes over the stones and has been infused with the vibration of amazonite. Allow yourself to relax. Slow your breathing and gently hold your breath for a count of two when lungs are full and again when lungs are emptied. Think of yourself as being healthy and happy, and outdoors, playing. You may get the best results if the sun is directly bathing the beads as one lies down. Amazonite responds to feelings of joy and hope, so recall circumstances when you were really happy as you work with this breathing technique.

As you lie comfortably, breathing deeply, close your eyes. Tell yourself that only by your own effort will this state of health return. State your commitment to work with the amazonite daily until you get results. Form a detailed image of yourself, bending and walking about with total health and ease of movement. Continue breathing deeply for five minutes.

Picture yourself shaking hands with amazonite. Imagine amazonite is a large blue-green man with powerful charisma. Make a pact with him. You will follow through with the necessary steps to health if he will guide you to the right methods and substances that you will need to restore yourself. He will help anyone who is really desirous of his help. Believe in his restorative powers. He can show you the way to good health. You are the only one with your special weaknesses, and he will help you get to know them. He will work with those who truly are open to better health.

Bloodstone

Bloodstone (sometimes called heliotrope) comes in many colors. Its most effective variety is colored deep green with red flecks. Some of the other varieties come in colors that include orange, brown, tan, gray, charcoal gray, blue green, brick red, and autumn yellow. They all have red flecks through them. The red flecks are important, and the more of them present the more effective the action of the bloodstone. Each of the various colors focuses the energy of bloodstone on a different area of the person—a different organ in the physical body, a different feeling center in the emotional body, or a different mental function in the mind. Primarily the bloodstone works on the physical body, but in combination with color-ray–bearing gemstones it will work on other levels. To work with bloodstone, begin with a necklace of mixed bloodstone that has more of the green bloodstone than any of the other colors.

Those who judge themselves often and harshly have personal judgments attached to almost every memory. Most of us have made serious charges against ourselves because of our mistakes. We have filed mistakes in the category of things never to do again because we have failed to find the learning we gained. Sometimes we even make up fantasies of denial to cover up this file and carefully hide it from our mind. This is a sad state of affairs because our mistakes contain the body of our learning experiences. Shutting off parts of the mind causes one to become fearful of other people and to tend toward isolation.

To overcome this harsh fate, we must learn to love ourselves. As we love ourselves we can forgive our mistakes and begin to learn from them. Only by doing so will we ever be able to love ourselves more deeply and thereby fill ourselves with love until we begin to love others. We may love ourselves and others when it is easy and times are good, but we may find ourselves unable to love when the pressure is on. Why is it so difficult to maintain an attitude of love, especially when it is most needed?

To see the problem, you could imagine your personality as a large pickle barrel. Each time you judge yourself harshly, you put another sour pickle in the barrel. Sometimes, however, you accept yourself. Sometimes you see your mistakes as gifts. Each time you do this, you are putting in a sweet pickle. Sweet pickles do not make the sour pickles less sour.

Notice the sour pickles sink to the bottom and the sweet rise to the top. When someone asks for your attention, you give them a sweet pickle off the top. Soon most of the sweet pickles are gone, and gradually the sour pickles begin to dominate the barrel. They become really sour with age. Now someone comes along and gives us a hard time. We are squeezed by the increase in internal pressure. Suddenly, out come sour pickles.

We can give out only what we take in. Each time we think a sour thought about ourselves or others, we are throwing another sour pickle the barrel. Eventually, all we have in there are really sour pickles. No one likes a really sour pickle. Our ability to choose what we give out is limited by what we have in our storehouse of preconceived possibilities.

Bloodstone has the capacity to bring to the forefront all the issues and decisions we have made that are having a negative impact on our lives. It brings those sour pickles to the top where we can see them and gives us a chance to sweeten them. These issues may be deeply rooted beliefs of inadequacy or just past decisions made in haste or on the basis of some-one else's opinion. We may not be aware of how these thoughts and feel-ings are affecting our lives. We may not even be aware that they exist.

Wearing a strand of bloodstone spheres that has many green stones with one each of a wide variety of other of the bloodstone colors works the most deeply and thoroughly. As the necklace becomes interactive with our bodies, it will begin to highlight the negative attitudes that have held us back from realizing our potential and allow us to see them. They will be exposed to the inner light of spirit. Negative thoughts can be made into positive thoughts just as someone who has been victimized and is fearful of other people can learn to become an open, giving, cheerful person. Simply wear this necklace and take every thought that strikes your consciousness with negative impact and deposit it gently into the inner light stream.

Our subconscious mind begins to see these negative thoughts before we become consciously aware of them. It learns tolerance for our mistakes and the strict judgments we have made of ourselves in the past. We learn to see our mistakes as learning opportunities and our hardships as gifts rather than failures. As we become conscious of these mistakes we learn compassion.

Gradually we become aware of the fact that the origin of these negative thoughts is negative judgments made in our own conscious mind. We are given the opportunity to see our judgments and to change our attitude. This process is referred to as "re-framing the past."

When used in combination with ruby and rose quartz, bloodstone is especially effective in helping us learn to love ourselves. The three stones work together to teach us a better, more compassionate attitude toward all life. We can set a goal to love ourselves, and the stones will support our efforts and provide us with clues as to how to overcome our limitations and embrace our experiences and love them.

We start by learning to make less harsh judgments of ourselves. We begin to see the deep relationship between our thoughts and our surroundings. Instead of judging each of our incomplete, inaccurate, or ineffectual thoughts and actions as a failure, we learn to see them as opportunities for improvement. Eventually the three stones will remove all vestiges of tyranny and self-abuse if you follow all promptings to improve your attitude with love.

Bloodstone focuses on disharmonies. It brings any memories that are associated with disharmony to the surface. Eventually we will learn compassion for ourselves and others. We realize that we can relieve from his duties the harsh judge who sits on a high, imposing throne behind a towering wooden podium and replace him with a gentler, more giving judge who helps us see the gifts in all our actions.

So, as you wear bloodstone, let the thoughts come up. Separate the disharmony from them, and recategorize or relabel them. Put them in a place of light with high ceilings and colorful skylights. Let the experiences placed in this room be separated from the judgments you made about them. Walk among your experiences and notice how they have taught you many spiritual lessons. Notice that the experiences in your inner room have plaques under them that title them. Suspend harsh words of definition—like failure, loser, fool, idiot, and incompetent—that once described the person you were in these experiences and replace them with moderate terms of a compassionate nature. We may think we are the sum of our experiences, but we are soul and soul has the power to be free of the past and all titles and limitations.

It is for us to see our place in the whole of things. We need not necessarily change. Beauty and splendor are a part of everyone. Let us show ours, and let us acknowledge the beauty in everyone. This is not a fantasy cover. It is a wide-eyed search for the jewels within the ordinary.

The green bloodstones with red flecks work on the heart. They bring to our heart an awareness of the disharmonious thoughts that our minds have been entertaining and the consequences of these. Green bloodstone heals the heart by allowing it to release all disharmony. When worn as a strand of all green stones, it teaches the heart to love the body and all within it with such compassion that we obtain the ability to spot and let go of all negative manifestations within it.

The heart is the most capable of the human systems in using the compassion inspired by bloodstone. Each organ has a corresponding color of bloodstone that will teach it of love, and, as long as the heart is given the support of the green bloodstone, it will help each of them learn. Bloodstone has one color for the kidney, one for the liver, one for the gallbladder, and one for every major organ. In this way, a well-crafted strand comprised of alternating green and other color bloodstone will work with each area of the body, allowing it to release its disharmony.

If you are able to take the point of view of soul through this process of learning love, you will find it an easy process to work through. Great release will be possible, for soul is not attached to any particular identity. Because we have identified so thoroughly with these deeply disharmonious thoughts, however, they have become part of our perceived identity and also have become lodged in our organs as part of our physical makeup. As these thoughts are released into the inner light stream, the organs begin to energize and thrive.

Bloodstone may bring up these issues and turn your head in their direction, but you must make the effort to look at them with detachment and let them go. If you have a guide or guru or inner master you can call on, it may benefit you to seek help in order to gain some spiritual perspective on your actions. This new perspective should be in contrast to that of the stodgy old English judge with a white wig who ruthlessly reprimands you for every action. Instead, allow yourself to view your actions with the eyes of a loving spiritual being who wishes for you only the happiness and joy you so richly deserve as a loving soul.

Be sure to open your heart. Strive to keep the heart open during this process, and you will be amazed at how quickly and dramatically you are able to change your response to emotional stress. You will be able to love others in a way not previously possible. By the time you have worn bloodstone for several months, you should be able to withstand the pressure of tense, difficult situations without losing compassion for yourself and others.

Wear a leopardskin jasper necklace with the bloodstone necklace, and you will have help maintaining a stronger sense of who you really are. This assistance will allow you to maintain better balance while you go through this process.

Other benefits of extended use of bloodstone include greater self-confidence, more courage, deeper empathy, and better connection with your spiritual path. You will feel stronger, be more aware whenever there is any disharmony in your physical body, and know how to rid yourself of such disharmony without letting it build up to dangerous levels again. You should become able to identify your own problems much more easily and keep them from getting mixed up with those of others.

Bloodstone is a perfect friend who teaches you to love yourself and to let go of self-limitations, judgments, and negative identifications so that you can be free of the pain and distress caused by these.

Howlite

This mostly white stone helps the wearer deal with problems or situations about which they are procrastinating. Howlite is insistent. It finds the areas where you resist the most and builds up your ability to circumnavigate the stuck point. It insists you face the reason you are delaying making decisions or taking action on your decisions. It may bring about the fall of your walls of denial if you stick with it even when it seems to be relentless.

Procrastination stops the open flow of color-ray energy. You may feel that not getting to some things you know you should do is not that big a problem. As color-ray energy is slowed or cut off, you may experience a lack of drive, an inability to focus energy, a waning in self-confidence and a general inertia. When you begin wearing howlite it does not feel good, nor does it seem to help you to be more confident because you feel pressured as it pushes you to get into motion. It is not a pleasant prodding, but the release of color-ray energy is tremendous when it is finally restored to its full potential, rather than being directed by stuck thoughts.

Howlite works subtly at first. It slowly adds to the forces within that are building a positive energy vortex. Each thought we stubbornly hold on to carries a resistance that has been built around it. The beliefs we protect are like feudal lords. They are fortified within their energy castles made of feudal thoughts. All light is kept out. Though these castles seem impregnable, they are in fact poorly constructed. These lords, or thoughts, that keep us toeing the line of negative limitations are afraid. They know their castles are easily toppled. They fight to keep their territory as long as possible.

Soon the walls come tumbling down. At this stage, the wearer will believe chaos has invaded the realm. Do not be alarmed. Let the feelings come. A certain feeling may predominate, or a number of feelings may come at once. Feelings are the foundation of these castles. Just one feeling will generate the cement necessary to create a castle of negative blocks. Often these lords of distraction will employ many feelings. Do not expect this construction to last. Once you begin to experience the feelings, the castle is nearly destroyed.

Soon the old feelings will all be torn asunder and the foundation scattered. As the storm settles, some work will be necessary. Life in the kingdom requires some inner protection, but modern towers of positive energy will do a much better job than the old castles. These towers can be built from modern materials. Blocks of pure color-ray energy are best. Each block will fit in perfectly if you take care to build a better structure that supports a new monarchy in which all the needs of the body are being cared for and no projects that drain the kingdom's resources are undertaken. Positive constructions are much stronger. They will protect the inner castle much more successfully. Howlite helps you determine what projects are positive and will feed the kingdom.

Peace can come to the inner kingdom. What is required is a complete restructuring of every construction on the inner landscape. Howlite alone cannot do the work. It can only prepare the way and open cracks that allow an understanding. Look within these cracks and see the faulty construction for what it is. Faulty constructions are based on fear, envy, anger, lust, and other powerful emotions. The walls are built of thoughts associated with these emotions. Each thought in a negative construction is loosely built on another thought. Each reasoning is based on the reasoning of another thought that is materially faulty. Once the structure begins to topple, you can see the construction made of faulty reasoning crumble. Each faulty thought cannot be sustained without the support of the faulty thought that it was based on.

During this process, when the going seems tough, relax as best as you can and take note of the thought structures. Observe each stone in the old castle as it begins to shake.

Howlite works into the cracks. It widens these breaches until the light gets in. Whatever color-ray stone you wear with howlite begins to get in. At first the lords are quiet, hoping this process will not affect them. Then they begin to lash out. At this stage, a flood of rationalizations will fill the mind. A hundred reasons will come up as to why the lord should be kept in power. Each thought will seem related and convincing. After all, this lord has been unchallenged for a long time.

Change the color-ray stones you use with howlite often. Short durations ensure that the mind will be unable to detect the cracks and will not begin thickening the walls or building a new castle somewhere else. At first, red or orange will work best to give strength to the resolve to oust the lord and find his weak points. Later, blue will help shed light on the truth hidden behind each thought in the flood. Then, as the walls crumble, yellow will help rebuild an energy construct on a more positive foundation. Indigo will give insight into the subtle workings of the mind and teach the wearer how to develop positive structures. Finally, try alternating violet and green to develop a connection with the positive constructions as inner symbols that support the spiritual kingdom and bring feelings of harmony and peace.

Do not underestimate the incredible power within. Each person holds the pass to unblock that power. Each person must learn for himself that all roads are not the same. Each person has his own road. Each can find a direct route to spiritual freedom. Release the blocks, and all the energy ever needed will become available. Howlite shows the way to apprehend and eradicate the forces you have set in motion to distract yourself from the road to greater love. This is not an easy road and the tests it presents are difficult at times but it will only strengthen the traveler whereas the castle life will weaken the traveler.

No matter how powerful these mind lords may seem at first, they cannot rule the kingdom forever. Their power is built on our own beliefs. Beliefs are protected by thoughts. Sure, all of our thoughts seem reasonable. After all, it is we who maintain these thoughts. Would we create thoughts that do not serve us? Would we create and maintain thoughts that protect a tyrannical feudal lord who threatens our harmony?

Before answering these questions with a firm "no," consider the conditions that prevail in your life. Ask yourself if you are happy with the amount of love you enjoy. Ask yourself if you have a clear sense of continuity and purpose in your life. Ask yourself if you have the kinds of relationships you can truly believe in and with people you trust and respect.

While looking at these questions, does your mind begin to make a fast list of rationalizations as to why things aren't quite what you would like? Are you satisfied with these rationalizations? Perhaps you deserve better. Perhaps you could use howlite to roust out the old lords of tyranny who keep you down. Try howlite for three days. If you don't see any changes that result in greater effectiveness and clearer directions for your life, then perhaps you are among the few who can honestly say they have no false mental concepts, no beliefs that limit them, and no feelings of resentment toward life in a subjective world with the structure of a feudal society.

Procrastination is the first sign of this condition. It is the signpost that marks where the work needs to be done. The second sign is a lack of energy. Large amounts of energy must be expended to maintain the castles of beliefs that limit. This energy would otherwise be available for more productive things. The work of howlite is the liberation of our useful energy.

Think of the negative constructs as being formed out of noncolor-ray energy. This energy is negative. All energy that does not support life to the fullest is negative energy. Someone who has constructed beliefs that do not support life and in fact limit the energy available in life can be sure they have been creating castles of noncolor-ray energy. Tear down these castles and construct beliefs from color-ray energy, and life will be easier. You will find that an abundance of energy is available to manifest every inner desire. These new constructions will be like fountains of positive energy that invigorate us, and replace the heaps of stone block that held us back.

Leopardskin Jasper

Leopardskin jasper has two primary missions with respect to humans. First, it strengthens our magnetic attraction to people, places, and things that would most support who we really are. It brings us what we need in our process of becoming more of who we are capable of being. Second, it helps us identify the cycles in our lives. It helps us answer for ourselves the following questions: What cycles are active in my life? How can I differentiate between them? Where do these cycles originate? Where do they begin and end? How can I change the way cycles affect me?

Leopardskin jasper can be worn for long periods of time. Its ability to strengthen your relationship with beneficial objects and forces will improve every area of your life. As you wear a particular strand, this strand will imprint your energy within its matrix. When you wear it for long periods of time, its energy goes out in ever-widening circles of influence and interaction. It strengthens your inner "radar" and improves its effective range, while teaching you how to subconsciously read the information your radar provides with greater detail and accuracy.

Each of the wide range of colors within its makeup carries a different vibration. These individual vibrations act as carrier waves. The energy that is us becomes superimposed on these carrier waves and is broadcasted, just as music is superimposed on and modulates a radio station's carrier frequency. Each of these vibrations comes into contact with the forces, objects, and people in our lives. Each vibration acts as a carrier wave to maintain a two-way, open interaction with everything within our lives that is there for our benefit. As they do, the carrier vibrations are subtly modulated by the influence of these interactions. The more we wear the necklace of leopardskin jasper that has become imprinted with and in tune with our vibrations, then the more that we become able to discern the exact benefit that each thing it connects with has for us.

The information about how influences around us will help or hinder our efforts returns to us in the circle or reflection of each returning modulation or sound wave. Learning to interpret these waves is a process that goes on at a subconscious level within our minds. Our ability to ascertain the value and specific characteristics of these influences improves with time and exposure to the leopardskin. In other words, we gradually learn to better judge how entering into a relationship with the people and things we come into contact with in our daily lives might advance us.

Imagine for a moment how you might benefit from this kind of discernment and the knowledge it brings. You meet someone for the first time, and before you even find out their name, you know what effect they will have on you. You are offered a food you have never tried before, and you just know it will greatly improve the way you feel. You pick up an object from New Mexico, and you immediately know you will achieve a better understanding of personal balance by visiting the place it came from.

In every case in which we interact with an outside influence, it is up to us to decide what we will do and if we will benefit. Leopardskin jasper cannot decide for us, though it will give us a new way to know when a certain medicine will help us or a certain food will make us sick. We must learn to decipher the nature of the vibrational interaction beyond a simple attraction or repulsion without getting ourselves confused trying to decide what to do with this information. Leopardskin will teach us what things are in harmony with us. Learning that we can walk away from things that bring us disharmony is up to us.

As an added benefit of wearing this stone, we will begin naturally to attract the very people and things we need to help us find greater balance and inner strength. We must first initiate the change for the better and desire the benefit of new attitudes and new outlooks on our circumstances. Leopardskin will teach us how to attract people who will support our efforts and help us understand the significance of the changes we make.

Life is a cycle. Every aspect of life exists in relationship to a set of cycles. Without knowledge of these cycles, we operate at a serious disadvantage. Timing is everything.

Have you ever noticed that some days you could run a mile without effort, and other days you find it difficult even to get out of bed? Some weeks we can focus on learning, and it seems no matter what we learn, we remember it. Other weeks we can hardly concentrate enough to stay with what we are reading. This shift is similar to the changes that occur in the results we get from our vegetable garden. Some years we get plenty of rain and the potatoes grow extra large. Other years the sun is out at the right time and our corn does exceptionally well. The results we get from planting a certain seed depend a great deal on the cycles in which we plant. Imagine knowing the precisely best time to plant your seeds or begin a new career.

All things change according to a natural cycle. Understanding the cycles and the way they change gives an advantage. We can learn to begin a lot fewer projects and yet enjoy much greater results. We will be less likely to waste time trying to get something accomplished when the time is not right.

Cycles have a beginning, a high point, a low point, and an end. You can direct the way a particular cycle will affect you by controlling the thoughts and goals you have at the time a cycle begins. At the beginning of a cycle of growth, the mental circumstances that exist will determine the way that cycle develops us and how we grow during it. Your mindset, feelings, attitudes, and physical health at the time a learning cycle begins determine what you will learn during that cycle. In the high point of a cycle of initiation you can create major internal changes in the way you make plans and manifest your life. The low point in a cycle of integration is a good time to be taking it easy. The end of a cycle of surrender is a good time to let go of some old habits that are no longer serving you.

Each situation in our lives brings us an opportunity for the particular kind of development unique to that moment. Leopardskin jasper brings us information about the current opportunity so that we can be sure to decide to act appropriately for this incomparable moment. It helps us determine when to act and what to act on. We sharpen our ability to refrain from action when we are at a low point in the cycle. It shows us when to feed and when to fast. At the high point in a cycle, the time is right to press on. At the beginning of a cycle, we must be grounded firmly. We learn to work with the ebb and flow of whatever energy we are currently tuned to. Resistance is futile.

Each time another cycle begins, we can make changes. As the cycle moves through its wavelike course, we can easily ride the crest if we remain ahead of it. Yet we must hold carefully to our direction when we are in the trough and visibility is obscured.

Picture the leopard. He waits silently and alone in a tree. His efficiency and grace are in his favor. Soon, along comes opportunity. He pounces. Easily overcoming his prey, he is able to feast. He is not involved with trivial pursuits. He never needs give up his prey to the hyena for he is always ready to defend his territory. He need not outrun his meal. Unlike the cheetah, he is not too tired to enjoy the fruits of his efforts when the time comes. We can learn, like the leopard, to take opportunities with total commitment when the time is right. We also learn to simply relax and hold our energy when there is no obvious goal.

Leopardskin jasper draws experiences into your life that aid in profound growth. All the while, you remain in balance because times of growth are controlled and deliberate. In much the same way, it encourages you to use beneficial foods and herbs that will help the inner regulatory functions of the body maintain balance. Your personal leopardskin jasper necklace will teach you to regulate your body's intake. It will teach each organ to work in harmony with the others. Place your strand on the skin above any organ centers that have yet to learn cooperation. Your strand will teach each part of your body to rely on and support the other parts. It will help identify the specific needs of each organ, and once you learn to fill those needs, your organs will communicate more. A body that is made of various parts that communicate and cooperate is a healthy body.

By this same mechanism, we will learn to show others our abilities, our talents, and traits that have served us. We may teach others how they may benefit from our unique capabilities. In just the same way, we will learn to recognize others in ways that invite them to participate productively in our lives. You will recognize methods and benefits of cooperation that may have been elusive or mysterious. You will learn that it is possible to live with people in a wide variety of different relationships that are beneficial.

Wear your strand while your mate wears theirs, and you both will learn how to harmonize with each other. Recognize the special gifts you can give the other and take time to share those gifts with love. Find a deeper gratitude for the special gifts they bring to your life and thank them in a way that gets this message across.

We will learn to interact with groups, teams at work, our families, clubs we frequent, and our sports teams in a way that supports the whole group while fulfilling our wants from that group. Each individual in the group will form a unique bond with the other individuals when their trust and spirit of cooperation are high. Wearing leopardskin jasper will help you become an example of good sportsmanship and inspired teamwork while putting no limits on your ability to be all you can be.

No one in a group need feel separate from the group. Leopardskin will show us how to give to each and how to benefit from each. If everyone in the group wears their own necklace, this process could be greatly expedited for all. In this world it is a pleasure to belong.

Each little spot of color on the surface of leopardskin jasper spheres is like an eye. Each one sees a different point of view. The more variation in the variety, color, size, and patchiness of the different beads in a necklace, the more we can expect to learn. Different eyes see different energies and energy is the essential element of life. A thousand eyes of every different color and size will bring us information from every spectrum of vibration.

Remember that all matter is energy with a specific vibration. If we wish to grow, we must learn how to interact with all the different energies in its myriad packaged forms. A necklace of this kind will treat the wearer to a vast array of subtle knowledge about these forms and their uses.

After all, there is nothing in creation that cannot be useful to us if only we know how to use it. Even poisonous plants and snake venom have tremendously beneficial properties in the hands of one who has mastered the application of such substances. Thus, leopardskin jasper is a tool that can be used to show us the precise tool that would best serve our purpose, is practical, and is most easily accessible. It also helps us learn when and how to use these tools. Whatever the job, having the right tool makes the job easier.

Wear your strand often and with understanding of its mission, and it will bring you to what you need. Let it guide you and be your friend for life. If at any time it becomes out of tune with your vibrations, simply place it in the sun for five or six hours and it can be reintroduced to your vibrations. As it reads your aura and the auras of everything in your world, it will be your personal guide to balance, health, and joy. It will teach you how to balance your body, have better relationships, get along with groups, master the cycles of life as they relate to you, and follow the path of least resistance to your greatest goals.

Poppy Jasper

Activity is the result of wearing a necklace of poppy jasper. It creates the kind of positive spiral of energy that directs itself at the atoms and molecules of the human body. It serves as a tonic for the whole body. Its action at the atomic level increases the activity of the atoms. Its positive charge will light you up. Most of all it works to invigorate the emotional body.

Wear this stone with leopardskin jasper at first. Leopardskin jasper finds the weak areas of the body. It focuses the poppy jasper energy to the areas that are weakest. Disharmonies are highlighted and treated with the positive poppy jasper energy. Together these two form a powerful attraction to the elements or substances these areas of cells need. They create a spiral of energy that will circle the weak areas with an energy of positive support. Poppy jasper will move us forward to meet with joy the challenges that would bring positive change to weak cells.

Wear these two together for a few weeks and you will find yourself on the move. Making changes will be easier. Your diet may alter to support the new energy. Your emotional energy will seem more positive all the time. You will begin to find things in your life to feel good about. This outlook can bring a new sense of gratitude for the challenges of life.

You will be able to view the hurdles you face as your friends. Pretend, for a moment, you are the greatest runner ever to run the hurdles. Each hurdle is the very challenge that separates you from the rest of the pack. The hurdles make you great because you love them. Each jump puts you more in command of your life. Each race gives you greater power over gravity that would pull you down and make you fall. No matter how much you run, each effort to clear a hurdle is a singular effort. Use this attitude with poppy jasper. Let it help you defeat gravity and keep your attitude up.

Now let your imagination place you on a well-trained horse. You are a trained rider and have worked hard to learn the course. Poppy jasper is like the greatest jumper ever to challenge the great jumps. It has all the grace and surety of a seasoned horse. You can learn to ride him to victory. Just go with the rhythm. Allow the strength and pace to take you. The truly great jumper makes it seem almost effortless as it hurls itself and you over the eight-foot wall. Poppy is like the horse that carries an emotional rider over every jump as if it were nothing. We can learn to ride it over our emotional hurdles and remain seated, as if our emotions were there to carry us where we want to go rather than to overcome us.

For those who drag their heels, poppy jasper is the tonic. It begins to address reluctance at all levels. Wear one particular necklace until it becomes part of your nature. It will move energy from chakra to chakra and will teach you to use the chakras you are reluctant use. For example, you may find it difficult to speak up for yourself. Your throat chakra is weak from being constricted. You work with poppy jasper and it encourages you to practice using your voice. You may decide to join a choir to express your newfound emotion. After a few months of this practice you begin to enjoy speaking. Maybe you even join Toastmasters to learn to speak in public. Poppy fills the throat chakra with good feelings.

The flood of energy into weaker chakras will help remove the blockages. Fear of your own potential will diminish.

If your energy is frozen in some areas of the physical body, and organs or limbs are weak, poppy jasper will relax these areas. As they become calm and more flexible, forward movement will be the natural outcome. Combining exercise with any physical treatments of poppy jasper will be essential to maintain the effects of rejuvenation.

If you have been lazy like a couch potato, you no longer will be when you wear poppy jasper. Your core energy is like a huge coil extending from the top of the head through the torso. Once it becomes activated, it will draw its energy from the etheric energy that surrounds us all the time. This energy is present everywhere, in abundance. Once it is attracted into your core, it will cleanse negativity present and poppy jasper will begin to work on the emotional level, clearing sadness and purifying the emotional body energy receivers, making them clear where they were covered with non-color-ray energy. The white-light energy will fill your emotional body through the newly opened receptors. You may experience a feeling of rising.

Poppy jasper attracts this white light into a pattern flow within this coil. Wearing it against the skin and in full sunlight will enhance this process. Sunlight enlivens the stones even more than they usually are. Sunlight removes the collections of disharmony as quickly as they are drawn out.

This process will lead you to further open the heart to the celestial sound of creation. This sound will uplift the wearer. A deep sense of joy will resound through you. Hold this joy in your heart. Let it fill you and spill out to touch all. This is the act of a true warrior of the heart. A warrior who is one with spirit need never be violent. It is love that transforms the enemies of life into allies.

Within you is a core. Picture a cauldron of lava that must be heated by the white light. This light is always shining. As the core fills with this light, it begins to radiate the light back out to touch the eyes of those who can see this. The spiritual adepts throughout the ages have been recognized by this light. It seems to glow around them. The Bible refers to a fire that radiated from the heads of the disciples when they spoke. You too can fill yourself with white light.

Picture your chakras as large lenses with a membrane surface and a liquid center. These lenses can become distorted, flattened, cloudy, shrunken, and generally inoperative. When they are inoperative, we stop functioning as transformers of the light. We eventually shrivel up our chakras and we slowly lose energy and ultimately die.

Poppy jasper moves energy through the chakras. In the process, they begin to adapt to the increased flow. We must ask for this energy. We must want to become clear. We must picture our chakras becoming open if we wish to see results. This means opening up to feelings of joy. This means seeing the lenses as full of clear liquid and perfectly formed, round, smooth, and curved to accept and focus the most light. It also means giving out this energy in the form of love.

We can store a certain amount of energy in our core. Like lava, this core will hold a tremendous amount of light energy in the form of heat (infrared light). We must learn to move this energy out into the world in the form of love; that is, the kind of love that is for the highest good.

To understand how this works, we can imagine an old warrior. He wears a suit of armor that has become tarnished, dented, and worn. He is a timeless youth inside, and yet he is limited by his armor. The armor keeps him moving like an old man and he comes to think of himself as an old man. The light cannot get in to nourish him, nor can the light get out to accomplish the deeds of love that he was once capable of.

Now picture poppy jasper as a servant. This servant wears a cloak of white and brown and orange and red. He is the servant of all races and creeds. He begins to work on the suit of armor. He polishes it. The rust falls away. The dents are reshaped. Soon it shines with luster and brilliance and begins to sing with radiance.

The knight, seeing himself as youthful and radiant, is now rejuvenated. He is brought to his former vitality by the white light. The light fills him and he becomes strong. Soon he is radiating this light through the land in the name of all that is good and right. The servant may move on and still the warrior moves forward, activated and full of the light.

Once the poppy jasper has worked to cleanse the chakras and reintroduce them to the flow of energy, it need do no more. We ourselves are the transformers of this energy, which is so abundant. We can choose to use it for good purpose, and we will have an abundance of vitality and all the joy we can handle. This is the cure for the heavy heart.

Compare the energy we speak of here to the energy lovers share when they are falling in love. It is a binding energy. It brings people together in a celebration of life. We are like the rose that needs direct sunlight to open up its petals and flourish. As the sunlight gives to the rose, the rose gives its beauty to all. Until we open up, our beauty is hidden. Until we reach for the stars with our arms wide, no one will ever know our bounty.

Poppy jasper has a cyclical energy pattern. Its vibration is similar to the vibration our hearts put out when filled with love. This energy fills the heart in pulsations and comes out in waves of love. We are a tuning fork being struck over and over until we begin to resonate on our own with the sound of love. Love is not exactly an act of will, yet we must want it to happen with all our heart before we can be open to it. It is not a function of our imagination, yet somehow we must be able to imagine it filling our senses before we can experience it.

Love may not be the answer to all your challenges. Poppy jasper will simply teach you to invite better outcomes and to accept that which cannot be changed. We will learn to love without interfering with another person's space or right to privacy.

This stone helps us find joy in the simple things of life. Wear poppy jasper when you are at work, and you will rediscover a love for your work. Each of the activities we do that once brought us joy will begin to appear vital and necessary. We may be encouraged to drop those that are no longer necessary. We will be encouraged to do what we do with joy. The stagnant feeling of apathy will leave us, along with the patterns and activities that accompany this feeling.

Once the log jams of negative emotions are cleared from our river, we will be less likely to flood with emotion. We will be more likely to experience a steady feeling of joy punctuated by emotional reactions to our new-found compassion and devotion. Our direction will become straight and our power more steady. We will laugh freely again. Our sense of humor will begin to blossom in the atmosphere of the free-flowing river.

Red Jasper

Red jasper is a wonderful brick-red color. The color may vary a bit with material originating from different locations. The preferred variety of red jasper for therapeutic uses is a deep brownish-red. It has few or no inclusions that form black or gray stripes or blotches on the surface. The color is both soothing and earthy. As in the colors of fall, this variety of brown has a similarity to Egyptian red.

The active word here is *earthy*. Red jasper helps you become attuned to the earth. Our earth element is one of the primary ingredients for life. We must learn about this element. Understanding the earth will be easy for some, elusive for others, and nearly impossible for a few. We all have certain aspects of life to learn about that are elusive and others that are foreign. It is good to work with lessons that are difficult, after having some success with lessons that are easier.

In a quest for spiritual purpose and spiritual meaning in life, one can become inclined to ignore the physical world. Associations with suffering and pain may serve to convince one that the physical world is a harsh and unhappy place. One may come to believe that spiritual insight can come only when one is tuned to some higher realm.

Red jasper teaches the wearer to appreciate a physical connection to the spiritual by becoming aware from soul's perspective while still conscious of the physical. Spirit is present at all levels. All of the inner worlds are spiritual, and so is the physical world. As soul, we are aware of this connection. Soul awareness is greatly expedited when, as it is after we have assimilated the wisdom of red jasper, the physical connection to Earth can be appreciated as a spiritual connection. This connection enhances our ability to bring the learning and the broader perspective of soul into the physical world to help us and others with daily life problems. For even greater connection to Earth, try combining red jasper with other jaspers.

For those who have difficulty making the connection between the spiritual, mental, and physical, red jasper is indispensable. Say you have need of a plan for a new business. If, while creating this plan, you are unable to consider physical concerns like store layout or ease of access to facilitate interaction with others, the business will suffer. On the other hand, and equally important, is the significance of supporting the spiritual needs of customers, although this may not be the primary service of the business. After all, you must consider serving customers on all levels if you wish to keep those customers returning again and again.

Red jasper keeps these channels open in times of trouble, too. If you have difficulty remaining in touch with the spiritual aspect when the body is sending out messages of discomfort or need, you can learn to take care of your body while at the same time maintaining a higher perspective. You can learn to develop this connection with spirit while remaining present to the body and the messages it sends. Your body can become a finely tuned instrument for detecting the presence of the spiritual. After all, our bodies are created of the same color-ray and noncolor-ray energies as all creation. You can also learn to perceive what others' bodies are saying when you learn to listen to the physical with the "ears" of soul. Physical body messages are normally seen as mundane. They do, however, have spiritual significance.

Red jasper builds this channel of awareness between the physical and the spiritual. Once information begins to flow from the physical to the spiritual self, or soul, then the information begins to flow from soul to the physical body. The connection gets stronger and stronger, the more this stone is worn. In time, we may begin to be able to interpret physical stimuli from the spiritual level. The ability to comprehend the physical will help us to create detachment from physical need, thus allowing the wearer to be free of any enslavement to the pursuit of physical satisfaction while being more capable than ever of providing for themselves. Soul can find solutions for physical situations that seem impossible from the physical perspective. This is because the causes of all physical situations have their roots in spiritual precepts.

Anyone who suffers from a physical condition in which an organ is at risk—like heart disease or emphysema—should consider using red jasper. It can bring information about the condition from its origin in the spiritual world directly to the cells. Once the cells understand why a condition has developed, they can begin to let it go. Our cells are not programmed to develop disease. However, they will serve us in any way they can, even including taking on a disease. As soon as the body has done its job and revealed to soul the cause of the disease as being an ignorance or pretense about a spiritual principle, the body can heal.

It may seem unlikely that disease is given to us as a spiritual experience. Understanding the spiritual gifts locked in the experiences we have in the physical world is one of the greatest challenges we face. Red jasper, a seemingly unimpressive earth stone, can build this incredible bridge to understanding between soul and the body. This connection could be the cornerstone to a learning that allows soul to develop the body as the eyes and ears of soul on the physical plane. We could begin gaining our experiences expressly for the enrichment of soul without the intensely distracting problems that can be associated with disease.

This stone is not a cure for all life's ills. Not all ills are a spiritual message. Everything that happens here in the physical world to challenge us spiritually and allow us to stretch our spiritual muscles is most certainly important. We are the beneficiary of a stone that takes us through a revealing, insightful look at the spiritual precepts in physical form.

Those who have difficulty connecting with the physical body could try red jasper. Problems with daydreaming will be lessened when red jasper bridges us to the secret spiritual meaning of events in the physical. Having difficulty getting into life? Perhaps getting up in the morning is difficult? Let red jasper give you a new connection to your motivation. Providing us with a strong sense of our spiritual purpose in the physical world is the mission of red jasper.

A need for purpose in life cannot be miraculously fulfilled by the use of red jasper. However, this stone can lead us to influences, practices, and procedures that will help us in a directed way to discover true purpose.

Also, red jasper can help you "translate" symbolic information into a more familiar, physical form. Try working with red jasper and malachite. Malachite will bring through information on such things as the significance of numbers and cycles. Red jasper will allow you to easily apply this learning to the physical aspects of life.

Red jasper is easygoing and comfortable to work with, even for those who have great difficulty with their physical bodies. Anyone who is clumsy, nonmechanical, forgetful of dates, or neglects to pay attention to what is going on physically should use this stone. It will gently remind you of what is currently going on that could affect you physically.

Many other uses can be found for this stone that creates a vibration harmonious with Earth. Use red jasper and discover new benefit in physical harmony.

Obsidian (Snowflake Obsidian)

Obsidian serves to purge negativity. Negativity—negative thoughts and patterns—collects in our auras, particularly those thoughts associated with strong feelings. Negative feelings like jealousy and anger are often strong and, connected to negative thoughts, they can be dangerous. Obsidian can give us a reprieve from these thoughts long enough to decide the merits of the thoughts.

The best variety has a deep black color with bright white snowflake patterns over the surface. To deal with negativity in the aura or in the physical atoms and molecules of the body you must use only the finest natural snowflake obsidian. Negativity will usually be present in the physical body if you have a habit of expressing negative thoughts and emotions. When seeking relief from the pattern of negative expression, seek first a repair of the physical distress caused by negative compounds within the body. Negative compounds can be complex toxic substances or simply negative ions of atoms of calcium or other elements found in the body.

A necklace of this stone will, over time, generate a vibrational "bubble" around those atoms and molecules within the body that are potentially harmful. The body is quite capable of removing harmful molecules, but at times, the removal system gets overworked or taxed. At these times, the body will store these molecules in fat cells or lodge them in deposits around joints or cartilage. The body becomes used to the presence of these molecules and works around them. Snowflake obsidian works to identify them.

Once identified and tagged for removal, these molecules become surrounded with this energy bubble. The body will remove them immediately or in short order as they can be replaced by neutral or positive molecules. Always be sure to drink lots of distilled water when working with snowflake obsidian. Water-soluble molecules will be disposed of easily in the presence of lots of pure water. Plus, the kidneys will be flushed so as not to cause clogs in their ducts or tissues during cleanses.

In a similar way, obsidian creates a "bubble" around harmful pockets of emotion in the subtle bodies. Sometimes, harmful buildups in the aura are in places correlated to deposits of molecules located in the physical body. Once a harmful thought like resentment is encased in a bubble, it is easier to view with dispassion. It can be seen for its damaging characteristics.

Work with a single large sphere of obsidian—or a small sphere if a larger one is not available—to identify and clear negative thoughts from the aura. Move the sphere throughout the aura to begin the identification process. Once you have worked through the entire aura, place a strand of eight-millimeter obsidian over the navel and slowly repeat the scan of the aura. As any area of the aura responds to the treatment and negative thoughts occur, take note of the location. After the second scan is complete and all locations that hold negative thoughts have been documented, pick one location that has held a negative thought that you could clearly identify and focus your intent and the vibration of the obsidian on. One or two treatments of fifteen minutes on a single location should be all you attempt in a seven-day period.

This treatment will allow you to begin the process of disassociation with negative thoughts. For a person to relieve the tension caused by negative thoughts, all personal feelings for the thought must be neutralized. Focus of intent is the key to clearing all forms of negative thought in your personal space. Ultimately you must consider taking long term care of the aura with your primary color-ray gemstone, particularly if more than six locations are found.

Snowflake obsidian cannot remove emotions or thoughts; it can only work to encase them so that a person can see them for what they are. You must work to neutralize harmful emotions. If you have a damaging emotion toward yourself, you can work to gather evidence that could diminish the emotion. Ask for help from others. Perhaps someone out there who is more objective than you can be about yourself could give helpful feedback.

Obsidian may be useful in meditation. With focus on a strand or sphere, the practice of meditation is enhanced. You may find an easier time clearing the mind of thought in its presence. Even simple techniques are more easily practiced with the help of obsidian. Practice your normal routine. With no special thoughts in mind, allow your attention to be held by the sphere for a few moments. Then, just continue the meditation as usual. Expect access to the causal portion of the mind, which may provide information on the causes of any negativity in your aura. You may notice no sudden awareness of a change, yet a change will occur in the way you relate to your habits. This change will be observed when you repeat a habit and notice the habit is different.

Obsidian is said to help put one in touch with the actual consciousness of Earth, sometimes referred to as Gaia. It promotes this connection for those with the ability to perceive such mental states, and though it is not as effective as red jasper at grounding, it can be used to gain some insight into the akashic records (long-term memory) of the planet itself. Obsidian is also useful to help you understand how the earth's natural processes can create global healing if you wish to help in this mission.

Obsidian may help those who wish to focus their thoughts, particularly where the focus is on relationships. Use obsidian with red jasper for grounding your relationships.

Use a strand of snowflake obsidian in a pile over affected areas that you have identified as holding negativity. Allow fifteen to thirty minutes for the vibrations to fully penetrate into an area. Obsidian may be particularly useful over eyes, chest, abdomen, gut, and any area where lymph glands are located. It will not clear lymph areas, but will identify and mark molecules with potential to harm.

Care should be taken to cleanse affected areas after a treatment of this kind. Try physical exercise of the area, massage and deep relaxation, and take an herbal cleanser as recommended by a nautropathic doctor (also see the section titled "Amazonite" in this chapter). It may seem like nothing has happened. Do not let the subtle way this stone works deceive you.

Follow all treatments with lots of pure water and do repeated deep breathing exercises that virtually stretch the chest to its limit of capacity.

Breathe slowly so that you do not hyperventilate. Breathe easily and gradually. Let all the breath out. Getting the carbon dioxide out is very important to good health, and oxidizing trace elements will return some ionized elements to a nonionized condition for assimilation within the body.

Daily tub baths are helpful. Use Epsom salts, sea salt, baking soda, or bentonite clay in the bath water, following the directions on packages for proper amounts. Cleansing the skin is as important as cleansing the digestive tract. To cleanse the digestive tract, consult one of the many books available on the subject; or find a local source for cleansing herbs, salts, and naturopathic remedies; or use other procedures like enemas or colonics.

You may wish to consult a physician. Remember, this information on gemstones is simply a documentation of results achieved by personal research, and results may vary. These procedures and therapies are not meant to replace medical procedures. In fact, gemstones are best used in conjunction with other, more physical remedies. Where emotional problems exist, you may find support from Bach Flower Remedies, or you may wish to consult a counselor. Snowflake obsidian is a wonderful tool. Simply augment its use with direct physical support for best results.

You may wish to work with gemstones in a group. This practice is very effective and useful when trying to evaluate the results. Twelve-step groups may be adapted to include the use of gemstones where agreement is reached to try it. Many obsessions are eased through the use of snowflake obsidian. Substances that you may overuse are not easily rejected by the body without help.

When a body becomes used to repeated intake of large quantities of the many substances we overuse, we must want to change this habit before obsidian can help. Review the conditions that result from their overuse. Decide if these conditions are harmful to yourself or others and if you wish to change. To retrain the body to identify these substances as harmful, one may employ obsidian. It can be very effective in putting an energetic "bubble" around harmful molecules. The more powerful or mood-altering the substance, the more difficulty you may have with the process of quitting its use. Snowflake obsidian is not a cure, but it will help those who make the sincere effort to quit.

Replacing the need for escape and the habit of employing harmful or overused substances isn't possible with gemstones. It is possible, however, to use this stone and others like indigo, citrine, and amethyst to rebuild the damaged structures. Use rhodocrosite to break up patterns. Use other earth stones to clear harmful energies. Then, when you are doing all you can on your own, you may wish to get help from a qualified specialist.

Snowflake obsidian works like an inner snowfall to erode negativity. Large, flat flakes of white energy float down through the body. Gradually, the entire body is filled with the energy. The largest accumulations of this energy will be found where protrusions of negativity or rough edges of negative emotions are jutting out. The more rugged the inner terrain, the longer it will take for the energy to cover certain slopes. After a time, all will be covered in a blanket of white. Under this energetic blanket, the negative compound surfaces will smooth as they "cool." Later, when the obsidian is removed and its vibrational energy recedes, the body will be able to remove some of this negativity. Each successive snowfall will further cleanse the surfaces of the inner terrain and the body will learn to identify and remove negativity before it has a chance build up.

Black Onyx

Black onyx draws all the color rays into its deep black depths. Just as the color black absorbs the energy of all colors of the rainbow, so black onyx draws all color-ray energies into the aura and thus into the physical body. When worn in a necklace of spheres, it brings the color rays more strongly into the base chakra than other chakras, and gradually teaches the body to move these color rays up into the solar plexus and heart chakras.

From the solar plexus, we are able to use this energy as a form of protection. The body more easily senses the invasion of forces from outside itself when this chakra is full of color-ray energy. We are able to ward off influences that are not for our true benefit. Having a surplus of energy present in this area allows us to feel more complete and self-sufficient.

Those who have difficulty with compulsive, self-defeating habits that persist despite their best efforts at resistance will find black onyx most helpful. It concentrates on our motivation and so is an excellent adjunct to the use of snowflake obsidian. It helps with all sorts of repetitive behaviors, particularly those that destroy self-esteem.

With black onyx, procrastinators will find relief from their inclination to put off action. It works differently than howlite because it fills the body with energy and creates a rising need to get motivated, whereas howlite seems to agitate the procrastination. Together they really get you into action where action is needed.

Black onyx teaches us about our habits. It will not simply remove them, instead it will highlight our actions. We will begin to see just what goes through our minds at the time we are triggered to carry out the repetitive behavior. We will begin to feel the negative effects of our habit as soon as we engage in the initial part of the action. This perspective will strongly associate the habit with the negative or harmful result. Each time we repeat the harmful habit, the anchor to the unwanted result will become stronger. In this way we will feel the pain caused by our habit sooner and therefore be able to see that the pain we feel is a direct result of our own action.

We will no longer be able to enjoy the temporary mood change we had enjoyed from the habit. The temporary "high" or mood shift will now be eradicated. The "fun" will be taken out of these bad habits. The longer we continue to wear the onyx, the more strongly its effect will manifest. Soon the cycle of the habit will be surrounded with onyx energy, and we will have to break through this onyx barrier to engage in the habit.

The longer this repetition persists, the more the situation will become magnified for us. This action is the same one the onyx energy initiates to help protect us from outside influences that are harmful. Should an old habit try to return, we will be ready for it if our onyx sphere necklace is close at hand.

This energy is especially useful for those of us who have a difficult time maintaining our boundaries around people who try to take advantage of us or use us in some way. Black onyx teaches us how to employ the understanding and energy of the male protector archetype.

Another fundamental effect of onyx energy is to stabilize us in every way while raising our vibration very gradually. Do you have a tendency to light headedness? Do you find difficulty focusing? Try a strand of black onyx on the forehead. This treatment should take only ten minutes or so. Repeat often if the results are less than satisfactory, as this process of stabilization takes time.

You might say that anything we think of often makes us its disciple. To change the beliefs we follow, we must learn discipline before we can consciously choose what we wish to become a disciple of. We will soon become aware of the areas of our lives in which we will need discipline to change. After all, if we keep on doing what we are doing, we will keep on getting what we are getting.

We may believe we are the innocent victims of a life that has wronged us. This may even be true. We cannot change what has happened to us, but we can change our relationship to it. We can learn from our past how to intuitively sense danger. We can learn how to protect ourselves better and how to stop being victims.

Look at the earth, for example. We who are dependent on it have so far survived the large number of toxic chemicals produced from its resources. We must, however, learn the discipline to stop our old habits of wanton pollution and wasting of resources before new solutions will be developed. Our attention must be focused and directed to change our habits. The change starts with each one of us individually before we change as a whole. Onyx does not tell us what to do, but it makes us aware of the part we play in creating what happens to us.

Black onyx can help us strengthen our personal determination and resolve to act in a health-conscious manner. Awareness is the only cure for ignorance. We need not resist forces that might harm us in order to protect ourselves and eradicate these forces. We simply focus on a positive outcome and put our creative energies into seeing that something is done about our solution. Science and aikido teach us this. Solutions are created by those who are capable of clear, focused thinking.

Strong reactions to others' behaviors muddle our thinking and may involve us in destructive thinking. Black onyx teaches restraint and clear thinking. It shows us how to separate ourselves from our grief and anger long enough to create alternatives. We can learn to feel our feelings and even empathize with others while pulling together our thoughts and separating them from circumstances that cause powerful emotions. This ability allows us to deal effectively with the present without being overwhelmed by negative thinking that erupts from overidentification with the emotions.

Black onyx teaches us to identify our vibrations and the energy we hold as individuals. Once we learn our own vibrations, we can begin to learn to emulate the vibrations of others by subtly shifting our perspective to one they identify with and allowing the vibrations they put out to come through us. As we become proficient at this art, with the help of black onyx, we can help others learn how to stabilize their lives. This skill is used by some actors who represent characters by living their perspective and the vibrations they embody. Each physical form has a unique vibration as does the mind, the emotional body, and soul itself.

Onyx teaches empathy. This stone in spherical form is most useful to those engaged in helping the victims of abuse and severe trauma. Wearers can help these victims learn to deal with their strong emotions. They can learn to work through the issues with the help of someone who can feel their pain and teach them how to strengthen their vibrations.

Onyx is especially helpful to those who suffer from insomnia. Wear a strand at night and use an affirmation that states your intent to learn about the secret or unknown cause of your condition. Trace the cause deeper than the first thing you find when you wonder what worries you. Be aware of any hints that may come to you, no matter how unusual they may seem. Keep a log, especially during the first week of wearing black onyx, of any dream or conversation or passage from a book that seems to stand out for you. Onyx will subtly draw hints into your sphere of perception and highlight them. You may be surprised at the real cause.

Black onyx may also help with circulatory problems and nervous disorders, though not in all cases. It may seem to provide a sort of thick, black blanket that soothes and warms.

In all sorts of combinations with rose quartz, clear quartz, aventurine, rhodonite, mother-of-pearl, bloodstone, all jaspers, opalite, gold beads, rubellite, lapis lazuli, pearl, and others, onyx helps us assimilate change. Onyx helps ease the stress caused by resistance to change as well as supporting us during the actual changes themselves. It helps the wearer understand unfamiliar vibrations.

Black onyx is one of the most helpful and accessible companions, yet it is not for everyone. If you are drawn to it, wear it often and it will show you much about the way you think and how this contributes to your circumstances. If you do not feel comfortable with it, then you must approach it only when you have developed the strength to be able to handle what it is trying to teach you. Those who feel trapped by the circumstances of their life will often be drawn to its support. Some who feel trapped will be unable to deal with this condition at first; so it is with other conditions that black onyx focuses its energy on in the human circumstance. Breakthrough is possible even in cases where one is afraid to proceed.

The black color will draw all color rays to areas that suffer the greatest need. This infusion may seem uncomfortable at first and should be undertaken in short, small steps until your balance is not so easily upset. Use this stone over the lower chakras for the most powerful effects. Easy does it, for the best results are obtained from repeated short uses.

Those who feel uncomfortable with black onyx may notice they are not having an easy time remaining present in the body. These are people whose thoughts wander. They may be prone to daydreams or fantasies about possible futures. Being held in the body is not comfortable. Black onyx will help with this if you let it. Numerous traumas or long-term neglect will force one to this condition. Undoing the tendency to escape and bringing back some of the personal power lost during repeated escape will take time. Let this deep, black stone be your guide. It is safe.

The mission of black onyx is to help us separate ourselves from our trauma, intense emotions, destructive tendencies, self-abuse, negative attachments, and power struggles for control for long enough to become grounded in a positive search for self-esteem. Let this stone teach you to be outstanding in your own way.

Riverstone

Known primarily for its ability to speed things up, riverstone should be used with caution. Its powerful vibrations will move you through processes of change rapidly and sometimes without regard for the consequences. Use this force when you are stuck or having difficulty getting on with whatever is next.

Use a full strand of riverstone carefully and sparingly; using spheres no larger than eight millimeters is recommended. Six-millimeter spheres are sufficient for most applications. An hour or two is sufficient time for most wearers to progress to the next stage in whatever process they are in.

Riverstone will speed up physical processes like labor, digestion, or some healing processes like scab formation; and emotional processes like grief or forgiveness. Its powerful vibrations go to work immediately. It establishes what is going on for the individual that causes a delay, and sets in motion the regulatory functions of the body to speed up these processes.

There is a danger that you would move through a cycle too quickly and neglect to learn the lessons the cycle has to teach. This may result in having to repeat a cycle that you otherwise might have completed. On the other hand, once you have gleaned the fruit from the lesson, there is no further point to moving through the cycle at a slow pace. To avoid repeating a cycle after having used riverstone to speed it up, take time to write down all the habits that may have hinged on the cycle and attempt to discipline yourself to avoid repeating these habits for at least a week after the cycle has been completed so as not to trigger the cycle starting again.

For really stuck processes where you are finding it nearly impossible to get going, riverstone is invaluable. For instance, suppose you are repeatedly going through a cycle where you find yourself confronting your fears. However, whenever you reach the point where you are beginning to face them, you stop. Riverstone can help you see that next step, whatever it may be. It may show you that you can feel the fear but do what you need to do anyway. You may have a habit of calling your sister and talking about your fear each time the fear overcomes you and stops you. If you can avoid calling her as you walk through the fear, you may not have to repeat the circumstances that caused the fear. You may need some help from indigo to discover how this cycle got started and what made you so susceptible to fear in the first place.

Understanding may come only in circumstances like these when the cause of the fear is located. If you run every time you face your fears, you will be destined to repeat the process of confronting them often and repeatedly. On the other hand, you could use riverstone to carry you to that next step.

Suppose you are using riverstone to help you overcome a debilitating emotion like fear. Imagine your fear is like a wild dog. Without warning, it comes at you, seemingly from out of nowhere. Each time it does, you grab its neck and hold it away from you to avoid being hurt. Over and over the dog comes at you, just as your fear does. Then one day you decide to take the next step. You let go of the need to struggle with and resist the dog. Now it comes at you and you do nothing, but allow it to happen. Perhaps it will bite you or perhaps it will sense your new confidence and hightail it out of there rather than engage in a face-off.

Either way, you win. Fear may bite you, but it will only hurt for a time, and because you did not resist it, the fear will be unable to attack you again. You may learn the origin of the fear, and soon you will be able to understand it more clearly and with greater detachment. Trust riverstone. It may help you realize that wild dogs may just as likely lick you as bite you, if you are unafraid or at least control fear.

To affect physical processes, you can wear a strand around your neck and direct it to aid you in moving a certain physical process more quickly, or coil a strand over the area of the body where the process is taking place. In a very short time the body will respond to the vibrations of riverstone. If the process you are in is similar to most other processes in that it cannot be reversed, riverstone will predictably move the process forward. If the process can be reversed, and it is your desire to do so, riverstone can help move you into a reversal.

Use riverstone when the process you are in is one you are familiar with and you just want to get through it, or when you are at the point in a process where you would normally stop it and now you wish to complete the cycle. When you are in an unfamiliar process, it may well be better to let it take its natural course.

Riverstone is perfect for those who have a sluggish metabolism and find it hard to get going in the morning due to a weak thyroid or a sluggish bloodstream. Try wearing a strand for just half an hour or so in the morning. If results are obtained maintain this practice for three weeks and then see if the sluggishness has been removed, you may wish to gradually lengthen the duration to an hour or more if sluggishness is not completely relieved.

Always use riverstone with a definite focus on the results you wish to obtain. This mental focus will ensure that you get results only in the particular cycle you wish to affect and not in other cycles, which may be moving along at a fine pace. After all, you don't want to create a cacophony of chaotic cycles. Each time you start a new task or each morning when you first put on the strand, declare your intention for that session. State how long you will wear it and what you expect to accomplish. Remember to remove the strand when your appointed completion time is reached.

In this way you may be able to help raise your blood pressure if it is low, or improve digestion if it is slow. Similarly, with any unconscious or habitual activity that you would like to speed up or improve, try wearing this stone. Perhaps you are practicing a serve in tennis and you wish to improve your speed, but each time you try you misdirect the ball. Try wearing riverstone during a practice and see if the physical movement can be quickened without losing accuracy.

Riverstone acts like a well-oiled machine. It always works. It will help you stay alert when you are performing a repetitive task. It moves you through each phase of a repetitive motion, keeping you feeling like you are engaged in this activity for the very first time. Operators of heavy machinery, which is dangerous if taken casually, may benefit from wearing a strand of riverstone when concentration starts to fade or the hypnotic effects of repetition are felt.

In any situation when you might require stimulation to the nervous system or assistance to keep from falling asleep, try wearing a necklace of six-millimeter riverstone spheres for fifteen minutes. If concentration wanes after a while, wear it again for another fifteen minutes. Next time you are on a long drive at night or trying to stay awake during meditation, try riverstone.

If the effects are helpful but a bit strong, try rebuilding the necklace and put a three- or four-millimeter bead of twenty-eight-carat gold every eighth bead or so throughout the strand. This will help regulate riverstone's effects, since the effects build in proportion to the number of beads in a single grouping and gold will interrupt the flow enough to create a series of separate groupings that are less powerful. If the strand is still too strong, try a gold bead for every six beads. It is best to use even numbers to divide your groupings of this stone as even number groupings have a more balanced effect.

A necklace of riverstone directed to speed up a particular process and worn at the same time as a necklace of sodalite or of frosted quartz will be less likely to affect the balance of one's other normal processes. This may be helpful for those who have trouble focusing or directing this energy to one particular process, or for those in whom processes like body heat or heart rate are affected. The necklace of quartz or sodalite will help focus riverstone energy on any process that is not functioning smoothly or in harmony with the rest of the body. Quartz also focuses the energy on the lower processes of the mind as they relate to the physical body, and sodalite focuses the energy on the higher processes like the generation of thought and use of imagination for better body functioning.

You may also wish to try black onyx as a stabilizer. Riverstone will "shoot" much energy into the area of focus, and onyx will keep the effects of this energy focused on the area you have chosen to concentrate on as it keeps other areas insulated from the influence of riverstone. You may wish to place the black onyx over the physical location of the stoppage if the effects you are trying for are physical.

Howlite will also act as a stabilizer for riverstone in certain treatments where resistance is felt. Use a strand of howlite to ease the effects of speeding up as they begin to get intensely active and internal resistance to change builds, which can happen shortly after application and as the riverstone begins to charge the area.

Prepare yourself each time you plan to put on your riverstone necklace. Take a moment to imagine just the effect you wish to get. You may wish to write out instructions for the course you wish to follow. The stone will not read your instructions, but you will have to focus your mind to write them out, and this will help suggest to your subconscious mind an agenda for its use of the riverstone. This part of the mind can control the charging of an area with riverstone energy.

Riverstone creates stress. Therefore, if you wish to practice a speech at home, one that you will have to deliver later under conditions of stress, try wearing riverstone to simulate the stress. In this way, what you learn will be learned in the same state as the state in which you wish to perform. Thus, the learning will be consistent and you will be familiar with the state you will be in when you eventually perform. The learning will work much more effectively to prepare you, as all learning is at least somewhat state-dependent.

Assume that whatever ruts you have created in the past are going to be broken up by the increase of energy brought on by the riverstone. You can expect the very atoms that are participating in this pattern to be affected. Blocked emotions will be encouraged to release as the energy builds up around them. In fact, you may wish to have a counselor present if you are working on blocked emotions, for they can release with a great force if you have been repressing your emotions for any length of time. A counselor may be able to keep this release safe for the wearer and those nearby.

Using an analogy of the mind as a house with many rooms, assume that some rooms have been sealed up since the day you were last in them because they contain memories you do not wish to recall. The emotions present at that time may be frozen within the room. You may be blocking any manifestation of similar emotions to those frozen within this room to avoid reminding yourself of what else is in the room. Perhaps something happened to you at that time and place where your mind and emotions generated the energy to lock this room that made you afraid to revisit this room. Certain emotions could have been blocked totally since that time. If you wish to unblock the emotions, you must revisit the room and come to a better understanding of why you have the beliefs you do that keep this room locked and how those beliefs restrict your thoughts and emotions today. Riverstone may be a catalyst to help you find the motivation to unlock the doors of this room. Once open, the emotions stored there may erupt. This process is not generally dangerous as the mind will not allow any releases that it can not handle. However, if you are inexperienced in dealing with these releases, you could benefit from the help of a counselor.

A counselor will help you integrate such cathartic experiences of release and understand that they are not euphoric transformations or religious experiences but merely releases of pent-up emotion.

If you wish to use riverstone to help release blocked emotions, you could benefit by wearing a necklace of leopardskin jasper and carefully thinking about what you wish for yourself in your ideal world of the future. Make a wish list for your ideal world. Ask yourself questions to help you discover what you would do if you were living life just exactly the way you would like to. What would you say and do? What would you believe? After making your wish list, remove the leopardskin jasper.

Then put on the riverstone and allow yourself to search your memory for a time when you were first as happy as you have ever been. In your imagination, experience that time again. Allow yourself to feel what that was like. Then gradually look for the incidents that may have changed your course along the way. What happened to cause you to stop believing in happiness? Was there a violent incidence? Did a loved one die? Perhaps someone you needed left or began to ignore you. Make an inventory of these incidents, and soon you will begin to experience the block. You may become aware of feelings that are blocked. You may become physically ill at the awareness of how much you have missed by not feeling the blocked feelings. Soon the riverstone will help you initiate a breakthrough into that locked room. The frozen feelings will thaw.

Always direct the energy of riverstone or use another gemstone that directs energy for you, such as those mentioned in this section. Riverstone is a marvelous tool, especially if used by an experienced therapist for specific purpose. Always direct the changes you wish from riverstone, for it will fill the aura with energy, and this energy will disrupt your life if it is not directed.

Riverstone will help you discover feelings you may have lost and help you remove blocks. It will teach you how to speed up the metabolism and control certain bodily functions that are normally controlled unconsciously by the autonomic nervous system. It will help to create breakthroughs. Use it wisely and take breaks between uses for you can deprive yourself of balance if you do not take the time to assimilate a breakthrough.

Tiger Eye

Tiger eye is a fascinating stone to gaze into. It may be largely black with areas that seem to show a brown-gold luminescence, or the whole surface may be covered with the luminescence. Either way, the stone is mysterious. One way to work with this delightful stone is to simply look into its depths and let the mind wander. Let the intuition guide the mind to discover new vistas within.

For those who have trouble with creativity, tiger eye is a real mentor. It will act to free up the mind. Sequential, logical thinking could be useful in many jobs, and in certain circumstances, it may be well rewarded by the system. If thinking is too linear for too long it becomes rigid and inflexible. Intuitive, systemic thinking is creative and operates across logical lines, but is not always productive. Tiger eye teaches the mind to stay on track as necessary and to develop new cross-references. Cross-references improve flexibility of the mind without destroying its ability to focus.

Tiger eye works with the lower, instinctual, primitive areas of the mind. We may believe our way of thinking is predominantly taking place in the higher, more esthetic area of thinking. We do not realize when we are functioning at a more primitive level and doing things that are prompted by primitive purposes. The primitive level of thought is instinctively patterned and not usually open to revision. Instinctive patterns will overlay our higher thoughts and cause them to appear to remain logical thoughts while being subtly slanted by issues of survival, reproduction, domination, or other lower level purposes. These patterns are static and predictable, though they seem to operate without our permission as they affect us in ways we are unaware of. This fact may help us understand why we, as a culture, have developed high levels of communication, and yet we have been unable to use this advanced communication skill to cooperate with each other or stop threatening each other.

Tiger eye teaches the mind to review the lower mental patterning and change patterns that serve purposes we no longer wish to advance while learning to respond instinctively when appropriate. It teaches us to use the lower mind instead of having the lower mind use us—and occasionally misuse us—as we hurt someone we love or become distracted by the apparent need for secrecy, control, or conformity.

Lower mental patterning is helpful to the higher mind. It aids the mind by taking care of many repetitive tasks and allows the awareness to remain uncluttered by thoughts of everyday decisions like how to walk or drive a car. It is necessary to retrain the lower mind to new patterns at times, like when we go into the local grocery expecting to find all we need just where it was the last time we were in the store. If the manager decided to move everything around since we were there last, we may have trouble shopping the next few times through the store. After a short time, we have the new store map in our heads again.

Certainly we don't memorize every item in the store and where it is. Instead, we learn the categories. We organize our minds the way grocers organize stores: by category. Some people's minds remain organized a certain way and never change for a lifetime. They tend to be rigid thinkers. Others move the items around often in less important categories, but always keep certain items in categories that remain toward the front of the store. Some of us are scattered and can never find a thing. These people are always changing things one at a time and losing track of the categories and their parameters. Tiger eye can teach you to be flexible and organized; keeping an eye to simple elegance in organization while recalling specific placement of memories for ready use.

Tiger eye can afford us some insight into how we use our minds. It will guide us through the mind and show us the patterns. Whether you are very organized or so creative that you can't find a thing, understanding the patterns will give you a map. Further, it will show you new ways of mapping. To work with this stone, you must be ready for some rearranging. At first, this process is messy and cumbersome. Only after repeated efforts will you begin to value the process of tiger eye.

Look into its shape. Notice the black and the gold and brown iridescence. The black material sets up a safe kind of continuity. It finds your strong points and holds them in the awareness. The bright gold begins to take you on a tour of the mental landscape from a position viewer. Images will be presented to the mind in a way akin to a picture show where you can view short sequences of your life. At first, the sequences will be made up of simple thoughts that are well categorized and always come to the mind in the same way.

It will take some concentration to work with patterns and notice what purpose they are designed to advance, particularly when studying sequences of scattered thoughts. Use the visual aid of the stone itself. Hold a sphere just a foot to a foot and a half from the eyes (closer if comfortable). Look at the lines. What do you see? Let your mind wander, but at the same time be aware of it. Notice the associations. This stone tracks associations. Associations are catalogued in the mind and held together by a kind of track. A useful analogy for this track is the pattern of a train track. A train track is supported by timbers every yard or so, and the track is held in place and separate from the ground by these ties. Associations, thoughts that are related to each other along some theme, are also parts of a system that support a mental track. All thoughts are catalogued and saved along with other thoughts with a similar theme on the same track to allow the thinker to consistently further some mental purpose. It's as if thoughts are ties, strung out along a track. Without the ties, the track would be useless. Ties keep the tracks up off the ground and spaced apart so the train can proceed down the track easily without falling off. Tiger eye will show us our associations by taking us down our mental tracks. It will show us how these tracks further certain purposes. It will teach us to evaluate these purposes and eliminate those we no longer wish to advance while building tracks that serve better purposes as directed by the higher mind. You may even learn to direct these patterns of thought from the soul as you become a willing conduit for color-ray energy.

At first all thoughts seem the same. Each thought is simply another timber. After a while, the track becomes visible. Soon, if you keep following the track, it will lead into valleys and around mountains. You may notice all the landscapes of your life along the track.

Before long, you will begin to notice that some tracks are bigger, longer, and more major. A single, major track probably extends through nearly every experience of one's life. Major tracks have branch tracks. Once the tiger eye has begun to move us along a track, it will teach us to explore branch tracks. Some will be dead ends, some will lead into several smaller branches, and some will interconnect to other major trunk lines.

We will learn to identify immediately the branch tracks, the dead ends, and the major trunk lines. Tiger eye keeps going. It shows us how to recognize main stations and interspersed depots. These are places where big life-changing events took place. Tiger eye will make clear the distinction between stations where several trunk lines originate and others where we merely stopped and set a new course.

Main stations are places to get off and explore. We have been to each one before. At these locations we can discover the underlying beliefs that support the creation of our lives as we know them. We created this whole network. We can change it. At first we may recognize only a few landmarks to help us identify when these stations were created. Perhaps we recognize the date or a nearby city or a house where someone very important in our lives lived. We are revisiting a moment where we made more than one life-changing decision about how we were willing to interact with life from then on.

Tiger eye will take us farther. Stay with it. Find out what was decided at this juncture. You cannot have found the origination for more than one major trunk line without finding a set of global unconscious rules, limitations, goals, and structures within which you now live. We may think our thinking is random and free, but the fact is that most people think well within some broad definitions of life. We color inside the lines.

Perhaps at age six back in our home town, we met another kid of the same age and the opposite sex. Suppose we wanted this person to like us. We offered marriage. Certainly at age six, this offer was not a worldly engagement, but we were sincere. Suppose further that this person rejected us after some deliberation. We may have decided we were rejected wrongfully. We may have been trying to overcome this rejection when we offered a marriage proposal to another person later on in fourth grade. When we were rejected again, we lost some of our abandon and hope. We may have decided that marriage proposals led to the end of a relationship. This decision could then lead us down a side track or two. Along the way of life, we may get into other relationships. All the rest of our lives we seem to drop love relationships when they start to get to a point of commitment and rationalize our decisions with a variety of plausible excuses without realizing we made a decision at six that led to a decision a few years later that led to our unwillingness to take a chance on commitment.

Eventually we will again be faced with that decision to ask or not to ask someone to marry us. Should we try to marry someone who may reject us? It may sound simple when stated so plainly, but this would be a difficult question to face and we may not be dealing directly with the fear of rejection but with our rationalizations instead. If we had the benefit of tiger eye, we would see the true questions we face. Without it, we may figure we cannot marry the person. Why? We must not, we think, because the momentum of the associations developed on a major trunk line won't let us stop. After all, we made that decision long ago and it has seemed right for us so far. The problem comes in where the decisions of long ago do not fit the current life and we are unaware of how we came to earlier decisions. That sneaking suspicion that we are doing the wrong thing by throwing away another opportunity for a real test of love's commitment will be proved one more time.

Tiger eye will not grant freedom from tracks. You must learn to make new decisions for yourself. You may need the support of your primary color ray to relearn how to make appropriate decisions. What decisions would suit you? Your life can be everything you wish for if you can maintain the strength of will to hold to an original new track. Once we get on a new track that is laid as we create it, we will be in charge. Tiger eye will always show us when we are revisiting an old track. It will provide the vibrational support needed to follow a track back to its origination to see if it is one we still wish to follow. We will learn how we pattern our responses and how to change the pattern to serve our current purposes.

Decisions made now could take into consideration all the wishes of the subconscious mind, conscious mind, emotions, physical body, and even the atoms and subatomic particles. A decision like that would bring challenges. Such a decision would propel us to new purposes. To meet those challenges, we may use other gemstone tools. These may show us how to meet the challenges. We may not find an easy way or a way to avoid challenges, but certainly we will find a way that gives rewards for every little accomplishment because we will be following our hearts and our higher minds instead of our primitive patterns.

Most primitive patterns only provide goals that bring satisfaction in the final moment. Unfounded decisions and worn-out rationalizations create goals that become dead ends and lead nowhere. We find out nothing until the end of the line. There may not even be an end of the line.

Ideal goals afford a degree of satisfaction with each step, and deep, significant, lasting reward with each hurdle cleared. At the end of an ideal goal is total satisfaction. Such ideals do not generally exist in the real world—except in the movies.

In the physical world we must be prepared to accept the challenges along with the moments of satisfaction. Most goals are not ideal and tiger eye helps us deal with the real goals and enjoy the benefit of the challenges. At the end of most goals is another challenge that may be taken up or not. Most goals only lead to greater goals if we take up the challenge, but if you have indeed gained in wisdom along the way, then each successive goal is more satisfying and the process becomes empowering as you become filled with love. You develop better, more personal, and more current goals that provide incentives and mini-breakthroughs along the way. Knowing the best path for you will lead to the only place worth going and this is through the challenges provided by goals that are less than ideal.

Tiger eye cannot teach you what goals are best. It cannot help you to directly make decisions. It can show those who wear it the many ways we repeat old decisions in old arenas that neither suit us nor provide much benefit except occasional, partial satisfaction. It shows a wearer how that person is the victim of their own limitations. It may inspire you to set goals with a more clear understanding of the fact that you will not achieve perfect results. Tiger eye will help us see when we are on the wrong track. It will help us gauge our mistakes. It will teach us much about the lower mind and help us use the lower mind to build a better track for the future.

To learn to set up whole new ways of thinking and to learn to lay new track in directions that will positively challenge us, we must find our primary color ray and build our strength for the long haul. Tiger eye helps us relieve the feeling that we are proceeding in a fog and gives us the basis to develop a new determination.

Moonstones are given their names because they take the wearer into the psychic realm. This is the realm that exists between the physical and the spiritual. It is the realm in which we have powers like the ability to see the future, to hear the thoughts of other people, to manifest thought into feelings, to create our dreams, to walk through walls, to sense what is happening in a remote area, to influence the thoughts of others, to bend reality, and the like. These powers are only useful as they open you to the higher realm of the spiritual. To get in touch with the spiritual realm, you must become aware of the psychic and realize the limitations of the psychic.

The spiritual realm supersedes the psychic and is finer and more rare than the psychic. In the spiritual realm there is no division between things. You are faced with the pure light and sound, not the paler versions of these that we apprehend as psychic or physical energy. This pure light and sound does permeate the psychic and physical and can be found in the physical gemstones or in the psychic-realm gemstones. It can only be seen and heard using the spiritual senses. To develop these spiritual senses, one must learn to discriminate between the three levels of impressions. Working with moonstones will help you to develop such discrimination.

12
Lunar Insight

Moonstones open the consciousness to the greater possibilities as they exist in the psychic realm and hint at the transcendental nature of the spiritual realm that exists at a finer vibrational level not visible to the physical or psychic senses but certainly perceptible to soul.

Moonstones open the inner senses and prepare you for the spiritual realms as they teach us to do all we do for love. In this sense the moonstones show us the way to the higher realms. Spectrolite is included because it contains the properties of the mystical moonstones. Let them help heal the psychic wounds that have disturbed your mental and emotional sheaths as they ease the effort one makes to learn the way to the pure positive spiritual worlds.

White Moonstone

For many centuries this stone has been used to help develop latent psychic capabilities. Most often it has been used to help wearers see into the future or into another's destiny. Kings, queens, pharaohs, and emperors have always kept a staff of seers at their beck and call. These men and women who made predictions were expected to tell the outcome of battles, the yield of crops, or the best direction to go for a successful hunt. These seers were treated well, but the art of foretelling the outcome of all the important events of a kingdom can be a dangerous task. If one prediction did not come true or was not entirely accurate in its substance, the individual who made the prediction could be put to death.

White moonstone was highly prized as an aid in the process of remote viewing of the future or even of current events. Its vibration would bring the wearer into a disassociated state where his or her fears and doubts were reduced. Once relaxed, the wearer's third or spiritual eye could open. Opening the spiritual eye is not possible in a state of fear or doubt. White moonstone would also stimulate this spiritual center and allow it to receive information more easily. Only the rare individual could be so relaxed to receive this information as the threat of death was very real. Then the person needed to train themselves to focus clearly on a single intent so their answers were relevant and to recognize whether information was from the near or distant future.

Today this stone will still open the spiritual centers and receptors and ease the wearer into a detached state of receptivity. White moonstone will gently ease a person's resistance to the forces at work in creating their own destiny. It opens us to the inner forces and shows us the way they work as they manifest our lives within the parameters and limitations we have set. Concentration of the ability to focus our attention is important to attaining this state of receptivity. White moonstone will encourage us to concentrate and will relax the mind so it will not continue to bring up the doubts and fears that often plague us in our attempts to concentrate. This attribute of moonstone is especially helpful to those who are afraid of the inner forces.

The religions of the world have for centuries told us that we must entrust our spiritual development to priests and spiritual masters who have passed on. They often present the fires of hell as reward for those who would seek to open themselves to spiritual contact with the forces of karma (cause and effect). The saints and saviors of the world have been the bold and adventurous souls who have been able to contact the Holy Spirit. Yet, seeing, hearing, and knowing the truth through contact with the Holy Spirit often is discouraged or forbidden.

I do not recommend that individuals open themselves to the lower psychic forces or to entities who inhabit the lower astral plane. These astral entities may have their own tricks and hidden agendas, which can ensnare the individual in illusory psychic phenomena. These entities are quite harmless until we choose to open ourselves to them. They can disrupt and destroy our dreams, and in worse cases lead seekers into insanity or death. Their trickery is responsible for many of the apparitions seen by those who are susceptible.

White moonstone will reduce our emotional reactions so we can more easily discriminate between the different forces we are able to contact. Entities who wish to fool us into believing their subjective reality is the one true reality will give us partial truth, which has been charged with emotional content, in order to hook us into believing their information is the complete story. Without the emotional hooks, the false information will be easy to separate from truth, and you will not be led astray.

Do not allow your fears of the subtle forces to stop you from honest inquiry into the workings of these forces in the universe. White moonstone can lead you safely and gradually into a greater state of consciousness in that your natural abilities to see, hear, and know are enhanced. The truth can become a vivid and real part of your subjective reality as you become open to the light of spirit. Spirit is the force that sustains us and carries us forward in our journey through this lifetime and beyond. Always remember to stay focused on your determination to reach the spiritual realms, and you will be guided through the psychic safely. Do not stop too long to view the many psychic phenomena.

By the act of living, we are channels for forces. We choose which forces we will work with by dedicating ourselves to certain beliefs. The forces of love have an entirely different outcome than the forces of power, control, and fear. We can use white moonstone to help us discriminate between beneficial forces and those that would lead us to our own ruin or the ruin of others as well as ourselves.

Wearing white moonstone helps us to recognize the influence of other souls that have intentions for us. People who have worked with entities who are "dead" and are now in the psychic realm may be learning, yet they may also be the pawn of a soul who is lost in a struggle with the forces of fear and control. Discarnate souls do not necessarily intend to interfere in the lives of those who come into contact with them; often, they sincerely have the best intentions. Good intentions, however, do not necessarily create good results. In any case, they are not a substitute for love.

Use white moonstone to help you discriminate between harmful forces that masquerade as friendly and the true spiritual force. The true spiritual always moves you toward love. Using this stone will open channels to the inner workings of spirit and allow us to access truth directly. We will begin to be able to find our own inner connection and learn to direct our own ability to discover the workings of the beneficial forces of spirit. We will learn to perceive spirit and to see and hear the way it works. In this way we can take responsibility for our actions and redirect our energies away from creating negative situations for ourselves and others. Instead, we can set up new patterns for ourselves, which will also benefit all those who come into contact with us.

As long as we refrain from manipulating those in our lives who trust us, we will build our ability to access truth. Once we begin to use our knowledge of truth to control others or manipulate them for our own purposes, we will surely bring about the retardation of our connection to spirit.

Moonstone has no power to force us to do anything. It does emit a vibration that will open doors to certain inner capabilities when we are ready. We must specifically seek to open these doors, and spiritually we must be fully prepared before these doors will open. White moonstone will not grant us access to any realm we do not have the level of consciousness to reach on our own. It acts as a guide and prepares us by making us aware of capabilities that lie dormant within us. It helps us work with the capabilities of inner perception by activating the subconscious mind and compelling it to become interested in, even hungry for, the natural connection to spirit that we have earned through our efforts. It acts like a Jedi warrior who teaches us to trust in this force.

White moonstone will help us begin to understand the subjective nature of our world. Our perceptions and all sensory data are constantly filtered by our subconscious mind. We are shown only the data that support and maintain the viewpoints that make up our chosen identity. We will never see or hear anything that is in conflict with our closely held beliefs about ourselves and our world unless we open ourselves to a greater viewpoint of soul that takes us beyond our ego and its limitations. In this sense we are living in the illusion that we are the center of our universe. To the extent that we believe that what we see in our subjective consciousness is all there is, we are living in a bottle made of colored glass. The more we believe our own view represents all there is, the darker is the glass. To lighten the glass we must open our awareness to what is going on outside of what we know. This requires an extremely open attitude, because we all believe that what we see is what there is. Just as Galileo was put to death by the leaders of his time for suggesting that the Earth was not the center of the universe, we may discard, ignore, or destroy any evidence presented to us that would suggest our suppositions about the world might be incomplete or inaccurate.

Getting control of this filter system is the trick to getting past it. Creating a subjective reality that truly serves us and generates the attitudes and actions that bring us the life we want takes effort. Moonstone in the white form will lead us into the unexplored territories of our own inner world. It will introduce us to our own premises. It will show us how they control our world. Gaining this knowledge puts us in a better position from which to consciously create our world.

Many people consider themselves quite open-minded; however, even the most open-minded thinkers throughout history often have based their conclusions on false premises. Scientists have often failed to see what is later obvious to those who have come to accept new premises. More accurate premises provide consistently better explanations for the data. All of scientific theory is being reevaluated or radically changed with each new advance in our ability to comprehend the universe. Yet for each scientist who goes beyond the accepted norm of scientific theory, there are a thousand scientists who will ignore or refute the new theories, especially if they challenge an accepted theory that is the basis for some favorite belief.

We have come a long way, but we have a long way to go to fully explain the workings of the visible universe. We have a longer time to go before we agree on the explanation. We have a very long time to wait before humans as a whole are aware of and accept the truth about the nonphysical worlds. No one argued that Galileo was incorrect in his calculations. They admonished and exiled him because he would not denounce his conclusions. The scientific glass is somewhat less dark now. We no longer exile scientists, we simply don't fund them. It may be a while before we recognize the science of the psychic realm, and perhaps it will never be popular to believe in the spiritual science.

White moonstone will show us the decisions we made early in life that affect our lives so deeply now. For instance, suppose that as a child you were slapped in the face by an uncle who was wearing a heavy beard at the time. The shock of the unexpected blow to the cheek sent you crying to the safety of mother's room. As you sat there feeling appropriately sorry for yourself, you formulated the belief that all men who wear beards are not to be trusted—they may suddenly hurt you without warning. One day, later in life, you meet a wonderful man for whom you have a deep attraction. You would have accepted his proposal for marriage except for this unexplainable feeling that he cannot be trusted. As you break the engagement, you are unaware that your fear of men with beards is responsible for ending the possibility of a life of joy with this wonderful man.

White moonstone will assist us in revisiting the past. It will help us remain detached from the old scenes as we relive them. It will bring us insight into our psychic reasoning and how this reasoning led to decisions we have made based on old beliefs that don't serve us. Most of our early decisions were appropriate, and yet some led to beliefs that don't empower us. Many fears, like the fear of jumping off precipices, may still serve us, while others, like a fear of all men with beards, will be better left behind. The prejudices that keep us from a balanced, proactive life may need to be changed. After all, some men with beards may be quite gentle, good-hearted souls.

The fact that we are individuals who can completely create our own subjective reality is not bad. We were given this ability for a reason. After all, to create is to emulate the divine. White moonstone will open us to greater clarity and light. It will allow us to create a subjective reality that is in greater alignment with truth. We will operate from a more enlightened state. It will allow us to see the truths that are outside our accepted explanation of reality.

White moonstone will also teach when it is not safe to share our awareness of truth. Disrupting another's reality is not what we are here for. At times, challenging the beliefs of another is not wise or prudent. We must allow the inner understanding of truth to become strong and clear before we go blasting another in the name of truth. White moonstone will help us know when we are in a clear enough "bottle" to see the best outcome and what actions on our part will help create this outcome easily and efficiently.

Other benefits that come from wearing a necklace of white moonstone are realized in its ability to access areas of our inner mansion that we have not yet explored. We may have talents and abilities that we have neither noticed nor nurtured. The vibrations emanating from a necklace of white moonstone spheres will penetrate the walls of every room in our inner mansion. It will begin to report to the unconscious mind on the contents of these rooms. One day, as you are wearing your moonstone, someone will ask you to participate in some activity you would never have tried before. You will find yourself getting excited about the prospect. Many opportunities you never noticed will become endeavors you love.

You may never associate white moonstone with this new opening, yet it has led you to a part of yourself of which you were unaware. Its action will bring the potential of your untapped abilities and interests to just below the surface of consciousness. It will create the feeling that this new interest just fits. This feeling will be based on the information moonstone has brought into the unconscious mind without the filtering and processing of the conscious mind. Moonstone then will attract the circumstances in which you can express this unrealized interest. It will bring you closer to realizing a life of great diversity and richness—a life in which you do all sorts of things you love.

These thoughts and feelings will originate in areas of the mind where thought is not linear. This part of the mind thinks through data and sensory input in ways that defy logical analysis.

Although indigo is the true governing stone for the intuitive mind, white moonstone is the one stone that provides the wearer with a clear line of access to the mental region where we first process perceptions. This unconscious region is a little-understood area of the mind. Thoughts that come from this area come to us in a flash of insight. They are complete to the last detail. This area of the mind is between the subconscious and the conscious minds and communicates to both. It is referred to as the left or intuitive side of the brain by some. This part of the mind will work on problems that we have given to it. The rational mind will gather all the data it can, and then, if it is still unable to resolve the problem, it will release the problem to the intuitive area. The greater the feelings about the problem, the more attention it will receive in the intuitive mind.

Often the solution will come in a wearer's dream. Many scientists have reported getting an insight into the solution to an unsolvable problem in a daydream or a night dream. Sometimes the fact that this insight is a solution is not obvious and the application of this insight as a solution will only come to them later, when their mind is wandering, or as if by accident.

To improve your communication with this area of the mind and thereby benefit from the seemingly magical way it resolves complicated problems, begin by wearing white moonstone regularly. Each day or several times a week, sit quietly in a comfortable seat and place your attention on the inner screen. Allow your mind to relax. Let all thoughts of daily problems or circumstances go by. Begin to watch the problem you most wish to resolve. Let it play across your inner screen like a movie with an incomplete or unfinished ending. Let the movie play through again, only this time, speed it up. Now watch the screen as your unsolved problem comes up and put your problem inside a sphere of white moonstone. Then, see the sphere of white moonstone steadily grow larger. Watch the speeded-up version of the problem in its milky white form as if it were projected like a movie on a spherical cloud. See the white absorb the movie. Watch as the sphere shrinks, and know that it is going to take the unfinished script to the intuitive mind. Watch it fly off to this intuitive mind like a white space ship. Allow yourself to accept as a certainty that this problem will soon return to your conscious mind, completed, with an ending so perfect that it will astonish you.

For anyone who has difficulty solving their daily dilemmas, this technique is foolproof. Rather than accepting the usual makeshift solutions, you will find yourself becoming decisive and acting on your newfound and eloquently intuitive solutions.

For best results you must also work at developing a repertoire of metaphors for your life. Develop moving images that represent your life as colorful cartoons with characters that represent the forces at work in shaping what happens to you. The subconscious mind works with a symbolic language, while the intuitive works with metaphor and simile. This part of the mind does not discriminate between what actually happened and what you made up or felt and thought about what happened. All subjective experiences are weighted equally if the relative emotional response is the same.

Therefore, it is most important that you gain control of your imagination. Imagine all metaphorical scenarios you create that are relevant to your current greatest problem as if they were reality. Be careful not to imagine outcomes that you do not wish for. Create metaphors for yourself that express your secret inner longing in a way that truly inspires a deep emotional response, and your intuitive mind will not rest until it has developed a method for getting what you want for you.

Once you have gained control of the imagination and can use it to generate the inner experiences you wish for and know are in harmony with soul's purpose, then you will have a powerful tool indeed. White moonstone will start you on your way by creating the initial links between the intuitive mind and the analytical mind. When worn with a strand of indigo, the two will work together to expand this link and create many new ties. All your life you have used your analytical mind to work on problems. Try a complete change of pace. Avoid looking for what can go wrong. Instead of looking for problems, use your analytical mind as a tool for interpreting the rich language of the intuitive mind. Let intuition work out efficient resolutions that surpass your expectations and that take into account factors that would never be considered by your analytical mind.

White moonstone will help you reach beyond the mind. Using white moonstone to strengthen the communication between soul and the intuitive mind will create integration within your mind. You will experience an inner congruence. All your future actions will be harmonious with soul, your true self and its priorities.

Soul has ways to access information that defy modern science. The limits of time and space are ignored by soul. Soul need not be in physical contact with the source of information. Hence, your strength of will improves as the mind becomes focused on a self-realized, proactive lifestyle. An attitude of "why wait when you can act as if you already have exactly what you want" will replace your attitude of "what can I think of to distract me from having to think of all the reasons why I'm unhappy with my life."

Furthermore, this mysterious stone will help the wearer identify the lost dreams of childhood . . . dreams of a wonderful life with few limitations . . . dreams the adult analytical mind has convinced you are not logically available to you, given all your limitations. Only the nonjudgmental part of the mind, with its ability to believe anything we tell it, is open enough to accept the possibility of a life of childlike joy and simplicity. Have you discarded your most cherished dreams? Do you think they are impractical? Is it possible they could become the motivation to enter the door marked "Eternal Happiness?"

Begin to take the advice of the intuitive part of your mind, and you will find yourself using talents you did not know you had. Continue to add new metaphors to your repertoire. Each analogy you create that describes some aspect of your life in terms of the obstacles you face as being exciting challenges that you are eager to take on, will add to your ultimate success.

At first, it is enough to imagine that you are doing the very things you would thrive on most. Picture what this looks like in detail. Spend a few minutes a day contemplating on the you that you would be if you were exactly as you would hope to be. What do you really love? What sort of details—little things—make you most happy? Can you picture yourself free from the complications of a life that runs you? Are you ready to take control? Ask yourself empowering questions. Write down the ones that really get you going.

Hold a strand of white moonstone in your left hand and picture it as a gift given you by your mentor. Imagine it is the symbol of your intention to get free of limitations. It is given you by the lords of karma as a token of your commitment to break the chains that bind you.

Now, hold the strand in your right hand. Know that you are offering this strand as a token to the universe of your commitment to give back all that you have been given and more. Offer it as a token of the good faith you have in your heart to give back to life.

The strand of white moonstone is your focus. The palms of your hands directly connect to your heart center. The left is receiving, the right is giving. Picture activities that open your heart as you do this exercise, and you will surely clear out your old notions of giving and receiving. You may even learn to allow yourself to picture a life of freedom and joy for yourself. It starts with you.

For best results, you must keep the judgmental part of the mind busy. Occupy it with the task of observer and chronicler. The judgmental mind says things like, "Oh, that will never happen for me" or "I'm just not ready for that." Do not allow these thoughts to become connected to the movies you create. Let your movie star you. You are bigger than life. You are the hero. In your movie you can do anything. Most of all you can choose the simple solutions, the sweet meat, and let the rest of the world buy the really tough cuts if that is what they need to help them.

Use humor, love, compassion, hope, strong positive feelings, and courage to outwit the challenges presented by the judgmental mind. Never use force. Force will only reinforce the opposition. Negative thoughts love to argue. Arguing only gets you into a duel with a force that always equals your best defense.

Simply acknowledge your pessimistic side as an old friend. He just happens to have a sarcastic form of sharing. Acknowledge his intention to help you by providing you with failure scenarios. Go forward. Don't stop and turn to tackle the opposition. It will create more opposition as fast as you can fight it.

Watch the conjurings of your old friend, pessimism, fall like leaves in a river. They flow on downstream and you don't have to dive in after them. They are sort of beautiful. They make patterns as they float on down toward the sea. Your friend is trying to keep you from embarrassing mistakes. But don't react to his overtures. Don't let the insidious nature of his comments stop you. Others' opinions of you are their business. Mistakes are perfectly acceptable.

Let white moonstone come to your side. Use its powerful vibrations to protect you from negativity. Learn to allow it to insulate you with a layer of white light. This is the divine light of spirit. White moonstone will be your companion in your visits into the unconscious. This is a world where anything is possible. This stone will be your agent. It will get you starring roles in movies that represent your dreams. You can get the roles you love and become that person in the movie.

Gray Moonstone

Gray moonstone is similar in energy to the white moonstone with some distinct differences. White drives us to reach for higher levels of consciousness just beyond our grasp, while grey moonstone draws us deeper into the deepest part of ourselves where we can learn to discover ourselves.

It is best worn as a necklace rather than placed on the body, except when worn around the ankles and wrists to remind the feet and hands of their purpose. That is, to serve us and those we choose to give to. Our feet can be reminded to take us to places where we will thrive; our hands can be reminded to interact with the world by grabbing all the vitality we can get and giving it out to those we love.

Gray moonstone takes us on a journey. A quest into the unknown, inner recesses of our being awaits us. This journey is not into the mind but into the larger, abstruse realm of our inner dimensions. Gray moonstone will introduce us to experiences that are beyond our current awareness in a realm we have not yet imagined. Such a realm is entirely outside our familiar world, yet is very similar in that it constitutes a conglomeration of all our experiences.

Here new things are possible. There are ways of being we have not considered that are commonplace in this realm. Gray moonstone gives us a look at all of what is possible and helps us achieve emotional detachment from these possibilities. With such detachment we can recognize which possibilities are for us and which are remnants and hand-me-downs.

As we become accustomed to gray moonstone, it will open up deeper layers of reality, like peeling an onion reveals new shapes within. As we allow it to deeply penetrate our bodies to remind us of their origins and our prior existence apart from them, our relationship with this stone will grow. We will begin to see how much we have grown. We will learn to value this gemstone and see its mission to reveal secrets of origins. It will teach us to be trustworthy. It will get to know us and gently remind us when we step too far outside our commitments.

Working with gray moonstone can by quite unnerving at first. The subtle, inner realm has different natural laws than the physical ones. Each layer has its own set of laws, and initially you may have the sensation of being lost when you wear a necklace. Working with gray moonstone may be easier in your dreams. In the dream state, you are more apt to accept things that do not follow the physical laws of matter, sequential time and non-bendable space. If you want an adventure, wear gray moonstone at night.

Before you retire to bed, spend a few minutes relaxing in a comfortable, seated position. Practice deep breathing. Breathe in, hold your breath a moment, and breathe out. Let the worries and concerns of the day pass by your inner screen rapidly. See these concerns as small, distant, and dim. If one demands your attention, simply suggest to yourself that tomorrow, after your night's journey into the dream world, you will have some new information that will ease your concerns. Let each concern shrink to a smaller size and intensity.

Then, when you have addressed all the concerns and worries of the day, just let your screen go blank. Do not direct your experience. When you have a blank screen, suggest to yourself that gray moonstone will take you someplace in the dream world where you will find out something new about what is possible for you. The exact nature of the experience you have during sleep need not be recalled. It is enough to know that you will discover some new aspect of your nature. Know that you will wake with the experience stored in the causal, or deep memory, part of the mind, and tomorrow you will operate as if you had always known what you are about to learn in your dream.

When you wake and are going about your daily routine, pay attention. Sometime during the day, something someone says or something that happens will trigger an awareness in you. Whatever the trigger is, it will surely jump out at you. During the day there will be one or more significant things that happen. It could be anything. Observe the ordinary events to find clues. You may see a few geese or be offered a popsicle stick by a child. Once the trigger is pulled, an image is given, and you must follow up on it. It is up to you to follow the clue to an understanding.

Gray moonstone will have prepared you for a significant disclosure but you must first discover the meaning of the clue. It will engage a trigger like setting a trap. If anything comes along that happens to fit into the opening, it will spring. Let your mind wander. Allow it to investigate correlations while remaining open to any reason why this particular clue has come. Watch as the various associations come into your mind. Sort through them for more clues. It may take several triggers and several clues before you get the message. You can be sure there will be a message that relates to the worries you put aside the night before. The new information from your dream will provide an insight into your situation that may remove the need for worry. Your attitude toward your situation will be directly affected by the experiences in your journey. In fact, as seen from the point of view you will have tomorrow and cast in the increased light of gray moonstone, the situation will not be the same at all. The fog will lift.

Whatever the connection is, it will lead you to a solution or opportunity or new possibility for you. A new way of thinking may be required to see the connection. Some clues lead you to ways of doing things that will be foreign to you.

At first you may not get the answer to the meaning of the clue. If so, let the question go unanswered. Write down the clues, the trigger events, and any associations in your own shorthand. These clues will be necessary for you to establish the connection later. This process will be quite mysterious at first, but not for long. Your mind will love the game of search and uncover. The game will make the learning fun when you get the hang of it. The reward will be in the process as much as in the new understanding if you let yourself get into it as a game.

Gray moonstone works best if worn in a necklace made from beads of graduated sizes. The various-sized stones each reflect different subtle energies. Each size is attuned to a different layer of the inner world. Each stone will reflect a different subtle energy. A necklace that increases in bead size from three millimeters to twelve or fourteen millimeters is perfect.

Use a necklace that fits closely around the neck for best results. The throat chakra is the best receiver for moonstone vibrations and the experiences they bring. Before putting on the strand at night, place it on the third eye for a few moments to introduce the third eye to its vibrations. This chakra should relax in a minute or so. If it does not, you will need to use indigo or amethyst to relax it. Then, put on the necklace and visualize a steady connection of sound vibration flowing from the throat to the forehead. Picture this sound and listen to the special quality, pitch, and timbre of it. It may remind you of flowing water, or it may be a humming or other familiar sound.

As each stone in the graduated necklace becomes attuned to a different level in your inner world, the sounds may change. Pay attention to the sounds, they can provide access to the different levels. In this way, you will gain access to many different dimensions and different parts of yourself will be activated as you access these levels. As soul we can enter all worlds, but we must work to develop the ability to consciously remember our experiences in these worlds and maintain our access to them as we go about our daily activities.

Your strand of gray moonstone will respond to many other sounds as well. During spiritual exercises you may wish to chant, sing a personal mantra, tone a vowel sound, or use a spiritually uplifting word at different pitches. Experiment. Let your senses open to the clues for when a particular sound or word will have a beneficial effect. These sounds can be used during the above-described process of bringing the awareness you have during dreams to the awake state.

While toning try using different pitches along with different harmonics by shaping your mouth, nose, cheeks, lips, and chest. You can bring out different overtones and create quite different qualities from one root sound. Particular sounds will resonate with the individual beads in the strand. Note which sounds work and what the sounds do.

You can work with a single sound that is especially active for one to fifteen minutes, as long as it is comfortable. Do it for long enough to remember the sound and imprint its vibrations into the aura. Catalogue the sounds that most deeply resonate with the gray moonstone. Those interested in maximizing their ability to recall dream metaphors and symbols, and learning to correlate these to circumstances in their lives that would be changed using certain sounds, should keep a sound library of these sounds on tape so as not to forget the exact sound. This may seem like a lot of trouble, but a small tape recorder and a single tape could dramatically change your life for the better.

Listen carefully for inner sounds that may occur when wearing grey moonstone. The moonstone will bring out your ability to hear vibrations from the different dimensions. These sounds are "not really there" in the physical sense, so you may be inclined to believe they are simply a ringing in the ears or some far-off humming or buzzing. Do not overlook these. Most inner sounds are indicative of the presence of another dimension, and you have accessed it. Training your inner ears to hear is not hard, training your mind to recognize the importance of these sounds may take some time, but with moonstone the mind will begin to process these inner sounds and categorize them distinctly and you will recognize them for what they are.

You may wish to simulate the inner sounds, when possible, on your tape to help you access these inner dimensions at will.

Accessing another reality may not be accompanied by any sort of profound sensations. You may not hear grand music. You may not see a spectacle of lights. Some people experience the other dimensions as an extension of the one they normally occupy, while other people experience these dimensions as profoundly different. You may experience a sensation upon entering one level or dimension, but none on accessing others. Each of us is an individual.

These levels are actually in the same place as the physical plane of existence; they simply exist at a different vibration. One of the benefits of working with grey moonstone along with many of the color-ray–bearing gemstones is the awareness of the difference between energies that exist on different levels. This difference may be difficult to visualize at first. It may be difficult to understand how the different dimensions can coexist without seeming to overlap.

Moments when you experience profound sensations, like the hair standing up on the back of your neck or your stomach lifting, can be moments when you are aware of this overlap. No person can go through life without having these sensations. Those of us who decide to develop the senses of the other bodies will profoundly change their view of the universe and will indeed be blessed. We will share a different way of understanding the incredible wonder of life.

Over time and with the help of gemstones, you will begin to recognize the inner realms you are accessing when you have these sensations. The astral and mental senses perceive much the same way the physical senses do. Pleasurable sensations usually accompany brushes with positive inner experiences. A sense of foreboding or danger is usually present when something powerful and not necessarily benevolent is near.

Many people have chosen to ignore these senses. It is not acceptable to speak of them in many circles. Consequently, many people do not believe in vibrations. They do not understand how atoms that vibrate at a higher level can occupy the same space as atoms that vibrate at the level that we can see with our physical eyes, even though everyone can accept that there is much within the physical realm that we cannot see. As Dr. Wayne Dyer says about different ways of understanding the universe, "You will see it when you believe it." Believing in these dimensions is essential to opening yourself to the experience of them. Do not be afraid. We already simultaneously exist on these different levels, we just do not experience the shift as we move our attention from one level to another, so we have no subjective experience of a change, nor do we notice a difference in our perception. We can develop empirical evidence of the other levels by using the sounds of a certain level to remind us of the change in perception as we move to a different level and then noting the difference in attitude and behavior that accompanies such a shift.

The inner realities may not appear any more vivid than the physical world when "seen" because we tend to only see the inner worlds in our memory. Memories are adjusted in the mind to reflect our beliefs, and so we never actually see the inner worlds except as if they were existing only in our imagination and were memories of dreamlike scenes. Many see the astral plane as being the same as this one. Some may see equal intensity, brightness, contrast, and color. Others may see an incredible brightness and intensity difference because they are fully aware of shifts in consciousness as they move their awareness to another level. Some have their inner eyes open much of the time and can be aware of either level at will. Still others will perceive vivid differences at times and no difference at other times. A very few can see both levels at the same time. This phenomenon is a purely subjective matter.

Working with gray moonstone will sharpen the senses. It will open us to these realms and allow us to sense what level we are operating from. Our ability to notice and our reaction to awareness shifts is up to us. If we react with fear, we will shut down. If we are having a good time and we want more, we will have more.

We are quite capable of being on two or more levels at a time. Soul is not limited to one, or even four dimensions. Gray moonstone is here to teach us about this. If your effort is diligent, you will get results. You will learn to see and hear the other dimensions. To have the experience of the multiplicity of existence, we must be very open indeed. After all, this multiplicity is not possible within the bounds of what we normally feel safe in accepting. Self-discipline is required to gain this perspective. Even for a few moments, the experience of multiple dimensions would be disturbing for most people.

Do not dismay. Your inner censor will not allow you any experience that you cannot grow from. You must decide to give the perception of other dimensions great importance before they will open up to you. Gray moonstone will not induce any premature experiences as they would seem to be hallucinations or druglike experiences. It simply gives you a bit more sensitivity to the other worlds.

Of course, the physical world is the place where we live. It is the dimension in which the most profound changes are possible because, while your life is here, you face a tremendous challenge remaining grounded in life if you try to believe in anything beyond the physical plane. Such beliefs must be very strong before you can see beyond the limits of the physical senses. So, do not denounce the physical world or seek to leave it before your time, as this proclamation is antilife and leads to regression.

To access the inner dimensions while in the physical body takes great effort and concentration, you must really want to do it—more than you want to have physical rewards or security. If your thinking is focused on physical pleasures, you will not be able to use the inner senses at least until these senses are more developed. This takes practice and you must prove your ability to handle the increase in energy that results before you will be able to "see." Being responsible opens us to greater responsibility. Access to the inner worlds is a great responsibility. It is also a freedom that is beyond the description of language.

Gray moonstone will help a person direct their attention to what matters. It will introduce soul to the desire for greater freedom. It will help you decrease your preoccupation with material goods. By focusing your attention, you can become aware of what goes on in the inner world, and learn to love the spiritual essence of life on all levels. It will give you an appreciation for the benefits of emotional detachment to physical pleasures, while leading you to forms of nurturing available only on the inner planes. Soul will find more pleasure in sharing such nurturing with the world than in pursuing pleasure for pleasure's sake.

Gray moonstone teaches you to see with "soft" vision—a way of seeing in which you can see the physical reality at the same time you have perceptions of inner realities. Like peripheral vision, it is indirect. Only with soft vision will you be able to see the subtle dimensions and the things that exist there while in the waking state. This is a state of heightened awareness. Usually only available in emergencies, this vision is quite useful. When you can control the inner senses, you can slow time or sense things that are outside your immediate space. You can learn to know things that have no substance but are nevertheless important to growth.

When working with grey moonstone energy for the purpose of opening the inner senses, always dedicate yourself to the highest purpose. This dedication will help you avoid the interference of psychic beings and the disruption of fears. Before opening yourself to the inner worlds, you must have complete confidence, and it helps to have the guidance and the protection of the spiritual-level beings around you. If you know that you are doing right by yourself and those within your inner circle who are honestly trying to improve themselves, good will follow you wherever you go. There is no long-term danger to those who are pure of heart and continue to do the right thing.

Beings who are permanently rooted in the spiritual worlds beyond the psychic level are committed to making it easier for all who come after them seeking the spiritual worlds, and will always respond to a sincere request for help. They will not intercede to replace your karma, but they can give a guiding nudge. Look for their help and they will protect you by helping you avoid pitfalls.

If you are filled with anger or resentment, you should deal with these feelings before attempting transactions with the inner-level beings, for you may attract controlling astral entities. There is no place for hatred in the inner worlds, and nothing will bring you bad karma faster than entering the places of power with intentions for destruction. Release all thoughts of anger. Hold no one in judgment lest you call the forces of judgment upon yourself.

Gray moonstone does not teach humility, but humility is needed to enter the secret temples of golden wisdom located in the inner worlds. Let this stone help you overcome unnecessary attachment, and humility may follow if you can let go of vanity. Work with the gemstones that carry the color rays you are deficient in, and you will learn what you don't know. Let gray moonstone guide you through uncharted regions where you can apply this new knowledge to spiritual benefit. There is far more that we don't know than that we do know.

Do not enter the other worlds if you seek power over others. You will find there entities whose sole purpose is to feed off those who seek power. They will create delusions and manipulate you into seeking more power. These entities have no qualms about misleading us to gain control over us even as we would gain control over others. They are often much more knowledgeable than we and can easily drive us mad with desire.

Let gray moonstone show you inner peace. After thorough investigation of the attitudes that gain this state, you will never lose it. Enter the other worlds as an emissary for freedom, inner peace, and a bearer of joy-giving love and you will be unimpeachable. You will have nothing to fear, for if you are pure in intention, you will find only love wherever you go. For help in clearing the heart of violence and harmful intentions, seek the red stones, these will teach you love.

Only with a firm grasp of love will you have the protection of the inner spiritual guides. Even alone, we can expect to be invulnerable when we surround ourselves with divine and unconditional love. Do everything in the name of all you hold as sacred or holy, and only love will come to you wherever you go.

Gray moonstone is especially helpful for those with a troubled spirit, especially those green-ray individuals. Its energy is gentle, and its vibrations smooth the rough edges. Those who suffer from uncontrollable fear of the unknown will benefit. They will gradually learn to overcome their fears after long-term contact with gray moonstone.

Anyone with cloudy vision will find this stone clarifies their view. Let gray moonstone help you find your way within, to the secret rooms that exist in your inner mansion that you have been afraid to visit.

Orange Moonstone

Orange moonstone epitomizes the feminine qualities of moonstone. Women have used its calming and stabilizing effects for centuries as a way to regulate their internal cycles and synchronize them to the lunar cycle. Women are deeply affected by the cycles of the moon, their bodies are living on a monthly cycle in many ways. Their hormones are affected by the cycles of the moon as are the other regulatory chemical interactions in the body. Men, of course, are affected by these cycles as well.

Getting in touch with the fundamental nature of cycles within the human body and adjusting these to be in sync with external cycles will greatly benefit those who suffer from irregularities or intense swings in their moods and bodily functions. Women who suffer from emotional imbalance often need to get centered in their cycle and learn when to move ahead and when to rest. Since women will affect each other, and those whose cycles are strong will dominate those whose cycles are not, having an understanding of cycles will help you to stay stabilized in your own cycle without becoming influenced by the cycles of other people. Staying on track with your own natural cycle can be quite difficult for some women. Orange moonstone teaches you about your own cycle, as well as the general importance of cycles by teaching about the influences of the moon.

All life happens in cycles. Orange moonstone can work with a woman to help her understand the spiritual significance of her own monthly cycle as it relates to the lunar cycle. Men have more to learn about their cycles than women, for they are often farther out of touch with their feelings. Men see their relationship to society in terms of their career or their ability to perform certain jobs. Our society is not run with consideration to cycles. We are expected to perform our jobs consistently from day to day. Those men who become out of touch with their cycles do not recognize the body's need for rest during low periods and need for stretching during high periods of a month. Women quickly learn from orange moonstone how to adjust their clocks. Men need more time to get used to the idea of the need for this sort of adjustment. All people will benefit in a host of ways by getting their internal clocks reset.

As many will testify, a cycle's effects can be masked so thoroughly that you are unaware of any cyclical changes or movement. This masking is not proof of some ability we have to dominate nature, rather it is proof of our foolishness with regard to our power over nature. Are we really getting the most out of life by trying to dominate things without regard to consequences? Learn to adjust your behavior to get in time with your natural cycle and you will go much farther when it is time to move, just as you will revive more completely by resting when its time to rest.

All growth and change occurs in a cyclical pattern. Anyone wishing to change their habits, their social position, emotional response, diet, or any other aspect of their outer life should be aware of their cycle. You must be aware of a cyclical shift in your strength in order to predict at what moment you will be strongest. Observe the moon. Watch your moods, your energy levels, your emotions, and your motivation as the moon waxes and wanes. Notice correlations. Put information about your physical changes on a calendar, and note when the moon enters each quarter. After several months of note taking, patterns should emerge.

Our ancestors were more aware of lunar cycles because these cycles obviously affected every aspect of their lives, from harvesting crops, to hunting, to human interactions. They were astute followers of the natural ebb and flow. They had to rely for their very existence on their ability to predict these changes. Today we tend to think of predicting cycles as some sort of esoteric astrological art. Women who practice the art are often categorized as eccentric. Their knowledge of astrological relationships to one's natural cycle is seen as superstition. However, personifying the phases of a cycle is an important method to understanding the aspects of any cycle. Try looking at the astrological signs as a key to understanding the phases of a cycle. These symbols contain much significance and you can learn to understand much from their teaching. Orange moonstone teaches the mechanics of what seems to be an esoteric art, prophetic access to future inclinations through symbolism.

All life is vibration. Energy is vibration. Matter is made of energy that manifests in one form or another, depending on its vibration. Movement is generated by vibration. Even thought exists as a form of vibration. Sound, color, light, feeling, everything is vibration. Vibrations are cyclical—a wavelike motion that goes up, then down, then back to the center again. Working with amethyst and lavender will help you to understand the higher purpose to life through understanding the vibrations of its elements. Use orange moonstone to relate this understanding to your own cyclical patterns.

If you are the type of person to occasionally suffer huge overreactions to some seemingly ordinary situations and then to return to normal without noticing how you got back, maybe you are out of sync. Lunatics are actually normal people who happen to be completely out of sync with their normal cycle. The word "lunatic" is derived from the word *luna,* which means moon. Extreme cases of psychological derangement result in panic disorder and dangerous phobias. Orange moonstone will bring people who suffering these disorders back to a relative state of stability after perhaps a month or more of continuous work.

In order to get fast results when working with orange moonstone to help alleviate psychological problems, you must wear a strand continuously every day or at least have the strand within the aura. You must make every effort to study the effects of and learn about the disorder you are suffering from. Read books, get counseling from a knowledgeable friend, and perhaps go to an astrologer for advice as to how to learn more. Learn about the phases of the moon. Begin to notice your behavior during these phases. Meanwhile, consult a psychologist or psychiatrist to address the mental aspects of these syndromes so you can see clearly how the mental habits you repeat also create an out-of-tune cycle.

Take a long look at your life. Perhaps work with a close friend who has known you for many years and can objectively evaluate your cycle. Create a calendar and log the different swings in the intensity of your psychological condition during your recent past. Start to write a journal of your development, paying attention to the overall characteristics of the different phases of the moon in relationship to your life. Make this process a study, and you will certainly identify the pattern to your own psychological shifts and emotional mood swings, and better learn to accept them and assimilate new ways to govern them.

Orange moonstone works with the heart center. All learning it imparts comes through the heart center. Strands will be most effective if they are just long enough to reach down to the heart area. The orange color nurtures the heart area. Its soothing vibrations ease a troubled heart—old wounds to the heart will gradually heal. You can expect the initial effects of moonstone to bring tears as the wounds are gently reopened during the healing process.

Heart wounds are largely emotional-body wounds. They generate a matting and knotting of the emotional body fibers. As orange moonstone helps these fibers become unknotted and free to move, they will feel tender and sensitive. Try to allow yourself time to soothe the sensitive areas, and give yourself the gift of creating a safe place with lots of loving support in which to practice this sort of healing. If your wounds are deep and the pain is still fresh, back off from stress-producing activities while you are healing. Trying to heal heart wounds under stress is quite a challenge and could cause more severe wounding.

In cases where the heart has suffered at the hand of another or several others, healing should be done in the presence of a professional counselor or in a group therapy setting. Those who have suffered the most severe types of emotional trauma, such as violent sexual abuse as a child or intense alcoholic battering accompanied by emotional abuse, should wear orange moonstone only during therapy for the first few weeks. After the trauma has been revealed or uncovered, the sufferer may begin to wear the strand all day. Wear it at night after all traumas have been processed to avoid suffering the severe nightmares that could result from unaided deep healing. In all cases, the person who is suffering will be able to process only as much of a past trauma as the heart center can safely deal with at one time.

Orange moonstone will also help strengthen the tissues within and surrounding the heart. It soothes and supports internal healing of these tissues as a very gradual process. Tissues will be encouraged to rebuild damaged DNA and to recall their blueprints for correct functioning. Cells do continually reproduce, however damaged cells will usually reproduce incontinent cells when one has sustained damage to the structural integrity of the mitochondria (an interior cell organ) or other cell bodies. The orange moonstone will support the restructuring of your mitochondria. These tiny organs are like separate life forms within your cells. This restructuring may require the additional assistance of other therapies, especially naturopathic remedies that support nucleic rebuilding.

Those who suffer from severe immune system deterioration will see improvements as the heart center becomes stronger. These people may see some improvement in the speed of recuperation from any diseases that may affect them if they wear orange moonstone along with green aventurine and follow a course of traditional medicines as prescribed by their doctor. Always use gemstones in combination with physical remedies to heal the immune system. Changing the energy patterns in your various bodies to improve health will be much more effective if the physical body is simultaneously receiving herbal or allopathic treatments.

All fertility problems that are based on energy deficiencies or imbalances due to the deterioration of cyclical hormonal production can be eliminated rapidly with the aid of orange moonstone combined with physical remedies. For the complex interaction of catalysts and active compounds produced by the body to prepare it for reproduction, releases of each must be timed correctly. Ovulation is governed by internal clock-like mechanisms.

Orange moonstone will reset these clocks to synchronize a woman's reproduction cycle if she uses a simple visualization technique while working with the stone.

Visualize the production of various hormones as processes governed by separate internal clocks. You must learn enough about these processes to be able to clearly develop a mental picture of what happens in the body with the release of each hormone. This may take some advance research in books about reproductive cycles. Now, picture a beautiful woman in orange chiffon robes coming into the area where the clocks are located. She has a wonderful aura of love and grace. See her carefully adjusting the internal clock for each hormone, setting it to properly work with your natural cycle. Repeat this procedure each day for three days starting just after the ovulation period, and then cease it for four days. Now, repeat again for three days and then cease for four. Then a third time, repeat for three days. Your reaction to your next month's cycle should be less emotional and more positive.

Female bodies must have love. This statement may seem nonscientific. It is, however, true. We all need to feel loved. We are the only ones who can create the internal state of love within ourselves. Others may love us or they may not, but we create the feeling of love in our hearts. Our minds can either aid us in this ability or completely eradicate any feelings of love we might have felt by repeating thoughts of poverty and scarcity. It is essential that the female feel love. The whole emotional body will become weak and inept if kept from love.

This does not mean that a woman needs sex. Sex may well be an adequate trigger for feelings of love, but it also may not. A woman must learn to generate feelings of love by herself, though she will be more successful if she can see the love coming from a divine source that is limitless. She may wish to see the love coming in to her heart from a parent, lover, husband, child, or friend. It is best to associate love with some higher power that never fails you. This sort of love will carry you through the really tough times. Orange moonstone can teach you about love. Feeling unconditional love for yourself may be the single toughest challenge of your lifetime. You must rise to the challenge if you are to enjoy inner peace.

Orange moonstone may work most efficiently with women because they are generally more in touch with their natural cycle as it relates to the lunar month, however men should not assume that this stone is not for them. Men can learn to become more balanced if they get in touch with their feminine side. Men can get support for this part of themselves by engaging orange moonstone to teach them about the benefits of being in touch with their inner femininity. Often this effort will lead to a deeper appreciation for feelings and the power they hold to direct men's lives and to help them accept more love.

Spectrolite (Luminite)

Spectrolite is indeed an awe-inspiring stone. The magical light show of rainbows within its surface is truly wondrous. Like an aurora borealis, the colors seem to swirl. The beauty appears and disappears as the viewer looks and looks again. Some varieties have only a barely visible sheen. The best varieties have myriad color reflections almost like opalescence. Its dark gray-black body is like thunderclouds. This stone is reminiscent of the far north, where time passes differently and cycles of life have a super-real quality that causes one to wonder more. The greatest deposits are from Finland, where the reindeer roam the frozen tundra.

Relatively rare until recently, this stone is now available in high-grade therapeutic quality beads. Necklaces are hard to wear for any length of time. The provocative effect of this stone is difficult to describe. The beams of flashing color seem to penetrate the darkest corners of our being. Like sparklers in a dead-black cave, these beams appear to implode on contact with painful corridors where we once found solace.

Many of the people drawn to gemstones as tools for growth will relate to the idea that deep, dark corridors of painful memories and feelings that accompany them are places to visit when life seems too much. Spectrolite changes this idea. It shows us better ways to get needs met than visits to private places of self-pity. We can still go to them, but their aura will be uncomfortable to us. No more self-indulgence in the woeful whining that brought us temporary solace. Prickly, tingling, itchy, healing energy will be in these corridors now. This is the same kind of energy that forms around a surface wound when the skin is healing. This energy is hard to endure, for its healing may leave you frustrated. Just as you cannot scratch a serious wound when it itches, likewise you cannot be comfortable upon entering these corridors when the prickly energy is there.

Healing is not always pretty. It is rarely comfortable. With spectrolite, it can be downright uncomfortable, partly due to the nature of its healing energy and partly because you will be forced to look at why you wallow in self-pity when change awaits. It is, however, very effective.

Overcome this initial discomfort. Put out of mind the desire to throw off the spectrolite. Pick someone safe, and spill. Let out the pain. Place trust in another individual. Trust opens these corridors to the light.

Before you get too far with this, you should build safe havens in the inner world. Let a "safe" stone like mother-of-pearl guide you to inner sites best suited for construction of a safe haven. Take hints from white coral as to structures that will support feelings of trust. You can feel the support of Biwa pearl as it soothes and builds a protective shield that can afford you the space to create such a place without interference. Let mother-of-pearl prepare the ground for this safe haven. Choose the stones that feel most safe and comforting to be the ornaments and build gates from your color-ray gemstone. Use leopardskin jasper to construct walls for a secret room. Fill it with the light of your primary color ray to uplift the very molecules of the physical body to higher vibrations.

Choose a center stone, perhaps a large single diamond of perfect clarity and colored with every color ray in perfect balance for your human signature. Build a fountain or other beautiful adornments for the gardens that may surround the inner site. Set a tone of healthy joy while building by playing a favorite piece of music to create a sweet, soft mood that expresses serenity.

Create your dream place. Put in only that which pleases you. Change it as needed. A place of safety can be there in the inner worlds whenever you need it. Revisit this room frequently to raise your vibrations.

You should be fully prepared for spectrolite. Its first effects can be disconcerting. Once you have gotten past the initial explosive pattern, look for flashes of insight. Come to spectrolite with a clear question. Focus on the question. Assume a posture of receptive openness and expect answers from the universe with the help of spectrolite.

Spectrolite is not an oracle stone. It can work with white moonstone or another oracle stone to provide the understanding and insight to interpret the language of the oracle as provided by white moonstone. An oracle expresses the mystery of a question. You sometimes get an answer from an oracle in the form of a riddle. If aliens could speak to us about things both wonderful and completely new, perhaps they would employ a tool like spectrolite to interpret their thoughts into our language. Spectrolite brings input to your conscious mind from far afield as its vibrations reach out to and become altered by external forces of higher consciousness and then, on return, reveal these coded variations in vibration to your mind, you learn to understand higher forms of consciousness. You must expand your consciousness beyond normal limits to develop consistently accurate interpretations of spectrolite flashes.

All profound insight into your life and the causes that produce your life start with a movement to higher, more expanded consciousness.

If you are feeling closed in, this stone provides space. Where no possibilities exist, it will show one. If you are in a corner, it will flash a glimpse of another dimension to you.

To help with the challenging effort of bringing these somewhat off-the-wall, spontaneous inputs to use, try the aid of blue sapphire. Its blue color-ray energy, carried on the steady vibration of sapphire, clarifies even the most obscure reference. Spectrolite will usually bring insights that are so far out that perhaps only one obscure reference affords any connection at all between us and what it is attempting to reveal.

As magical as all this may sound, the process is quite scientific—no mumbo jumbo here, no tricks. Stones are compressed vibrations that often have a very select set of frequencies at which they resonate. Every object has a signature resonance and this resonance radiates out in a sort of field. Gemstones have large fields. Live objects have a greater field than inanimate ones. We all have a field that can be contacted. Set a stone in the human energy field and the stone will become activated. Round gemstones resonate more clearly and consistently than other objects and feed that resonation back into our field from sources beyond our normal range of detection. Since the field of a human is also directly connected to sensory organs and emotional feelings, the vibration will be received by the person as a feeling. The reception will give us a feeling of well-being if the vibration we contact is beneficial to us, as though a vibrational harmony or combined chord between our energy and that of the stone has developed.

To feel this may take some practice, but those who have given it a chance have felt it. Spectrolite would be an excellent stone to help stretch a persons receptors to see and feel influences normally beyond their outermost abilities of subtle receptivity. Finally the person can either sit and enjoy the resonation that often feels like a visit from an old friend or can keep this stone in the field as the field fluctuates with the various influences life provides.

What makes this a spiritual tool rather than a psychic trick? Psychic tricks provide no useful input and may leave the recipient confused, scorched, tired, sick, or in some way feeling abused. This is because psychic tricks, really potent ones, are very humiliating and dehumanizing. Gemstones promote joy and abundant giving while improving receptivity and opening the heart. Only a spiritual tool can do this. We are in fact spiritual beings. We are made of an energy even science has a hard time defining or localizing. The gemstone energy is directly effective at building this energy for growth.

The result of this interaction can be a new integration of your lost capabilities and an attunement with your spiritual mission. Practice using high-grade spectrolite as a radar device to identify your greater capabilities. Hold it about eight inches in front of the brow and imagine spectrolite vibrations going out to the subtle unconscious reaches of our inner space where the waves of vibration contact inner locations filled with great insights. As these insights are contacted, adopt an attitude of openness and discover the insights into realizations beyond normally self-imposed limitations.

Use spectrolite to find help. The challenge is to take responsibility for your acts. Misuse gemstone energy to perpetrate a violation of someone's space or to trick a person psychically, as some have done in the past, and many will suffer, most of all the sender of the energy. Use this energy for your benefit and all will benefit as you enjoy raised consciousness and increased awareness and become a better, more productive, soul. We are constantly faced with the challenge to make the right decision.

With gemstones, the heart must be pure and without harmful intention or the results of their use for harmful purpose will be sufficiently disruptive to set one far back on the evolutionary scale of spiritual fulfillment.

Spectrolite will help you in every way when gaining aptitude and insight from your guides or guardians, as their spirit bodies can send and receive messages through spectrolite directly to your conscious mind.

Sea stones include mother-of-pearl, pearl, freshwater or Biwa pearl, and all three varieties of coral: red, pink, and white. In general, sea stones are refreshing and provide a strong sense of what is natural, basic to all life, and sustaining. They nurture the superphysical level of the energetic aura. Sea stones soothe in a way similar to the waves of the ocean. They provide a gentle, rhythmic flow of energy with a slow vibration that helps the body stay grounded.

These "stones" are not actually stones in the strict sense. They are formed by sea creatures. They are deposits made for specific use. Of course, the creatures are long dead, but the rhythm of the sea is carried in their vibration. The sea can soothe us like the energy of the earth mother—the mother of all life. Its vibration is the vibration of birth.

Sea stones do not carry color-ray energy, nor are they amplifiers for the color rays. They do, however, support the work of the color rays. For this reason they are included here. The work of the color rays is to bring us to our original, childlike simplicity with a comprehensive ability to give love and to understand ourselves. The color-ray energy is provided to show all people who they are and to help them realize their full potential. This mission requires the color rays to be capable of teaching humans about their nature. Sea

13

Treasures of the Deep

stones can help one get in touch with the primal—our origins. Creatures of the sea are our predecessors and have qualities that we also encompass within us. Even though we are mammals, we carry the traits of ancient reptiles and fish.

These origins are not relevant to our lives as we go about our daily duties. The human world long ago left behind its origins in the ocean. Energetically, though, we are still related to these creatures. To become complete human beings, we must ultimately come to grips with every aspect of our nature. We must understand our origins and make peace with the instincts and desires that are as old as life on this planet if we expect to live up to our potential.

Our physical bodies use energy in ways similar to other animals. Coral and pearl can teach us much about our instincts. They can help us rebuild our core energy, the energy within our core—a roughly cylindrical shaft of energy that flows from the center top of the head through the torso, legs, and feet to the ground—that we use to generate physical power. We must build our physical power to survive the trials of coming to grips with who we are and the forces of nature that will test our commitment to understanding the principals of a spiritual life. We must understand all the natural laws in order to work with the positive forces in life and avoid diminishing our physical strength or regressing spiritually. The spiritual law of power, for instance, refers not to the power of force or control of others. The law of power refers to the need for learning control over the forces of physical power, which requires the ability to gain the spiritual perspective of soul by transcending the mind while still being capable of using all our faculties.

The sea stones will also provide insight to controlling certain necessary auric energies, which will be required to maintain the momentum to attain the future goal of spiritual freedom. The freedom we seek is the freedom to create, without patterned reaction, a life we love. Learn what these sea stones have to teach, and you will have some important clues to achieving this freedom.

Mother-of-Pearl

This pearl-like material is cut from shell and made into beads. The most common color of mother-of-pearl beads is bright white. To obtain this white variety, a bleach is used in a process that is not particularly harmful to the vibrations of the material. Mother-of-pearl is soothing to look at and all shades and varieties are equally pleasing to most. If you prefer the natural color variety, a cream or light beige tone, then use this type.

We find mother-of-pearl to be most gentle, especially with those who feel they need love. The support of mother-of-pearl helps the wearer assimilate the powerful changes initiated by the color rays. Its gentle reassurance is a welcome presence in times of great change. Wearers will learn of love for nature in the simple things in life.

For those who feel they are just common folk or are not deserving of the good things in life, a strand of mother-of-pearl, worn for several months, will aid in creating a new point of view. Mother-of-pearl will also help you get in touch with your deepest self and see the grace and beauty there. It may even help us maintain that feeling of grace and beauty when we are being forced through a situation that will not allow us to proceed without letting go of some of our past security. Wear it in times of change as much as is practical.

Life originates in the ocean, and wearing even a four-millimeter strand will help you get in touch with your roots. This connection will enhance your sense of centeredness and help you develop a stronger relationship with Mother Earth. It is important when wearing the strand to have the intention of achieving this connection so that the gentle action will affect your subconscious mind and provide a direction for the subconscious impressions to follow. Mother-of-pearl helps direct the subconscious mind by subtle suggestion as this part of the mind does not respond to the force of will.

Creating this subconscious direction will affect your very presence, the aspect of your being that is perceived by others though not engaged in projecting the persona. Presence is an indefinable quality of being. Your being precedes you. People can sense how we are, removed from all our trappings, masks, and personality traits. The vibrations of mother-of-pearl teach us the profound nature of our being, how to reside in this being, and how to find serenity and peace there. Peace, an aspect of presence, is a quality of being, not an action, though it may be seen in one's actions.

Mother-of-pearl teaches you to sidestep trouble. Sometimes trouble comes in the form of negative thoughts directed at you. If you need protection from others' negative thoughts, mother-of-pearl will nurture a sense of well-being that will protect you from accepting harmful negativity even through the toughest times. Its milky white swirls enfold the subtle bodies and provide a stronger sense of your ability to form boundaries. You will become more sensitive to negative thoughts, though you will learn to walk around them as if they were mud puddles on your path.

Mother-of-pearl aids you in understanding fluidity and the nature and purpose of cycles. For women who resent, try to minimize, or deny their natural cycles, this understanding will be of great benefit. If worn during the "weak" part of one's cycle—that is, the part of the cycle that precedes any major, repeating symptomology, like premenstrual—these symptoms will be felt to a much less profound degree. This weak part of a menstrual cycle is usually forty to eighty hours before the major release of hormones.

Men, too, will benefit from a deeper understanding and respect for the cycles of life. Although men may seem to be above being affected by cycles, they are in fact, quite profoundly affected by them. The understanding of cycles affords the luxury of being in alignment with the forces of these cycles. In other words, you are not always trying to dry the laundry outside when it's raining or take a long trip when a storm is pending.

Few people are objective enough to realize how profoundly their attitudes and behaviors may change in the course of a day. Most of us believe we are more or less the same from hour to hour. Those of us who display internal changes too dramatically are considered insane. We are trained to act consistently and think predictably, but our consciousness is often moving through a whole variety of different states. Mother-of-pearl will lessen the effects of cycles on our inner being to afford us greater detachment from the effects of cycles. This will afford us greater flexibility in displaying our outer traits.

Mother-of-pearl will teach self-nurturing and will encourage you to nurture yourself and get the help and support you need. This support will greatly reduce the deep emotional changes that often result from the weakened state one falls into after experiencing the low point of a cycle. For many people, this low point is approximately three days before the appearance of any outward effects or symptoms. Deeper lows are experienced when several cycles coincide at a low point.

Consider a typical cycle. We can track the results in the physical world of an influence. This influence can be a cause set in motion by some outside force, by the universal creation, by us, or by the social consciousness of everyone in the country in which we live. Most cycles occur on a repeating basis. Common lengths of these cycles are a day and three-quarters, three-and-a-quarter days, just under seven days or approximately twelve days. As a cycle repeats it becomes less influential, just as a wound clock will eventually stop. All cycles return to a state of inactivity except cycles of physical force that are in such a perfect balance that they do not appear to run down, like the cycle of the tides.

For example, suppose we cause an eye infection by inadvertently forgetting to wash our hands and rubbing an eye. Unknown to us, a bacteria has been placed in the eye. This cause sets a cycle in motion. A war ensues between infection and immune system. If we track the growth cycle of the bacteria on a chart we will see that each day and three-quarters or roughly forty-two hours we would notice a surge in the speed of bacterial growth with spurts of growth occurring as the cycle is at a high and then, as the cycle moves to the low side, a slowing of growth occurs until the cycle reaches its low. If we track the activity of our immune response, we will notice a reciprocal cycle. The highest activity of our body's immune system, we will notice, will occur sometime after the bacteria is at its highest growth. Our bodies respond to the cycle of the bacteria with a delay. The cycle eventually will come to a stop and the length of time this takes is proportional to the delay time between the two growth cycles.

We will observe much more intricate interactions between forces than described here. This example is a simplification of a possible cycle meant to show some of the aspects of cycles. Mother-of-pearl will teach much more to those who experiment with cycles and make a study of them.

Mother-of-pearl helps regulate the flow of fluids in the body and teaches the body to accomplish this necessary task. When color-ray treatments include rest periods and bathing in water treated with mother-of-pearl or placing your feet in a foot bath that contains it, the soothing and nurturing effects will be very helpful to easing a persons resistance to improvement. Such baths are recommended prior to and subsequent to surgery or other trauma to the body. Mother-of-pearl spheres reduce inflammation and will promote healing and lessen the pressure and buildup of excess fluids. It will absorb negativity and can become useless when it has absorbed its limit of negativity.

Mother-of-pearl can assist someone who is emotionally or mentally unbalanced or who experiences intense or harsh emotions or thoughts. For those who find recurring abuse, anger, shame, or grief in their lives, wearing a strand will help a great deal both to soothe the wounds and to protect the wearer from the recurrence of abuse. It helps you mend the "fabric" of your energy field. Auric energy fields can have holes or weakened areas where you have been invaded in the past. These weak spots must be healed if you are to avoid further invasions.

To assist in mending these holes, take a strand of mother-of-pearl and move it gently and very slowly all over the energy field at a distance of approximately two to three inches from the body. Imagine the energy field as a soft cushion. It protects the body from attack the way a soft cushion would protect you from a physical blow. This cushion needs fluffing from time to time. Repeated blows to it flatten and mat the energy, reducing its elasticity. This "fluffing" is a gentle, in-and-out motion, like petting, which encourages the bodies to rebuild the aura. Work the aura with mother-of-pearl to regain the cushioning. As babies can fall and seem to bounce right back despite their fragile bodies, so we can regain this youthful cushion even in later years when we have lost most of its protection.

Babies have a fully functional energetic cushion. If a baby is repeatedly hurt, it will show greater signs of damage from each occurrence. Babies have no control over this cushioning. Adults can learn to direct a cushioning energy to protect themselves after letting mother-of-pearl teach them.

Children may find great benefit from wearing a strand. It helps them maintain and build their protective aura. They can regain a great percentage of natural layering.

Every person alive could benefit from mother-of-pearl. We all are constantly bombarded with wild energies thrown about by emotionally distraught people. Whether at work, on the road, or at home in your neighborhood, notice how a strand of mother-of-pearl creates a better cushion to protect you from others' outbursts. It is very effective, yet very gentle. It would make an excellent gift to anyone, since we all have occasion to suffer an unexpected blow. A necklace will teach the wearer to put out a cushion of energy rather than flinch as a blow strikes. This simple effort will minimize damage.

Mother-of-pearl teaches nonresistance. It subtly exemplifies the way negative energy can be deflected or sidestepped when you are not busy preparing to resist. We need not deal with all the energies that come our way. We can learn to sense negative energies as they approach and to better determine which ones we can avoid and which ones we need to contend with directly.

Mother-of-pearl also teaches discrimination. As it senses energies in the environment, it quickly responds to these energies and helps us evaluate their potential for harm to the aura and signal the subconscious mind to either accept or fend off the energy. In this way, we all can learn how to better distinguish beneficial color-ray energies and receive them to nourish us while rejecting the harmful noncolor-ray energies. This benefit alone is enough to justify the purchase of mother-of-pearl as a learning tool for all who wish to better manage their subtle energies.

Biwa Pearl

Biwa pearls are formed in fresh water. They are softer than saltwater pearls and tend toward a barrel shape with tapered ends. Larger, smoother, shinier Biwa pearls are preferable. The better-grade Biwa have a satiny, pearlescent sheen that glows gently. It is a beautiful material and the shapes in the higher grade are unique and pleasing. It pleases us in a way we should learn to please ourselves.

Biwa pearl promotes a sense of personal purity. You may find your vibrations reflected in its pearlescence. Its reflective ability teaches you to evaluate your energy-handling abilities, to respond to opportunities for growth more readily, and to discover your hidden potentials. When you use personal affirmations while wearing a strand, you will be able to overcome negative self-image and thereby reduce the tendency toward self-abuse. Simply affirm your worth and let the pearl energy support this action and keep your mind from debating or sending negative energy to disperse the affirmation.

Noncolor-ray energies are not always received from the outside; they can be produced within. We are capable of literally transforming color-ray energies within ourselves into noncolor-ray energies. Biwa works with a wearer to show them how to control their tendency to step down color-ray energies and to maximize use of available color-ray energies.

Biwa pearl shows us many sides of ourselves. Some of these sides are familiar and others are not. We believe we are who we would like to be.

Actually we are many things, and not all of them are acceptable to us. Biwa teaches us acceptance. It may reflect parts of ourselves we are not comfortable with, it will reveal the dark side of our natures. Our dark side is indeed a useful part of our nature if brought into the light of the color-ray energy and transformed into our agent devoted to teaching us how to gain spiritual strength.

Pearl will help you face the deepest, darkest issues within yourself. It can help you accept responsibility for the actions you engage in that arise out of this dark part of yourself. You feel a great deal more inner energy when you begin to integrate your darker side, for behind every dark intention lies the desire for love.

As in the act of standing in a river, wearing a strand of Biwa pearl will cleanse us and teach us a deeper sense of joy and satisfaction in our own potentials. Its smooth, swirling vibrations act in our aura the way a river's water swirls around our body as we bathe. It carries away the false belief that someone else can make us whole. It suspends our conviction that we must be someone other than who we really are to accomplish spiritual goals. Pearl works in this way to show us our potential, for joy in total self acceptance. We choose how we will react to life, and we can learn to create a reaction of joy even while acknowledging the dark side.

Biwa pearl heightens our appreciation of music and harmony in all forms. It can help us in learning the benefits of toning or chanting and singing. It is a pleasure to work with—its gentle energy will soothe the emotional body. The emotional body can learn resonance. At times dissonance is useful to dislodge negative stimuli. Dissonance breaks up patterns and can protect us. Inner resonance draws in the color-ray energies, forestalling our misguided resistance to the benefits of greater energy.

Like wearing a blanket of pure silk filled with goose down, Biwa will nurture and soothe the sick and weary. Anyone who has been buffeted about by the forces of life will find access to a softer, easier approach to learning than they have known before. After all, life is about learning; we can hardly change that. We can, however, affect how the lessons come. We can attune ourselves to a finer, more gentle way. Our mental shroud is made of vibration itself. As the vibrations of our thoughts change, our minds change; as our minds change, the thoughts we think create a different life for us. If our lives teach us by hurting us, we must raise the vibrations of our thoughts to a higher level such that our thoughts no longer bring us into the company of harmful forces.

We are our own melody. Our mind is the tune life will play by. If our song is a happy one, life will provide happy words to go with it. Biwa will soften our tune so that life can teach us the softer ways to learn. It will ease our worried minds and open our hearts to a gentler way. Life sometimes seems tough. Let it. Create a style and attitude that provide an insulation of kindness. Even though not everyone will respond by being kind in return, we can learn that others' reactions do not have to affect our choice to be kind.

Biwa pearl is a good listener. It absorbs your troubles and reflects them back more gently and kindly than you normally present troubles to yourself. You can always stand to be kind when making judgments about your life.

Accomplishment is important, but learning to develop love is more satisfying. Certainly we can set goals to accomplish things in life. This is a good way to remain on track. We must remember, however, that our goals are simply targets we have aimed at. The benefits we gain from the target practice need not depend on how well we do at hitting the bullseye. If our purpose is to enjoy the game, we will surely be more likely to enjoy the practice. If our purpose in life is to learn to love and to be more open to receive love as an act of love, then love will likely come our way. We will surely raise the vibrations of our minds in an atmosphere of love. As we raise the vibrations of our mind, love will seem easier. Whether or not we believe in God or a spiritual purpose in life, we can still agree that a life filled with love is hard to fault and more satisfying to live than one filled with disappointment and failure.

Mix Biwa pearl with gemstones to help the body accept the color-ray energy in those gemstones. Biwa pearl in a necklace of gemstones assists in the assimilation of the color rays. It helps soften resistance and generally eases us as we overcome the many blockages we may discover while working with color-ray energy.

You have no real idea how entrenched you can be in habitual ruts until you try to learn a better way of doing things with the help of gemstones. Color-ray energy presses us forward to meet our challenges and tests. It teaches us where we can improve. It brings us the experiences that will change us for the better. All the while, it insists we try a better way when the way we do things is less than loving to ourselves. Biwa pearl nurtures our feelings of purpose, improves our openness to love, and encourages us to find serenity in all we do.

Biwa pearl supports all positive, self-improving actions and especially supports the efforts we make to develop a belief in more abundance. Let love be the benefit we enjoy and the results we seek in the form of goals and accomplishments will come and go, bringing us what we need while we learn the greater measure of love.

Natural Pearl

The power that pearl once embodied has greatly diminished. The near-extinction of natural pearls because of pollution has generated great sorrow. Its reign in the sea has been a happy one, and though its power has waned it will be a positive influence on life on this planet to its end.

Pearls are the eyes of the sea. It may seem difficult to accept the idea that something amorphous like the sea can have intelligence or teach anything. You must perhaps believe in the idea that all life is spiritual, although simply being open is enough to contact this intelligence with a tool like pearl. Working with pearl, particularly for those who love the ocean, will open you to this knowledge and verification of a new knowledge in your consciousness is a purely subjective experience. Those who have not had this experience believe it unlikely, but those who have become aware of having knowledge available to them that originates in the sea believe this experience is undeniable.

The idea of asking a rock, a plant, or an animal for guidance is equally unlikely. Scientists today believe that "primitive" tribes were superstitious or worshiped fantasies when they spoke to these and received answers, but for those who have had this experience it is not superstition at all. A scientist could stand to learn something from a primitive on many subjects. The ability to listen to less-developed souls and learn something comes to those who respect and love life in all its manifestations and pearl can open you to this love. You must temporarily become open and loose the ego to understand looking to a "lowly" animal for advice, yet all forms have soul. Even a pet can give you valuable information on surprisingly complex problems. Many scientists like Albert Einstein would agree: all problems have their root in nature and all solutions are possible by studying nature.

The sea is where life began and was the medium for all the early evolution of the current Earth inhabitants. The sea is like a mother. It can hold our troubles and our dreams. A full heart is an open heart. Pearl fills the heart with appreciation and wonder helping us overcome barriers to initiating actions with the heart abased on what we feel, rather than with the mind based on what we think or what others want us to think. The wisdom of the sea is easily accepted by the heart because the heart can't judge. Pearl is attuned to the vibrations of this wonderful wisdom of the sea. It serves as a translator until the heart can grasp the intelligence directly.

The glow from a person's heart will radiate from a strand of pearl when worn around the neck. Each strand will have its own particular owner. A relationship of support and love will develop between a wearer and their strand.

At the time of Atlantis, pearl was at its height of strength and power. The early, sacred music of the lute and pre-Celtic harp arose out of appreciation for the love and devotion to life embodied in the natural pearls of that time. Very large pearls adorned the temples and courtyards of the time. These huge pearls created an energy that pervaded the temples. Those who entered the temples were able to experience deep benefit from the sacred music.

It is sad indeed that these pearls were destroyed. The devastation resulted from people who sought to control rather than to love. This devastation changed pearl. The consciousness of those who lived at the time could not value the work of pearl. Its fabric absorbed this consciousness. Pearl lost its ability to absorb and became less effective. Its mission was to teach people the benefits of love, but it was only able to help in absorbing some of the negative emanations of that time.

Its connection with the human species has been corrupted by the negative thought forms sent out by the Earth inhabitants. No single group is responsible for this. In fact, the same forces that brought negative thought forms to us caused us to develop in ways so different from each other that we can hardly relate to one another has also caused us to become alienated from pearl.

Pearl was once a grand and beautiful adornment for the most gracious. It was usable by those who sought to develop an understanding of love and how love transforms soul into a radiant light that can uplift all who contact it. Pearl—once a powerful tool for the benefit of the heart, though now a dim and weak force—is still useful to those who would listen to it.

The possibility of enjoying the once great energy of pearl does still exist. In the present time these energies exist primarily as reflections of the past. For those who can use pearl energy to travel into the past, this tool will be especially useful.

Red Coral

Red coral will not often be the strand of choice for people seeking the security of a life without change. Red coral brings fundamental shifts in the very core structure of the energy-producing foundation in the physical body. Ironically, those who would resist core issues the most may in fact have the greatest need for the strength that comes from red coral and from the physical changes it brings. It will work as described here only when worn as a strand of spheres. It affects you at the level of your energy core. Fundamental restructuring of the building blocks of your energy foundation is red coral's mission. It will actually rebuild your energy core according to your blueprint. The fiery wheels of the chakras will be balanced and brought into harmony.

Red coral is fundamentally safe. It may make deep changes in your very foundation, but it does so only as you are ready. This cooperative quality may explain why a few of those who most strongly resist change in the structure of their energy core find red coral so desirable. Since it never forces change that is not immediately beneficial, you need not fear it.

Red coral allows the body to relax its habitual maintenance efforts and focus on rebuilding areas of malfunction. Organs, glands, cells, even individual atoms of the body, have an energy of their own. These energies should conform to the body's blueprint. With the influence of red coral, the body will begin to alter its basic structure to a more perfect harmony and balance. This process may be upsetting, even painful as the body releases its attachment to the old forms, but red coral will never force changes more quickly than you can safely adjust to the changes. The benefits of this restructuring are phenomenal. Results are dramatic and yet seem effortless, especially when white and pink coral are used in conjunction with red. To improve the adaptation process, eat vitamin-rich, fresh foods, drink fresh vegetable juices, and get plenty of low-impact exercise.

Red coral helps the body rebuild the bone marrow. This action will create healthier red blood cells, which in turn will increase oxygen to the whole body. This process, in combination with the actions of white and pink coral, will create a stronger skeletal structure. To expedite this process, try drinking one ounce of wheat grass juice twice daily to provide oxygen and enrich the blood.

Red coral, in combination with white and pink coral, is highly effective in supplementing the treatment of osteoporosis. Women who are on the go and can little afford deeper changes that would otherwise disrupt their demanding schedules will love red coral. It holds the emotional body in place while building changes in the substructure. The effect is as if the emotional body were lifted off its foundation temporarily while the foundation is rebuilt. The emotional body need not become altered. It simply readjusts to the new foundation by altering its communication practices. Red coral easily makes major changes unlike other methods of change to the underpinnings of our false ego that cause deep emotional reactions.

Women are particularly susceptible to imbalances caused by emotional shifts. Although they are more effective than men at giving emotional support to others and receiving the emotional support of others, they must be careful to be conscious of their timing when inducing changes in the emotional body, as they rely on it and can become unbalanced if it were changed too rapidly at a time when they were heavily using the emotional body in such give and take. If these emotional exchanges were disrupted, it would be distressing and could cause unnecessary strain.

Men are less able to give or accept emotional support and therefore may not miss it if changes were to occur in the emotional sheath while support was suspended. This weakness is a strength in the short term when some of the more powerful color-ray gemstones shift the emotional sheath and men seem unaffected. Of course, no one is unaffected by deep emotional change but men are able to put off their reaction to such change and may assimilate changes gradually if they remember to take time to do the work and do not procrastinate.

Men and women alike will be much the better for allowing red coral to work with their emotional bodies. Wearers of coral will discover many benefits to having an emotional body that is fully functional. Most people have no idea what this would be like. Most of us live in and out of one or more destructive emotional states obviated by depression, guilt, anxiety, panic, rage, or other intense emotions.

Repair the emotional shroud and you become much more sensitive without susceptibility to invasive emotions of others. You can easily avoid the various forms of compulsion. You can enjoy serenity. You employ great creativity. You will feel exceptionally alive and vibrant, yet you can quickly relax or sleep. A healthy emotional sheath provides the basis for great passion in all activities and, with a strong astral conjunction, you can project your thoughts and easily influence others. Trust your feelings.

Specific designs that use red coral in combination with white and pink coral will be highly effective in rejuvenation. Red coral creates the new foundation. The other two help build the color-ray energies into new constructs cemented with the positive emotional energy of joy, as the white coral maintains feelings of security.

Note that both men and women have both the masculine and feminine qualities. Some men are actually more feminine than masculine and some women use more masculine energies. Our integration of whichever qualities of either of these we have trouble with is a worthy goal, but our efforts to achieve this goal can be out of balance. For example, men who are trying to be sensitive can act overly dramatic as they express their feminine sides, and in their eagerness to attain equality, some women prefer to emulate predominantly masculine qualities instead of improving the effectiveness of their feminine qualities. It can be precarious to overcompensate or overbalance in this way, yet some men and women must have this experience in order to understand the true nature of balance. Further, note that balance is not a set value. For some women, more of the masculine qualities are present, and this is quite a good balance for them. Some men are naturally more feminine. Each person must find the balance that is best for them at any one time. Red coral will bring the energy needed to create this balance as well as the security of knowing where your balance is for optimum growth.

Red coral introduces you to the inner "yardstick" for growth. This yardstick is marked with the milestones for growth that we can expect to be challenged with in our lives. Great satisfaction can be had in knowing we are right where we should be and that we have just the right abilities to meet our specific challenges. We learn from red coral not to measure our lives by the standards of others. Once we have been introduced to our personal yardstick, we will always know where we are and how far we have come. Our yardstick can even give us a sense of the challenges to come. This allows us to improve our trust in the positive intelligence of the spiritual energies that guide us. As we trust in the spiritual, our personal path seems more right and we can relax into the difficulties we face.

To find this yardstick we must first commit to finding out where we are. This may not be pleasing to our ego if the ego is currently in charge of our lives. Nothing could be more satisfying than knowing who we are and where we are going, but the initial challenge may put some seekers off.

Red coral works like a construction crew superintendent. Reconstruction is a multitask effort. You need all parts of your body to cooperate like a crew if you are to rebuild your body to blueprint specifications. Each bead of coral is like a separate foreman. One red coral foreman will take charge of work laying the foundation for new growth in the organs, another will manage the process of rebuilding the cell walls, and another will oversee the finish of new cell interior structure. Red coral will seek to insure that you build up the body to support a powerful energy core with the same care, and then some, that you would use for any important construction project.

The process of employing coral to rebuild this inner energy core is similar to employing a team of workers to build a new cauldron or furnace. It is important to think through just what you want. Any construction crew works best when the tasks are clear and the outcome is specified. Plan what you expect to be able to do with your energy when the reconstruction is complete. Let your subconscious mind be guided by coral to develop a plan to establish how this new cauldron will provide power. Know what the power will be used for. Take notes as you become aware of plans. Be specific in those notes. You must provide the goals. You must know your own priorities. Determine what your values are. Then produce a list of long- and short-term goals you intend to work on. This will set red coral in motion. Be sure these goals are in alignment with your true inner priorities or your plan will not succeed.

In a house design, you must plan for the kind of house that would permit openness and plenty of natural light differently from a house that would provide isolation and privacy. Many factors are different —orientation, location, landscaping, and placement of windows and doors. Similarly, your body must be constructed according to specific goals and intentions if you are to maintain good health while living in this body.

What do you value? Would you like more autonomy or community? Privacy or interrelating with others? Stillness or activity? Physical pleasure or exercise? Emotional emptiness or emotional intensity, or any other possible state of affairs? We are all different. A list of preferences will help one decide what kind of house to build. Establish clear priorities.

The deep red coral is a bit more aggressive than the more orange/salmon sort of red coral. This aggression is not for the average person but may help some who need the extra strength. The finest beads are formed well, have a fine grain, few imperfections, and consistent color. They seem to radiate a powerful yet smooth energy and seem to "like" people.

Red coral must be of highest quality to be a trustworthy ally. Do not use dyed red coral. Coral will be hard on your emotional body if it is dyed, reconstituted, or filled with debris. A single high-quality sphere of perhaps four or five millimeters will create major restructuring of our inner core energy handling furnace. This cauldron is normally heated to a low temperature as our energy is diverted to support what we are trying to avoid or force in ourselves. Unable to sustain higher levels of energy since such energy could only disrupt such a system, the cauldron must remain relatively cool. Coral will challenge our use of energy.

Once red coral begins to rebuild the blocks of our inner furnace, we will be able to sustain much higher levels of energy. Vitality can return to an old body. Once the cauldron is heated, it will stay hot even when energy is lower, such as during sickness. Our heat element is essential for proper disease-fighting capacity. All Chinese medicine speaks to the problems encountered by one who has no inner warmth. Heat or the fire element, as they refer to it, is one of the basic ingredients of good health. The Chinese have used coral for many centuries. Only now are designs being developed for necklaces that will generate deep restructuring.

The secrets of coral are revealed to one who wears it with expectation and gratitude. The benefits it can bring are many and once restructuring is complete, you can accomplish more in life with greater efficiency and less difficulty. This may not simplify your life but it will make possible the development of an ability to handle greater challenges with ease.

Pink Coral

Solid pink coral, as well as the pink swirled with white varieties, aid the body in the process of rebuilding inner strength. Within us we have a columnar-shaped field of energy. This field will become quite powerful when built upon a strong foundation. The physical body in conjunction with red coral will reform this foundation in alignment with our inner nature. The presence of pink coral, especially when worn in four- to six-millimeter beads around the neck, will greatly enhance the process of rebuilding the structure of the powerhouse. Worn for a period of three to six months, it will thoroughly reprocess all "building blocks" of the powerhouse. Pink coral will do much to teach us how to safely use this powerhouse as it integrates greater energy and removes blockages. Integration and cooperation in all interrelationships is the mission of pink coral.

Once we become more powerful, we must learn to deal appropriately with anger and other destructive emotions. If we do not, our inner powerhouse will have occasion to explode. Anger will fuel destructive energies. You will be in great danger if you fuel with anger a cauldron that is newly rebuilt and more efficient. You may be harmed deeply as a result. Not all anger is harmful, but all anger when sustained is harmful. Initially anger may motivate us to greater heights of achievement. If anger is wrongfully directed at those around us and sustained until it distills into rage or bitter resentment, it will become explosive. Explosive anger is quite different from a spontaneous, more normal anger. It is the explosive anger that is dangerous. Explosive anger can destroy what we build and set us far back. Usually, one who is plagued by such explosions is suffering from fear. Fear, especially frantic fear, will often trigger such outbursts.

The cauldron is fired by emotional energy. Indulgence in the negative form of the various emotions can damage the cauldron. Pink coral shows the person how to use the cauldron to build emotional power and how to use this power for the benefit of all. Use the power for self-aggrandizement, and the harmful emotions will surely get activated. If we worry about our own concerns to the exclusion of the interests of others, then we will be fueling the fire with vanity. Vanity will develop into envy. Envy will generate fear, and fear will produce anger. Anger begets rage when unchecked, and pink coral can do little to help one who is in a rage.

On the other hand, if you focus on the best use of power for all of life, you can generate positive emotions. Giving freely generates freedom from worry. Freedom serves gratitude. Gratitude engenders joy. Joy empowers one to compassion. Compassion is the cornerstone of love. Emotional power can beget love if used for the good of all without invading anyone's space or trying to change them. Grant others the freedom to have their life be just as they wish it to be. Pink coral challenges you to develop a lifestyle oriented to giving without expectation of changing someone. The riddle is how you contribute to others without expecting them to change. Solve this riddle for yourself with the help of pink coral. You have a special gift to give, and when you determine how to value your gift and give it freely without trying to change others, you can enjoy a profound feeling of love.

Let pink coral guide you through daily decisions and your emotions will become more controllable and more positive. You will develop the discrimination to choose wisely. Soon the decisions we make that create our situation and raise our emotions will be clear and within our control. Eventually, we can learn to make good decisions without its help.

As pink coral works with your body, so it works with even the smallest microcosm within you, that of the organic molecule. Once your body has replaced atoms that hold too much noncolor-ray energy with more positive atoms, and recreated each of the minute molecular forms in complete alignment with its blueprint, you develop a "consistent" extended structure. This structure will give you not only greater physical strength, but harmony, endurance, and vital energy.

Your perceptions of the outside world will become more detached and less subjective once your bodies are in complete alignment with your inner purpose. Having a more consistent interrelationship among your inner parts will give you a strong, clear reference with which you can compare influences as they come to you in life. The outer physical aspect of structure is nearly as important as the inner, mental aspect, which is affected by the indigo and blue rays. Physical structure is slow to change, and change is harder to accomplish, but the benefits are more immediate and are felt throughout all the bodies.

Picture a miniature colony. Everyone in the colony has their own cubicle. The colony is in space, and all the residents stay in their cubicles throughout their whole lives. Each resident has a task they must perform from their location. They have been divided into groups, and individuals work at the same jobs for their entire lives. They are born into the job. A few have the job of exchange, and these few bring raw materials and food for everyone, though each individual must regulate their own intake and outflow.

At the command center, tasks are assigned according to information received, catalogued, processed, and disseminated. At times the high command will send down new orders, and a restructuring takes place. Information is sent out along established lines, and communications experts along the route receive the information and pass it on. Their job is to relate the restructuring information to the groups in their area. Groups then interpret their jobs according to the restructuring as it relates to their function. All groups are expected to participate in keeping the system working.

The problem in the colony is that the various groups have gotten off on their own, doing what they do, and have lost track of the other groups and the effect of their work on others. Each clan must process information and raw materials that keep arriving, but otherwise they do not have to concern themselves with the whole.

Over the years, a colony that has been isolated in space a long time begins to suffer from this lack of cohesion. Each group develops its own specialty language. The command center gets so busy following its routine that it loses touch with the clans. For a long time now, clans in our colony, like organs in our bodies, have been failing long before they should. In fact, a colony could survive for hundreds of years, but most manage for only a few generations—sixty years—before total breakdown.

Along comes a dead spaceship that arrives at our miniature colony carrying the remains of a larger, more prosperous colony. This colony lived in the water. Conditions were quite different there, and this colony was made up of individuals who remained in their cubicles but did not interact much. They simply got all their food from the surrounding water. They learned to be individuals. They learned to survive by taking care of themselves. Their society was a much simpler and lower form that was effective.

This colony had no specialization. Every individual built their cubicle on top of the last. The record of their struggle was locked as a readable, vibrational resonance in the walls of their cubicles aboard this ship. The dead colony cubicles were like a hologram of a differently structured society. When our miniature space colony came upon this dead, undersea colony, they learned from it. They learned how to create a new structure where all clans looked out for the others, but even more, they looked out for themselves and stopped relying on the other clans so much. By using their communication lines to transfer the needs of their clan back to a command center that was now interested in forming a new more cooperative system of interaction and cooperation, the clans learned to thrive. They learned to do their jobs and take care of themselves. They learned to ask for what they need and get their message heard. A common language developed. Soon every clan could and did listen to every other clan at least in terms of their needs. As the communication developed, the colony grew stronger.

Now relate this little story to yourself. Understand that you are much like that space colony. Your organs and bodily systems have likely lost touch with each other. They obtain directives but are used to being ignored when their needs change. Problems have developed in your body. Organs and systems are struggling to survive.

When you begin to wear pink coral, it is like bringing in information from an undersea colony. The coral is dead, but the vibrations of the creatures are still within its very makeup. This hologram is complete in even the smallest beads. The rounded beads allow the vibrations of pink coral to emanate in all directions. Your body gets the message. Every part gets the same message—a restructuring can begin. A new language of cooperation is developed. A new language is spread throughout the colony—a language of hope from entities that work individually to carry the lineage of the whole.

When the process of creating a new communication and structure is well under way, the body develops a congruity. A consistent message goes out, and the organs and structures learn a common language. Soon the vibrations of each come closer to the vibrations of the whole. An inner clarity and mutual purpose develops throughout the system. Cooperation improves.

Understanding and wisdom come to those who have inner clarity and congruity. The lessons of life bring us greater joy and fulfillment when taken as gifts for the betterment of ourselves as well as all life. Learn the language of pink coral, and you will understand more of the language of life. You will learn to contribute to and receive from others in a far more productive way.

Pink coral works first on skeletal structure. Skeletal structure rebuilds every few months. This phenomenon seems impossible as we are used to thinking of skeletons as solid and unchanging, but it is a proven fact. Pink coral will aid the body in creating strong bone structure. It will condition the body to develop resilient infrastructures, resistant to collapse yet more flexible. This process happens quickly within the bone, as it has such a similar vibration to coral.

Worn with approximately twenty percent high-quality red coral in the same necklace, pink coral will greatly support the generation of bones that are much less brittle and improve flexibility of ligaments and support tissue as it develops conditions for mutual support throughout the body systems. Red and pink coral cooperate in this task. Though each has a different constitution and vibration, the two set up a syncopated rhythmic pattern. This pattern creates significant change easily when wearers constantly keep this necklace on or near them. Foundation and structure can be rebuilt within four to eight months.

You may wish to wear a necklace of white coral as needed to protect your partially restructured systems from the hindrance of other peoples' emotions. Many people have not begun this process or learned the value of cooperation, and some of them will resist the efforts of anyone who attempts to change. The entire body can be restructured without interference from others emotions when the occasional use of a separate necklace of white coral is included during the regime.

Necklaces of pink coral with white coral, worn regularly, will support growth. The two used together can help children who have growth problems. They will support physical changes in the endocrine system to promote growth. They will also help children protect themselves and sense when danger is present. If children learn the lessons coral has to offer at an early age, they can become highly coordinated and congruent at a much deeper level and stand a good chance of remaining so throughout their lives. Because children are more flexible to begin with, they will assimilate the lessons easily. The languages of each of their various systems have not yet fully degenerated into codes that the other systems won't understand. A common language is easier to learn and quickly replaces the various others. The pars of children's bodies learn to cooperate easily.

Red coral is generally too powerful for young children. They should begin with white coral and stick with it throughout formative years when problems arise. Pink coral can be introduced to older ones after a few months. With older children, only a few beads of red coral are needed to achieve results.

Adults, on the other hand, can start with necklaces of twelve red coral beads combined with pink beads. Additional necklaces of white coral alone should be worn when in the presence of those who demonstrate negative emotions. Combination necklaces of white and pink can be introduced after the combination of the red and pink has done its work (approximately four to six months). Always have that white coral necklace handy to help with the difficult moments when change seems intolerable or when others interfere.

Pink coral aids the wearer with color-ray work by providing a vibrational hologram that will allow the body to restructure. This restructuring supports the drawing in to the body of a much higher level of color-ray energy. The physical structure often is the limiting factor in the body's use of color-ray energy. The level of color-ray energy in the physical body will often determine the level of positive emotional energy in the emotional body. Utilization of positive emotional energy will be at a minimum in a body with an incongruent structure. Conversely, the congruence of a harmonious structure will promote a greater capacity for positive emotional energy.

Positive emotional energy attracts loving relationships. Wear pink coral as described above and your propensity to attract love experiences will improve. In fact, all internal and external relationships will improve when one has assimilated the lessons of pink coral and restructured the body to a system that works with greater efficiency and propensity for growth.

White Coral

During and after the process of rebuilding the central powerhouse with pink coral, white coral will help you recognize negativity, both internal and external, that can threaten the powerhouse. Our natural protective mechanisms will be triggered to come to our aid in sustaining the inner powerhouse. By wearing white coral we will learn to maintain an inner feeling of safety and security even in circumstances that might have frightened us at one time.

Negative emotions of others can be quite destructive to our energy flow, especially during the process of rebuilding our core. White coral may help us become aware of the source of this negativity and its effects. This awareness will go a long way toward keeping us out of the line of fire.

Negative thoughts can accumulate in our aura as well. These must be cleared if we expect to be safe from their influence. It is most helpful to wear a strand of white coral when clearing these thoughts. When doing so, we may find that we can more easily avoid situations that conflict with our purpose. For some, this may develop into an ability to sidestep harm in its earliest manifestations. Note that white coral may not stop conflict from arising as this is a natural occurrence in this world, but it will help you stay clear of any damaging effects that negative emotions would cause.

You may also notice a movement toward a natural affinity with forces that act to sustain life rather than destroy or damage life. This can be a tricky distinction if a wearer is out of touch with personal goals, and nearly impossible if the wearer's "radar" system has been denied or damaged. White coral teaches the individual to master the use of this radar system that tells one when harmful emotional energy is near. It will show them the steps they needs to take to repair the radar if such repairs are needed. It protects you from emotional harm, particularly from shame and fear, as you are learning to distinguish between beneficial forces and those that may not be healthy.

Not all forces that would distract us from our purpose are obviously negative. An example of this might be a friend who comes to us and asks us to join them for lunch. This good friend is someone we would like to spend time with. Suppose our initial inclination is to decline, but we do not, because we are afraid to disappoint them or to let out our feeling that we need to stay on track. Though we need to be back at work early that day, we let our desire to help a friend who needs emotional support interfere with our plan. We go to lunch. We are late returning to work. For the rest of the day we are concerned about our friend and distracted from being focused and deliberate at work. We do a less than adequate job that afternoon though we know we were supposed to be on top of it and finish an important project.

Later a coworker informs us that just after lunch the boss had come through the office and offered all present the option of taking a tough assignment. Unfortunately, we were still gone. No one wanted the responsibility. The boss assigned it to a new employee who accepted the assignment reluctantly. It turns out that this assignment is just the duty we wanted and needed to round out our experience and prepare us for the future. Our hunch to say no to our friend and be back early from lunch was correct. Not only did we do a poor job that afternoon, but we missed an opportunity for improvement.

We may be inclined to get caught up in emotional turmoil. We may miss such opportunities all the time. We may not always know we have missed something. White coral helps us maintain our inner strength, clarity, detachment, and focus, by reducing the impact other people's emotional turmoil has on us. It works to protect us and to show us how to make use of the emotional strength we gain by working with pink coral. With white coral, we learn to apply the internal language and connectivity we learned with pink coral to getting to what we need while staying on course and free from emotional entanglement. This is not to say that white coral gets us what we want. Rather, it brings us to a place where we can express our wants and needs clearly at any time, and if we don't get what we want, we are okay with that. When we miss a chance to improve, we know that soon there will be another opportunity to get what we want and we will be ready.

For those who have trouble knowing what they want, white coral can be their best friend. It will allow the heart to mend gently. The body needs, but it is the heart that wants, and the heart must be open to want. Coral protects the heart as it mends and learns to trust enough to open.

White coral shows us where we fit in in life. We learn the benefit of autonomy. White coral connects us to the whole. We learn how we are distinctively different from others, how to use our unique talents, and how to apply ourselves to more productive tasks using our special gifts.

White coral teaches us to apply the skills of communication. It teaches us to get the lines of communication open in a broader way. It teaches us to use our awareness to contact forces and support causes that are further afield. We may take up new hobbies, start writing a journal, join a group, visit different places, taste different foods, follow more hunches, make friends with different kinds of people, visit an attraction we previously avoided, or try any number of other new activities.

Wearing white coral we learn to participate in areas of life we may have avoided without noticing it. With gentle suggestion this coral teaches us that we are a unique part of humankind and able to contribute in our own way.

When we wear white coral in a strand with blue sapphire rondels, we will become inspired with higher thoughts. We will increasingly be able to regulate the energies of the higher mental aspect as we become more familiar with its vibrations. The pineal gland, which regulates the flow of many of the body and mind substances, in turn will become regulated by the higher mental functions. Wearers may learn the inner causes of their own self-negating thoughts. Once they learn the sources of their thoughts, they may learn to control them. Thoughts often generate patterns and connect with other related thoughts, forming powerful chains. The coral and sapphire strand will help to localize the effects and break up unwanted patterns as we direct it. With the sapphire, the blue ray is brought into the lower awareness from the higher and the coral influences us to regulate our thoughts, particularly those that affect the lower mental functions and the emotions.

Wearing such a mixture for timed periods of twenty minutes at a specific time of day, every day for twelve days or more, with the clear intent to bring the benefits of higher awareness into the lower mental functions and quietly contemplating this purpose, will set in motion a pattern of change that will improve our ability to produce positive emotions and enjoy their benefits.

White coral works with blue lace agate to cement the mental building blocks needed to achieve an understanding of life that is at once more flexible and more sure. Wearers of this combination learn to more completely assimilate thoughts derived from higher mental functions to create a new lifestyle, deduce new understandings of the way life works, and shape productive, efficient plans of action. You learn to improve your connection with the flow of higher concepts. You can begin to grasp what it is like to be thinking in alignment with this flow. You will feel more certain of your place in life. As this flow directs a receptive group consciousness, that is a number of like-minded people, such a group will at once discover a better way to do things.

There is always a next step. White coral works with the blue ray to reveal the next step and help us take our part in it.

Over time, the result of wearing white coral is the feeling of belonging— a feeling of knowing your boundaries and how to protect them. You will know when you are being supported by others and when it is time to keep away from certain people who do not have your best interests at heart.

White coral helps the wearer sense the flow of energies around them, interpret these radar-like images, and go with those that are helpful and empowering. It teaches you how to keep silent. Silence is the greatest protection from those who wish to control you. White coral can help eliminate from all thought and speech someone who is sending harmful energies. White coral will teach you how to shut off the flow of energy from one source while remaining open to energies from another source.

Hateful, fearful, and jealous thoughts will cause a person harm. If you maintain a close relationship with hateful, fearful people, you will be opening yourself unwittingly to mind attack. White coral does not stop mind attack, but it teaches us how to distinguish the thoughts of others from thoughts of our own. We learn to sense where a thought comes from. It helps us to stop inviting in someone else's harmful thoughts by reminding us that the one who sent the harmful thought can not take our attention unless we let them. It teaches us that silence in every regard about such a person will stop the invitation. By thinking or speaking of the person, we set up a link with them. Across this link will come the subtle messages of harm. White coral may post reminders across these lines in the form of symbols to remind us we can block destructive messages.

As the recipient of such messages, we may experience anything from headaches to deeply disturbing fright, and these experiences can have great effect on one's health. Problems like susceptibility to environmental hazards such as dust, mold, or chemicals can arise. Problems with depression and loss of energy can result. Low blood sugar and hardening of digestive tract can develop. All this can be stopped by taking the mind off the person. This breaks the link. White coral gives us the awareness of the cause of the problem and encourages us to silent building of our defenses. For deeply entrenched patterns of enmeshment, you may need to use rhodocrosite to break the pattern. Then, white coral will help keep you free.

White coral can teach specific techniques to a person who is open to creative self-protection. Each individual must find their own specially designed technique by carefully listening to trusted friends and being open to any lead that may take one to a book or tape describing a perfect technique.

For severe cases of attack, you must use greater precautions. You must develop a shield within. Build it out of white coral covered with turquoise and striped with pink tourmaline (rubellite). As you build such a shield, you must hold firmly in mind the intention to remain silent on the subject of another's problems. Hold on to the right to your individual space, free of the attacks of others. Imprint on the shield the symbols of your personal integrity, religion, or philosophy that support the right of autonomy and spiritual freedom. Place the symbols on the inside of the shield. From this side, you can see the symbols and be reminded of the promise made to yourself to stay silent on the subject. You may inlay your own color ray into the letters or symbols to give them the power to remind you to use the shield. A shield may be as big and fortified as necessary to rebuff any attacker. Remember, an attacker may not mean us harm, but thoughts of theirs that are directed at us with the intention to change us will interrupt our lives, and if those thoughts are highly emotionally charged they may cause considerable distress.

Whenever you feel tired, edgy, tense, weak, powerless, or susceptible, you can take refuge behind or within the inner shield. White coral can show you how to wrap yourself in white light and ensure protection from all harm.

You may seek within the light of coral the strength to discover the tie you have with a certain danger or a specific perpetrator. No one can harm you if you are truly within the protection of the white light. Within this safety, you are free to discover how you may have initially caused someone harm and unwittingly begun a chain of cause and effect that is bringing you this experience. Revealing how you may have started such a chain, the white light will help you heal the emotional pain associated with such an action. This is the direct route to removing your involvement with attacks.

As we build our inner strength with the color rays, we can use the help of white coral to keep clear of attacks. All the time we are building our bodily temples of pure color-ray energy, we may have moments of doubt. Doubt will cause no harm as long as we have white coral to immediately seal off any openings to harm that the doubt may cause. White coral ultimately teaches us to assume our rightful places as protectors of our own inner sanctum. Within this sanctum we may reign as beings of light.

Practice visualizing yourself sitting on a dais of pure white light. You sit in the middle of a large, circular room with many doors and as you watch the doors, images of different habitual interactions with other people begin to play like movies on the different doors as if they were being projected from behind the door. You watch these scenes of your involvement with ease. From your seat you are completely safe to view without involvement. If emotions arise, you can soothe them with a large strand of white coral you hold in your hand. Putting attention on this experience daily for a time and then as needed will dissolve the unwanted emotions that draw you into these experiences. Coral soothes the heart.

To remain safe during the gradual process of recreating your image of yourself and coming to an understanding of your birthright as soul, the prince within multilayered sheaths of nearly pure color-ray energy, you must inwardly hold the firm belief in the power of love.

Suppliers of Therapeutic Gemstones

Gemisphere

2812 N.W. Thurman

Portland, OR 97210

(503) 241-3642

Lightstreams

3272 California Ave. S.W.

Seattle, WA 98116

(206) 932-1671

1-877-321-4383 (toll free)

Visioneering

P.O. Box 21

Carlsborg, WA 98324

(360) 683-2385

(360) 681-8485 (fax)

Appendix

How to Use the Appendix Charts

The following charts are to be used to make a thorough diagnostic of physical organs and the various energetic levels of physical, astral, and mental bodies in therms of color-ray energy. You may wish to copy the tables and take inventory approximately every three to six months as you are working with the color-ray energies. After a series of these charts are

445

completed, you will be able to document the adjustments you are making in the relative color-ray levels in each organ area. Thereby, you will note the success you are having as you work with the gemstones for balance of color-ray energy.

I would advise you to write out a thorough and comprehensive statement of your current health each time before you fill out one of these charts and then when reviewing this document and preparing your next set of charts, note changes in your health. You can, with a little practice, understand the testing procedure and test yourself, but you may not be confident. You may wish to consult a gemstone therapist or a kinesthesiologist who can take readings of these factors using a muscle-testing protocol. Most naturopathic doctors are versed in the art of muscle testing to determine the health of a particular area, so it should be relatively easy to have this person test for the levels of color-ray energy in these areas.

Should you find that you must test yourself, follow these steps and note the results of every test on the charts. Gather strands of high-quality carnelian, rose quartz, citrine, aventurine, blue sapphire, indigo sodalite, deep violet amethyst, and white onyx and use these to test each color ray. Note: Use the carnelian first, as this stone will be the easiest one to "feel" on your first attempt at this test. If you do not have all of these strands, you can use single stones or do all of the tests with carnelian.

As you test each area where a particular organ center is located, hold the appropriate strand approximately two feet above the organ center. Slowly lower the gemstones toward the organ. If you can move the strand very easily down to the body, then the area is overactive in this color ray and you should note the area is in a state of expansion with respect to that color ray. Hyperexpansion may be the result of excess noncolor-ray energies along with excess color-ray energy of that color. If this is the condition, then the layer of resistance will almost certainly be twelve to eighteen inches from the body and will seem much more "dense" and repulsive to the gems.

Not all people will be capable of performing this test without personal assistance or instruction. Some individuals may simply know what the condition is by simply asking themselves and realizing the truth without testing, and others may have an emotional reaction or feeling for the color ray condition of a particular organ center. You may find that you can work with a friend to test each other and be successful. The idea is to establish a baseline for your condition and to relate improvements to the changes in color-ray signature for the different organs.

Every organ has a blueprint that indicates the precise levels of each of the color-ray energies. These levels change from moment to moment, but you can make a determination as to whether each of the organs is deficient (if so, note "-" for contraction on the chart). extremely deficient (note "--" for hypercontractions), overactive (note "+" for expansion), or extremely overactive (note "++" for hyperexpansion) as the particular organ or system receives or blocks color-ray energy. In extreme cases, an organ center will not respond at all ("0" for shut down). It will resist any focused input of any color ray energy. If this is the case, then you should consult a physician to run some laboratory tests. Occasionally an organ will test as healthy ("X" for healthy), in which case it will receive color-ray energies from all spectrums according to its blueprints, and it should react by drawing in the gemstone test strand with a gentle attraction.

Begin entering notations in the Diagnostic Chart for Energetic Healing with a similar approach to the above testing methods. Use the heart center, located at the sternum in the center of the upper chest, for all testing. In these tests you are looking to establish the level on which the person being tested is disrupted. With this information, as well as the Diagnostic Chart for Organ Healing, you can establish exactly what color ray is the greatest problem and on what level you should focus the healing gemstones.

As you are testing, simply focus your attention on the level indicated in the chart, for example the etheric/unconscious level and imagine a stream of the particular color being tested, like blue entering the etheric level of the mental body, and test the heart center to determine if the level of blue-ray energy entering this level is either more or less than optimum. For this test, use a strand of carnelian spheres and hold the spheres over the heart and test the "resistance" the subject has to the imagined color ray as it enters the imagined level. The heart center should give accurate results for all level tests, especially if it is functioning fairly normally. In cases where the heart is badly out of balance, the subject may have to choose another, healthier organ center to test over. Try the major chakra of your choice—like the solar plexus, located just below the rib cage in the upper gut, or the brow chakra, located just between the eyebrows above the nose.

When you have completed the charts and all organs and levels have a notation, you can look for major patterns like always contracted in the indigo ray or always expanded in the red ray. Then, refer to the chapters on these rays and use the described stones to "feed" the missing color ray until you are more in balance or until you have cleared excess build up if the condition was expansive. You may refer to the "Entries" portion of the appendix (page 452) for a reference to these demarcations.

Once the overall condition of excess or lack of a certain color ray has been addressed, then you can proceed to deal with each organ that has been shown to have a severe condition. Clearing these imbalances should clear the effects of past trauma and allow the organs to begin to build strength and after each treatment you will increase the health of one area of the body. Do not hesitate to make notes about any area that has a more specific problem than the chart allows space to explain, like the left ovary contracted in the yellow ray or the third thoracic vertebra showing signs of expansion in the red ray. Similarly, any muscle could be tested, as could any specific nerve pathway or lymphatic duct. Such tests could follow where tests indicate the person being tested is having trouble with a smaller, more specific area, cell, fluid, or structure.

As you become familiar with these tests, you may learn to make adjustments to the most out-of-balance parts of your bodies without taking time to complete such charts, but understand that this sort of chart is extremely useful because it gives you the complete picture of what is happening to you and why. Taking time to complete such a chart every six months will assure that you remain in good health because conditions will show up on this chart long before you would come down with any obvious symptoms or contract any disease. This way you will treat your conditions on the energy level before any serious physical reactions result.

Diagnostic Chart for Organ Healing

	red	orange	yellow	green	blue	indigo	violet	white
cerebral cortex								
pineal								
cerebellum								
hypothalamus								
brainstem								
eyes								
ears								
nose								
throat								
neck								
lungs								
heart								
liver								
kidneys								
solar plexus								
thyroid								
thalamus								
stomach								
spleen								
gallbladder								
small intestine								
transverse colon								

	red	orange	yellow	green	blue	indigo	violet	white
lower colon								
rectum								
sex glands								
sex organs								
bladder								
urinary tract								
blood/veins								
lymph system								
skeletal								
nerves								
nerve sheaths								
arms								
legs								

Diagnostic Chart for Energetic Healing

	red	orange	yellow	green	blue	indigo	violet	white
sub atomic								
atoms								
molecules								
somatids								
intercellular								
cellular								
organs								
body systems								
whole body								
supraphysical								
astral emotional								
causal/mental								
thinking/ mental								
etheric/ unconscious								
soul								
oversoul/ collective								

Entries

+	Expansion	– –	Hypercontraction
++	Hyperexpansion	0	Totally Shut Down
–	Contraction	X	Healthy Energy

Aura. A field of energy that surrounds any gemstone or life form.

Alignment. A state or condition of energy use that can be demonstrated by masters of chi (life force) by healing or destroying simply by imparting energy through direct contact.

Astral Body. A sheath that surrounds and protects the physical body and that produces emotional responses to our environment.

Balance. A stable state of being where a person is working without constraint with all types of energies and experiencing no disharmony.

Blockage. Refers to an obstruction in the free flow of energy through a body.

Blueprints. Packets of color energy that determine how a healthy cell will interact with its environment when conditions are optimum and no blockages are present. When functioning properly, blueprints will determine correct spectrum of energies for each cell or organ.

Causal Body. A sheath that surrounds and protects the astral body containing records of all experiences in our different lifetimes.

Chakras. Centers in the various bodies of great energy flow primarily located along the median line in the physical and astral bodies through which vibrational energy

Glossary

flows. Causal and mental bodies also have these centers, normally located along meridians as charted by Chinese medicine.

Chi. The oriental name for vibrational energy. This energy can be directed for the purpose of improving health.

Color-Ray Energy. The energy that can be directed, focused, and amplified by a crystal. Is "seen" to have a specific color by those able to view the human aura.

Denial. A process whereby an individual has lost control over the decision-making practice and has substituted a set of habitual responses for true freedom of action. By this process, some individuals may become the victim of their own unbreakable habits.

Divine Love. A kind of love that is never controlling, gives without limits or conditions, and always gives first without demanding reciprocation. This love can be demonstrated but cannot be claimed by pretense.

Divine Will. The flow of guidance from a consciousness that is both universal and omnipresent and directs events from a point of view that is fully aware of what is best for all life.

Energy Pattern. An habitual use of life-force energy in a very specific routine that is associated with a set of conditioned responses to produce ongoing life circumstances.

Inner Focus. To direct your attention to the inner screen and project a mockup of an image of something you wish to manifest in your life that allows you to hold this image in place for a time.

Etheric Body. A sheath that surrounds and protects the mental body and contains impressions we know as subconscious thought.

Harmony. A state where all of the different vibrations of the parts within a body are congruent.

Heart Center. The chakra located in the center of the chest at the approximate height of the heart or sternum.

Imagination. The singularly most spiritual ability soul possesses that allows one to direct events in life from the mental level, or when the ability is refined, from above the mental level.

Impulses. Sensory data is processed as it is received by the brain in bursts and stored as a whole.

Individuation. A process whereby a person makes their own decisions and becomes uniquely more themselves.

Inner Screen. When made blank, this screen can be used to project intentions for viewing by the mind's eyes.

Integration. Individuals have many points of view and as you mature, you develop sophisticated attitudes that are formed while uniting their many considered points of view.

Intention. The act of mentally carrying out a plan or purpose while maintaining the feeling of certainty that the mental action has initiated a perceptible thought form that will be realized when it manifests in physical form.

Life Path Point. A point on the back of the leg just above the ankle where the Achilles tendon joins the leg muscle that is used for placements of gemstones when you wish to affect your future life.

Lines of Force. Directed energy that is amplified and focused by crystals along a particular pathway.

Material Worlds. All levels of creation as defined by, experienced as, or comprised of matter, energy (noncolor ray), space, and time.

Mental Body. A sheath that surrounds and protects the causal body and contains thoughts and beliefs that control our lives.

Mental Construct. A set of ideas that when taken together represent a belief about the world.

Meridian. An imaginary line that connects points over the physical body that relate to a particular bodily system as in acupuncture.

Misalignment. A condition where the chakras of one body that should be located above the chakras of another body have been shifted and are no longer located in the same proximity.

Negative Energy. Any energy causing an undesired or disturbing effect.

Noncolor-Ray Energy. Forms of energy that are devoid of color and therefore cannot improve the flow of life force in cells and organs.

Perception. The ability of soul to apprehend the totality of some thing or idea of a thing in its fullness as opposed to eyes that see a detail at a time or a mind that thinks of things in a certain limited way.

Placement. The act of placing or taping a gemstone directly on the skin or clothing over a point where the energy of the stone will effect a specific internal change.

Primary Color Ray. The principal color of energy in a healthy person's aura. Each person has a signature of various colors of energy that comprise their aura, and when that person is fit, then a certain color characteristically predominates.

Psychic Space. A person's own space occupied by one's thoughts and feelings. This space should be considered sacred and sacrosanct—invasion of said space constitutes a transgression unless the person crossing such boundaries is invited in.

Resonance. Two bodies that share the same or similar vibrational signatures cause each other to sound, just as a tuning fork, when placed over a guitar string causes the string to resonate with its characteristic frequency. This is the principal by which gems create effects.

Rondel. A rounded bead that is somewhat flattened on two sides like a doughnut.

Saturate. Vibrations of a particular gemstone fill the aura with color-ray energy and the aura reaches a point where it can absorb no more of this vibration.

Solar Plexus. An area in the center of the abdomen just above the stomach from which you direct your will.

Spectrum. A set of color or noncolor energies that when taken as a group have a signature and can be identified by their effects. Could be defined by the amount of each constituent energy.

Strength Ray. This singular color ray is the most beneficial to a person's vitality and its presence strengthens an individual's entire system.

Soul. The unit of awareness of each being that learns but does not fundamentally change form despite outer changes in physical constitution, emotional response, and mental function.

Spirit. The name given to the consciousness exhibited by the life force itself.

Subconscious Thought. A process whereby thought proceeds from closely held beliefs without the conscious interaction of the mind or purposeful direction of soul.

Superphysical. A layer of energy that is located just over the skin and, when healthy, maintains your initial defense against trauma and invasions of directed noncolor energy.

Upliftment. A change accompanied by a feeling of well being.

Vibrational Change. An alteration of a person's characteristic energy that occurs through the influence of an outside vibration.

Vibrational Energy. Those energies that have a specific wave pattern and do not act directly on the physical body but when applied to or around it will cause an indirect reaction or change that is concordant with those energies.

Vibrational Healing. The use of light, sound, and other vibrational energy to adjust your energy patterns to allow an individual to make changes that are permanent and beneficial to them.

Visualization. The art of adding imagined visual detail to a fanciful scene so as to create enough realism to the scene to allow or generate an emotional response within.

Will. The direction of vital life force originating in the mind and often creating outward effects that generally cause an equal and opposite effect as well.

Window. A point on the skin where you can direct color-ray energy to effect change in a particular gland or organ (normally found above or near the organ).

Bibliography

Bassano, Mary. *Healing with Music and Color.* York Beach, ME: Samuel Weiser Inc., 1992.

Brennan, Barbara Ann and Thomas J. Schneider. *Light Emerging: The Journey Of Personal Healing.* New York: Bantam Books, Doubleday, Dell Publishing, 1993.

Chase, Pamela Louise and Jonathan Pawlik. *The Newcastle Guide to Healing with Gemstones.* North Hollywood: Newcastle Publishing, 1989.

Cunningham, Scott. *Cunningham's Encyclopedia of Crystal, Gem, and Metal Magic.* St. Paul, MN: Llewellyn Publishing, 1991.

Dinshah, Darius. *Let There Be Light: Practical Manual for Spectro-Chrome Therapy.* Malaga: Dinshah Health Society, 1985.

Dow, JaneAnn. *Crystal Journey: Travel Guide for the New Shaman.* Santa Fe, NM: Journey Books, 1994.

Gardner, Joy. *Color and Crystals: A Journey through the Chakras.* Freedom, CA: The Crossing Press, 1988.

Holbeche, Soozi. *The Power of Gems and Crystals: How They Can Transform Your Life.* London: Judy Piatkus Publishers Limited, 1995.

Katz, Ginny. *Beyond the Light: A Personal Guidebook for Healing, Growth, and Enlightenment.* Portland: Golden Age Publishing, 1991.

Katz, Ginny, and Michael Katz. *Gifts of the Gemstone Guardians: The Mission, Purpose, Effects, and Therapeutic Applications of Gemstones in their Spherical Form.* Portland: Golden Age Publishing, 1989.

Katz, Michael. *Gemisphere Energy Medicine, Books 1–5.* Gemisphere Publishing, 1996.

———. *Gemisphere Luminary.* Portland: Gemisphere Publishing, 1997.

Katz, Michael, and Dr. Pauline Alison Crouch, eds. *Gemisphere Source: Tools for Healing and Awakening.* Portland: Gemisphere Publishing, 1998.

Keyte, Geoffrey. *The Mystical Crystal.* Essex, Saffron Walden: The C. W. Daniel Co. Limited, 1993.

Lilly, Simon. *Crystals and Crystal Healing.* The New Life Library Series. New York: Lorenz Books, Anness Publishing Limited, 1998.

Melody. *Love Is in the Earth: A Kaleidoscope of Crystals.* Wheatridge: Earth Love Publishing, 1993.

Raphael, Katrina. *Crystal Healing: Therapeutic Application of Crystals and Stones,* Volume II. Santa Fe, NM: Aurora Press, 1987.

Richardson, Wally and Jenny, and Lenora Huett. *The Spiritual Value Of Gemstones.* New York: DeVorss and Co. Publishers, 1980.

Index

REACH FOR THE MOON

Llewellyn publishes hundreds of books on your favorite subjects!
To get these exciting books, including the ones on the following pages,
check your local bookstore or order them directly from Llewellyn.

Order by Phone

- Call toll-free within the U.S. and Canada, 1-800-THE MOON
- In Minnesota, call (651) 291-1970
- We accept VISA, MasterCard, and American Express

Order by Mail

- Send the full price of your order (MN residents add 7% sales tax) in U.S. funds, plus postage & handling to:

Llewellyn Worldwide
P.O. Box 64383, Dept. 1-56718-685-8
St. Paul, MN 55164–0383, U.S.A.

Postage & Handling

(For the U.S., Canada, and Mexico)

- $4.00 for orders $15.00 and under
- $5.00 for orders over $15.00
- No charge for orders over $100.00

We ship UPS in the continental United States. We ship standard mail to P. O. boxes. Orders shipped to Alaska, Hawaii, the Virgin Islands, and Puerto Rico are sent first-class mail. Orders shipped to Canada and Mexico are sent surface mail.

International orders: Airmail—add freight equal to price of each book to the total price of order, plus $5.00 for each non-book item (audio tapes, etc.).

Surface mail—Add $1.00 per item.

Allow 2 weeks for delivery on all orders.
Postage and handling rates subject to change.

Discounts

We offer a 20% discount to group leaders or agents. You must order a minimum of 5 copies of the same book to get our special quantity price.

Free Catalog

Get a free copy of our color catalog, *New Worlds of Mind and Spirit*. Subscribe for just $10.00 in the United States and Canada ($30.00 overseas, airmail). Many bookstores carry *New Worlds*—ask for it!

Visit our website at www.llewellyn.com for more information.

Chakras for Beginners
A Guide to Balancing Your Chakra Energies

DAVID POND

The chakras are spinning vortexes of energy located just in front of your spine and positioned from the tailbone to the crown of the head. They are a map of your inner world—your relationship to yourself and how you experience energy. They are also the batteries for the various levels of your life energy. The freedom with which energy can flow back and forth between you and the universe correlates directly to your total health and well-being.

Blocks or restrictions in this energy flow expresses itself as disease, discomfort, lack of energy, fear, or an emotional imbalance. By acquainting yourself with the chakra system, how they work and how they should operate optimally, you can perceive your own blocks and restrictions and develop guidelines for relieving entanglements.

The chakras stand out as the most useful model for you to identify how your energy is expressing itself. With *Chakras for Beginners* you will discover what is causing any imbalances, how to bring your energies back into alignment, and how to achieve higher levels of consciousness.

1-56718-537-1, 5³⁄₁₆ x 8, 216 pp. $9.95

To order, call 1-800-THE MOON
Prices subject to change without notice

Reiki for Beginners
Mastering Natural Healing Techniques

DAVID F. VENNELLS

Reiki is a simple yet profound system of hands-on healing developed in Japan during the 1800s. Millions of people worldwide have already benefited from its peaceful healing intelligence that transcends cultural and religious boundaries. It can have a profound effect on health and well-being by re-balancing, cleansing, and renewing your internal energy system.

Reiki for Beginners gives you the very basic and practical principles of using Reiki as a simple healing technique, as well as its more deeply spiritual aspects as a tool for personal growth and self-awareness. Unravel your inner mysteries, heal your wounds, and discover your potential for great happiness. Follow the history of Reiki, from founder Dr. Mikao Usui's search for a universal healing technique, to the current development of a global Reiki community. Also included are many new ideas, techniques, advice, philosophies, contemplations, and meditations that you can use to deepen and enhance your practice.

1-56718-767-6, 264 pp.,5 ³⁄₁₆ x 8, illus.   **$12.95**

Cunningham's Encyclopedia of Crystal, Gem & Metal Magic

Scott Cunningham

Here you will find the most complete information anywhere on the magical qualities of more than 100 crystals and gemstones as well as several metals. The information for each crystal, gem or metal includes: its related energy, planetary rulership, magical element, deities, Tarot Card, and the magical powers that each is believed to possess. Also included is a complete description of their uses for magical purposes. The classic on the subject.

0-87542-126-1, 240 pp., 6 x 9, illus., color plates $14.95